The
International Antiques Market

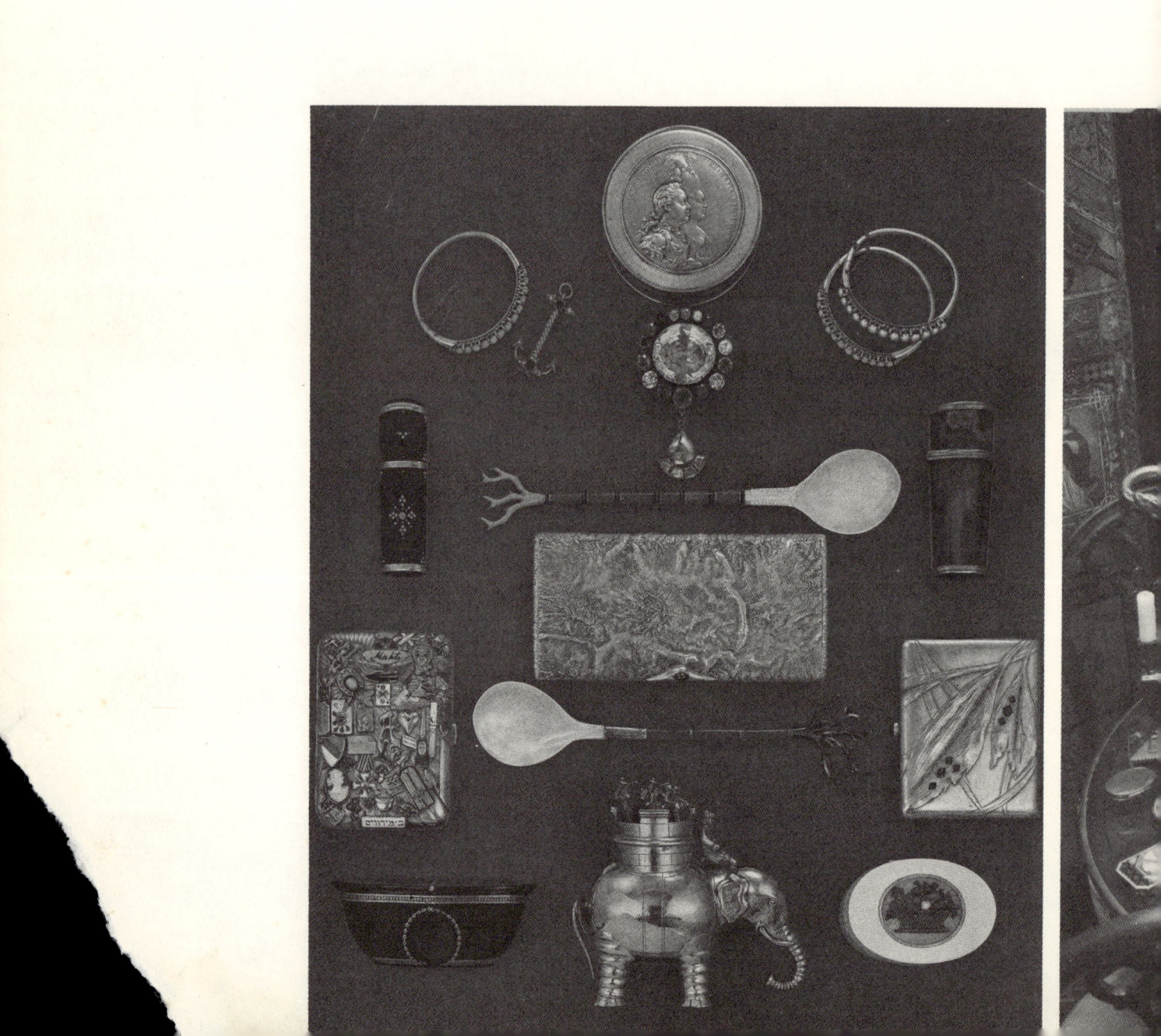

The International Antiques Market

A Guide for Collectors and Investors

Marjorie Ann Luecke

South Brunswick and New York: A. S. Barnes and Company
London: Thomas Yoseloff Ltd

© 1979 by Marjorie Ann Luecke

A. S. Barnes and Co., Inc.
Cranbury, New Jersey 08512

Thomas Yoseloff Ltd
Magdalen House
136–148 Tooley Street
London SE1 2TT, England

Library of Congress Cataloging in Publication Data

Luecke, Marjorie Ann, 1947–
   The international antiques market.

   Bibliography: p.
   1. Antiques. I. Title.
NK1125.L75   745.1   77-84576
ISBN 0-498-01989-6

PRINTED IN THE UNITED STATES OF AMERICA

To Michael

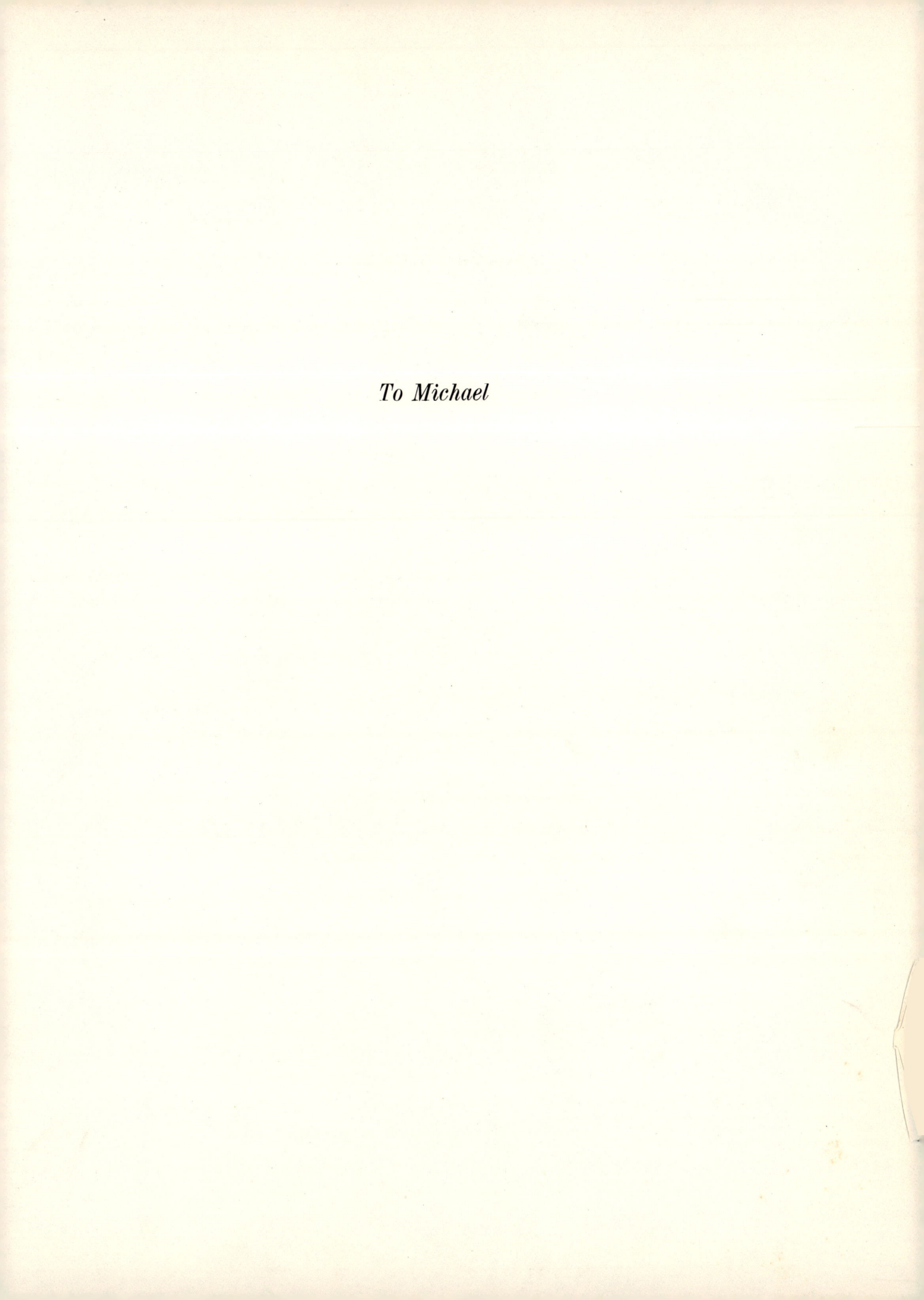

Contents

Acknowledgments
Introduction

PART I *Collecting Antiques*

1 Porcelain 17
2 Collector's Plates 87
3 Enamels and Boxes 101
4 Silver 103
5 Pewter 117
6 Brass and Copper 128
7 Clocks 131
8 Folk Art 151
9 Fraktur 163
10 Packaging Collectibles 165
11 Furniture 168
12 Glass 188
13 Paperweights 206
14 Bottles 215

PART II *Investing in Antiques: An International Price Guide*

15 Price Guide to England 223
16 Price Guide to France 274
17 Flea Markets of Europe 304
18 Price Guide to Germany 314
19 Price Guide to Holland 338
20 Price Guide to the United States 359
21 A Pictorial Study of Prices in Belgium, Switzerland, and Denmark 381

Bibliography 396
Index 399

Acknowledgments

Without the expert help of the many antique dealers throughout the world, this book could not have been completed. I would like to thank the following: Randolph Antiques, Dark & Rendleshan, Portmeireon Antiques, Clinkers Antiques Ltd, Simon Kaye Ltd, Limner Antiques, W. R. Harvey & Co., M. Chrestian Rosset, Karl Modschiedler, Butterfield & Butterfield, Goffery Godden, Earle D. Vandekar, Libreurie Halbart, Jean Sewell Ltd, Dr. Ernst Hauswedell, Fritz Nagel, Charles Morse, N. Bloom & Son Ltd, Vanderborght, Belgium Shipping Company, Finkielstein, Juvel Kunst, Kunstvelingen Mak Van Waayy B.V., Wilhelm Henrick, Premsela & Hamburger, Rumens Antiques, Nicolier, R. H. Pinquier, Jan Becker, De Hermitage, Mess. Ader Picard Tajan, Kunst en Antiekhandel Oosterpaark, A. Aardewerk, Simon A. Bul, Pieere Lecoules, Xavier Petitcol, Jeanne-Marie Bealu, Galerie Du Coq, Dickson Antiques, Derek Green Cedar Antiques, Arne Bruun Rasmussen, Kark H. Polk, F. Dorling, Daniel Chatelain, Aux Trois Arcades, F. Dervieux, Nicole Rodrigue, Michael Zeller, Galerie Du Lac, White Boniface, Rolex, W. Graham Arader III, John H. Collings Ltd, and G. E. March.

Introduction

Antique prices are skyrocketing, but how many antique buffs understand what these increased prices mean? A new and very lucrative market developed several years ago when the first antique price guides were published. These books filled a gap, giving the collector the first conception of what his antiques were really worth. But in reality, are the prices that appear in these books valid? Do they represent the true market value of a piece or the inflated price that was actually paid?

The intelligent collector must try to understand the spiraling prices and analyze them over a period of several years. Comparative price evaluation is the only way to predict future price trends. The press, which loves sensationalism, often reports fantastic prices paid at auction, but these are the plums of the market and frequently of museum quality. The average collector is interested in antiques that he can afford and, in addition, that provide him with an excellent hedge against inflation.

Today's salesroom figures read like an impressive banker's investment book, but on closer investigation, what do these figures tell us? Most collectors assume the entire market gives solid advances regardless of the field of specialty. In many fields this is true, but in others changing fashion trends can cause unexpected fluctuations. The astute buyer will analyze existing trends and try to anticipate future market direction. Economic factors have recently brought about some important market trends. The so-called new antiques made after 1832 were until recently not considered collectible. The dramatic price increases seen in the pre-1832 antiques directly caused the tremendous interest in the Victorian era. This new search for fields of collecting has expanded the market to include late nineteenth-century antiques, special edition plates, Tiffany glass, as well as pieces representative of the Bauhaus school.

Economic forces have also played a major role in collecting trends in recent years. Until recently the United States was the major buying power in the European antique market. The dollar has lost much of its purchasing power in the last few years, and the Japanese yen and German mark are rivaling for first place on the investment scene. Therefore, now many of the prime auctions held in the United States as well as in Europe are populated by enthusiastic Germans, Japanese, or representatives for the oil-producing countries.

This new trend in purchasing has brought about changes in taste. The new Japanese buyers have had a profound effect on the market, stimulating interest in Japanese artifacts found on the European and American antique market almost 400%. Chinese ceramics, favored by both Japanese and German investors, have been increasing at a compound annual rate of 23%. Future market trends point toward an increase in buyer demand. Orientalware still holds an aura of mystery for the collector. Western porcelains are a more stable market and have correspondingly appreciated at a much lower rate. The best eighteenth-century German or English porcelain has only doubled in value over the past seven years. But the dramatic rise in Oriental ceramics may have begun to taper off, or at least progress along more realistic lines. This fact can only be determined by studying market and price trends, not price guides, which obtain their data from prices paid.

Antiques are steadily increasing in value every year and remain a prime source of investment for the astute collector. Since 1968, the stock market gained only 2.6% per year, which is less than half of the rate of inflation. Most antique categories easily outperformed inflation since 1968 and remain an excellent inflation hedge.

This book will provide the antique investor with the knowlelge required to collect, plus the needed price information to intelligently compare price trends in various markets. There is no such thing as the American antique market or the British antique market. Today all antique dealers fall into one category: the international antique trade. With more than 70% of all dealers in the United States getting their wares from foreign sources, the astute collector will arm himself with the actual price paid at country of origin, plus dealer markup, to evaluate whether or not his price is fair. Until now, few people knew what the dealers actually paid abroad. In many cases it could be cheaper for the interested collector to go to Europe himself and buy directly, making valuable contacts for future purchases.

This book will provide the collector as well as the dealer with valuable price trends to help understand the international antiques market of today and to prepare for the future.

The
International Antiques Market

Part I
Collecting Antiques

1 Porcelain

AMERICA

There was very little porcelain produced in the American Colonies until after the Revolution, which caused the first real economic as well as cultural break with the mother country, England. Up until this time porcelain was exported to the Colonies by the shipload from both England and the East. Many of the Staffordshire potteries produced wares geared especially to the new and very profitable American market. Much of this export Staffordshireware depicted historic American scenes as well as buildings and famous people and became very profitable as well as popular in the Colonies. In fact, many of these patterns have been in continual production since the early nineteenth century, and special productions have been made for both the centennial and bicentennial celebrations.

Bergen, 1825

In 1825 in Bergen, New Jersey, the Jersey Porcelain and Earthenware Company was founded, and although the factory won several awards for the production of specialty pieces, no volume porcelain was ever made. Due to financial reversals, the factory closed several years after it was started.

Lenox, 1889–Present

Background

Walter Scott Lenox founded the factory that bears his name in 1889. Scott spent his entire life in the porcelain industry and founded his factory in order to prove that an American factory could produce an equal quality ware to that made in Europe.

Characteristics

Lenoxware consists of a hard-paste porcelain body that is ivory colored in appearance as well as being translucent. The majority of production was centered on dinner sets, but small, decorative accessories such as figurines, vases, and bowls were also very popular.

The majority of decoration was accomplished by painting freehand and was of the highest quality, but transfer-painting was also used on certain pieces.

Marks

The Lenox mark is usually the single letter L carefully drawn in script and enclosed within a laurel wreath—also found in the mark is the name "LENOX" printed, as well as "Made in U.S.A."

Philadelphia, Southwark China, 1769–73

Backgrouud

Two men, Gousse Bonnin and George Anthony Morris, were the founders of the Southwark, Philadelphia, porcelain factory. One of the founders, Mr. Bonnin, learned his trade at the Bow factory in England and made an honest effort to train local men in this field.

Unfortunately, not even their expert experience

could make up for lack of finances, and in 1771 they applied for aid to the government of Pennsylvania. Apparently the request was denied, since no records exist to confirm the decision, but the factory closed less than two years later.

Characteristics

Southwarkware was soft paste, and granular in consistency. The majority of production was everyday porcelain that greatly favored the shapes and decorations of the more popular English factories, especially Bow, where Bonnin received his experience.

Marks

A small letter P was drawn in blue under the glaze.

Philadelphia, Tucker, 1825–38

Background

A Quaker named Benjamin Tucker was a china merchant in downtown Philadelphia during the first twenty years of the nineteenth century. Tucker's son, William Ellis, worked for many years as a painter in his father's shop, as well as experimenting with various formulas for porcelain production.

In 1825 William Ellis, together with his brother, Thomas, founded his own porcelain factory. The factory flourished even after William Ellis Tucker died in 1832, and it was not closed until several years later in 1838.

Characteristics

It is difficult to qualify the actual formula used in Tuckerware, but comparatively speaking it is much closer to hard-paste porcelain from the East than either its English or Continental counterparts.

The majority of Tuckerware produced during the later years of production were white, but a slight yellow hue can be noticed on the earlier wares. Although the composition is closer to the Oriental, the designs and forms were mostly copied from the great Sèvres factory in France.

Marks

All marks on Tucker porcelain were very distinct and always included the names of each maker, and varied only as they changed at the factory. Unfortunately, some of the wares were not marked at all, but these pieces can always be cross-referenced to the original pattern books, which are still in existence. The Philadelphia Museum of Art has an extensive collection of these books.

AUSTRIA

Vienna, 1718–1864

Background

The famous Vienna factory was founded by Claude du Paquier, a Dutchman, in 1718. Du Paquier had unofficially experimented with the production of hard paste porcelain several years earlier, but it was not until 1718 that his work permit was granted by Charles IV, who was the Holy Roman Emperor.

Two former employees of the Meissen factory provided the much-needed technical assistance: Christoph Conrad Hunger, an enameler-gilder, and Samuel Stölzel, an expert in arcanum (the science of mixtures and experimentation in the field of porcelain production). The porcelain produced during the du Paquier period was of an excellent quality, but unfortunately the factory suffered from poor management and declared bankruptcy in 1727. The state provided financial support until 1744, when the factory was purchased by the Empress Maria Theresa. Unfortunately, by this time, due to lack of wages and the uncertainty of the factory's future, both the talented Stöltzel and his new protégé, Höroldt, a very promising enameler, had returned to Meissen to further their careers.

Under state ownership the Empress Maria Theresa appointed a new director, Matheus Mayerhofer, who managed the factory from 1744 to 1764. Much of the work done during the first ten years of the state period was only decoration of earlier-produced du Paquier wares. The *Modellmeister*, Johann Josef Niedermeyer, produced figurines from 1747 to 1784. His production could best be described as endearing figures with a doll-like charm done in rococo styling.

Vienna was always striving to compete with the production at Meissen, and took advantage of this by expanding the factory while Meissen was affected by the Seven Years' War. Following this expansion the factory entered a period of experimentation that caused its eventual collapse due to financial failure once again.

The state decided to sell the factory in 1784, but found no one willing to take over the facilities. Therefore, a new director was found—Konrad von Sorgenthal—and production was once again begun. Sorgenthal was a dynamic manager and determined to have the factory succeed. He hired Georg Perl, who devised a new method of gilding, as well as Joseph Leithner, who introduced several exciting new colors, a very dark violet-blue and a light lilac luster, both of which were immediately very well accepted.

The designs became overly decorated and poorly

executed during the last years of operation. The factory stopped production in 1864.

Characteristics

The du Paquier period is noted for the quality of wares produced. Any available pieces from this period show a distinctive grayish tone to the paste and are very expensive. Styling favored baroque forms with scrollwork and leaf and strapwork decorations. Very few figures or groups date from this period. Colors for decoration were limited at this time, but gold, pink, and the favored brick red were most often used.

The state period is noted for its designs patterned after those done at Meissen, Sèvres, Frankenthal, and Nymphenburg. Although nothing spectacular was developed in designs, the figures molded at this time were of superior quality.

The Sargenthal period shows a definite trend toward neoclassical styling and excellent decoration. New colors were added, but later production in this period tended to be overdecorated and imitated previous production.

Marks

1720–30.   1744–49, impressed.

1744–49, red.

1749–70, blue underglaze.

1750–80, blue underglaze mark used on imperial court-produced ware.

1820–27, blue underglaze.   1820–27.   1850–64.

Marks were used by individual Vienna artists.

DENMARK

Royal Copenhagen, 1775 to Present

Background

The Royal Copenhagen Porcelain Manufacturing was founded on May 1, 1775, after more than twenty-five years of very expensive research and experimentation. In Denmark it became almost an obsession to carefully duplicate the Chinese secret of porcelain production. Interest was stimulated from such various areas of the economy as political economists, scientists, and the monarchy, who all joined forces to perfect and make a profitable industry for the country. Denmark patterned its policies of production after the various other Continental manufacturers, which viewed porcelain production as an affair of state, contrary to Britain, where private enterprise was encouraged. King Frederick V of Denmark, together with his prime minister, Count Adam Gattlob Moltke, both lovers of the arts, encouraged the experimentation in the new field of porcelain production. Although experiments started in 1752 and no known samples have existed from this workshop, enough interest was stimulated to help discover the native deposits of kaolin on the island of Barnholm in 1755. Additional interest in porcelain production was stimulated by the beautiful gifts of porcelain sent from Louis XV of France in 1757–58 to the King of Denmark.

The following year, 1759, Louis Antoine Fournier was invited by Count Moltke to Copenhagen. A well-known expert, Fournier had previously been employed by the Vincennes, Chantilly, and Sèvres factories. As early as 1762 he showed successful soft paste production of which only 171 piece of his work exist today. Fournier remained at the factory until 1766, when he returned to his native France.

Franz Henrick Müller succeeded Fournier in 1765, but the work was not supported by the king, due to severe financial problems affecting the crown, and because the wares previously produced were so expensive that only the very wealthy could afford them, thus eliminating one of the major incentives, savings on imported foreign porcelain.

Frederick V died in 1766 and was succeeded by his son, Christian VII. That same year Count Moltke was dismissed, thus killing the last hopes that Denmark might become a great porcelain-producing center.

Franz Henrick Müller was not discouraged by this political disadvantage, but decided to proceed on his own in 1768 by renting a blacksmith's workshop and establishing his own factory. By 1772 Müller submitted his first samples of hard paste production to the Board of Trade for official and financial support.

The year 1772 saw severe political difficulties with the king being replaced as ruling head of state by his half-brother, Prince Frederick, and together with his mother, Queen Juliana Marie, he gave royal support to porcelain manufacturing.

After the factory was officially formed, expert personnel were required, and many workers from Meissen in Saxony were employed. In 1776 Carl Anton Luplace, Master Modeler of Furstenberg fame, came to the factory, and remained until his death in 1779. Many foreign artists brought their talents to Copenhagen. One of them was Johan Christof Bayer, who came from Nuremberg to design the botanical work *Flora Danica* in 1761. The complete design of this motif consumed his entire life until he retired in 1804.

The factory experienced a decline during the nineteenth century, but by 1885, with the employment of Arnold Krug, it began to make a dramatic recovery to the modern factory of today, which produces a magnificent quality of porcelain.

Characteristics

The first production under Fournier's direction was a soft-paste porcelain with a slightly yellow tint, but at the same time the ware was translucent. The glaze had a unique soapy quality that also was soft and lustrous. At the beginning production was very limited, but it gradually increased to include dinner sets, plus all kinds of decorative accessories. Also, impressive clocks and figures, both biscuit and glazed, were produced.

A definite French influence was evident throughout production, although at the beginning slight traces of German styling could be seen. Rococo styling was popular, but by 1780 it had been substantially replaced by neoclassic and later by the neo-Grec.

Müller produced a soft-paste porcelain that had a slightly grayish tinge, but the hard-paste wares that were at first made also were slightly gray and darker in tone. By 1780 Müller's production had greatly improved and was very white and translucent. The glaze first used by Müller also had its imperfections and showed to be slightly yellowish, while later attempts were both clear and brilliant.

Most of the decorations were patterned after the new French porcelain factories such as the polychrome flowers of Chantilly and the cornflower motif made so popular at Sèvres. Chinese designs as well as battle scenes and blue and white decorations were very popular.

On May 1, 1775, at the founding meeting, the mark of the factory was decided. The future trademark was to be three wavy blue lines symbolizing the sound, the Great Belt, and the Little Belt, thus stressing the factory's position in a country that had considerable maritime interests.

Royal Copenhagen Commemorative Plates

The commemorative plates are a unique, underglaze artware that have enjoyed increased interest among collectors both in Denmark and abroad since the first plate was developed in 1888 to commemorate the Great Scandinavian Exhibition of Industry, Agriculture, and Art in Copenhagen. While each plate issued varies in motif as to the theme it commemorates and as to the artist's interpretation, they all have a common styling that sets them apart from other similar plate series produced by other factories. To the connoisseur, this unique quality is as distinctive to Royal Copenhagen as Jasperware is to Wedgwood.

On January 1, 1885, Arnold Krug, a young architect, was appointed to the Royal Copenhagen factory as Director of Art. Having first completed his degree in architecture after several years in Italy, he was very interested in majolica wares. Krug was also a very talented artist who could master any artistic style, and this ability brought him to the attention of

Philip Schou, director of the factory. Porcelain as an art medium was new to Krug but posed a challenge, especially since he was to be allowed complete artistic freedom to find a new styling concept.

His first experiments with underglaze painting were an immediate sensation at the Paris World Exhibition in 1889. Krug's was such a deviation from everyone's preconceived idea of what porcelain should look like, that his was perhaps the first innovative work done in the European porcelain industry since the Meissen factory was founded 180 years before.

Until this time all underglaze porcelain was limited to tableware with either stylized or geometric designs. Landscapes up until now were only painted as overglaze decorations. Krug at once realized the advantages of using underglaze decoration compared to overglaze, since the underglaze becomes an integral part of the porcelain, while the overglaze decoration obstructs its beautiful texture. Krug felt that if he used the soft, hazy effect of cobalt blue under the glaze he could much better achieve the naturalistic styling that he sought and also enhance instead of obliterate the beauty of the porcelain.

In order to accomplish his new theory a new technique of painting was imperative, and he began experimenting immediately. At first the plate was dipped into a suspension of cobalt blue, and the excess was later taken off by brush to reveal the design. This process was repeated many times until the layers of blue covered the plate in various thicknesses. After the glaze and firing the design appeared in various hues of blue from intense to pure white.

This type of decorating proved to be not only time-consuming but complicated. The process was then refined to begin by using the brush and eventually spraying on the additional layers of color, which is essentially the method used in producing the plates today.

The Technique

Arnold Krug has been recognized as one of the greatest innovators in the field of applied art. All of the commemorative plates designed by Krug were to be done by hand, and transfers were not intended to enter into this type of decoration. The tradition established by Arnold Krug has been carried on until today, and this careful handwork is what sets the Royal Copenhagen commemorative plates apart from other commemorative wares.

Each plate motif appears in relief that has been accurately hand-carved in the master mold. After a plate has been cast and bisque-fired, the painter sprays on an even layer of cobalt blue and then removes the excess paint with a brush. This method is

1. 1775–1820, about 1850–70; 2. 1820–50; 3. 1870–90; 4. about 1892; 5. 1894–1900; 6. 1894–1922; 7. 1905–, so-called Juliane Marie mark; 8. 1922–; 9. about 1923; 10. 1929–50, used on so-called matte porcelain only; 11. about 1863, on earthenware; 12. 1868–1922, on earthenware; 13. 1872–1930, on earthenware, best quality; 4. 1903–69 on earthenware with many-colored decorations under glaze.

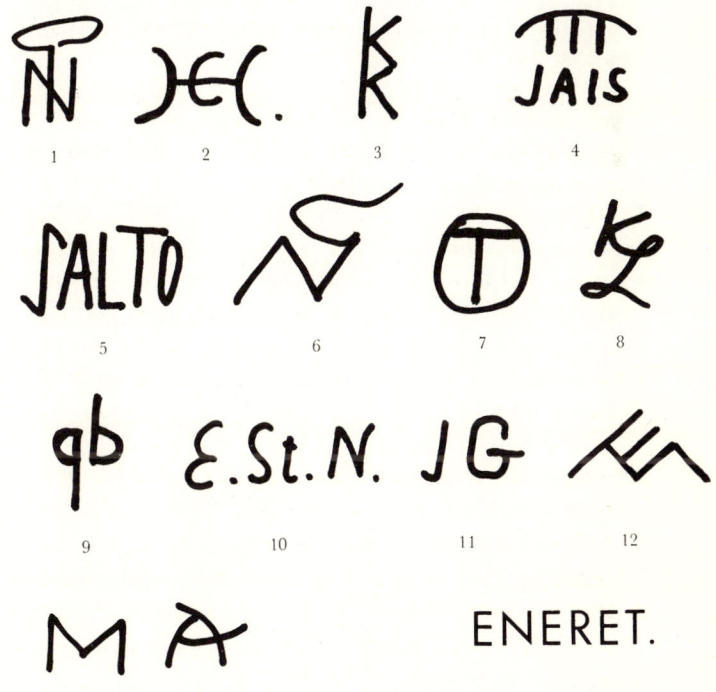

1. Patrick Nordström, 1912–22; 2. Carl Halier, 1913–48; 3. Knud Kyhn, 1903–67; 4. Jais Nielsen, 1921–61; 5. Axel Salto, 1930–61; 6. Nils Thorsson, 1918–; 7. Thorkild Olsen, 1908–68; 8. Kaj Lange, 1934–; 9. Gerd Bogelund, 1946–; 10. Eva Staehr-Nielsen, 1968–; 11. Jeanne Grut, 1959–; 12. Ellen Malmer, 1965–; 13. Mogens Andersen, 1970–; 14. ENERET = Copyright on biscuit, 1835–.

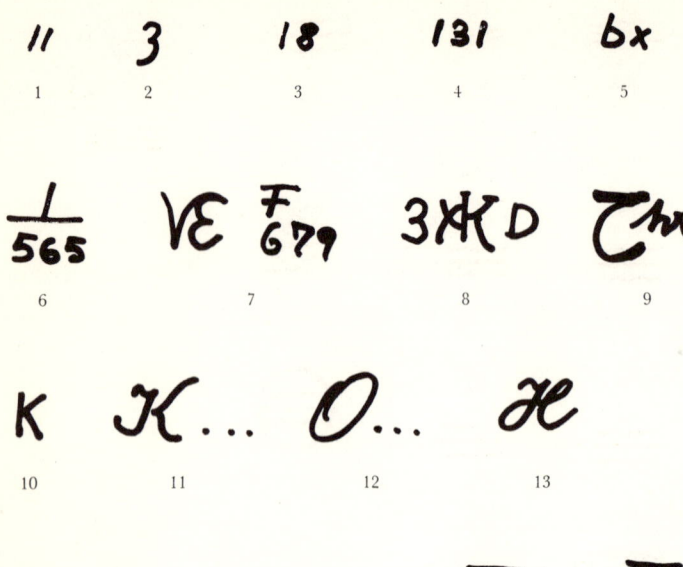

1–2. Blue-painter marks, 1175–1814; 3–4. 1863–1931; 5. Letter-mark on blue painted porcelain, 1931–; 6. Fraction-marking, 1894–; 1 = decoration, 565 = shape-number; 7. V. Engelhardt, F = yearmark, each letter with numbers 1–1000; 8. Arnold Krog, 1884–1916, 3 = March, D = 1888; 9. Christian Thomsen, 1898–1921; 10. V. Kock, 1842–51; 11. C. L. Klein, 1825–91; 12. E. Orth, 1869–1902; 13. F. A. Hallin, 1885–95; 14. Gotfred Rode, 1896–1933; 15. Marianne Host, 1885–1904; 16. C. F. Liisberg, 1885–1909; 17. Th. Madsen, 1900–35.

repeated from three to five times until each area has the intended thickness of color. In the final stage a piece of cloth and various sizes and textures of brushes are used together to remove any excess color.

The success of each plate depends on the skill and deftness of the painters and the feeling these people develop for their work. Only the most trained painters are employed, since errors that are made during decorating do not appear until all of the plates come from the kiln.

Arnold Krug retired in 1916, but not before some of the most talented painters from Europe had been attracted to the Royal Copenhagen porcelain factory to join forces with the famous Krug.

ENGLAND

During the last half of the sixteenth century Britons were using imported stoneware from Germany and fine porcelain from China. About this time the potters of Great Britain began experimenting with a tin-glazed earthenware, known as delft. This domestic production was an immediate success, and was an ideal substitute for the more expensive porcelain being imported from China. At first delftware was produced in London, and as its popularity grew various other areas such as Bristol and Liverpool began making the ware.

By the end of the seventeenth century the newly founded industry had expanded and was producing large quantities of stoneware, which imitated the German stoneware. Small factories sprang up all over England, but by the beginning of the eighteenth century most of the pottery was in Northern Staffordshire, where it remains even today.

Individual experimentation was encouraged in England; therefore small potteries were established throughout the Staffordshire countryside. Many potters, men of determination, such as Woods, Astbury, and Josiah Wedgwood, began experimenting with various earthenware forms, glazes, and clay blends to further produce unique artwares. Some of the best products of this experimentation were made during the first struggling years in the eighteenth century. Unfortunately, just as the industry began producing wares showing originality and an art form worthy of recognition, the secret of porcelain production in 1740 was discovered in England.

At first this newly discovered porcelain was only produced by imitating both the European and well-known Chinese imports. The body of the ware was soft paste, and quality varied greatly from one factory to another, since each had its own closely guarded secret recipe for porcelain production. It was not until 1768 that the formula for hard-paste porcelain was achieved, but this was much too late for any artistic recognition in the European marketplace. By 1794 the formula for bone china had been perfected (supposedly by Spode), and sofe paste production was suspended at all but a few factories .

Most of the pioneer factories that played such an important role in the development of the porcelain industry of England are still in operation today.

Today, with the age of mechanization, the porcelain industry that previously relied so heavily on expertise and work done exclusively by hand has begun producing mass-made wares. Fortunately, the original standards that gave the industry such a world renowned name have remained high. Today, specialty products such as limited editions, geared to today's changing lifestyle and fluctuating economics, are being produced with the same meticulous workman-

WEDGWOOD & SONS	Very rare mark used for a short period in 1790.	WEDGWOOD ETRURIA / WEDGWOOD ETRURIA / Wedgwood Etruria	These marks are rarely found on pieces of a very high character. Adopted about 1840 but used for only a short period.
JOSIAH WEDGWOOD Feb. 2nd 1805	Mark of Josiah Wedgwood II. Supposedly a new partnership or change in the firm. Found only on some basalt tripod incense burners. It may be the date when the design was first registered, 1805. Sometimes '2nd Feby' appears instead of 'Feb. 2'.	WEDGWOOD	This mark, now in use on bone china, was adopted in 1878 when the manufacture of bone china was revived. It is printed in various colours.
WEDGWOOD	The mark upon the bone china or porcelain, made 1812–1822, always printed either in red, blue or in gold.	ENGLAND	England was added to the mark Wedgwood in 1891 to comply with the American Customs Regulation known as the McKinley Tariff Act.
WEDGWOOD / WEDGWOOD	From 1769 to the present day this mark has been impressed in the clay on Queen's Ware, or printed in colour. In recent times the words Etruria and Barlaston and the name of the pattern have in many cases been printed in addition to the trade mark. From 1780, ornamental Jasper, Black Basalt, cane, terra cotta and Queen's Ware are always marked with this stamp. The name 'England' was added in 1891.	WEDGWOOD Bone China MADE IN ENGLAND	Mark used today on bone china, developed from mark of 1878. In 1974 the circled R was added to backstamps to indicate that the name 'Wedgwood' is a registered trade mark.
		OF ETRURIA WEDGWOOD MADE IN ENGLAND BARLASTON	This mark, printed in colour, is being used today on Queen's Ware, starting in 1940. In 1974 the circled R was added to backstamps to indicate that the name 'Wedgwood' is a registered trade mark.
wedgwood	Probably the first mark. Supposed to have been used by Josiah Wedgwood at Burslem 1759-1769.	Wedgwood & Bentley	Unique script mark, Wedgwood & Bentley, 1769–1780.
WEDGWOOD	This is a very rare mark, used at the Bell Works 1764–1769.	Wedgwood & Bentley 356	Mark used on Wedgwood & Bentley intaglios, with the catalogue number varying in size, 1769–1780.
WEDGWOOD / Wedgwood	Used in varying sizes from 1759–1769.	W. & B.	Very small intaglios were sometimes marked W&B with the catalogue number, or simply with the number only, 1769–1780.
WEDGWOOD & BENTLEY (circular)	The circular stamp, without the inner and outer rings, and without the word Etruria is doubtless the earliest form of the Wedgwood and Bentley stamp, 1769.	Wedgwood & Bentley (circular)	Rare mark found only on chocolate and white seal intaglios, usually portraits made of two layers of clay with the edges polished for mounting, 1769–1780.
(circular seal)	This mark, with the word Etruria, was fixed in the corner, inside the plinth of old basalt vases. It is sometimes found on the pedestal of a bust or large figure. 1769–1780.	WEDGWOOD & BENTLEY / Wedgwood & Bentley	These marks, varying in size are found upon busts, granite and basalt vases, figures, plaques, medallions and cameos, from the largest tablet to the smallest cameo. 1769–1780.
(circular stamp)	This circular stamp, with an inner and outer line, was always placed around the screw of the basalt, granite and Etruscan vases, but is never found on Jasper vases. 1769–1780.	WEDGWOOD / Wedgwood / WEDGWOOD	Varying in size, these marks are attributed to the period after Bentley's death (1780) and probably used for a time after Josiah's death (1795).

ship, which could possibly be the collector's pieces of today for future centuries.

Understanding the English Registry Marks

The British Patent Office established the registry mark system from 1842 to 1883, which greatly helps in identifying porcelain produced during this period in England. In fact, it is possible by understanding how to interpret these marks to tell the exact date, month, and even year of production. The following are two examples of Registry Marks:

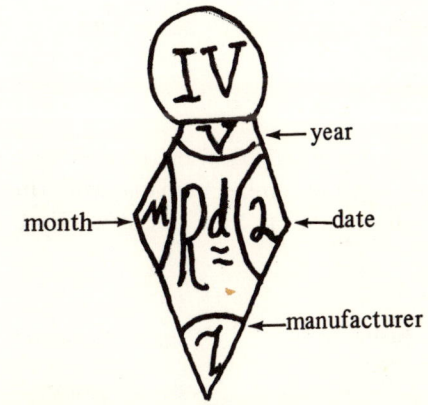

1842–67, shows the year letter at the top.

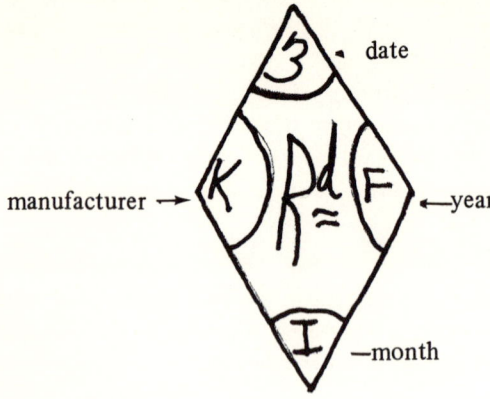

1868–83, shows the year letter at the right.

The following are the index numbers to interpret the various British registry numbers.

Registry Numbers Type I: 1842–67

A = 1845	N = 1864
B = 1858	O = 1862
C = 1844	P = 1851
D = 1852	Q = 1866
E = 1855	R = 1861
F = 1847	S = 1849
G = 1863	T = 1867
H = 1843	U = 1848
I = 1846	V = 1850
J = 1854	W = 1865
K = 1857	X = 1842
L = 1856	Y = 1853
M = 1859	Z = 1860

Registry Numbers Type II: 1868–83

A = 1871	L = 1882
C = 1870	P = 1877
D = 1878	S = 1875
E = 1881	U = 1874
F = 1873	V = 1878
H = 1869	W = 1878
I = 1872	X = 1868
J = 1880	Y = 1879
K = 1883	

In 1884 the registry numbers were revised due to the fact that they were becoming unmanageably high. The following shows the revised registry chart of numbers.

Registry Numbers	Registry Numbers
1884 = 1	1895 = 246975
1885 = 19754	1896 = 268392
1886 = 40480	1897 = 291241
1887 = 64520	1898 = 311658
1888 = 90483	1899 = 331707
1889 = 116648	1900 = 351202
1890 = 141273	1901 = 368154
1891 = 163767	1902 = 385500
1892 = 185713	1903 = 402500
1893 = 205240	1904 = 420000
1894 = 224720	1905 = 447000

Belleek, 1863 to Present

Background

Ireland, long famous for its beautiful crystal, also produced porcelain in the town of Belleek, for which the factory is named. The factory was founded in 1857 shortly after native deposits of feldspar and china clay were discovered. The hard-paste parian-ware produced at Belleek used the same basic ingredients as other porcelain factories, but the basic formula was considerably altered. Large quantities of feldspar were used, sometimes as high as three to one. In fact, this new procedure created the effect of delicate seashells or coral and was an immediate success. Belleek was a great favorite in the United States, where several factories began copying the original production. The largest wholesale copying of Belleek was undertaken by the Etruria pottery company of Trenton, New Jersey, in 1883, who even hired many employees of the original Belleek factory in Ireland. The production of this factory was an admirable reproduction that enjoyed much success in the United States.

Characteristics

Besides the famous shell-like appearance that this porcelain displays, the surface very often is covered with a quite distinctive, pearl-like luster. Since naturalism was stressed, a full range of marine figures such as sea horses and dolphins were produced, as well as a normal line of dinner and tea services. Belleek is easily recognized by its graceful shapes and gentle coloring, which could be compared to the Oriental *blanc-de-chine* wares.

Marks

The mark combines the greyhound, three-lobed Shamrock, harp, and round tower, which is either stenciled or printed on the wares in either brown, red, or green.

1750.

Bow, 1744–76

Background

The Bow factory, also known as "New Canton," was located in London's China Row not far from the Bow Bridge. The factory no longer exists, and the exact position of the factory had all but been forgotten until the last part of the nineteenth and beginning of the twentieth century, when excavations in the area uncovered original Bow kilns, wasters, and molds, which have helped establish definite Bow characteristics.

Thomas Frye and Edward Heylyn were issued a production patent in 1744, and later in 1749 the second factory patent was issued only to Frye. The factory passed to the ownership of John Crowther and John Weatherby in 1750, and it is from this period that the first existing Bow porcelain was produced. The majority of wares made at this time were limited to teacups and saucers decorated in the Chinese style of underglaze blue.

The factory continued under John Crowther's management until 1775, when he sold out to William Duesbury of Derby, who closed the Bow factory. Duesbury took the majority of the equipment, molds, and models from not only the Bow factory, but also Vauxhall and Chelsea, to the Derby factory.

Characteristics

The Bow factory from 1747 to 1754 produced large quantities of blue and white porcelain as well as the raised prunus and famille rose designs done in polychrome. Figures were produced in the white and decorated outside the factory by the workshops of James Giles and William Duesbury. The period between 1755 and 1760 shows a definite European influence on both shapes and design stylings, copying Sèvres, Mennecy, Meissen, and Chantilly, as well as the traditional Oriental.

The quality of the Bow paste was constantly changing; for example, the early soft-pasteware was not a specific white or had very little translucency, and compares favorably to the wares produced at Chelsea. Later production was a very hard body of a much better quality, thinner, and a distinct white body. The first glazes used were yellowish and satin-soft to the touch. As the lead content was reduced the glaze became much more brilliant and considerably harder.

Marks

Much of the first Bow production was not marked. The following are some of the known symbols used at the Bow factory. The famous arrow and dagger marks are usually done in a red or reddish brown.

1750–60.

1760–75.

Bristol, 1770–81

Background

William Cookworthy, together with his manager, Richard Champion, founded a hard-paste porcelain factory at Bristol in 1770. The factory, which did substantial business with the American Colonies, was severely hurt financially by the American Revolution. Richard Champion, due to these financial difficulties, sold his patent for producing hard-paste porcelain to some potters working in Staffordshire. With this advantage a very simple ware was then made by these men at New Hall.

25

Characteristics

Two qualities of porcelain were produced at Bristol; the first, known as "cottage china," was made for everyday usage, while a first-quality porcelain, similar to Dresden, was also produced for the more sophisticated market.

Both form and decoration favored the simple elegance of the Chinese and neoclassical. Delicate flowers and ribbon borders adorned the simpler porcelain, while the fine ware was decorated with much more ornamentation.

Marks

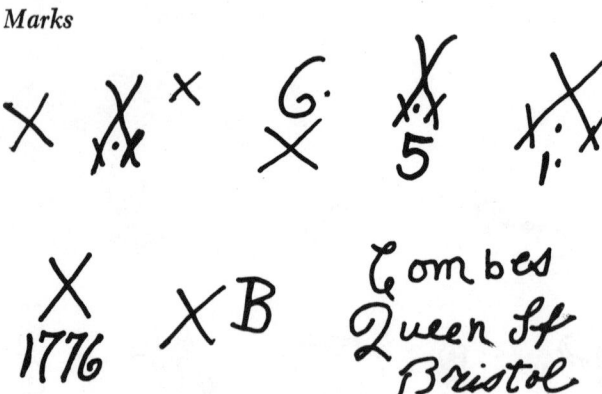

Caughley, 1772–1815

Background

Thomas Turner, an engraver from Worcester, started his own porcelain factory in Caughley in 1772.

At first production was based almost exclusively on blue and white transfer decorations with the very popular "Broseley Dragon" and "Willow Pattern" being produced at the factory.

Turner sold the factory to John Rose in 1799, who annexed the operation to Coalport porcelain factory, and continued production until 1815, when the factory was closed.

Characteristics

The glaze and body of the ware was of an excellent quality, being both translucent and the paste very white. Of course, decoration was centered on the blue and white patterns, which were at first painted in underglaze blue but quickly changed to transfer printing.

After 1780 there was a slight change in style, which was influenced by painters brought back to England from France by Turner. Flowers, landscape, and birds became popular at this time.

Marks

There is a definite similarity between the first marks at the Caughley, the C, and the crescent commonly used at Worcester. The mark "SALOPIAN" was impressed, while the remaining factory marks were painted in underglaze blue.

Cauldon or Ridgway, 1813–58

Background

Since the later part of the eighteenth century the Ridgway family had been very active in the pottery industry in Staffordshire. The Cauldon factory was founded by Job Ridgway in 1813 and produced various types of earthenware and porcelain until 1858. At this time the factory was acquired by Brown, Westhead, Moore, and Company, later known as Cauldon Ltd.

Characteristics

A large majority of the ware produced were of the blue trasnfer printed type, and geared to the American market, specializing in American scenic views.

Marks

1813.

Until 1830.

CAULDON CHINA
ENGLAND

Chelsea, 1745–84

Background

Little is known about the first few years of production at Chelsea. Although at first the Bow factory was credited with producing the first porcelain in England, Chelsea experts firmly established Chelsea's claim to this distinction. Several pieces, such as the "goat and bee" cream jugs, having "Chelsea, 1745" scratched in the paste to substantiate the earlier operating and production of the Cheosea factory, were found.

Nicholas Sprimont, a silversmith from France, joined the factory in 1749. Under his management the factory prospered, with styles greatly influenced by Sprimont's Continental background. The factory continued to thrive, and upon the death of the owner, Sir Everard Fawkener, in 1758, Sprimont purchased the factory.

In 1769, James Cox purchased the factory and several months later sold it to John Heath and William Duesbury of Derby. Production continued until 1784, but only a limited variety of tableware was made, which was known as Chelsea-Derby ware (but favoring the later style).

Characteristics

The first wares produced at Chelsea could be favorably compared in composition to milkglass. Much of this production has small pits and an extremely heavy, glasslike glaze that at times shows either white or ivory in tone. Very often the small imperfections found in the glaze were decorated over with delicate nature subjects such as insects, birds, or leaves.

The factory produced some of its best wares during the 1750s, better known as the red anchor period. During this time the famous "Chelsea Toys" were made. During the gold anchor period produced during the 1760s, large figure groups decorated with vibrant colors and gilding were popular.

Marks

Very rare.   **Very rare.**   **1745–50.**

Underglaze blue on wares inspired by the Meissen factory.

Underglaze blue on wares inspired by the Meissen factory.

Red or gold anchor period, 1750–60.

Red or gold anchor period, 1750–60.

Red or gold anchor period, 1750–60.

Chelsea-Derby period, 1784.

Marks one and two are from the first and very rare production period, while mark number three is from the 1745–50 period. Marks five and six are done in underglaze blue and appear on wares inspired by the Meissen factory. Marks seven through ten are from either the red or gold anchor period, 1750–60. Mark ten is from the Chelsea–Derby period, 1784.

Collector's Note

It should be noted by collectors interested in the gold anchor period that this mark was widely copied by various hard-paste porcelain factories on the Continent, especially France. These forgeries were made during the nineteenth and twentieth centuries.

Coalport, 1796 to Present

Background

John Rose founded the Coalport factory about 1796, and in 1799 he purchased the Caughley factory, as well as both the Nantgarw and Swansea factories in 1820. The factory continued to be operated by the Rose family until 1862, when it was purchased by William Pugh. On Pugh's death many of the old wares from the Rose production were decorated and sold for tax purposes in 1875.

At this time the factory was purchased by the Coalport China Company, which immediately began improvements to make Coalport an equal in the great English porcelain industry.

Characteristics

The porcelain was very like Caughley production, being very white and translucent, and the glazes used were of an equally high quality, producing an almost mellow effect.

Production centered around dinnerware, but vases and other smaller decorative pieces were made, mostly copying the styles of both Dresden and Sèvres.

Constant experimentation during the nineteenth century took place at the factory to better the quality of the paste. Production after 1820 was extremely fine and closely resembled Nantgarw porcelain.

Marks

JOHN ROSE & C^{ic}
COLE BROOK DALE
1850.

 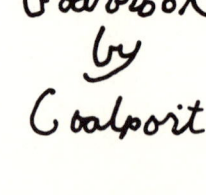

Davenport, 1793–1882

Background

John Davenport purchased a pottery factory at Longport, Staffordshire, in 1792. The following year production was started and included both porcelain and earthenware. The factory was very successful and received the Royal Patronage of William IV, who ordered his coronation porcelain service from the Davenport factory in 1830. Queen Victoria was also a patron of the factory, but this was after John Davenport had retired in 1831.

The factory continued under the management of John Davenport's two sons to produce first-quality wares, with a great part of the business centering on export to the Europeans as well as to the United States.

Characteristics

Davenport is perhaps best known for its blue-printed decorations that mostly adapted popular Oriental designs. Although all types of porcelain were produced, tea sets became very popular during the last part of the nineteenth century.

Marks

Sometimes after 1806 the Davenport mark included a crown to signify royal patronage.

Derby, 1755 to Present

Background

William Duesbury founded the Derby porcelain factory in 1755. Duesbury, who once was a painter for both the Chelsea and Bow factories, purchased them together with the Longton Hall works shortly after acquiring Derby.

After Duesbury's death in 1786, his son, William Duesbury, Jr., managed the very successful operation until his death in 1795. The factories continued under the management of William Duesbury III and Michael Kean until 1811, when the works were sold to Robert Bloor. Unfortunately none of the quality that established Derby's fame was retained under Bloor's management, and the factory eventually closed in 1848.

Almost immediately the factory was reopened by some of the original Derby workmen, and in 1876 the present Royal Crown Derby Porcelain Company was established.

Characteristics

Besides the usual dinner sets and decorative accessories the Derby factory produced many small figurines. It should be noted that at first the glaze was velvety soft, and only in later production did it become hard and brilliant.

All forms, such as rococo, neoclassical, and neo-Grecian, can be seen as dictated by popular demand. After the acquisition of the Chelsea factory, much of the decoration followed in the typical Chelsea manner, but at times some pieces were overdecorated. One favorite decorative form was an adaptation of the Japanese Imari patterns, but these were overdone.

Perhaps the factory reached its best period under the management of William Duesbury, Jr., where great care was taken with painting as well as some of the best biscuit medallions and statues.

Collector's Note

Many of the excellent Derby statues were produced from the original Chelsea molds, but these have been widely copied. Some of the larger and more elaborate forgeries were done by Samson of Paris. One of the most obvious defects concerns the marks on these pieces, which are very clear and bold. A much less devious forgery was done at the Derby factory itself from 1850 to 1870, when some of the best of the earlier pieces were copied, but these pieces were adequately marked as follows and in no way should be judged with earlier works of the Derby factory.

Marks

Lane Delph, c. 1800–1850
Mason's Ironstone, 1804 to Present

Crown Royal Derby Porcelain Co. since 1890

Background

Miles Mason during the eighteenth century was established as a well-known importer of Oriental porcelain, but due to wartime delays together with increased duties, he was forced to close his business.

Mason was determined to develop a domestic ware that matched the imported Chinese porcelain on every level, so he studied porcelain production at both Derby and Worcester. By 1780, Mason felt himself qualified enough to operate his own factory at Lane Delph, in Staffordshire. He succeeded in producing a very fine porcelain, but because of its expense, production was stopped and experimentation was once again started. Later Mason developed a ware that combined the good qualities of true porcelain with added durability, known today as ironstone.

Characteristics

Ironstone was an immediate success. Due to Mason's prior experience with Oriental porcelain much of the decorations followed the designs of the East, with floral and pictorial scenes being very popular.

Marks

Liverpool, 1754–1800

Background

Liverpool gained its reputation as a ceramic center producing delft during the eighteenth century. In addition, hard-paste porcelain was produced during this period, although very few pieces exist today.

From 1800 to 1841 the Herculaneum factory operated and produced porcelain that was not terribly distinct, but favored the popular wares produced at Davenport.

Characteristics

Besides the locally produced delftware, which was often labeled as porcelain instead of pottery, the wares of Liverpool were mainly transfer-printed. The paste as well as the glaze were of an excellent grade and the decoration colors tended toward deep shades of green and red, as well as black and brown.

Marks

Richard Chaffers 1769.

The marks are easy to identify, usually incorporating the name of the factory and sometimes the crest of Liverpool.

Longton Hall, 1751–60

Background

The earliest known porcelain factory to operate in Staffordshire was established by William Littler in 1751, but due to various problems it closed several years later in 1758.

Characteristics

The major aim of the Longton Hall factory was to copy and undersell both the Chelsea and Bow production. The soft-paste body was of a good quality, but the glazes used were much thinner than Chelsea and Bow and did not tend to crack. Much of the production was limited to dinnerware, and the decorations often used bright enamel colors.

Marks

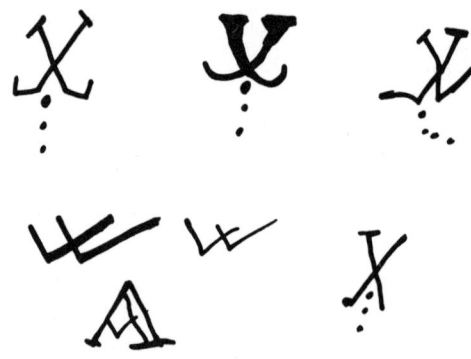

Unfortunately, much of the production was not marked, and collectors sometimes confuse Longton Hall wares with either lesser quality Chelsea or Bow.

Lowestoft, 1757–1802

Collector's Note

It should be clarified at this point that many people use the term *Lowestoft* erroneously. The town of Lowestoft is located in Suffolk, England and is itself a porcelain center that made a fine quality soft-paste ware that was very popular with the middle class.

During this same period in China a hard-paste porcelain was made and exported to England in large quantities and became known by the name Lowestoft. This ware should be referred to under the name of Chinese Lowestoft.

Background

First started in 1757, the Lowestoft factory produced a good quality soft-paste porcelain that has very often been compared to production of both the Bow and Worcester factories.

Characteristics

The paste was composed of bone ash, and was very often decorated in underglaze blue. The wares are primitive and very often engraved with such slogans as "A trifle from Lowestoft" as well as both marriage and birth plates.

Enamel colors were widely used after about 1770 and in 1775 Chinese patterns were copied, with mauve being a favorite color used in decoration.

Marks

Many of the marks used were copies of other factories. Workmen's numbers are usually found very near to the foot rim and are between 1 and 30.

Minton 1798–present

Background

Thomas Minton began producing hard-paste porcelain in 1798, but the factory up until then only made earthenware decorated in blue, which copied Nanking ware. Production was stopped in 1811 but was started again with the aid of several employees of the Derby factory in 1821.

The factory continued under family ownership until 1883, when the present-day company, Mintons Limited, was established.

Characteristics

Minton production was always very well accepted. The body was extremely white and almost never showed flaws and as a result decorations on this ware were very light.

Perhaps the height of production took place from about 1820, when some of the pieces were on the level produced and decorated at Sèvres. In fact, much of the decoration showed a definite French influence both in color and format.

Marks

Minton production was always clearly marked, with much of the first wares bearing the name Minton or only an M impressed in the paste. In 1841 the mark of Minton and Co. impressed was adopted. During this same period a mark was used that closely imitated the crossed L mark of Sèvres. The Globe mark was used in many different forms starting in 1868.

Madeley, 1827–40

Background

Thomas Martin Randall founded the Madeley factory in 1827 after being associated in the firm of Robins and Randall, who were decorators of fine porcelain.

The majority of production reproduced not only the styles but decorations of the Sèvres factory that were sought after at this period.

Characteristics

The ware was soft paste that was almost creamlike in color. Although shapes and decoration were forgeries of the old Sèvres factory, many collectors are now beginning to take an interest in Madeley porcelain for its exquisite quality.

Marks

Although other factories not only forged the Sèvres wares but also the marks, Randall must be complimented for his honesty, since he never copied the old Sèvres marks. In fact there is no record mark for the Madeley factory.

Nantgarw, 1813–23

Background

William Billingsley founded a porcelain factory in Nantgarw, Wales, in 1813. The factory was moved to Swansea for two years from 1814 to 1816 and eventually closed several years later in 1823.

Characteristics

An exceptionally white and translucent soft-paste porcelain was produced at Nantgarw during its short period of operation. Production was limited to dinnerware and small, decorative accessories fashioned in the neo-Grecian styling.

Marks

NANT·GARW C.W.   C.W. NANGAROW GW

Nantgarw

Most marks at Nantgarw were impressed.

Collector's Note

Nantgarw marks have been readily forged and all marks not impressed in the paste should be carefully researched and examined.

New Hall, 1782–1835

Background

A group of six potters started the New Hall factory in Staffordshire, England, in 1782. Although the men had the good fortune to purchase the patent for making hard-paste porcelain from Bristol, none of the original workmen or molds were acquired. The aim of the New Hall factory was quite different from that of Bristol, and a much more commercial ware was produced.

Characteristics

Although a similar style ware to Bristol was produced at New Hall, the quality was not equal. A hard-paste porcelain was made until 1810, when production was changed to a bone china. This later ware was noticeably glassy in appearance besides being opaque. Mainly tea services were produced, with decorations being limited to blue and white transfer designs.

Marks

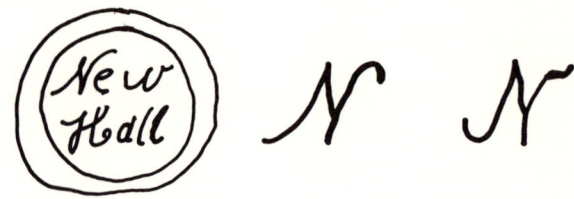

At first, most wares were not marked. It is not known exactly when this practice was established but, it is estimated to be between 1810 and 1835. The earliest marks were the letter N incised in the paste; while the later circular mark was transfer-printed on the glaze.

Plymouth, 1768–70

Background

The first hard-paste porcelain made in England was produced at Plymouth sometime between 1768 and 1770. The factory was founded by William Cookworthy in the hopes of discovery of the exact formula for reproducing the famous Continental porcelain with local material found in Cornwall.

Unfortunately, the enterprise was too great an effort for the aging Cookworthy, and eventually he transferred to Bristol.

Characteristics

Much of the ware produced has noticeable defects in form, but the consistency of the paste was very hard, white and translucent, the three basic qualities of hard-paste porcelain. The glazes used had more problems and very often tended toward thickness with bubbles and a distinct grey tone. This greyish color was caused by smoke stains.

A good variety of wares were produced from dinner sets to figurines, mostly styled in rococo.

Marks

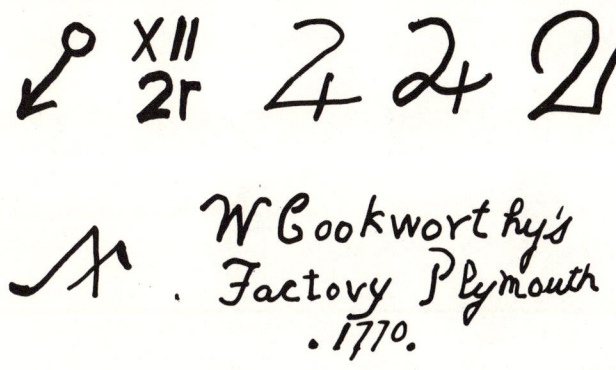

Many of the Plymouth marks closely resemble the alchemical symbol for tin.

Rockingham, 1820–42

Background

Thomas Brameld founded the Rockingham porcelain factory in 1820 together with his royal patron, the Marquis of Rockingham. The quality of production was excellent but did not yield a great enough return for the Marquis, who was the sole financial supporter. Therefore, the factory was closed in 1842.

Characteristics

Rockingham produced a very high-quality bone porcelain that displayed a very transparent glaze. A great variety of wares were produced that included dinner and tea services as well as a good selection of decorative accessories. Many of the decorations as well as shapes were fashioned in the Derby form.

Marks

The marks that were used on Rockingham ware are either impressed or printed and depict either "Royal Rockingham Works, Brameld" or "Rockingham Works, Brameld." After 1826 the crest of the Fitzwilliam family was included in the mark and either painted in red or impressed in the paste. A royal crown has also been noted on several pieces after 1826.

Royal Doulton, 1877 to Present

Background

The factory was established in 1815 and produced both stoneware and earthenware. It was not until much later under the direction of Henry Doulton that an active interest was developed in decoration. The results of these experiments were very well accepted, and eventually this popularity aided in the firm expanding production to include fine porcelain in 1877.

Henry Doulton took a personal interest in refining the staff of artists, modelers, and designers employed at Doulton, and expanded the factory once again in 1844. Henry Doulton dedicated his life to constant improvements at the Doulton factory as well as throughout the porcelain industry in England and in 1887 received his reward by being knighted by Queen Victoria. Ten years later, Sir Henry Doulton died, but the factory was continued by his son, Lewis. It was not until 1901 that the Doulton factory was granted permission to include the "Royal" title in their name.

Characteristics

The Doulton factory produced an exceptional quality bone china that is composed of almost fifty percent bone-ash. Both the porcelain and glaze due to good research has been painstakingly perfected.

The factory's production includes a wide range of dinnerwares as well as decorative accessories and figurines. During the first years of porcelain figurine production the decoration was overdone, but modified when the factory received sharp criticism. Fortunately the factory responded to public demand and experienced a great success with the simpler forms in figurine production.

Marks

The mark found on Doulton porcelain represents four intertwined "Ds" surrounded by the words "Royal Doulton" above with England, below. The British lion and royal crown surmount the entire mark.

Spode, 1770 to Present

Background

Josiah Spode I established the factory in 1770, and together with William Copeland developed the firm into a successful operation that has been in continuous operation since its foundation. William Copeland, a London tea merchant, supplied the Spode factory through his contacts in the East, many of the Oriental patterns that guarantee Spode's popularity.

Spode sent his son, Josiah, to apprentice under Copeland to learn the business side of the firm, and Josiah took over after the death of his father in 1797.

The firm prospered under the management of Josiah Spode II, and his partner, William Copeland. Copeland died in 1826, but was replaced by his son, William Taylor Copeland. The partnership continued under the name of "Spode, Copeland, and Son" until 1827, when Spode died. Several years later, in 1833, Copeland purchased the surviving Spode heirs' interest in the firm, changing the name to "W. T. Copeland and Sons."

Characteristics

Josiah Spode I has been credited with discovering the most favorable combination formula for china paste, which eventually influenced the rest of English factories. The paste was very white and extremely translucent. During the nineteenth century under the management of William Copeland the first parian body was produced.

The factory throughout the centuries has produced a very complete line of wares including dinner sets, decorative accessories, as well as vases and figurines. Much of the decoration was greatly influenced by Oriental motifs, but other patterns of both French and English origin were popular. The colors used were deep and rich, which greatly enhanced the interpretation of the most popular floral, fruit, or bird motifs.

Swansea, 1814–23

Background

Although a pottery factory operated at Swansea as early as 1764, it was not until 1814 that soft-paste porcelain was produced. The factory experienced many financial as well as production reversals and was eventually closed in 1823.

Characteristics

The soft paste produced at Swansea showed many of the same qualities seen in earlier Nantgarw production, being very translucent with an exceptionally white paste. During the first years of operation a definite greenish tint can be noticed exposed to light. This gradually changed to a somewhat more yellow tone as different formulas and production methods were tried.

A good selection of tableware was produced mostly decorated in the neoclassic period with birds, flowers, and fruit being favorite motifs.

Marks

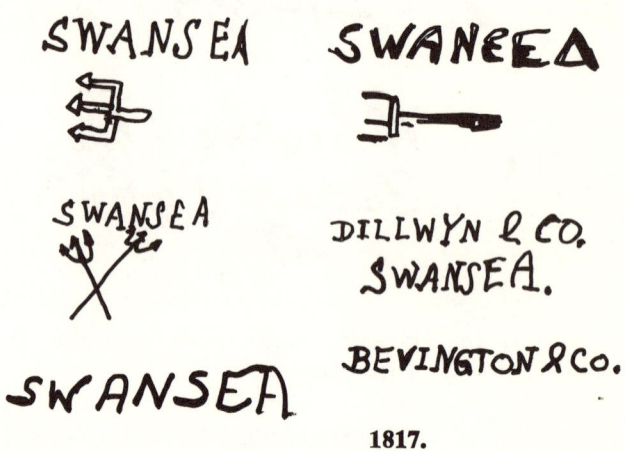

Wedgwood, 1759 to Present

Background

Josiah Wedgwood, member of a well-known Staffordshire potting family, started his own small factory in 1759. At first he produced creamware, which was an immediate success because of its great similarity to porcelain at a much more favorable price. Josiah Wedgwood produced a special service for Queen Charlotte in 1762, and due to her approval of his workmanship she appointed him "Potter to Her Majesty" and allowed the name of creamware to be changed to Queen's-ware in her honor. Queen's-ware became immediately popular not only in England, but throughout Europe. The popularity of this ware had a disastrous effect on the many faience factories, forcing them to close down one by one.

A very astute businessman, Josiah Wedgwood had the further good fortune to marry a very wealthy cousin in 1764, which allowed him to expand his already very successful business. In 1766 he bought the Ridge House estate, which he renamed Etruria in honor of the Etruscan background connected with his new basalt production.

By 1774 the factory produced four basic wares: white terra-cotta (better known as Jasperware), black basalt ware, white biscuit, and terra-cotta.

During the time the factory was developing Josiah Wedgwood encouraged both experimentation with decoration and molding and employed many qualified people. Also, his three sons, Josiah, John, and Thomas, together with Thomas Byerley, his nephew, were trained in managing the various aspects of the business and in 1790 were made full partners.

Josiah Wedgwood died in 1795 and his nephew took over the management of the factory.

For a short period, about 1812 to 1822, bone china was produced at Wedgwood, but this was discontinued because of the expense and the competition, and not produced again until sometime during the 1880s.

Worcester, 1751 to Present

Background

The Worcester porcelain factory was founded in 1751 by several businessmen and was first known as "The Worcester Tonkin Manufacturers." Doctor Wall is perhaps the most famous of the founders, and is attributed with influencing much of the early forms of production. In fact, the Dr. Wall period is established from 1751 to his death in 1776. After Dr. Wall's death, production continued under the general manager, William Davis, until his death in 1783, when the factory was then sold to Thomas Flight, who continued to run the porcelain factory together with his two sons, Joseph and John. Several years later Martin Barr became a partner, and for many years the factory alternated names such as "Flight and Barr," "Barr and Barr," and "Barr, Flight, and Barr." It was not until 1862 that "Worcester Royal Porcelain Company" became the name.

Characteristics

During the first period of production the paste could be best described as soft soapstone. The factory was constantly experimenting with the consistency of the paste between 1770 and 1805, and during this time developed paste of a good quality that was somewhat thin and translucent. Very often the glazes used tended to have either a blue or grey tint.

The Worcester factory was perhaps the most productive porcelain factory operating in England, and never did the volume of its production take away from the excellence of the decoration. Only the Chelsea factory could be rated before Worcester in artistic merit and influence on other phases of the industry.

The quality of production was excellent. Decorations tend to be very English in design and flavor, and transfer-printing was avidly used, first in black and then in various additional colors.

Marks

ROYAL WORCESTER TRADE MARKS

FRANCE

Everything ends this way in France—everything. Weddings, christenings, duels, burials, swindlings, diplomatic affairs—everything is a pretext for a good dinner.

Jean Anouilh, *Cecile*

Perhaps the above comment on French society was in actuality the basis for the foundation, out of necessity, of the great porcelain factories of France.

Historians for centuries have written and researched the despotic reign of Louis XIV (1643–

1715). Volumes have been filled with evaluations of his politics, policies, and fantastic parade of mistresses, but very little has been said about the king as a patron of the arts. The entire world recognizes the majesty of his architectural achievements at both Court of the Roi Soleil, and Versailles.

The reign of Louis XIV established a life-style for grandeur that spread throughout Europe. Each court tried in vain to outdo their French god.

Besides being a patron of the great artists of the world, the king was also very interested in porcelain, which was imported from the Orient. Perhaps Louis XIV could be called one of the first truly great porcelain collectors of the world.

With the death of his minister, Colbert, in 1683, Louis XIV found himself for the first time completely free of governmental obstacles to his extravagances. With friends of the king now in key cabinet positions, French royalty entered the road to financial destruction. After several years of wars and poor management she found herself near bankruptcy.

The French aristocracy stood behind their erring king, and the Duchess de Gamont magnanimously donated her gold and silver plate to benefit both king and country. Although this was not a popular act with her contemporaries, the entire court reluctantly followed suit, to the delight of Louis XIV and the exchequer. This national generosity left the splendor of the French tables bare, and in a country where the preparation and presentation of food was considered a heavenly act, where each dish had to be fit for a god, this became almost a sin. The people at first replaced their precious plate with faience, which was totally impractical and produced active interest in porcelain.

Porcelain production started at Rouen, France, about 1673, and slightly later in 1702 at Saint-Cloud. The first wares made at these factories was not true porcelain, but *pâté tendre*, soft-paste, better known as artificial porcelain. The German Meissen factory succeeded as early as 1709 to produce hard-paste porcelain, but this was not achieved in France until much later, about 1769. Development was slow due to severe regulations established by the guilds, especially the gold and silversmiths, who considered this new product merely an extension of their trade. In fact many of the first designers and decorators were from these guilds, and very often their marks were seen on the earliest production.

By the first quarter of the eighteenth century the art of soft-paste porcelain was well established and under the direction of the regent Philippe, Duc d'Orleans. In 1728, when Louis XV became thirteen, he was already very interested in porcelain production, and by 1745 the king took a personal interest in the new factory started at Vincennes and became part owner of the Sèvres factory. In fact he issued several royal edicts designed to protect the Sèvres factory against competition.

The porcelain of the period, like the silver it replaced, became a luxury for the rich. In 1765 kaolin was discovered at St. Yrieix, and many small factories were established to produce a much cheaper hard-paste porcelain.

Unfortunately, most of the French porcelain factories did not survive the devastation of the Revolution, but the new government demanded a different, but equally gracious, living style, and Napoleon extended his patronage to the factory at Sèvres, to supply these needs. As the empire grew, many of the social boundaries were also extended. The porcelain factories were unable to maintain their former excellence and meet the new demands for production. Perhaps if the patrons of these factories were as quality conscious as before, this degenerate trend would have been stopped, but their clients now came from a much less exacting class, much more interested in prestige than quality of production.

Arras, 1782–88

Background

The factory was established by four ladies, the Demoiselles Deleneur, under the patronship of the governor of Flanders and Artois. The main reason he extended financial support was to produce a product that would stop the extensive china imports from England.

Characteristics

The Porcelain produced was soft-paste and yellowish white in color. It can be most closely compared to the paste produced at either Sceaux or Mennecy. Mostly copies of Chantilly and Tournay were produced and very simply decorated, chiefly in blue. During the nineteenth century some Arras porcelain was redecorated to imitate the more important factories of the original time.

Marks

The major mark consisted of either the letters AR in separate or monogram form painted in underglaze blue. Painters' initials can often be found beside the mark.

AR 20 A.R
             P
de Ce AA AR

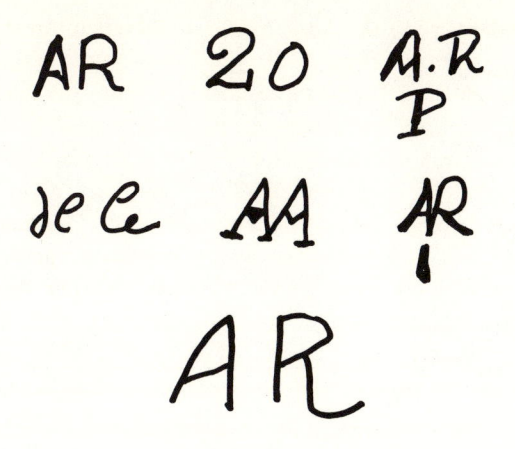

AR

Bourg-La-Reine, 1774–88

Background

The factory was founded by Jacques and Jullien in 1774. Both of the men were experienced as previous managers of the Mennecy-Villeroy porcelain factory. The Comte d'Eu extended his financial support to start the Bourg-La-Reine factory.

The wares produced at this factory, instead of being new and innovative, were merely continuations of the work started earlier by these two men at Mennecy and Sceaux.

Characteristics

It should be noted that some of the production of the factory was left unmarked, and identification between the unmarked wares of Bourg-La-Reine, Sceaux, and Mennecy is almost impossible. Very little gilding was used, and along all the edges a fine line of rose coloring can be seen.

Marks

MO + Moitte B.R.

B la R   ⟊OB

BR

All of the above marks are found incised in the paste.

Caen, 1739–1808

Background

The small factory at Caen, near Limoges, was founded in 1798 and prospered for several years until the political and economic conditions of France caused it to close in 1808.

Characteristics

The wares produced at Caen were of an excellent quality hard-paste porcelain. The factory relied heavily on the abundant local deposits of both feldspar and kaolin. The forms produced closely followed the styles of both the Empire and Directorire periods, which portrayed much beauty and grace.

Yellow was a favorite color, and can be seen quite often as a ground color. The porcelain produced combined excellent quality of workmanship in the glaze and body as well as design and decoration.

Marks

The marks were mostly printed in red.

caen   CAEN

Le françois
à
caen. **Early part nineteenth century.**

Chantilly, 1725–89

Background

The prince of the fabled White Castle, Louis-Henri de Bourbon, became the leading patron both financially and managerially in the famous works at Chantilly. After finding the master craftsman Ciquaire Cirou to supervise to production, the Prince de Condé assembled a collection of the finest Japanese Aritce ware to be used as factory models.

The prince felt that the quality of porcelain produced would be accepted not only in France, but throughout Europe, and the King extended a license for twenty years for the factory at Chantilly to produce a first-quality porcelain that would imitate the Japanese.

The factory enjoyed success and popularity; although no new styles were produced, the beauty and charm of the wares prevailed. Production continued almost until the eve of the Revolution, in 1789.

Characteristics

The body of the ware produced at Chantilly was soft paste, which very much resembled Saint Cloud production at that time. A comparison between the two factories shows the Chantilly products to have a slight yellow tinge and a tendency toward a granular texture.

The first glaze used at the factory was tin oxide, which produced an opaque, milk-white finish. Because of the aesthetic restrictions caused by this glaze, and economic pressure caused by the competition, Mennecy-Villeroy and Sèvres, a transparent glaze was substituted.

Chantilly produced mainly porcelain for use in the home, for example large dinner services, tea and chocolate sets, flowers, knife handles, covered jars, and many more. At the beginning the shapes were directly copied from their Oriental prototypes, but gradually the French styling was adopted.

The majority of decorations produced were the polychrome Kakiyemon, and Imari motifs, but excellent Sèvres style polychrome fruits, birds, and flowers were produced.

Marks

Red was used at first, but later in the eighteenth century the colors varied, with blue being used quite often.

The following marks are from the factory started by M. Pigorry in 1803 after the closing of the Prince Condé factory. This factory produced general table services as well as tea and coffee sets. Many of these marks are confusing to new collectors, who often confuse them with marks on the earlier Chantilly production.

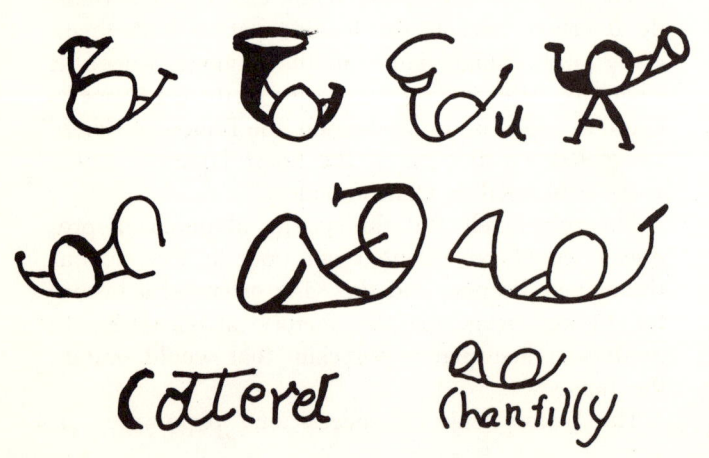

Haviland, 1842 to Present

Background

Frustrated by the difficulties in importing French Porcelain into the United States, David Haviland moved to France, built a factory, and began producing a product, Haviland, that in grandmother's time became a household word. His factory started in 1842, and was called Haviland and Company.

Charles Field Haviland, David's nephew, managed the Alluaud Factory, which about 1850 became part of the Haviland group. It was originally founded by M. M. Greflet, and Massie in 1771, and continued under the Haviland name until 1880.

Theodore Haviland, David's son, started his own factory in 1892. He took great care to be sure that his factory was one of the most modern and largest in Limoges. After much experimentation it was decided that special patterns and shapes intended especially for the American Market could be more profitably produced in the United States. Therefore, the American subsidiary was founded in 1936, under the name of Theodore Haviland and Company, and operates under this arrangement today.

The Theodore Haviland factory purchased the original David Haviland factory in 1939, combining for the first time the entire family porcelain interests.

Characteristics

The Haviland factory pioneered chromolithography, a process that is now used by almost all porcelain manufacturers.

The body of the wares produced at the Haviland factory was a fine feldsparthic one with an excellent glaze. Although transfer-printing was used primarily, some gilding can be found.

The shapes produced conformed mainly to Victorian styles that were liked in the American market. Large table services were produced, and flowering rococo motifs were very popular. Perhaps the most popular pattern produced was the Moss Rose.

Marks

There are two separate marks used in connection with the factories both in America and France. The mark for the French market shows "Theodore Haviland" printed above the town name "Limoges," and "France," while the American mark shows the name "Theodore Haviland" printed above the city "New York." The above is written in Old English and enclosed in a lobate cartouche, with "Made in America" printed underneath.

Other Important Marks

Haviland and Company, founded 1797.

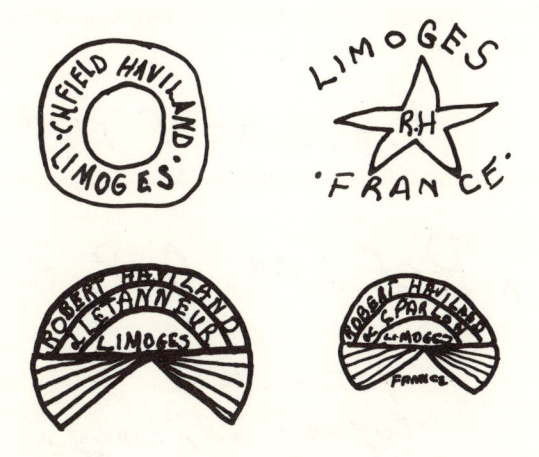

Robert Haviland.

Theodore Haviland Porcelain Factory.

Lauraguis, 1758–?

Background

Louis Léon Félicité (1733–1824), the Count de Brancus-Lauraguis, was very interested in hard-paste porcelain. He started his experimentation near Alençon, in the west of France, in 1758.

Characteristics

The production was a primitive grey-brown ware that displayed a very poor glaze. The quality improved, but the biscuit showed a slightly greyish hue. The majority of the pieces were very simple and decorated in only blue.

Very few pieces survive, and these are difficult to identify.

Marks

The "BL" was interlaced and painted underglazed blue.

Lille, 1711–?

Background

Barthélémy Dorez and his nephew, Pierre Pélissier, petitioned the City Council of Lille to establish a porcelain factory to operate simultaneously with their faience factory. The mayor and council were excited by the samples they were shown and extended financial support until the factory was able to operate profitably in about 1720.

The king became aware of the factory and, although impressed with the quality of production, decided not to extend his patronage, because it might affect the factory at Saint Cloud, which was supported by the Duc d'Orleans.

39

Without the support of the king, and denial of a factory warehouse in Paris, the factory lacked the necessary marketing operation to grow more successful, and gradually began to curtail production. The actual year the factory closed is not precisely know.

Characteristics

The porcelain produced mainly copied the wares made at Saint Cloud. Although the Lille production was an excellent copy of Saint Cloud ware, differences can be detected in the finish, since the glaze tended to blister ever so slightly.

Marks

All marks appear in blue.

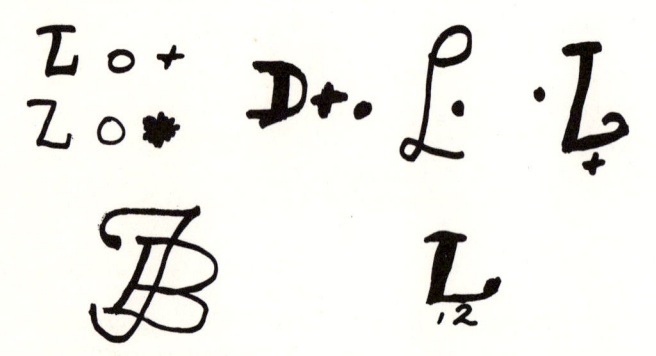

This mark usually appears on wares decorated in blue.

Following the decline of the original soft-paste porcelain factory at Lille, a hard-paste factory was established in 1784 by the Dauphin and M. Lepere-Durot. This factory closed in 1817.

Marks

A dolphin stenciled in red marked the wares, which were very similar in style to the "Paris" style of production.

Limoges, 1771 to Present

Background

The Comte d'Artois extended his patronage to the Grellet brothers for the establishment of a hard-paste porcelain factory at Limoges in 1771. Several years later in 1784, this factory was purchased by the king, and this is perhaps the accepted date for the foundation of Limoges production. Originally the factory was purchased to produce white ware to later be decorated at Sèvres.

Due to the abundant supplies of kaolin and petuntse found in the Limoges area, many porcelain factories flourished during the eighteenth and nineteenth centuries.

When the main factory at Limoges was no longer needed by Sèvres for white production, it was sold to M. Alluaud, and still operates today under the name of Pouyat and Alluaud.

Characteristics

Besides the white porcelain, which was supplied to the Sèvres factory for decoration, nothing of great importance was manufactured. The paste of the eighteenth century showed distinct ivory coloring and was decorated with small, nondescript flowers.

The production at the Alluaud factory showed great advancement. The body of the ware was pure white, and the glazes used were much improved. In fact, great technological advancements were developed here during the nineteenth century that helped the entire porcelain industry.

Marks

Among the marks used were either the initials of the manufacturer or the word "Limoges." The following is a list of various factories and marks operating in Limoges.

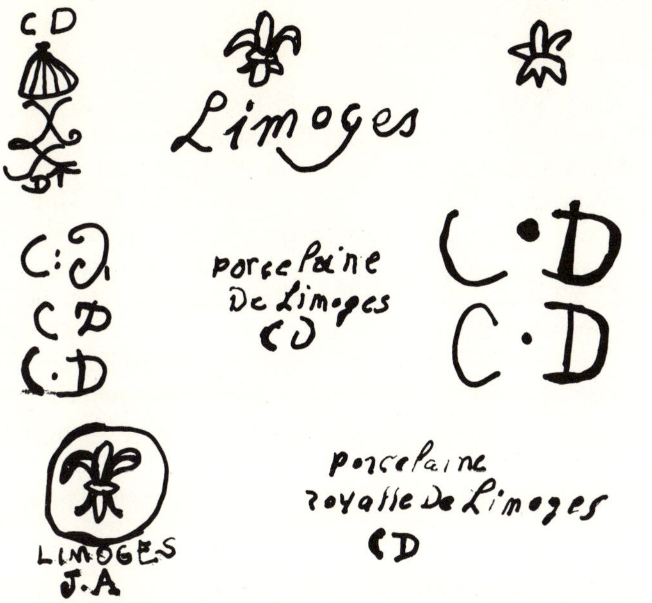

First factory founded by Grellet Brothers in 1771 and continuing marks through Crown ownership.

P. Tharaud, 1817.
Barbe Poncet, 1819.

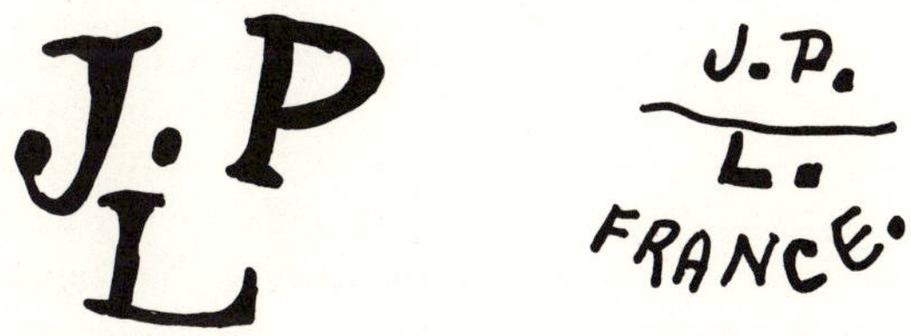

J. Pouyat, 1842. Mark in green under the glaze.

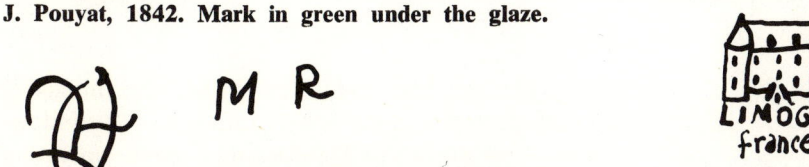

Montjoreis and Gorsas, 1882.

Small factory, 1842–98.

Small factory, c. 1875.

Small factory, nineteenth century.

Small factory, c. 1880.

Charles Ahrenfeld, 1894.

H. A. Balleroy Frères.

Julien Balleroy & Cie.

L. Bernardaud & Cie., 1863.

Beule, Reboissonet Parot.

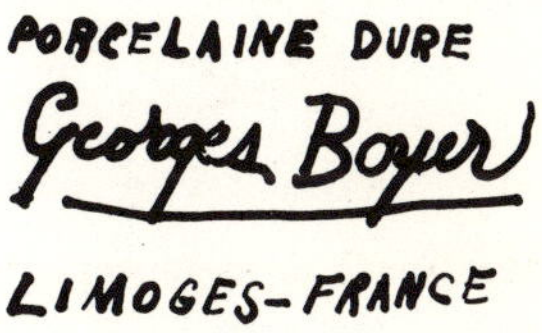

Georges Boyer, 1934.

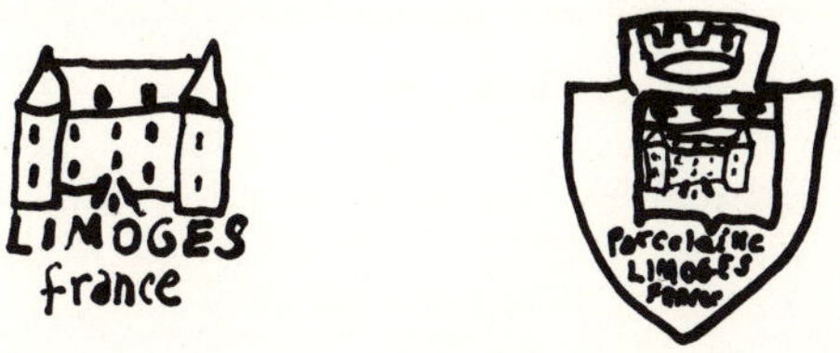

Porcelain J. Chateau or Porcelaines Limoges Castel.

Manufacture de Porcelaines Artistiques.
Fontanille & Marraud, 1925.

Maison Gerard, founded 1798.

41

A. Lanternier & Cie., 1855.

Raynaud & Cie., 1919.

Mennecy-Villeroy, 1734–1806

Background

The original factory was built directly in Paris in 1734, but was forced to move to Mennecy in 1748, because of pressure from the then very powerful Vincennes factory. Later the factory was moved to Bourg-La-Reine in 1773.

The factory was managed by Barbin, and later by his son in 1751. As a team they continued to co-manage the factory until 1765, the year of their deaths.

Characteristics

The first products from the Paris factory and Mennecy displayed a definite yellowish tone at first, which later turned a milky white. Although the wares produced were in essence only reproductions of the successful factories of the period—Chantilly, Vincennes, and Saint Cloud—they retained their own distinct characteristics in the glaze, which was extremely brilliant and could best be described as looking "wet."

Although the factory's patron, the Duc de Villeroy, was very powerful, he could do nothing to overrule the guidelines established by Vincennes against gilding. Mennecy porcelain edges are painted a blue or pink, but because of the above ruling are never gilded. Perhaps this gives Mennecy porcelain an air of delicacy, which is very appealing, both in form and decoration.

Delicate yellows and greens were frequently used, and all colors are noted to be crisp and cool. Shapes such as the "ozier" were favored, as well as adapting delicate scattered flowers from Meissire and Vincennes. Figure modeling was very popular and displayed an appealing simplicity.

Marks

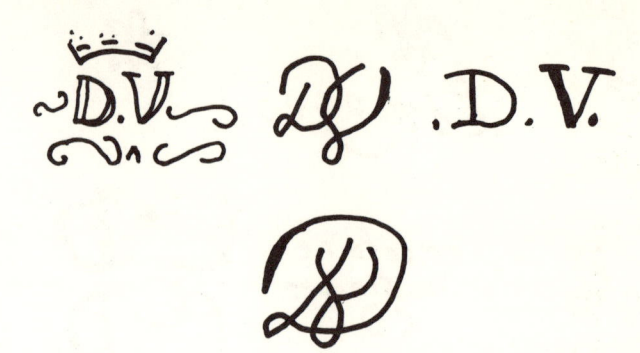

Most marks were painted in various colors, but the second mark pictured above was mostly done in red.

Although the wares produced at both Mennecy-Villeroy and at Bourg-La-Reine were very similar, adequate markings were used, and identification is relatively easy.

Niderviller, 1754–1850

Background

The first factory established at Niderviller in 1754 produced a fine faienceware. Porcelain production was not started until 1765. The Baron Jean-Louis de Beyerlé, the factory patron, imported kaolin from Germany at first, and then decided it was a better investment to purchase some of the kaolin mines found at St. Yrieux.

The famous sculptor Lemire was employed at Niderville in 1780, when the factory was purchased by the Comte de Custine. It was during this time that famous figurines and vases styled in the Louis XVI form were produced, which have made the factory famous.

Characteristics

The first paste produced was very translucent, but this quality lessened slightly over the years. There was a definite favoring of rococo styling at first, and these products were greatly influenced by Strasbourg and are some of the most important wares produced. Decorations were expertly done, and figures were often painted in crimson monochrome.

Marks

Painted in blue.

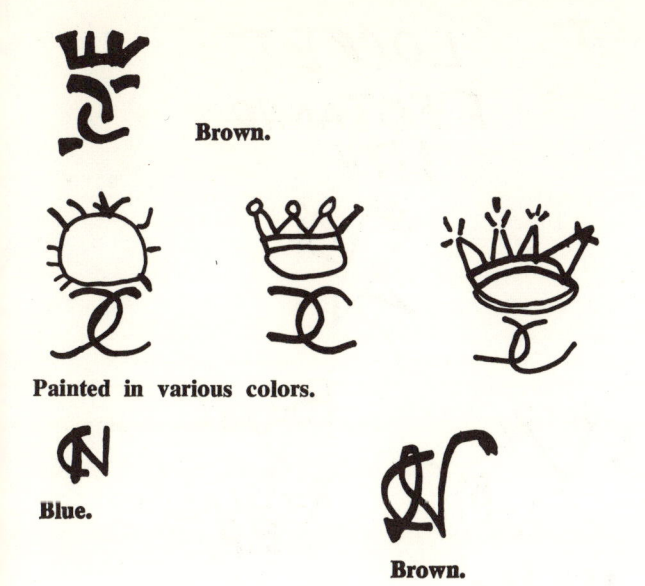

The CC stands for General Comte de Custine; the monogram CN represents the combination of the Custine and Niderviller names. Some of the first wares were monogrammed with the letters JLB, and represent the period from 1755 to 1770.

"Old Paris" or Paris, 1770–1850

After the factory of Sèvres was well established, some of the very strict rules that governed the competition were slightly relaxed, and the area directly surrounding Paris during the 1770s saw the development of many porcelain factories that enjoyed the patronage of members of the royal family.

Due to the success and pressure applied to the Sèvres factory by the various new Paris factories, many of the noted designers and staff members joined the new factories. Due to this migration of workers from Sèvres, this style was avidly copied in production.

The hard-paste porcelain produced at the various factories can both in form and decoration be favorably compared to the wares made at Sèvres. This elegant style of decoration, known as Louis XVI, was favored until the Empire style became in vogue and was produced until around 1814, when the various factories began producing many different styles that were in vogue at the moment.

The different factories produced mainly vases, dinnerware, tea services, and various decorative items. At present, Old Paris porcelain is favored by interior decorators and specialty shops.

The following is a detailed individual listing of the various Paris porcelain factories.

Vincennes, 1767–86

Background

The Hannong family, who originally were potters located in Strasbourg, France, freely negotiated with M. Boiheau, the managing director of the Sèvres factory concerning the secrets of hard-paste porcelain production. After surrendering this much guarded family secret, the Hannongs were forced by the all-powerful Sèvres factory to stop any further production of porcelain in France.

The production of hard-paste porcelain was not seen again until 1784, when the Sieur Lemaire protested the severe restrictions placed against the factories. It is also known that Louis-Philippe, while he was the Duke of Chartres, gave his patronage to the Vincennes factory.

Characteristics

Vincennesware has a noticeable yellow hue to the body, which is also vitreous hard paste. The glaze used has a definite pitted and uneven appearance. Most of the production was limited to everyday dinner sets that resembled much of the soft-paste procelain produced earlier, but tended to favor contemporary styling.

Polychrome flowers were very often used in decorating, and definite coloring flaws can be noticed in the violet and rose colors. This fading is due probably from extensive overfiring.

Marks

The first four marks were painted in underglaze blue and date from the foundation of the factory, during the Hannong period.

These marks represent wares produced under the patronage of Louis Philippe, Duc de Chartres and done in underglaze blue.

43

This mark, seems to be the only official mark produced and was done in underglaze blue and registered by the factory in 1777.

La Courtille, 1773–94

Background

The factory was founded in 1773 in the rue Fontaine-au-Roi to produce copies of the wares made at great German porcelain factories, especially Meissen. The height of important production came directly after Russinger joined the factory in 1784.

1790 saw the introduction of the first casting of hard-paste porcelain done in France at the factory. All significant production came to an end during the Revolution.

Characteristics

The body was of an excellent quality white hard paste, and the glaze was of the same purity, showing the prime property of clarity.

Mostly dinner, tea, and coffee sets were produced and were decorated primarily with small Meissen-type flowers and Pompeiian Scrolls done on colored grounds.

Marks

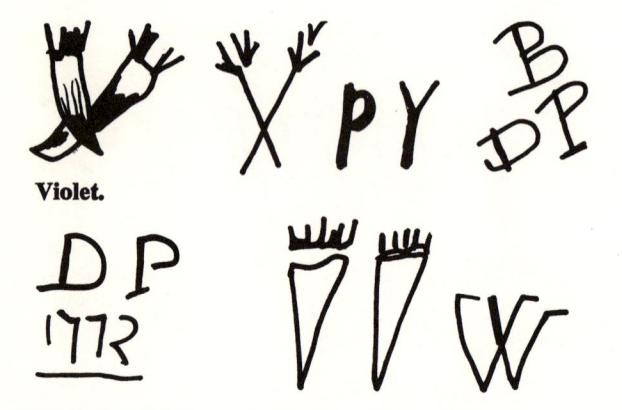

Violet.

Painted in blue and gold under the glaze.

Painted in blue and violet.

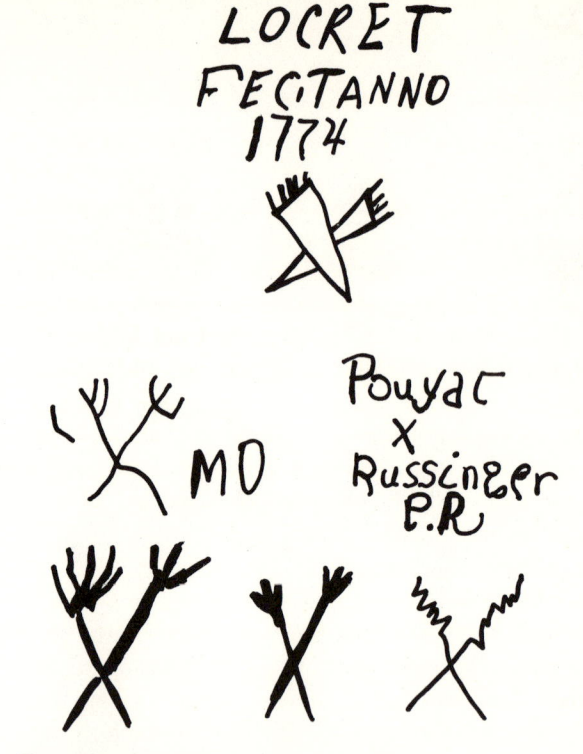

Reproduced in blue under the glaze.

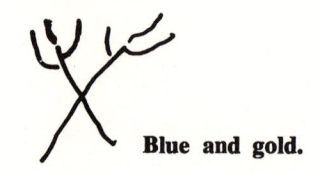

Blue and gold.

Painted in red.

Faubourg St. Denis, 1769–1810

Background

Pierre Antoine Hannong, the prior famous director at Vincennes, took over the direction of the factory in the Faubourg St. Denis in 1772. Hannong remained only a few years and was replaced by Barrackin in 1775. About this time the factory came to the attention of the king's brother, Comte d'Artois, and was under his patronage granted permission to call the factory the Manufacture du Comte d'Artois. Production was centered around biscuit and continued to operate throughout the Revolution, not stopping until around 1810.

Characteristics

Due to the fact that the factory used coal instead of wood for production, a fact that alleviated a fuel shortage that was causing a serious problem around Paris at the time, the restrictive rulings governing porcelain factories were amended. This amendment was granted as long as only biscuit pieces were produced, and that each piece measured not higher than eighteen inches in height, and that the gilding could not at any one time completely cover one piece.

The beginning production shows either an amber or yellow tinge that shows a great similarity to Vincennes. During later periods the body of the ware became almost a milky white, and improved in quality so that it could favorably be compared to Sèvres. It should be noted that of all the Paris factories, the Manufacture du Comte d'Artois produced some of the most important and impressive pieces of the independent factories.

Marks

Fabrique de la Rue de Reuilly, 1774–1800

Background

The factory was officially established in the Faubourg St. Antoine by Lassia in 1774, but production was not begun on a large scale until 1781. The restrictive edict of 1784 caused considerable hardship at this factory, but production lasted until sometime around 1800.

Characteristics

The wares produced were of an excellent pure white hard-paste porcelain with a glaze that was extremely clear. Although the factory tried to specialize in porcelain stoves and mantelpieces and was denied permission, it did produce vases, tea sets, and dinnerware of excellent quality.

Shapes were basically in the neoclassical styling, with decoration favoring flowers and designs in the Renaissance and classic styling.

Marks

The L mark was registered by the factory's founder, Lassia, and retained in different variations throughout production. Also L marks have been noted done in underglaze blue.

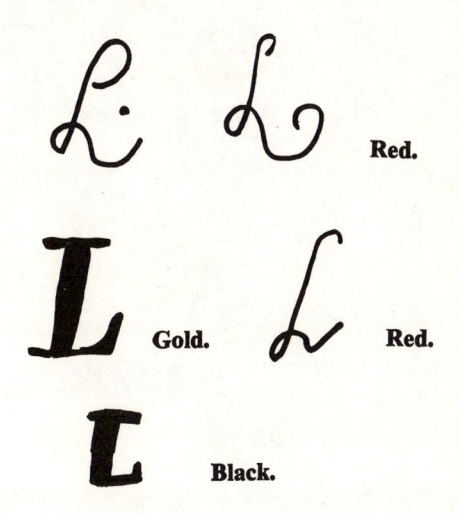

Mark number one and two were done in red while 3 completed in gold, four in red and 5 in black.

Fabrique de Monsieur à Clignancourt, 1771–98

Background

The factory founded by Pierre Deruelle was begun in 1771 at Clignancourt to produce hard-paste por-

45

celain. Although the factory operated for several years without official approval, in 1775 the brother of Louis XVI extended his patronage and allowed the name of the factory to be changed to favor his name, Fabrique de Monsieur à Clignancourt.

The products produced were of an excellent quality that daringly crossed the boundaries set up by Sèvres. In fact some of the pieces were even decorated in the exclusive Sèvres styles, and these wares were confiscated, and the director of the factory was heavily fined.

Characteristics

The production of this factory patterned itself so closely after Sèvres that it was very difficult to separate the wares of the two factories. Gilting was favored, as was the neoclassic styling that was very popular in this period.

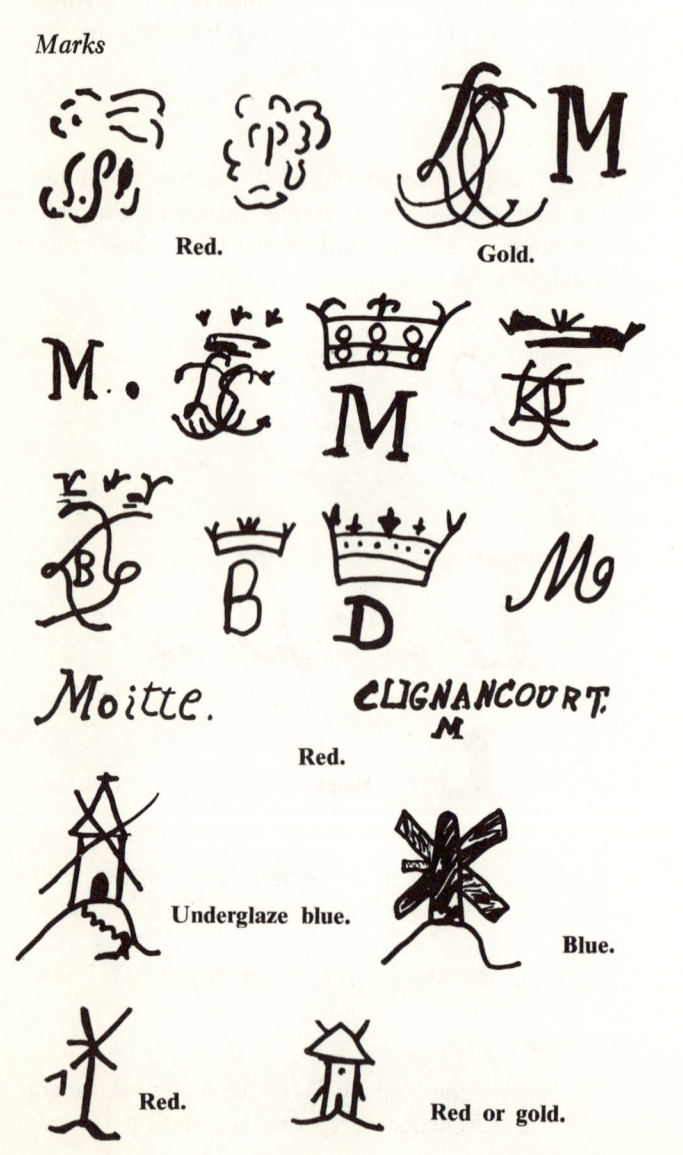

Marks

Fabrique de la Reine, 1778–98

Background

Andrè-Marie le Boeuf founded his hard-paste porcelain factory in 1778. Within one year his production was so perfected that the factory in the rue Thiroux became a definite competitor to the heavily protected Sèvres works. After incurring the displeasure of both Sèvres and the police, the factory acquired the patronage of the queen, Marie Antoinette. She allowed the use of either her initial or monogram on the wares produced. The queen purchased most of the porcelain for gifts and her personal use from the factory.

Marks

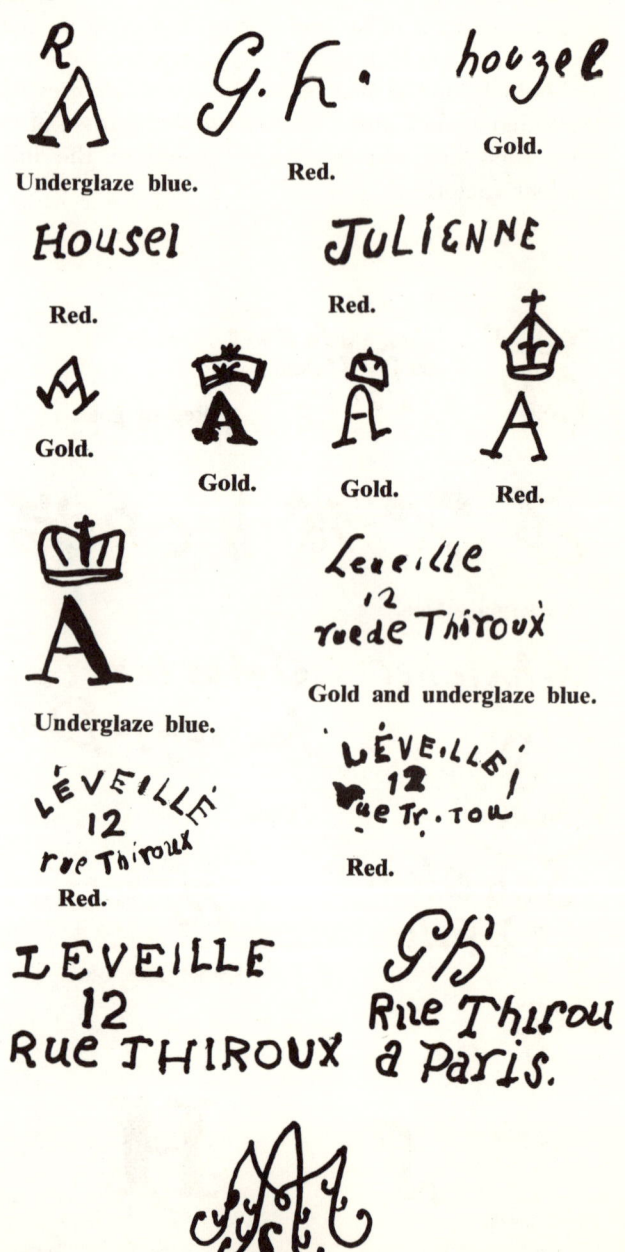

Other marks are either done in underglaze blue or gold onglaze, while the crowned "a" usually appeared only on the most beautiful ware.

Fabrique du Duc D'Angoulême, 1780–1829

Background

Both Dihl and Guerhard established a hard-paste porcelain factory about 1780 in the rue de Bondy. After much experimentation Dihl developed a broad range of colors for decoration. The factory enjoyed a successful operation under the patronage of the duc d'Angoulême until the Revolution, and after Dihl and Guerhard continued operation without any royal patronage.

Characteristics

The factory carefully copied the many colors used at Sèvres for both ground and decoration. Tablewares, tea sets, ornaments, and vases, as well as some biscuit pieces of exceptional quality, were mostly produced. The decorations were elaborate.

Marks

The marks showing a G.A. or with a coronet were used previous to the Revolution. After the Revolution the production was merely marked either with the names of the two founders, "Guerhard" or "Dihl."

Fabrique de la Rue Popincourt, 1760–1835

Background

The first factory was founded by Lemaire in the rue des Amandiers in 1760. J. N. H. Nast purchased the hard-paste porcelain factory from Lemaire in 1783. Nast's sons continued the factory until 1835.

Characteristics

The factory produced tableware in large quantities, as well as biscuitware. The majority of pieces show beauty and intricate designs. Although nothing new was developed, both shapes and painting followed the neoclassic styling.

Marks

Most marks bear the name "Nast" done in red on the glaze.

Fabrique du Duc d'Orléans, 1784–1806

Background

The first factory was established in 1784 on the Faubourg St. Antoine and operated for two years until 1786, when it obtained the patronage of the Duc d'Orléans.

Characteristics

The factory produced a good-quality porcelain that could be compared to the other contemporary wares made by the Paris factories. The basic form favored first the Louis XVI styling in both shape and decoration, and later the Directoire and Empire periods.

Marks

Basically two marks were used, both of which show interlacing monograms of L.J. and O.M.

Rouen, 1673–96

Background

The first recorded patent for porcelain production in France was given to Louis Poterat in 1673 for a factory to be built at Rouen. Poterat was issued the exclusive patent for a period of thirty years on the condition that he learn the secrets of porcelain production in order to establish a worthwhile industry for France.

In 1696, Louis Poterat died, but his brother carried on the family tradition.

Although Rouen had an exclusive monopoly, very little porcelain was produced, and what has survived is mostly in museums.

Characteristics

Rouen porcelain was soft paste, and shows considerable similarities to Rouen faience. The few remaining pieces are almost exclusively decorated in blue, although green and red have also been used. The blue used is soft and greyish, and the decoration was applied on the raw glaze before firing.

Most decorations followed the styling of Louis XIV.

Marks

No factory mark has been attributed to Rouen production.

Saint Cloud, 1696–1773

Background

The factory was established near the famous Castle of Saint Cloud, and enjoyed both the patronage and financial support of the Duc d'Orléans. Not only the Duc, but the king and the entire court at one time gave their approval of the work being done at Saint Cloud.

Production originated in 1696 as a faience factory, and by 1670 was so well established that it was supplying vases and pots for the gardens at Versailles. The factory's reputation grew, and it is believed that a painter from Rouen was employed to start production with the still well-kept secrets of porcelain. There is very little recorded about the original factory at Saint Cloud, and it was eventually destroyed by fire in 1773. The factory was not restored because of personal financial difficulties.

Characteristics

The production at Saint Cloud was limited to soft paste, which showed a definite mellow yellowish tinge. The glaze was exceptionally clear, brilliant, and rarely blistered. Mostly domestic tableware was produced, as well as vases and figurines. The majority of figurines were produced between 1710 and 1724.

At first the wares closely resembled the Chinese imports of the period in both form and decoration. At a later period production favored the European styles that were becoming more popular. Production in the white with molded ornaments favored Fuchien wares, which were very popular at this period. Decorations of sprigs in relief and Prunus flowers as well as rosettes and flowers frequently appeared in decorations.

Marks

All marks from the Saint Cloud factory were done in blue.

Saint-Amand-les-Eaux, 1815 to Present

Background

The factory was founded in 1815 by a Flemish porcelain master, Dorchies Herbo, to produce soft-paste porcelain. The factory is still in operation. This factory and the factory at Tournay are the only two remaining works producing soft-paste porcelain in France today.

Characteristics

Saint-Amand-les-Eaux produces a very fine white soft-paste body. Reproducers of porcelain avidly seek to imitate the original production at Sèvres. The majority of the wares are painted simply in underglaze blue.

Marks

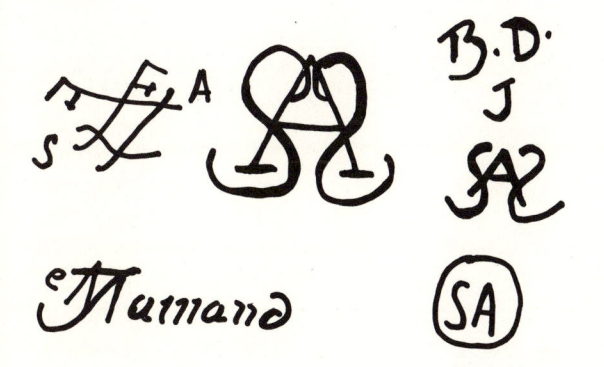

Date from the end of the nineteenth century.

All marks from the factory were done in underglaze blue.

Sceaux, 1748–94

Background

Under the direction of Jacques Chapelle a porcelain factory was founded at Sceaux in 1748 at the already well-established faience works. The factory was denied permission to operate even with the intervention of the Duchesse de Maine. Both the forces of the protection of the factory at Vincennes and the opposition displayed by Madame de Pompadour resulted in the continuation of a form of faience, Faience Japonée, as a substitute for advancement in porcelain production.

The factory was taken over by Jacques and Jullien in 1763, the same two men who purchased the factory at Mennecy several years later. The factory operated without royal consent until 1775 when the Duc de Penthièvre extended his patronage and porcelain was openly produced. This unofficial production continued from 1775 until 1784, when the Vincennes-Sèvres rulings were to some extent relaxed, and then the production was expanded to include gilding and polychrome decoration.

Characteristics

The soft-paste wares produced were similar, as were the glazes, to that of Mennecy, which should be expected, since the same two men operated both factories. The majority of wares produced were for use in the home, for example tableware, dressing table accessories, and other decorations. Decorations centered on birds and flowers much similar to those of Mennecy, but much finer designing was done at Sceaux. At first, rose-color edges were substituted before the ban was lifted on gilding.

Marks

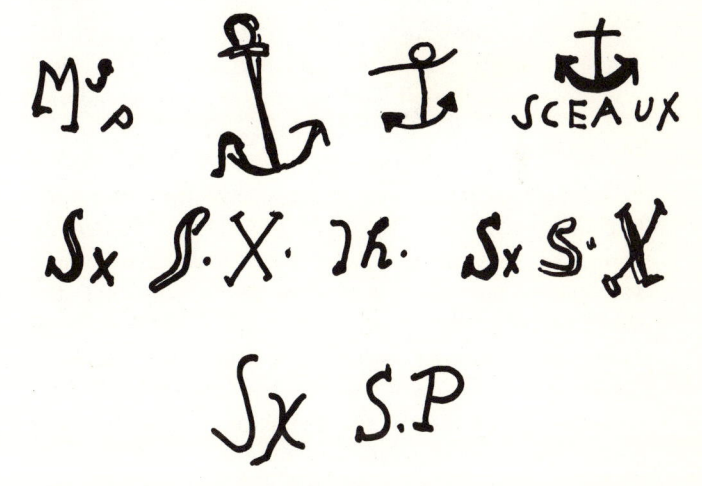

Most of the SX marks shown above were incised in the paste. Many Sceaux pieces have been found that are lacking the incised SX mark.

Sèvres, 1756 to Present

Background

The founding of the factory at Sèvres is directly

49

related to both the first factory at Vincennes and the beautiful and powerful Madame de Pompadour. With the king's favorite interested in the beauty of porcelain, she saw to it directly that the king took a personal interest in the development of the art in France. Therefore ground was selected and work immediately started for the opening of the Royal porcelain factory at Sèvres and the entire staff and equipment of Vincennes transferred to the new site.

Sèvres was very fortunate to have both the knowledge and craftsmen who had worked previously at Vincennes and, perhaps more importantly, royal patronage. Due to the interest stimulated by Madame de Pompadour and the money given by the king, the Sèvres porcelain factory was able to produce wares of fantastic beauty and excellent design. Unfortunately Sèvresware was very expensive and could not compete with the less expensive Oriental and German porcelain produced at the same time. In 1759 the king assumed full financial responsibility for the Sèvres factory to avoid total bankruptcy. In order to protect the now royal Sèvres porcelain factory, the king established severe laws restricting the production of other competitive factories.

During Sèvres' supremacy all other French porcelain factories were not allowed to use gilding, and any color decorations were restricted to only blue. This is very evident in both the production of the Mennecy and Chantilly factories of this period.

Even these severe restrictions did not help Sèvres prosper, since production was centered on much too expensive wares for the population. It wasn't until several years later in 1769 when the king could not afford to subsidize the large financial deficits of the factory that production was reorganized and began to appeal to the populace. At this same time the much needed secrets for producing hard-paste porcelain were procured and kaolin deposits were found near Limoges. Together, these two factors helped the Royal Sèvres factory to survive and prosper.

Royal patronage continued under the rule of Louis XVI and Marie Antoinette. The factory continued to prosper until the Revolution and was saved from total financial ruin by Napoleon in 1800. Alexandre Brogniart was appointed technical director, and he reorganized production. Soft-paste porcelain was completely discontinued, and improved decoration techniques as well as a wider range of colors were developed. The factory continued to prosper, and in 1876 new buildings were constructed and the Sèvres factory enlarged.

Characteristics

The hard-paste porcelain produced at Sèvres can only be described as extremely translucent, hard, and very white. The wares were flowers and possessed a resonant quality lacking in other less perfect porcelain of the period. The glazes for the soft-paste porcelain were basically the same used at the Vincennes factory, because much time and expense was allocated for their perfection. They displayed a distinct clarity, smoothness, and transparency that helped Sèvres attain its reputation for perfection. The glazes developed for the hard-paste porcelain were not as transparent or glassy because of the addition of lime to the composition. The glaze on this early hard-paste porcelain was almost opaque and gave the wares a slightly pearly white appearance. The glaze was once again changed under the directorship of Brogniart during the first part of the nineteenth century and could be best described as being glittering.

The Sèvres factory produced almost everything one could imagine to be reproduced in porcelain, but all wares were definitely French in design.

Rococo decorations, which seem to characterize Sèvres styling, were only produced from 1756 to 1769. Louis XVI and Marie Antoinette inspired at first a new elegance in decoration that displayed a reserved delicacy but that later inspired an almost fanciful unreality.

Although the original decorations were basically the same as those used at Vincennes, favoring flowers and birds, there were considerable developments in the colors, which showed a definite new richness. An impressive group of sculptors, painters, and modelers were employed at Sèvres. Impressive panels and busts were produced, as well as the endearing rosettes, cornflower, and forget-me-not decorations. Gilting was excellent at Sèvres and was developed to its highest form.

Marks

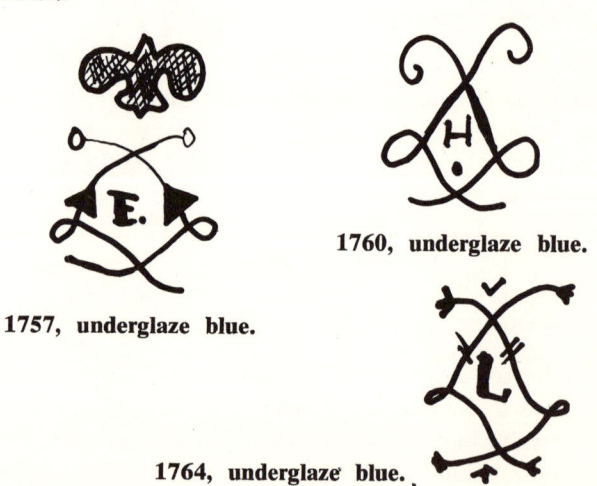

1757, underglaze blue.

1760, underglaze blue.

1764, underglaze blue.

1764, underglaze blue and occasionally red.

1778, underglaze blue.

Underglaze blue, 1830.

1831–34, blue or gold.

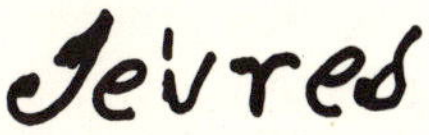

Sèvres — Gold or various colors.

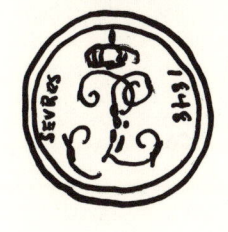

1834–45, blue or gold.

1845, underglaze green.

R.F Sèvres — Underglaze blue.

1848, gold or blue.

1803–4, blue.

First Empire, 1804–14, stenciled in red.

1845–48.

1810–14, printed in red.

Underglaze blue.

1851, green.

1848–49.

1849, red.

1850, red.

Underglaze blue from the period 1824–30.

1852–70, red.

51

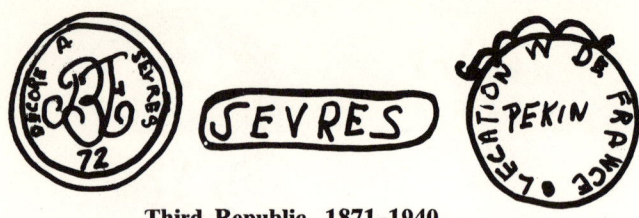

Third Republic, 1871–1940.

1871, underglaze brown.

1926.

1928–40.

From 1941.

From 1753 to 1793 the year of production was represented by letters of the alphabet. The following is a representative chart:

A	1753	M	1765	Z	1777	LL	1789
B	1754	N	1766	AA	1778	MM	1790
C	1755	O	1767	BB	1779	NN	1791
D	1756	P	1768	CC	1780	OO	1792
E	1757	Q	1769	DD	1781	PP	1793
F	1758	R	1770	EE	1782		
G	1759	S	1771	FF	1783		
H	1760	T	1772	GG	1784		
I	1761	U	1773	HH	1785		
J	1762	V	1774	II	1786		
K	1763	X	1775	JJ	1787		
L	1764	Y	1776	KK	1788		

Strasbourg, 1766–80

Background

Paul Antoine Hannong, famous for his faience, started experimenting with hard-paste porcelain production as early as 1726. About this time he gave some of his hard-paste wares to the Strasbourg factory as examples of his work. Almost nothing exists from this period, but Hannong's son Paul continued the factory and produced hard-paste porcelain as early as 1745. Paul Hannong hired several workers from the famous German Höchst and Meissen factories, and with their help Strasbourg produced a much improved porcelain.

Because production was so successful, Hannong's patent for production was denied as was his offer to sell his knowledge to the powerful Vincennes factory. It was useless at this time to try and fight the powerful Vincennes monopoly, and Hannong was ordered to stop production at the Strasbourg factory.

Paul Hannong moved his factory to Frankenthal and continued his work and the patronage of the Archduke Charles Théodore. Paul's son Joseph Adam Hannong remained at the Strasbourg factory and continued the production of faience after his father moved to Frankenthal. The factory again tried hard-paste production in 1766 and continued until 1780, but the wares that were produced were geared more to a commercial market, therefore passing the real threat to Vincennes.

Characteristics

The hard-paste ware that was first made, 1745–54, was white and slightly translucent. Joseph Adam Hannong produced a much thicker porcelain that displayed a yellowish hue. It is evident that both Hannongs had difficulties with glazes, since the wares are pitted and irregular in surface texture. Very little gilding was used but floral and Chinese scenes were favored.

Marks

The first two marks are written in capitals and the remaining marks are done in underglaze blue. Several of the biscuit figurines have an "H" directly in the paste.

52

Tournay, 1750 to Present

Background

Peterinck established a porcelain factory in 1750 at Tournay, which at the time was annexed to France. The factory, which today still operates in Belgium, prospered almost immediately.

Two distinct grades of porcelain were made, and both were well accepted in their markets. The finest porcelain, although quite as good as any contemporary French production, was discontinued after several years and the average grade ware was exclusively made and is still produced by the factory today.

Characteristics

Tournay wares used a slightly different composition from the other factories operating at the time that needed a shorter firing time. The finished product showed a slightly more porous texture, which was not as white as other factories' works, especially those of Sèvres and Vincennes. The glaze used was very smooth and clear.

Production included household products and tablewares that were styled in both European and Oriental lines. Most pieces were decorated similarly to those of Dresden, showing scattered flowers. Later the styles of Sèvres were very well imitated, showing landscapes and pastoral scenes, as well as all classic patterns.

The normal grade production was very often only decorated with flowers, and these were scattered and done in blue.

Marks

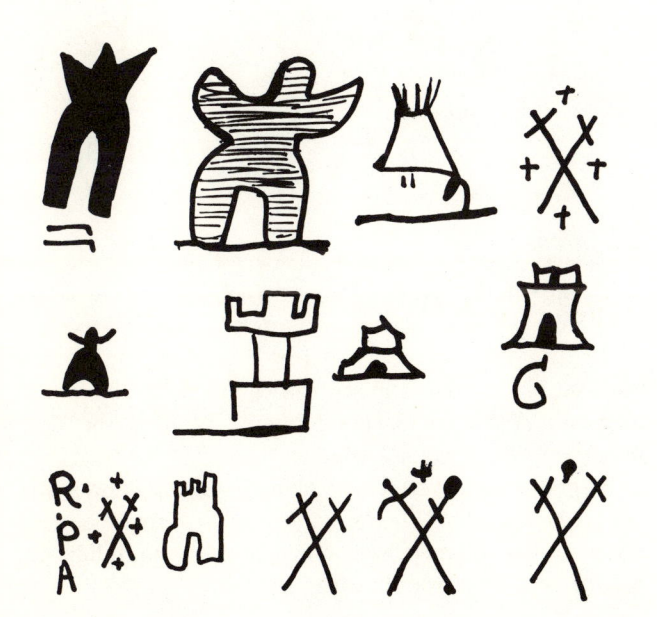

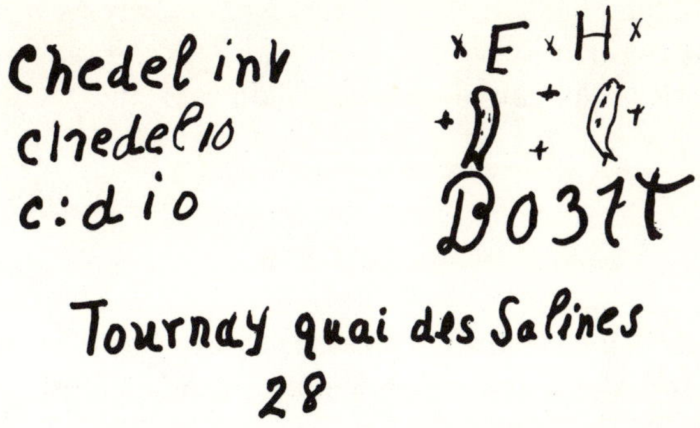

The first two marks are done in various colors, while the third is noted to be done in red. The remaining marks in various forms are usually done in gold or as onglaze color and appeared mostly on the better grade of porcelain.

Valenciennes, 1785–99

Background

Fauquez and Lamoniary were granted state permission in 1785 to operate a porcelain factory at Valenciennes. They planned to produce a fine quality porcelain that favored the style of the East. They were allowed to operate providing the ovens used coal.

Characteristics

The majority of wares produced were influenced by the current styles. Mostly good-quality dinnerware was produced, but a less expensive grade of porcelain similar in style and quality to Tournay was also made until the factory closed in 1797.

Marks

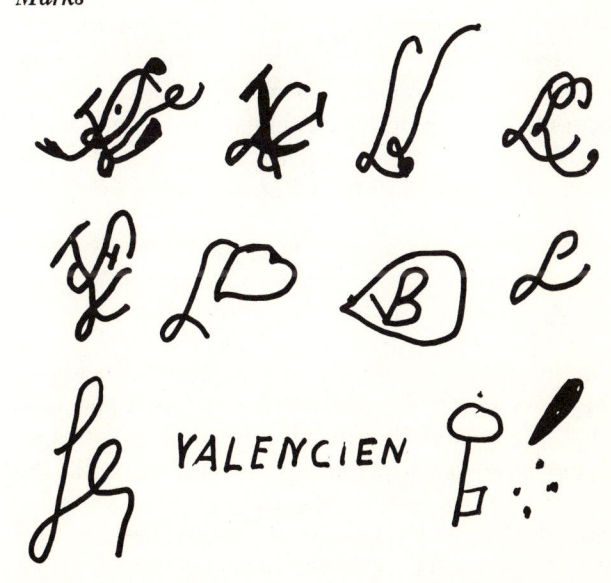

The interlaced "L & V" letters were mostly used on the better-quality wares, while the lesser-grade production usually used an abbreviation of the factory name.

GERMANY

Porcelain-collecting in Germany during the beginning of the eighteenth century could almost be described as a passion. The princes of the various German states, as well as wealthy noblemen, devoted entire rooms to displaying their porcelain collections in a desperate effort to show their culture as well as their prosperity. The French culture, as well as style of decoration established by the French court, was avidly copied by craftsmen of the various rulers of the German states. Perhaps there are more copies of the famous Palace of Versailles and the Hall of Mirrors scattered throughout Germany than anywhere else in the world, and one might speculate that an ambitious young French architect might have found the original style for Versailles while traveling through Germany.

Perhaps this hunger for perfect design form as well as beautiful porcelain prompted the formation of the Meissen Porcelain Factory and helped make it the immediate success that it became. Ironically, the Meissen factory produced a domestic product that could rival even the French, and production at Meissen increased so rapidly that the factory had an almost immediate monopoly on the market. As this occurred, coupled with increasing prices, various German noblemen decided to start their own porcelain factories to rival the great Meissen, and thus the German porcelain industry found its beginnings in the spirit of competition. Many of the talented arcanists from Meissen were persuaded to leave and help start these smaller factories. The world will always be grateful to their courage and inventiveness, because together they left a legacy of beautiful porcelain for many generations to take pleasure from.

Ansbach, 1758–1860

Background

The Ansbach factory was started by several former employees of the Meissen factory, perhaps the most noted of them being Johann Friedrich Kändler, a close relative to the famous Kändler of Meissen. After several years of production the factory was transferred to the castle ground at Bruckenberg so that their patron, Margrave Alexander of Brandenberg, could take a more personal interest in production. After the Margrave's abdication in 1791, the factory experienced a gradual decline, until it was eventually sold in 1807. The factory continued production until 1860, when it was closed, but produced nothing of artistic distinction during this period.

Characteristics

During the first several years of production before the relocation to the Bruckenberg site only a pure white porcelain was made. The best of all the Ansbach porcelain was made at Bruckenberg between 1762 and 1775, the majority of which was in the rococo style. Mostly, production was limited to small decorative accessories, as well as coffee and chocolate pots with cups and saucers that were decorated in a very similar style to that of Meissen.

Marks

The majority of the Ansbach marks were done in underglaze blue. It is interesting to note that the letter A represented in the marks does not stand for the town of Ansbach, but for the financial patron of the factory, Alexander of Brandenberg.

Berlin, 1752 to Present

Background

Berlin stands today a divided city, but in the eighteenth century it was a progressive cultural center under the rule of the Emperor Frederick the Great, and in 1751, with the aid of Frederick, the wool merchant Wilhelm Casper Wegely founded the first porcelain manufactory there.

Wegely was given every chance for success, since his materials were customs-free and his royal patron donated the factory site. Nevertheless, he failed to obtain the most sought-after Meissen secrets during the Seven Years War. Due to the devastation that followed the war, combined with the fact that Wegely fell from the king's favor, the factory closed in 1757. Porcelain of this period is relatively scarce, and was marked with the Wegely trademark of a blue W under the glaze. Production was largely limited to figures, which were mostly left in the white. The surviving colored specimens demonstrate the difficulty the factory experienced with enamels, since a considerable amount of flaking can be noticed. Colors of the period are strong, and lacquers were often substituted for enamels. The characteristic feature of the period is that the figures are short with large hands and heads.

Until 1761 Berlin was without a porcelain factory. The second factory was built by Johann Ernst Gotzkowsky and was located in the Leipzigerstrasse, which was to be the site of the famous Prussian parliament. Unfortunately, this porcelain factory lasted only three years and stopped production due to financial reversals. Because of the short time of production, Gotzkowsky porcelain is very rare. It was marked with a blue G under the glaze.

On September 3, 1763, Frederick the Great purchased the Gotzkowsky factory for 225,000 talers. The factory thus passed from private ownership to the Royal State of Prussia and from then on was referred to as the King's Porcelain Manufactory—KPM. At the same time, the king granted the use of the scepter, which was part of the Arms of Brandenburg, and this was adopted in blue under the glaze as the official mark. At the beginning of the nineteenth century the orb and the letters KPM were added to all pieces painted at the factory.

Characteristic of the Royal Period were the splendor and size of the table services produced. An example of such a service is one especially designed in 1793 for the wedding of Crown Prince Frederick William, and the "osier" shape, which has been in production since 1752. The plates of this service have borders of wicker-work, and all covers are adorned with cherubs for knobs. The decorations, if any, were motifs of rococo flowers. Frederick the Great used such a service for state occasions at his palace of Sans Souci, near Potsdam. Very good examples of this lovely service are still available from production of the later periods.

The success of this period was due to the perseverance of Frederick. The factory was purchased after the war primarily for economic reasons, since Prussia was at this time suffering from postwar impoverishment. The king decided to rebuild the manufactory and allow the art of porcelain to develop into a solid economic enterprise. At the time the Gotzkowsky factory was purchased, there were 146 employees. Some of the more famous of these included the chemist Reichard, the designer Frederick Meyer, and the painter Karl Frederick Boehme. Wilhelm Christian Meyer joined the factory in 1766 and is famous for his "Allegorical Children." His work can be distinguished by the notable French influence.

The royal period of KPM lasted until 1918. The factory was then transferred to state ownership, and is known today as the State Porcelain Factory, but still retains the mark of KPM.

On November 22, 1943, the factory was so severely damaged by a bombing raid that only twenty percent of its buildings and equipment survived. The Berlin manufactory was the hardest hit of all of the German porcelain firms during World War II. After the bombing raid the factory was to close its doors for a third time, but this was done with the security that the priceless and irreplaceable models and molds were safely hidden in central Germany.

Today, the factory maintains the same high standard of quality and reproduces the art forms of the past combined with designs for the future.

Marks

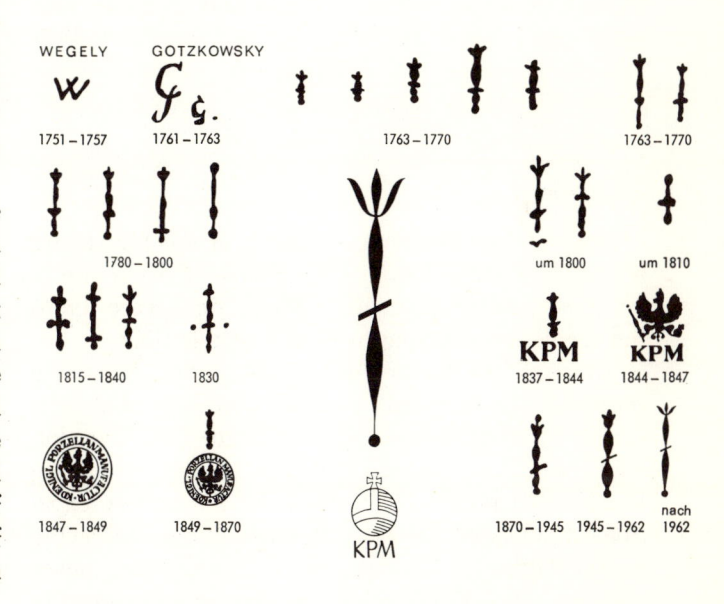

Production Numbers

Model numbers were always written or stamped under each individual piece. This number identifies the year the item was produced. The following is a listing of dates and model numbers from 1896 until the state took over in 1918.

1896	Nr. 5261-5484	1908	Nr. 8766-9090
1897	Nr. 5485-5700	1909	Nr. 9091-9375
1898	Nr. 5701-5950	1910	Nr. 9376-9695
1899	Nr. 5951-6300	1911	Nr. 9696-9985
1900	Nr. 6301-6500	1912	Nr. 9986-10200
1901	Nr. 6501-6765	1913	Nr. 10201-10405
1902	Nr. 6766-7195	1914	Nr. 10406-10625
1903	Nr. 7196-7545	1915	Nr. 10626-10740
1904	Nr. 7546-7785	1916	Nr. 10741-10880
1905	Nr. 7786-8110	1917	Nr. 10881-11015
1906	Nr. 8111-8515	1918	Nr. 11016-11180
1907	Nr. 8516-8765		

Artist Identification

A further classification was necessary due to the fact that many more pieces were produced in the white per year than could be painted. Therefore a letter was signed on the bottom of the finished pieces to indicate the year that the artist finished his work.

A	= 1901	G	= 1907	N	= 1913	T	= 1919
B	= 1902	H	= 1908	O	= 1914	U	= 1920
C	= 1903	I(J)	= 1909	P	= 1915	V	= 1921
D	= 1904	K	= 1910	Q	= 1916	W	= 1922
E	= 1905	L	= 1911	R	= 1917	X	= 1923
F	= 1906	M	= 1912	S	= 1918	Y	= 1924
						Z	= 1925

Frankenthal, 1755-95

Background

Paul Antoine Hannong, formerly of the Strasbourg factory in France, founded the Frankenthal factory in order to produce porcelain without the severe, limiting regulations existing in France at this time.

Although the factory was small at first, Hannong produced an excellent quality porcelain that was brought to the attention of the Elector Carl Theodor, who gave his financial support to the struggling Frankenthal factory. Unfortunately, the factory experineced financial setbacks throughout the following years. Although the quality of production never suffered, the Frankenthal factory was eventually closed in 1795.

Characteristics

An exceptional-quality white, hard-paste porcelain was produced at Frankenthal. Although a wide variety of dinner services and coffee sets were made, the greatest emphasis was placed on groups and individual statues.

The shapes and decorations were of the highest quality, but instead of an entirely individual style, Frankenthal decorators copied the styles of both the Vienna and Sèvres factories.

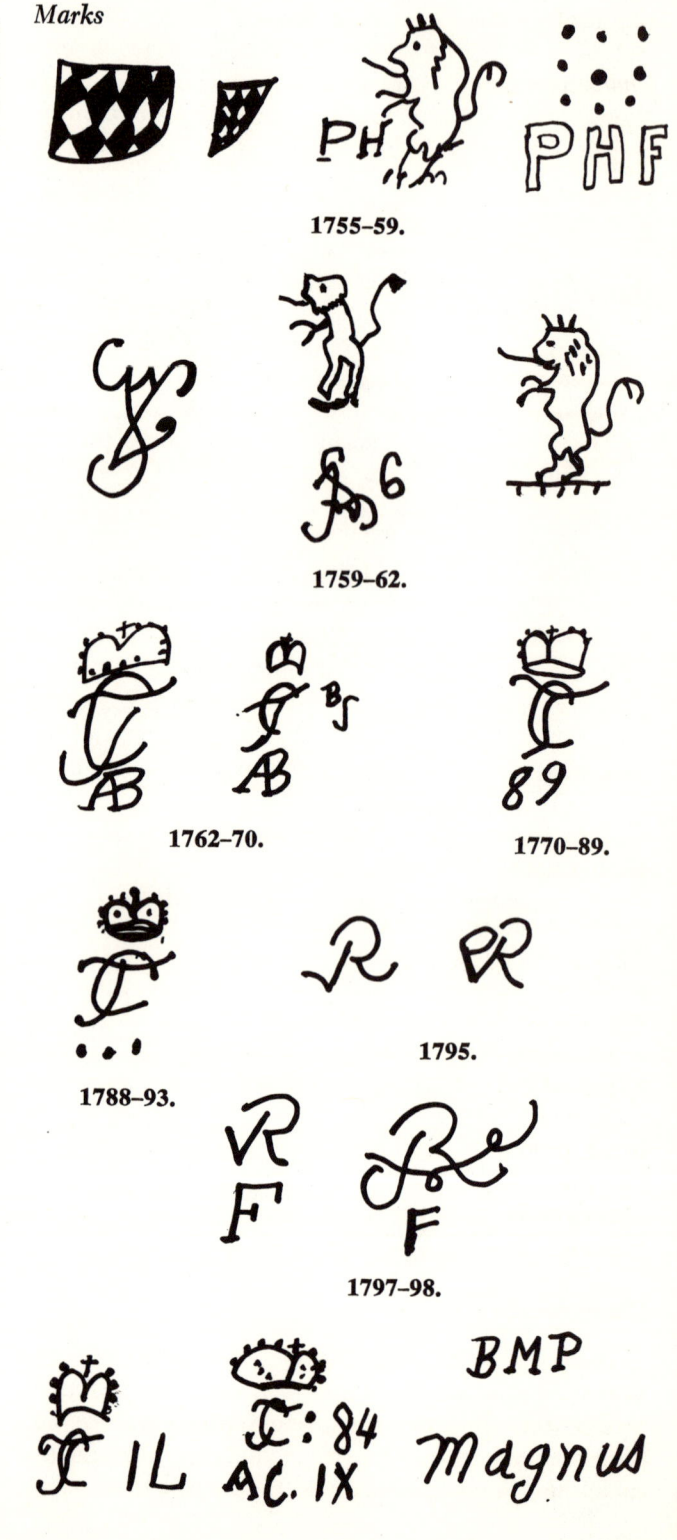

Marks

1755-59.

1759-62.

1762-70.   1770-89.

1788-93.   1795.

1797-98.

FULDA, 1765–90

Background

Johan Philipp Schick, together with his patron the prince-bishop of Fulda, founded a porcelain factory at Fulda in 1765. The factory was closed in 1790 after having produced some of the best-quality porcelain of all the German factories.

Characteristics

An excellent-quality porcelain with a very white paste and sharp sparkling glaze was produced at Fulda. Some of the finest figures were made between 1768 and 1775 and usually bear the cross mark.

Marks

1765–88.

1765–80.

1788–90.

Fürstenberg, 1747 to Present

Background

Karl I, Duke of Brunswick, founded the Fürstenberg porcelain factory in 1747, but very little was produced until 1753, when several expert craftsmen were hired from various other porcelain factories, the most noted being Benckgraff from Höchst. The factory continued to prosper until after the Napoleonic wars, when very little porcelain of any distinction was being produced, and it was eventually sold in 1876 to a private firm. After this date production improved considerably, and the Fürstenberg factory is still in existence, making a very good quality of wares.

Characteristics

The paste produced at Fürstenberg was very similar to that of Dresden despite difficulties at the outset of production when the factory was plagued with impurities and greyish tones. The glazes also experienced the same problems in production, but were eventually perfected to an excellent, brilliant quality.

A wide range of dinner services as well as decorative accessories were produced. The styles adapted by the Fürstenberg factory were copied from many of the other Continental factories, such as Berlin, Meissen, and Sèvres, but due to the close family connections between the factory's founder, the Duke of Brunswick, and the English royal family, Fürstenberg was the only German factory that freely copied the English styles.

Marks

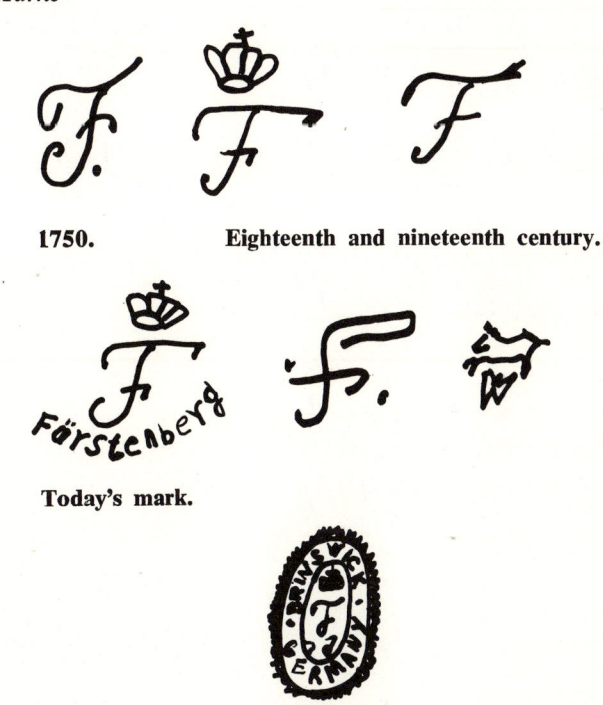

1750.　　　　　Eighteenth and nineteenth century.

Today's mark.

Used on wares exported mainly to United States, c. 1915.

Höchst, 1746–96

Background

Höchst is first known for the production of an excellent-quality faience before the porcelain factory was founded in 1746. The Höchst factory was established with the combined expertise of two businessmen and a former Meissen employee who brought the much guarded secrets of porcelain production. At first production was divided equally between faience and hard-paste porcelain, but many difficulties, both financial and production-oriented, plagued the factory. In 1778 the prince-bishop took over the management of the endangered factory and corrected conditions so that the factory prospered until political conditions caused its closing in 1796.

57

Characteristics

After only a very short period of experimentation when the paste had a slight grey tint, Höchst porcelain was noted for the extreme whiteness of its wares. The factory produced dinnerware as well as decorative items and beautiful figures, mostly in the rococo styling. The majority of decorations done at the Höchst factory were patterned after Dresden, with flowers, as well as Chinese-inspired designs, playing an important part in the motifs.

Marks

Kloster-Veilsdorf, 1760 to Present

Background

The Kloster-Veilsdorf porcelain factory was founded by Friedrich Wilhelm Von Hildburghausen, Prince of Thuringia, in 1760. The factory remained under its royal patronage until 1822, when it was sold to the Greiners.

Characteristics

The Kloster-Veilsdorf factory produced an excellent-quality hard-paste porcelain. Perhaps the best ware was made during the first twenty years of operations. Many of the designs favored both fruits and flowers done in clear and often brilliant enamel colors, mostly in the rococo style. Very fine figures were also molded, many from the Italian comedy.

Marks

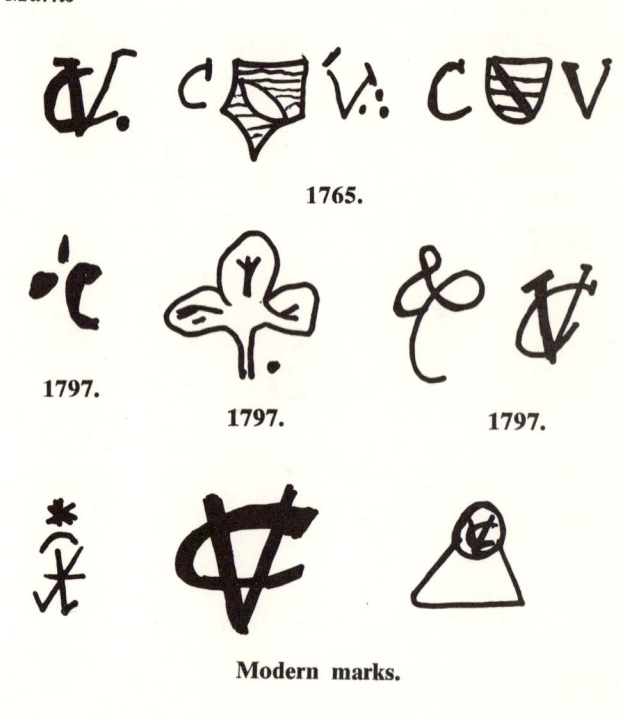

Ludwigsburg, 1756–1824

Background

The Duke of Würtemburg founded the Ludwigsburg factory in 1756, and due to his personal supervision and excellent taste established a porcelain factory of distinction. Duke Carl died in 1793, and due to lack of interest on his successor's part, the factory entered into a period of decline and was eventually closed in 1824.

Characteristics

The Ludwigsburg factory was located in Southern Germany not far from the town of Passau, noted for its large deposits of kaolin. The paste produced from this kaolin was very favorable to figure modeling, in which field Ludwigsburg made some of its best examples. The greatest period of figure production was between 1764 and 1774, and these were mostly in the rococo style.

Some of the best groups of figures produced at Ludwigsburg were miniature scenes depicting many different events, such as the famous Venetian fairs. Although a wide range of other porcelains were produced, perhaps these figures are the most noteworthy of the Ludwigsburg production.

Marks

1758–93.

1793–95.

1806–16.

1810–16.

1816–29.

1760–1802.

1762–72.

Meissen, 1710 to Present

Background

Augustus the Strong, elector of Saxony, together with Johann Friedrick Böttger, founded the Meissen porcelain factory in the castle of Albrechtsburg in 1710. The factory of Meissen, or Saxe or Dresden as it was known in France and England respectively, was completely unrivaled until 1756 and the start of the Seven Years War, when the monopoly on porcelain production was passed on to Sèvres in France. There was a desperate effort to regain the Meissen exalted position between 1774 and 1814, when the factory hired the very talented manager Count Marcolini, who was unable to attain the factory's former greatness in innovative designs. It could be said that Meissen was unable to achieve its former spontaneous individuality.

Kühn took over the management of the factory in 1814 and began the immediate revival of the earlier Meissen wares, which had greatly appreciated in value in design and monetarily since the factory began production at the beginning of the eighteenth century. The Meissen factory was moved from its original site at the fortress of Albrechtsburg sometime late in the year 1863, and every effort was made to modernize production methods, but unfortunately none of the originality of the art forms of the earlier periods were redeveloped.

Characteristics

During the beginning of the Böttger period the paste was often thick, and warping could easily be noticed on many pieces. The glazes used by Böttger were much thicker than latter glazes, but were clear and free of imperfections.

The Meissen factory produced, as it still does, a wide variety of dinner services, tea and coffee sets, and decorative accessories; but the figures were perhaps its most perfect and notable productions.

At first, the majority of shapes as well as designs were adapted from the much admired, imported Chinese porcelain. It was only after Johann Joachim Kändler came to Meissen in 1731 that the designs as well as shapes began to adopt a more traditional European flavor. The majority of the wares of this period show definite rococo styling until about 1764, when the gentle curves and scrolls were gradually replaced by first the more popular neoclassic and later the Empire styles.

Meissen porcelain was always copied because of the fineness of its decoration. Two of the most popular designs, the "onion" and "Strohblumen" patterns, were widely produced both at Meissen and other contemporary porcelain factories.

Johann Gregor Herold came to Meissen in 1720 as art director and began an immediate improvement on the quality of the porcelain as well as enamel ground colors. One of his most popular contributions was a new method of decoration inspired by the Japanese Kakiyemon designs, which was widely used at Meissen as well as inspiring interest throughout Europe and America.

Marks

The following is a list of the various production periods:

Böttger 1710–19
Höroldt 1719–31
Höroldt-Kändler 1731–63
Dot period 1763–74
Marcolini 1774–1814

All Meissen marks were done in underglaze blue.

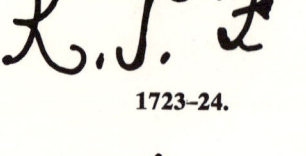

K.P.M.   1723–24.
M.P.M   1723–24.
K.P.F.   1723–24.
R   1733.
A   1733.
          1723.

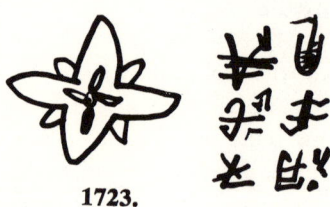

From 1923.

Marks confused with Meissen.

Bristol.

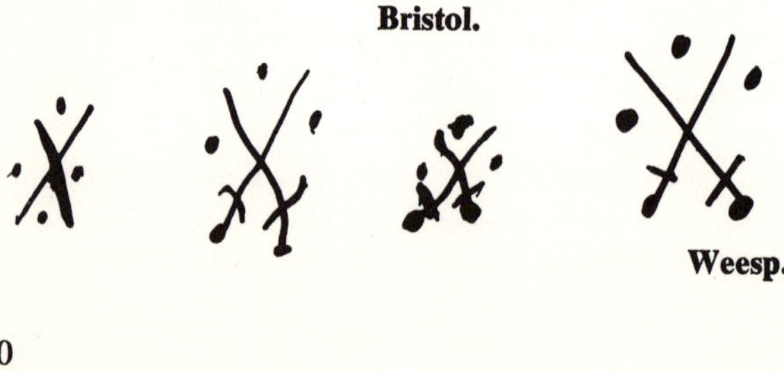

Weesp.

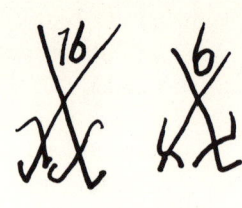

Worcester.

Volkstedt.

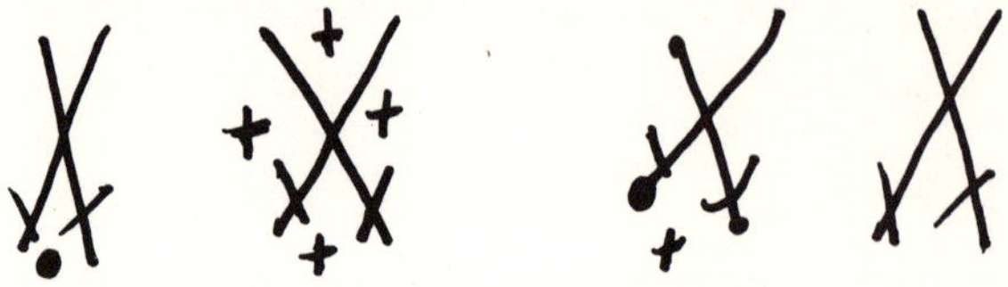

Tournay.

Chelsea.

Derby.

Lowestoft.

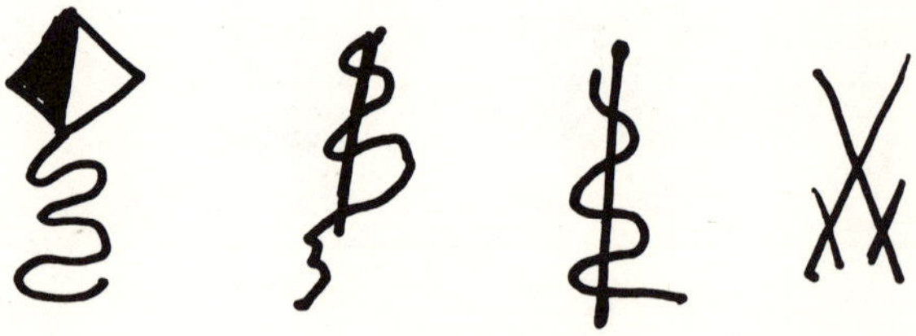

From 1723.

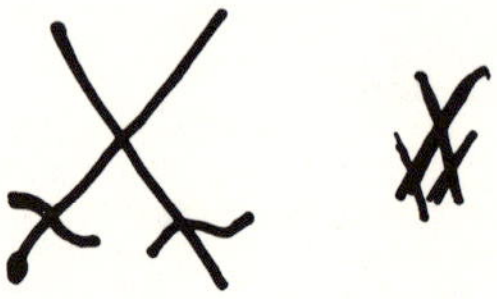

1725–63.

1763–74.

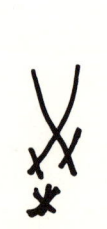

1774–1813.

1814–18.

60

Marks

From 1818.

1860–1924.

1924–34.

From 1934.

1755–65.

1760–70.

1780–90.

1763–65.

1810–50.

1850–62.

From 1862.

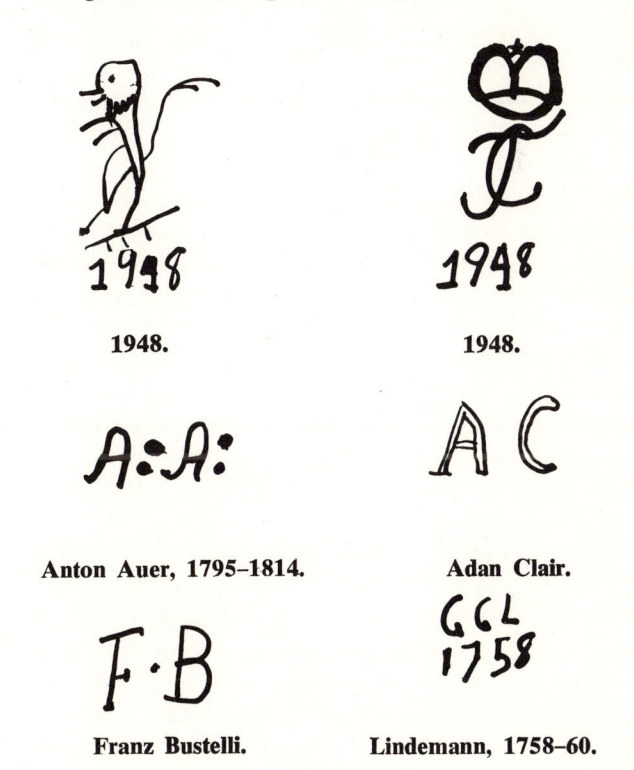

Modern mark.

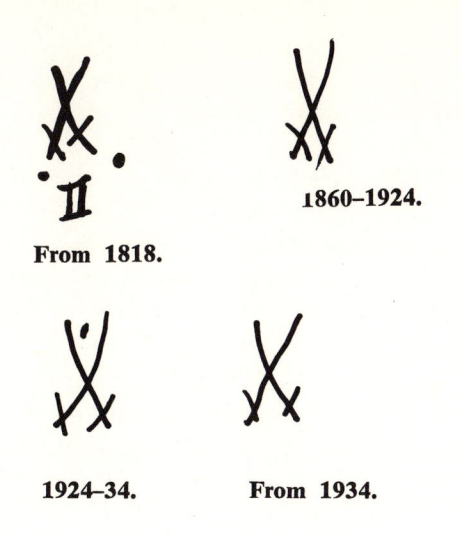

Nymphenburg, 1747 to Present

Background

The elector, Max Joseph III, helped found the state porcelain factory in 1747, but actual production did not occur until several years later in 1753. The factory was moved from its original location in Naudeck to Munich in 1761 and finally established near the royal palace of Nymphenburg from which the manufactory took its name.

The factory experienced great success, but from 1777 to 1799, due to a lack of political interest, the factory produced very little porcelain and was on the verge of closing when the new elector once again took a very personal interest in the Nymphenburg factory. The factory experienced a great revival, again producing some of the beautiful pieces of the earlier periods.

King Ludwig I of Bavaria, champion of the arts, sold the factory due to financial pressures in 1856 to a private firm, which still operates the Nymphenburg factory today.

Characteristics

The Nymphenburg factory produced an excellent hard-paste porcelain that was noted for the extreme whiteness of the paste as well as for the clear brilliance of the glaze. Although a large variety of porcelain was produced, the majority of production was centered around the beautiful figures that made Nymphenburg famous.

The majority of decorations copied the current popular trend of flowers, animals, and landscapes, mostly in the Meissen style. These motifs were noted for their beautiful naturalism without loss of detail. Unfortunately, much of the later works are overdecorated, losing the much admired simplicity.

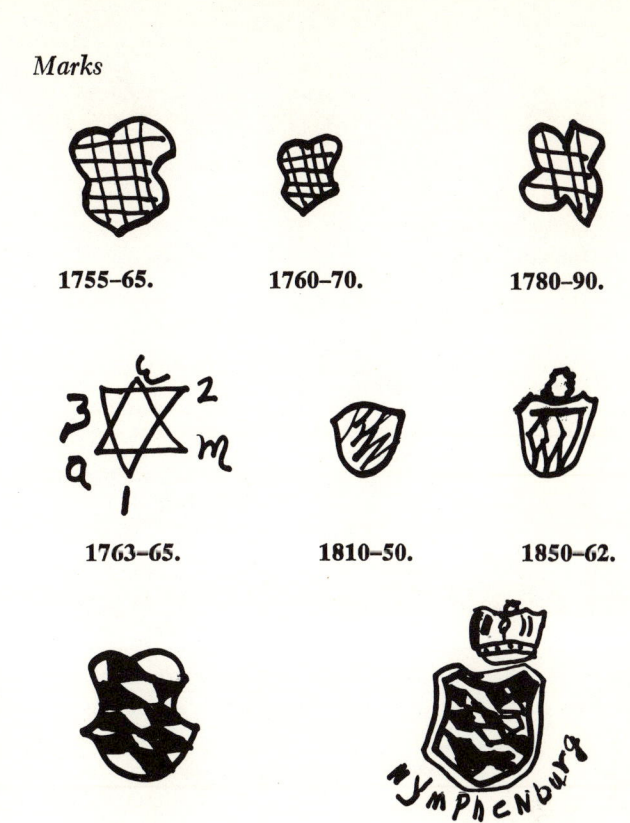

The following marks represent the various painters and molders working at the Nymphenburg factory during the different periods of production.

1948.

1948.

Anton Auer, 1795–1814.

Adan Clair.

Franz Bustelli.

Lindemann, 1758–60.

Huber. 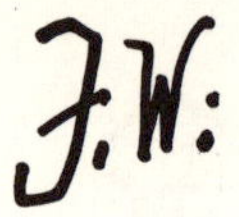 **Wielland.**

HOLLAND

Amstel, 1764–1810

Background

The chronological development of the porcelain that is generically referred to as Amstel is slightly confusing, and therefore the following is an individual breakdown of the various production.

Weesp, 1764–71

The first factory was originally founded in Amsterdam to produce faience by Count Gronsveldt-Diepenbroick-Impel in 1764. The factory was later moved to the small suburb of Weesp, and production was known by this name thereafter. The paste produced was of an excellent-quality hard paste that resembles closely the work done at Dresden, perhaps because of the large number of former Dresden workers employed at the Weesp factory.

At one time, because of the quality of hard-paste wares produced, the founder, Count Gronsveldt-Diepenbroick-Impel, directly negotiated with the famous Sèvres porcelain factory to sell them his perfected formula for hard-paste porcelain, but the project was never completed due to political and international difficulties. At this time Holland became a prime source for the importation of porcelain from Japan, which caused great financial difficulties at the Weesp factory. By 1770 most of the workers from Dresden had returned to their native land, and the factory was about to close when it was purchased by the Calvinist minister de Mol in 1771.

Oude Loosdrecht, 1771–84

When the Weesp factory was purchased by de Mol the production was immediately transferred to Oude Loosdrecht and operated very successfully. By volume the factory produced a considerable amount, and did so until de Mol's death in 1782. After de Mol's death production continued for two more years until the factory was acquired by another firm in 1784 and transferred to Oude Amstel.

Oude Amstel, 1784–99

The factory at Oude Amstel operated for only fifteen years, producing a good-quality everyday dinnerware and accessories that were popular.

Nieuwe Amstel, 1799–1810

The Oude Amstel factory was purchased by yet another firm in 1799, and production once again moved to another location, Nieuwe Amstel. The factory continued to make the same quality of porcelain until 1810, when production was finally stopped.

Characteristics

All four factories produced merely a continuation of the same basic wares. The body of the wares closely copied Dresden, due to the experienced workmen from that factory employed at the various Amstel porcelain works. The factory produced mostly dinner sets and small decorative objects. Of course, the styling was at first copied from the various German factories and, at a later date, greatly influenced by the French.

Decorations were patterned after the rococo and neoclassic stylings produced at the period.

The Marks

Weesp, 1764–71

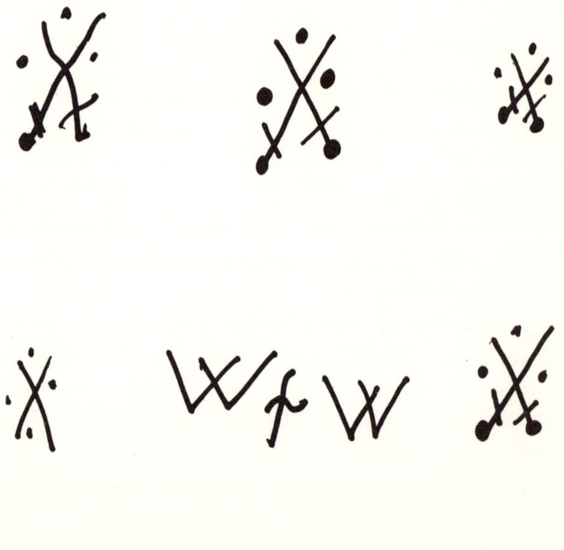

The marks found on the Weesp production are done in underglaze blue, and are greatly influenced in form (the Dresden crossed swords) by the number of former Dresden employees at Weesp.

Oude Loasdrecht, 1771–84

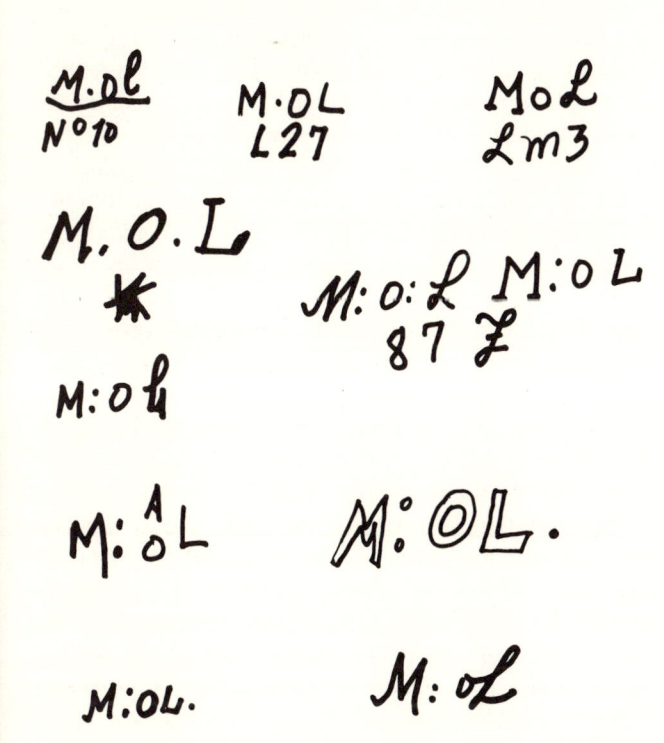

The marks of this period were drawn in various colors, but all represent the founders name, MOL, in some form.

Oude Amstel, 1784–99

Amstel
MOL

These marks depicted either the name of the factory, Amstel, or the monogrammed letter A

Nieuwe Amstel, 1799–1810

Amstel

Production was simply marked with the above name of the factory.

The Hague, 1775–85

Background

Anton Leichner founded a hard-paste porcelain factory in 1775 at The Hague. Unfortunately, the factory only operated for a few years, and because it decorated soft-paste wares produced at Tournay, much confusion has arisen as to what soft- and hard-paste porcelain was actually made at The Hague. The porcelain made at this factory was of the highest quality in both form and decoration.

Characteristics

The wares were produced after the styles of both Vienna and Dresden, the former being influenced by the founder, Anton Leichner, a Viennese. Although the majority of production was centered on dinner sets, some truly exquisitely decorated vases were made. Shapes and designs basically followed the neoclassic and rococo styling.

Flowers were mostly favored in decorating, but silhouettes, children, and landscape scenes were very often painted. One form produced at The Hague that was especially favored were the profiles set in medallions on pink grounds.

Marks

The marks of The Hague production favored the city shield and were done in underglaze blue.

63

Delft

"Delfsche Porcleyn," the faience of Delft during the second half of the sixteenth century, was worked mainly in the style of the Italian majolica: the brownish earthenware was covered with enamel, a polychrome decoration was then painted on the enamel, and both the enamel and decoration were burned together in the second firing. The newly established Delft potters relied heavily on the exported Italian wares for both style and form. They selected such exotic motifs as ripe, bursting pomegranates and grapes that were not readily available in their Northern climate. Toward the end of the sixteenth century, Portuguese ships carried the first exported pieces of Chinese porcelain to Western Europe; at war with Spain and Portugal, the Dutch captured many cargo ships transporting Chinese porcelain. The quality of the Chinese product was highly valued in the low countries.

The Asiatic product was first introduced into Europe by the famous traveler Marco Polo after his visit to China in the thirteenth century. For the next several centuries numerous pieces were seen throughout Europe, the majority centered in Italy, but there was no organized trade. Florence saw the first reproduction of the Chinese porcelain, under the patronage of the Medici family. Between the years of 1575 and 1585 a clumsy porcelain was made by mixing clay, sand, and glass, but proved to be a very poor imitation of the imported ware. This "Medici" or "Florence" porcelain was a soft porcelain and the forerunner of the porcelains produced in England and France during the eighteenth century.

After the establishment of the Dutch East India Company in 1602, the Dutch directly imported the Chinese porcelain in large quantities. The majority of the wares were in the blue-and-white style of the late Ming period, and especially popular were the so-called Wna-Li ware representing Buddhist emblems. The Dutch potters of the time began to neglect their own products and slowly began to change over and imitate the newly imported ware. The Dutch, unfamiliar with the art of making porcelain, retained their own technique, but refined the procedure to fit their purpose. They used their original grayish clays, fired the products, covered them with a white enamel, and painted the decorations in blue on the white background; a second firing was required to finish the procedure. The refined procedure was so successful that the finished product, when seen from a distance, was hardly distinguishable from the imported wares. Unfortunately, the Dutch products were rather thick, and did not possess the same brilliancy and translucency of the real porcelain.

Nevertheless the Dutch-produced wares found a good market during the first half of the seventeenth century. The pottery industry continued to grow, responding to the demands of the newly prosperous burghers, who, conscious of their status, demanded fine porcelain wares to display in their homes. During the sixteenth century the potters were located all over Holland. The town of Haarlem achieved the greatest technical perfection, and Rotterdam was noted for its quality and quantity of tile production. The beginning of the seventeenth century found the *galeyerspotbakkers* or the galleypot-makers, a name adopted to distinguish them from the numerous *tegelbakkers* or tile-makers, centered in the picturesque town of Delft, chiefly renowned at the time for its excellent beer. Delft claimed nearly two hundred breweries, which exported their brews throughout Europe. Due to economic pressure during the first half of the century, one after another of the breweries began to close down, until only fifteen were left open, enough to quench the thirst of only Delft.

The abandoned breweries were taken over by the new and growing pottery industry. Delft was not well supplied with natural potting materials and began to import clays from the Ruhr valley and England to blend with their own. The second half of the seventeenth century saw over thirty established potteries working at Delft. One such factory was the Porcelain Jar (*De Porceleyne Fles*), founded in 1653, and still in continuous production for over 322 years.

For over two centuries the main product remained the blue-and-white ware, but the old polychrome decorations became as popular as their blue-and-white prototype.

The potteries enjoyed a period of success. The painters who had begun by copying the Chinese patterns began to develop a definite style that was typified by traditional Dutch decorations, although there still remained an unmistakable Chinese influence. The potteries came under a commercial influence, and they were pressured toward mass production regardless of artistic merit. The stoic Dutch responded to a hereditary tradition of artistic quality and integrity and maintained the high quality of their work.

The second half of the seventeenth century brought competition again from China with the porcelain of the CH'ing dynasty, which was founded in 1644. This porcelain showed vast technological and design improvements. The designs were not only in blue, but the polychrome decorations were of incredible beauty. The main color of this type of porcelain was green and became known throughout Europe as *famille verte*, (green family). Many colors were painted under the glaze, while others called "enamel colors" were painted on a fired glaze and fused into the surface by refiring at a lower temperature.

Competition was also felt from the Japanese porcelain that began to be exported to Europe during this period. The "Imari" ware with underglaze decoration in blue and onglaze enamel of muffle-decoration in red and gold, was more than likely made especially for the Dutch trade. The competitive spirit of Delft potters was heightened by the overflow of Chinese and Japanese products on the European marketplace, and once again the Delft potters showed their skill in producing similar work in pottery. Close examination will show that the Dutch colors of red, blue, and gold even surpassed the Japanese in beauty, design, and color. For a third time the Dutch were called upon to match the Chinese, when at the beginning of the 18th century *famille rose*, (rose or pink family) was introduced onto the European market. Each time the Delft potters succeeded, but the blue and white still remained the main product.

In the eighteenth century, however, three events took place, the consequences of which led to the slow but steady decline of the old craft. The factories began to come into the ownership of merchants who operated them mainly for profit. Over the years, with an atmosphere of artistic suffocation, a deterioration set in with only a few of the older potters standing out for quality of work. The invention of making real porcelain in Germany by Böttcher in 1709 saw, during the next thirty years, the development of porcelain factories throughout Europe. Many of these famous factories are still in existence today, such as Meissen, Berlin, Nymphenburg, and Sèvres. Perhaps the most important development was by a Staffordshire potter named Josiah Wedgwood, who developed a white pottery body. This new body did not need the opaque white enamel as a covering, and allowed greater freedom with painting techniques. Decorations could now be protected with a transparent glaze. The new ware lacked the brittleness of the Delft products and was much harder and tougher.

The Dutch potters were this time unable to compete with the new European porcelain and English wares. They were only able to equal the outward appearance. The faience was made thinner and lighter, and copies of Meissen were tried with the muffle or decorating kiln. The old established method of underglaze decoration was discarded, and both technique and quality saw a decline toward the end of the eighteenth century. The manufacturers tried to produce porcelain and white pottery in Holland, but the cost of imported clays and materials was prohibitive. So to compete in the European marketplace they resorted to making their own products cheaper, but this resulted in a rapid deterioration of quality and designs. One pottery after another closed due to the competition with the cheap English cream-colored earthenware and new European porcelains. The French Revolution caused a great many of the remaining factories to close their doors, and in 1813, when Holland was declared a kingdom, only three of the original potteries remained, one of them being De Porceleyne Fles.

Of the three potteries that remained open at the beginning of the nineteenth century, two were closed within a few years. The Porcelain Jar survived but experienced hard times for more than three quarters of that century. To keep their doors open they produced no artware, but resorted to a cheap, printed product produced for overseas export.

In 1876 Joost Thooft purchased the Porcelain Jar and planned to revive the famous blue-and-white "Delft." After a relatively short production it was evident that the old techniques were useless. With the help of Mr. Labbouchire, a new type of blue Delft was produced that had all the properties of the hard-body Wedgwoodware. The mixture of clays were cast in plaster-of-Paris molds; the dishes, plates, and vases were then dried and fired. The fired product was called "biscuit," the decoration was painted by hand, and then fired for a second time. The decorations appear in blue under the transparent glaze of the second firing. The perfection of this procedure was arrived at only after many years of experimentation with body composition, color, glaze, and kiln type.

The new Delft only added success and fame to the world-famous name of "Delft," which remains popular to the present day.

Forgeries

Few ceramic groups have been so extensively forged as Delft, and for various reasons. Perhaps the most important one is that faience is easier to imitate convincingly than is hard-paste porcelain. The standard of skill in the best forgeries is very high, but the following points may prove helpful.

Suspect and piece in which the blue has an ultramarine tinge, or in which the paste feels hard or faintly granular. In genuine pieces the exposed body of the clay feels soft to the fingernail. There is the further problem of distinguishing Delft from German wares, such as those made at Frankfort and Hanau. It should be remembered that on the German wares the blue used is much starchier and brighter, the use of "treck" is rare, there is a preference for lobed dishes and narrow-necked jugs, which were uncommon in Holland. It should also be noted that Delft plates are remarkably thin and light. Good-quality Delft is always very highly glazed yet soft to the touch, and crazing is very rarely found on any genuine pieces.

Markings

One effective, but not foolproof, method of identification is to know the marks of each factory. The following marks are representative of various factories in operation in Delft throughout the centuries.

De Griekse A (The Greek A), founded in 1645 by G. L. Kuryk.

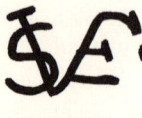

S. V. Eenhoorn, 1674.

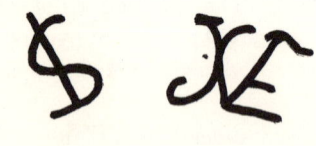

S. V. Eenhoorn, 1674.

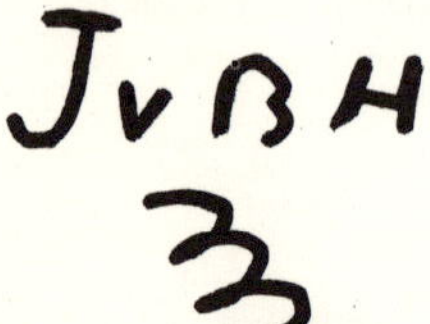

P. Kocks, 1701.

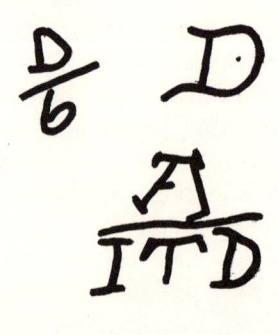

A. Korks.

J. T. Dextra, 1759.

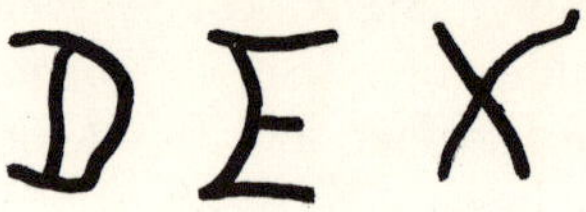

J. T. Dextra, 1759.

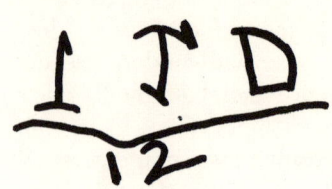

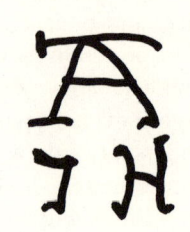

J. T. Dextra, 1759.

J. H. Adriaens, 1765.

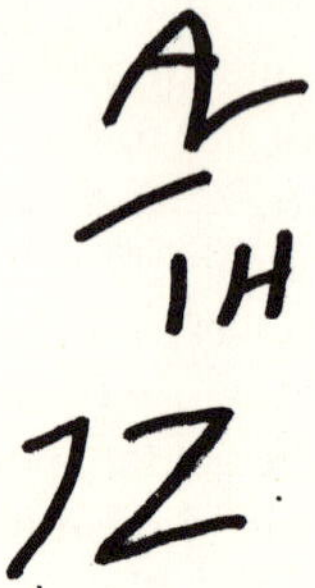

J. H. Adriaens, 1765.

De Klaew (The Claw), founded in 1662 by C. V. der Hoeve.

C. Corneliz V. D. Hoeve, 1662.

C. V. Schoonhove, 1668.

66

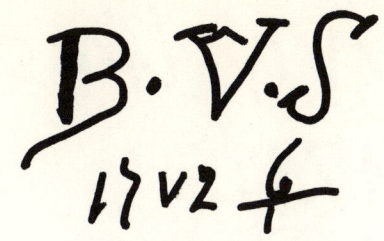

L. V. Schoonhove, 1702.

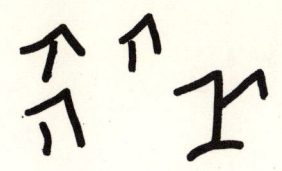

B. Rottewel v.j.v.d. Lanen.

j.j.v.d. Laen, 1675.

L. V. Schoonhove, 1702.

K. V. Dyck, 1759.

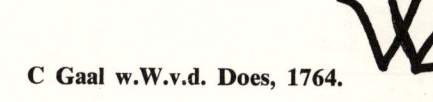

C Gaal w.W.v.d. Does, 1764.

De Porceleyne Biji (The Porcelain Axe), founded in 1679 by H. Brouwer.

L. Sanderus, 1764.

H. Brouwer, 1679.

De Drie Klokken (The Three Bells), founded by S. Mesch in 1671.

J. Brouwer, 1759.

Simon Mesch, 1671, Peter Simon Mes, 1700, W.V.d. Dols, 1759.

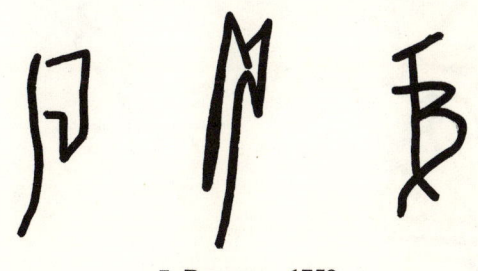

J. Brouwer, 1759.

De Porceleyne Fles (The Porcelain Jar), founded by J. Pynacker in 1680.

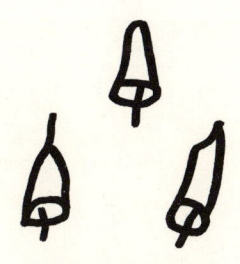

W.v.d. Dols, 1764.

Knotter, 1698.

P.v. Doorne, 1759.

67

j. Harlees, 1770.

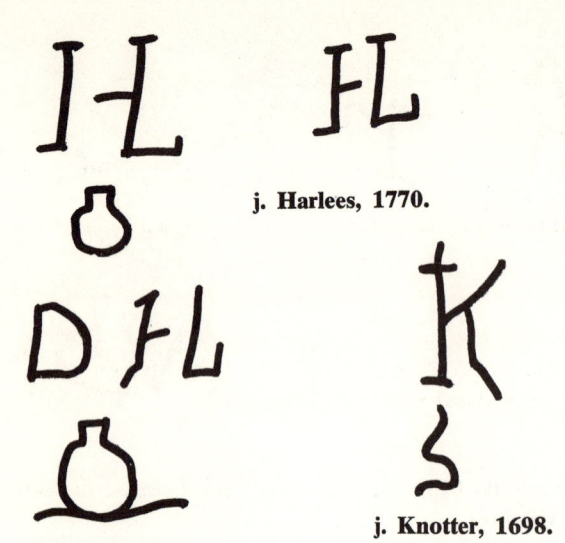

J. Aalmis.

D. Harlees, 1795.

j. Knotter, 1698.

J. Aalmis.

De Star (The Star), founded in 1690 by T. Witsenburg.

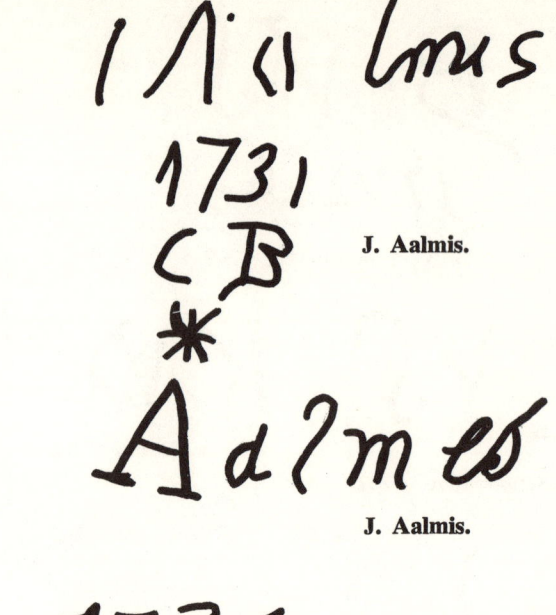

T. Witsenburg, 1690.

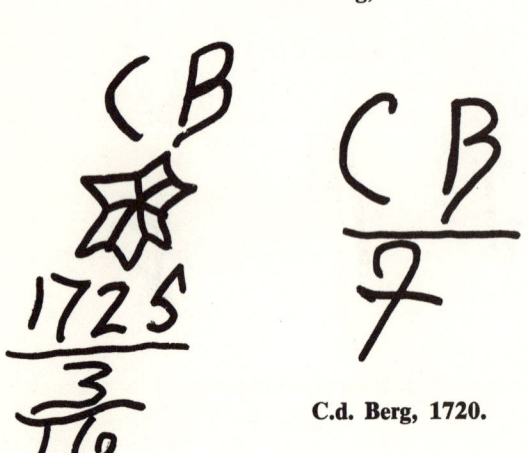

J.d. Berg, 1759.

C.d. Berg, 1720.

A. Kiell, 1764.

C.d. Berg, 1720.

HUNGARY

Herend, 1830 to Present

Background

Moritz Fischer founded a hard-paste porcelain factory in 1830 in Herend, Hungary.

Characteristics

The wares were very good copies of both Capo di Monte and Sèvres porcelain. One of the most favored copies represented the beautiful Chinese imported enamels. The decorations were brilliant. Production was limited to dinner services, decorative accessories, and figurines.

Marks

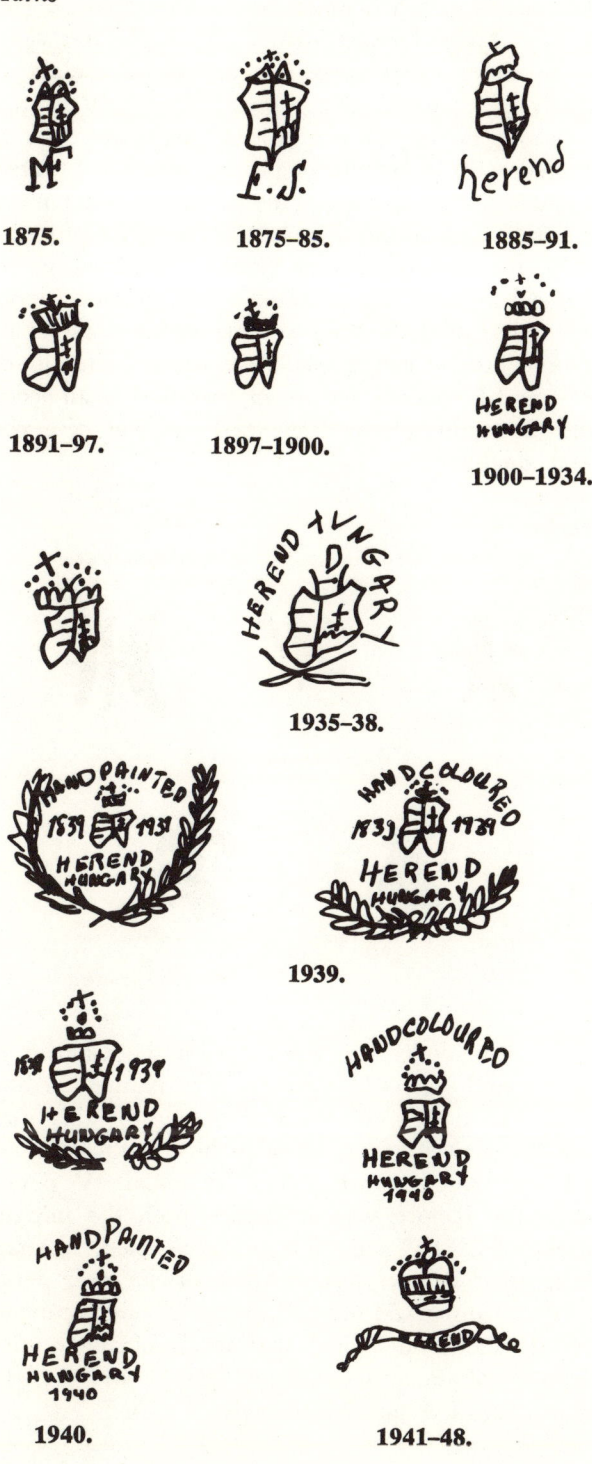

The Marks were very often applied directly over the glaze.

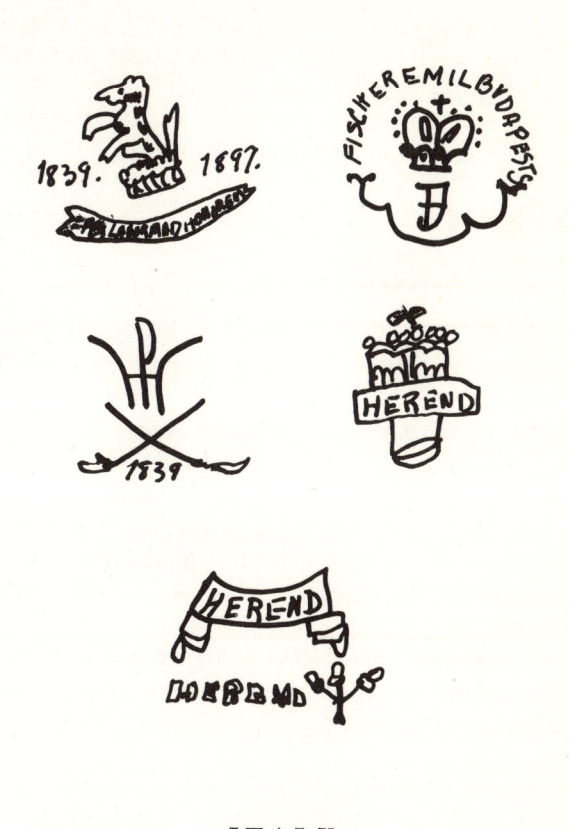

1875.

1875-85.

1885-91.

1891-97.

1897-1900.

1900-1934.

1935-38.

1939.

1940.

1941-48.

ITALY

Italy, long known as the cradle of art to the rest of the world, greatly began influencing other European countries during the fifteenth century as the awakening of the Renaissance brought the civilized world out of the darkness of the Middle Ages. The atmosphere of creativity was cultivated, and many new forms of art were developed.

Maiolicaware was developed and became a success immediately. This new type of ceramics was introduced to other European countries, which began copying the new ceramics with great enthusiasm.

Although the first record of porcelain production has been attributed to the Medici factory in 1575, there is evidence that an earlier ware, referred to as *porcellance contrefacto*, was produced as early as 1470 in Venice. Unfortunately, no wares have survived from this time, and authentication is impossible.

More than a century after the first factory was established in Florence, the new King of Spain, grandson of Louis XIV, and ruler of Italy, became the patron of a new factory being established in Naples. He became more than the money behind the operation and carefully supervised all forms of production. This passion for porcelain continued throughout his

69

life, and, when appointed, King Charles III of Spain in 1759 established a continuation of the Italian production near the palace in Madrid.

Unfortunately, production during the later periods in Italy was not nearly as imaginative and lacked originality.

Capo di Monte, 1743–1834

Background

Charles III Period, 1743–59

Charles III, king of Naples, and his queen founded the Capo di Monte porcelain factory in 1743. The queen, daughter of Augustus III of Poland and an elector of Saxony, showed great interest in the arts and especially porcelain, perhaps due to her background in the cultural center of Dresden.

The factory was established directly in the Palace of Capo di Monte and continued until 1759 under the direction of the chemist Schepers and his painter assistant, Caselli.

When Charles succeeded to the throne of Spain in 1759 he took some of the best workmen and models with him to Madrid.

Ferdinand IV Period, 1771–1806

The factory suspended operation for about twelve years after Charles III succeeded to the Spanish throne. King Ferdinand IV opened the factory once again and moved the operation to the Royal Villa Reale at Portici in 1771. The king transferred the factory once again to the Royal Palace at Naples in 1773, where production continued until 1806.

Post-Royal Period, 1807–34

The factory was sold to a private company in 1807, and production was continued uninterrupted until 1834, despite several successive owners. The post-Royal period produced very little porcelain of artistic importance. The molds and models of the factory were purchased by the Doccia factory.

Characteristics

During the Charles III period, soft-paste porcelain was produced, which either showed a subtle grey, green, blue, or yellowish tint to the body. The wares of this period showed an exceptional translucency. The glaze used was like satin and exceptionally smooth to the touch. Production during the Charles III period was centered on dinnerware, vases, and small, decorative objects, which were lavishly decorated with vibrant colors that are most often associated with Capo di Monte production.

Both soft- and hard-paste wares were produced during the Ferdinand IV period. The glaze developed for the new hard-paste production was extremely brilliant and very clear. Production was continued in decorative accessories and dinnerware, but a good quantity of biscuit pieces were produced. Most production showed a definite neoclassic influence. Decorations favored either harbor and landscape scenes or motifs inspired from Pompeii or Herculaneum, which also became very popular throughout Europe.

During the post-Royal period production was increased with a definite emphasis on volume instead of quality of production. Production of biscuit pieces also increased during this period. The wares produced while the factory was at Naples continued in the classical trend in form inspired by the previous period but exaggerated the lines to some extent. Some of the favored ground colors used were yellow, blue, green, gray, and Pompeiian red. Black was used as an accent color and gilding was often used and was of a very good quality.

Marks

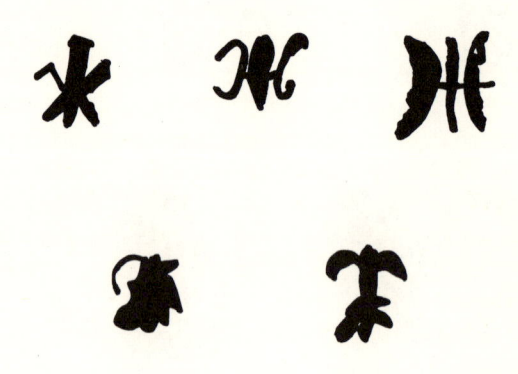

The fleur-de-lis was used during the Charles III period, and was either impressed or painted in blue. Although there were many variations of this mark and the majority were done in blue, both gold and red were used. During the Ferdinand IV period, while the factory was at Portici, both the initiated marks of "R.F." and "F.R.F." were used, although these are relatively scarce. Much of the later period wares were marked either with an "N" or a crowned "N". It should be noted that much of the original Capo di Monte production of applied and modeled figures was left unmarked.

Forgeries

Capo di Monte porcelain has been blatantly forged. Perhaps the most noted forger was the Marquis Ginori, who purchased many of the original models from the factory and established his own porcelain factory near Florence. His factory produced both a majolica and hard-paste porcelain. These wares were marked with the crowned "N" that was either scratched or drawn in blue on the paste.

Marquis Ginoris's factory produced some of the best forgeries on the market, but unfortunately many German and French factories also produced exceptionally poor forgeries that have flooded the market. The majority of pieces made were vases, tankards, bowls, and plates that were pretentious in design, badly finished, and coarse in character. These pieces were usually marked with a crowned "N" painted in either blue or gold. The productions of these factories were done in quantity and are worthless to the collector.

Doccia, 1735 to Present

Background

The Marchese Carlo Ginori founded a porcelain factory on a part of his Tuscany estate during the nineteenth century. A patron of the arts, Ginori wanted to revive the porcelain industry near Florence in the tradition of the famous Medici factory. Therefore production centered on imitations of earlier wares. This was made considerably easier after original Capo di Monte molds were purchased by Ginori for the Doccia factory as well as permission to use the Capo di Monte mark on wares produced from these original molds.

The factory today still remains in the control of the Ginori family.

Characteristics

At first the body was almost a hybrid soft paste, which quickly developed into a true hard paste patterned after the quality of the ware produced at Vienna and Dresden.

At first, because local clays were used, there was a slight gray tint to the paste, but later materials were imported from France with the addition of the French kaolin, and a hard, white, and extremely translucent ware was produced, which has become characteristic of Doccia production.

The factory made an extensive list of dinnerware as well as decorative accessories, which displayed a distinctive rococo influence at the beginning. After the middle of the eighteenth century the styling followed the neoclassic, which was later replaced by the neo-Grec and Empire stylings.

The first ten years of production was mostly experimental and quite often done as the wares were decorated. Since the factory was noted for copying famous porcelains, no distinct style was ever developed.

Marks

A hybrid soft-paste porcelain was produced by the Antonibon family until 1802, when they lost the factory and did not recover it until the year before it was officially closed. During this time only faience and earthenware pieces were produced.

Marks one through eleven were done at the factory from 1737 to 1860, and were either impressed or painted in blue, red, or gold.

Collectors Note

Reproductions made from the original Capo di Monte molds are marked with the Capo di Monte crowned "N".

Medici, 1574–1620

Background

The first soft-paste porcelain factory was established by Francesco I de'Medici, Grand Duke of Tuscany, in 1574. The first several years were mostly experimental, but the major production of wares took place between 1581 and 1586.

Characteristics

Although fewer than forty documented pieces exist today, the majority of production centered on vases, bowls, dishes, bottles, and ewers. Decoration was simple, mostly done in blue with purple sometimes used for definition. Although painted figures were seldom used, foliage that displayed a distinct Chinese tone was often painted. The glaze was often plagued with small bubbles.

Marks

The marks were always carefully painted in blue and represented the dome of the Cathedral of Florence with the capital, F appearing, below.

Le Nove, 1752–1832

Background

Although porcelain production was not started until later, the factory originally was established to produce faience by Giovanni Battista Antonibon. The quality of the wares attracted many talented people including Sigismund Fischer from Dresden.

Characteristics

The porcelain produced during the first period of production was of an exceptional quality with the paste being a cream white with a clear and distinctive mellow glaze. Much of the decoration followed the Sèvres style, favoring flowers either in polychrome or gold, purple, or green. Also, mythological subjects and figures were often used.

Marks

The name NOVE often appears, as well as the six-pointed star, which is either done in red, blue, or gold. The GB monogrammed marks represent production between 1802 and 1825, when the factory was leased by Giovanni Baroni.

Venice, 1720–40

Background

Although the first porcelain production in Europe has been credited to the Medici factory in Florence, it is believed that an earlier factory was started in Venice about 1470 by the alchemist Maestro Antonio Lodovico. Unfortunately, no known pieces exist to substantiate production from this factory at a prior date. Later, the Vezzi brothers started a porcelain production at the beginning of the eighteenth century in Venice. The Vezzi brothers were from a family of goldsmiths who appreciated both talent and quality of workmanship, and they were determined to hire only experienced, well-known men at their factory. Christopher Conrad Hunger, who had worked at both the Vienna and Dresden porcelain factories, was hired. Hunger brought several expert workmen from Dresden, which greatly influenced the quailty and design of the production, both of which were of an excellent quality.

The factory was closed in 1740 with the death of one of the founders, Francesco Vezzi.

It was believed that a couple from Dresden reopened the factory from 1758 to 1763, but very little is known about this period of production.

It was not until 1764 when Geminiano Cozzi opened a soft-paste porcelain factory that Venice once again had a successful factory. The factory did extremely well until 1812.

Characteristics

There was a definite Dresden influence during the first five years of production due to the management of Christopher Conrad Hunger. The hard paste was a warm white with very clear glaze very similar to that used at Dresden. After the departure of Hunger the styling changed to conform with popular rococo style of the mid-eighteenth century.

A great variety of dinnerware, vases, and decorative accessories were always produced that favored both impressed and molded ornamentation. Painted decorations were widely used, as was gilding with favorite motifs such as landscapes and animals being used very often.

Cozzi

Since only soft-paste porcelain was produced at the Cozzi factory it cannot be directly compared to the Vezzi factory, but it should be noted that the glaze at Cozzi had more of a satin appearance and the paste showed a somewhat grayish tone.

Cozzi produced tableware, figures, and accessories for the home that reflected the neoclassic style of the time. Decoration followed the styling of the neoclassic period, and gilding was very often used, as well as monotone decorations exclusively in gold.

Marks

Vezzi

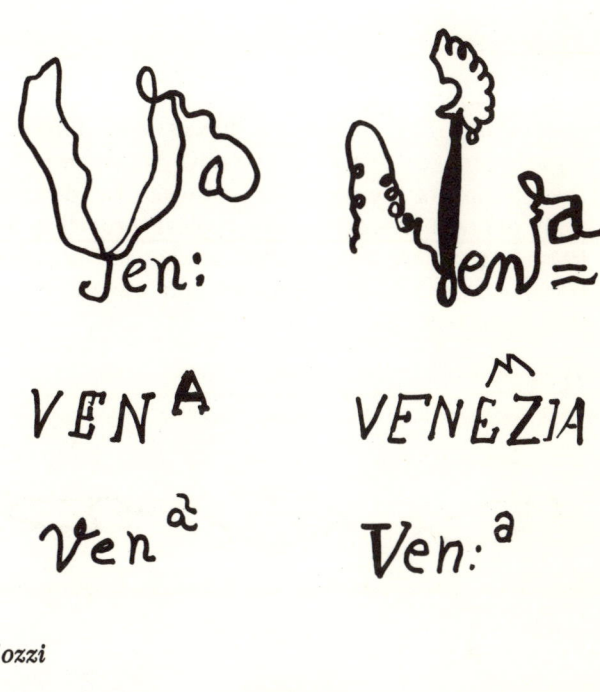

Cozzi

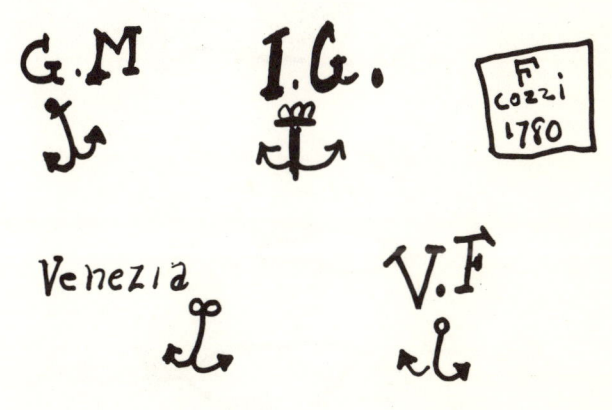

During the first period of production under the direction of Hunger the wares produced were unmarked. The Cozzi factory adopted the distinctive anchor mark painted in gold, blue, or red. Painters' initials or names are very often included in these anchor marks.

SWITZERLAND

Nyon, 1790–1813

Background

A soft-paste porcelain factory was established in the Swiss canton of Vaud in 1790. The director of the factory, a Frenchman, Maubrée, was a former employee at the Sèvres factory, and this experience led to a definite French influence in the production.

Characteristics

The wares produced were extremely white and very translucent. The majority of pieces were limited to dinnerware and small, decorative accessories. Although most of the porcelain produced was decorated with delicate flowers in the typical French motifs, some of the earlier production showed a definite German influence in decoration, favoring birds and landscape scenes.

Marks

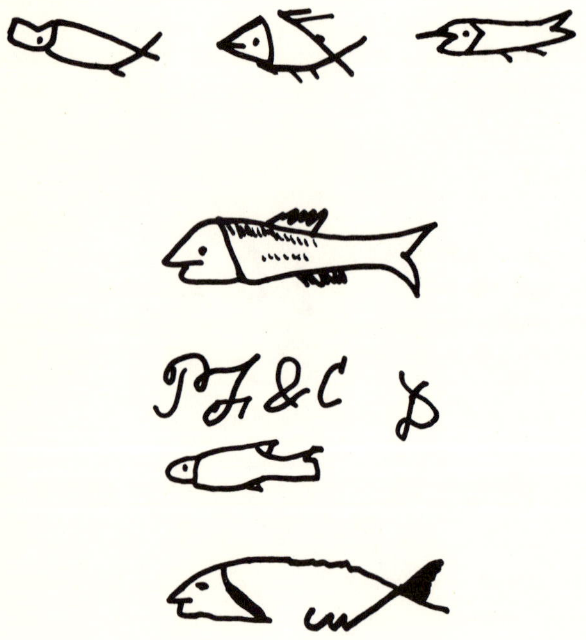

The fish marks of the Nyon factory were drawn in underglaze blue.

Zürich, 1763–91

Background

The first hard-paste porcelain factory was established at Zürich in 1763 by Heidegger and Spengler. Both men encouraged workers from the German porcelain factory Höchst to join the new production.

Characteristics

The majority of the production was very similar to the wares made at the Höchst factory. At first, soft-paste was produced, but it was found to be not financially profitable and almost immediately was discontinued. The hard-paste ware showed a grayish tone, and were mostly decorated with flowers and landscapes of the Swiss countryside. The best quality of workmanship was done during the last fifteen years of production.

Marks

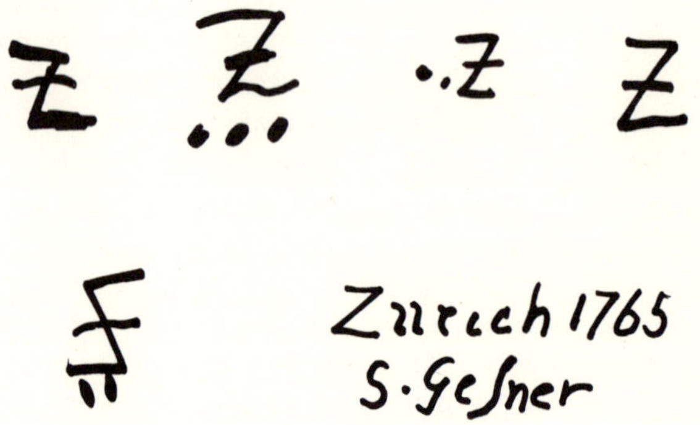

The first five marks were done in underglaze blue. The sixth, dating from 1765, is carefully drawn in gold for the city and date and violet for the name, Gesner.

UNDERSTANDING THE DECORATION PROCESSES

Printing from Hand-engraved Copper Plates

Engraving

The engraver cuts the design into the copper plate either with a graving tool (lines) or with stipple punches (dots). The depth of color of the finished pattern will depend on the depth of engraving. The style of engraving is often known as intaglio. The engraving is done on copper, and in order to render the surface hard-wearing, it is plated with chromium before being passed to the printing shop.

Printing

The traditional method of printing uses a hot engraving and hot color. The color, being a mixture of metallic oxides with printing oils, is applied to the engraving and rubbed well into every line and dot before the surplus is scraped off and further bossed away by the skillful printer to leave a surface free of any unwanted color. To this surface he applies a fine, fiber-free tissue paper that he has soaked with a soft soap "size" (to prevent it sticking to the hot copper plate). He then passes the engraving with the tissue paper under a printing roller press and immediately removes the tissue paper from the engraving, pulling with it the color from the engraved parts. This printed transfer is then handed to the team of skilled workers who will apply it to the piece of ware to be decorated.

Transferring

The surplus paper is first cut away, leaving only the essential parts of the design. These are then carefully placed in position on the ware in such a way that the decoration conforms to the standard pattern laid down for that piece. Pattern books and registers of how each particular piece in each pattern are to be decorated are kept in the pattern safe. The wide variety of shapes and items and the patterns that decorate them in the Spode range are so numerous that it needs considerable knowledge and much skill to decorate them in the correct way: many of these patterns possess "continuous borders," which call for great ability on the part of the printer and transferrer to ensure an imperceptible join. When the parts of the design have been placed in position, they are rubbed down with a piece of felt, using a little soft soap as a lubricant.

They are then strongly rubbed down by a girl using a stiff, bristled brush.

The process so far is similar both for earthenware and china. At this point earthenware is placed in a tub of water so that the tissue paper is softened and then removed, leaving the oil-based color intact on the article, which is then inspected, any faults corrected or touched up before being sent either to the hardening-on kiln (if a plain print) or to the underglaze painters if the outline print is to be filled in with other colors before the hardening-on fire.

With bone china, some colors enable the same procedure to be followed, but others that require a stronger tone will have the tissue paper carefully teased away from the item and color or gold rubbed into the printed design either to strengthen the tone of color or to force into the print a greater quantity of gold than would otherwise be the case. After inspection in these cases the printed designs on bone china will then be sent to the enamel fire to fasten them into the glaze.

Murray-Curvex Printing

In 1954 a new principle of printing was introduced by Spode whereby the design was transferred from the engraved copper plate on to a plastic pad, which reprinted it onto the article. This is called the Murray-Curvex process of printing; it yields a very high standard of reproduction on plates and saucers.

Hardening-on Fire

This fire is to fasten the printed and painted color indelibly to the biscuitware and to drive off the oils before the dipping process.

Hand-painting

Although most designs are applied complete as waterslide transfers nowadays, Spode still produces many popular patterns by hand-painting the colors onto a printed outline. For underglaze patterns, the colors are applied directly onto the biscuit (unglazed) earthenware, while for many other patterns the colors are painted onto the glossed ware. Luster, as used for Indian Tree pattern, can only be applied by hand.

Water-slide Transfers

Many decorations are now applied as transfers, preprinted either by lithography or silk-screen process, and carefully placed into position using water to permit the transfer to be slid carefully into the correct position. This process permits designs of great intricacy to be developed that would otherwise be beyond the range of profitable production.

But Spode permits no compromise to this valuable new technique by altering an established pattern for easier application. Great skill is needed to ensure that continuous borders and colored bands pass uninterrupted behind handles to retain the high standard of Spode designs.

Gilding

Many bone china designs are completed with a gold edge and/or other embellishments in gold, which is usually applied by skilled hand-gilders, although gold edges on flatware may be gilded by a machine.

Metallic gold is mixed with fluxes to bond it to the glaze and oils to make it possible to apply. (This makes it appear brown or blackish.) After firing, the gold is dull and needs to be rubbed with fine sand to brighten it.

The gold on Spodeware will withstand detergents and washing in dishwashers provided it is treated with reasonable care.

Final Selection

Throughout manufacturing, the inspection of pieces at each stage is carried out carefully, but because human judgment is involved, it is possible that a fault may be overlooked occasionally.

The final selection is especially stringent so that every piece of Spode will be a joy forever.

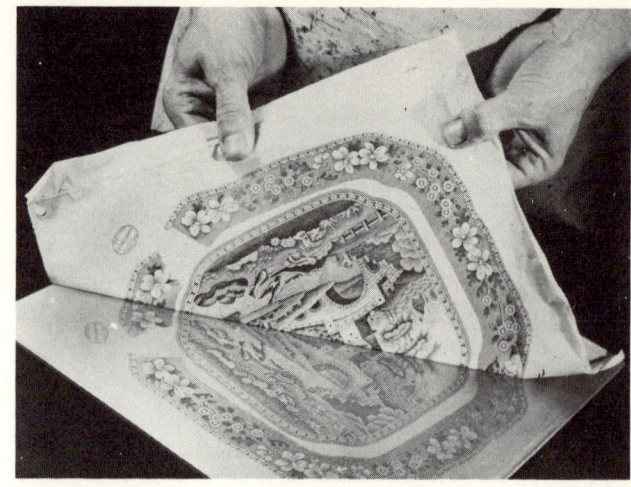

The "flat press" printer pulls the printed transfer from a copper plate.

Engraving a copper plate by stipple punching.

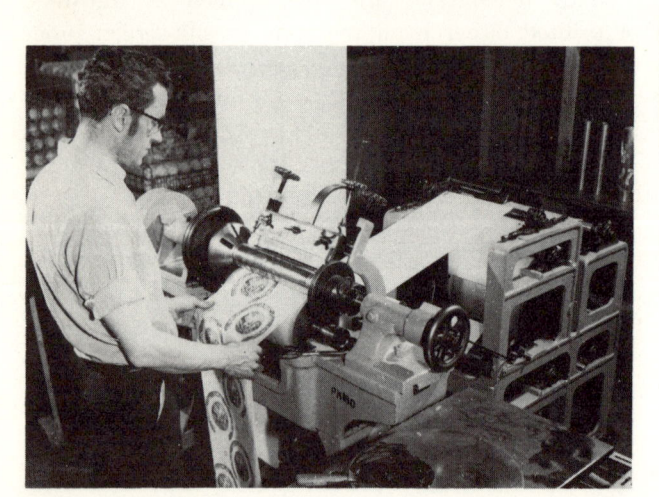

Roller press. Most patterns today are printed on roller presses.

Transferring the printed tissue to the article.

Rubbing down the transferred print.

Queen's Ware tureen, hand-painted border, c. 1780. Courtesy Wedgwood.

Careful inspection.

Items of Queens Ware showing the trial pieces (a selection of) made by Josiah Wadgwood I in connection with the production of the famous Dinner Service for Catherine the Great of Russia, 1793. Courtesy Wedgwood.

Items of 18th-century cameos mounted in cut steel showing the use of Jasper in jewelry, c. 1790. Courtesy Wedgwood.

Chocolate cup and cover with saucer. Vincennes, c. 1753. Yellow ground with Putti and trophies in monochrome blue. Courtesy The Walters Art Gallery.

Derby-English, 18th century. Statuette, young woman with basket of eggs, 9⅞ inches. Statuette, young man with lamb and basket of fruit, 10¼ inches. Courtesy The Walters Art Gallery.

Bowl, pot, and saucer. Bohemia, c. 1820–30. White painted in colors with gold and figures. Courtesy The Walters Art Gallery.

78

Bristol (1770–81), sauce boat. Courtesy The Walters Art Gallery.

Oil and vinegar set. Ceramic, c. 1780. Flower motif; Luxembourg. Courtesy Villeroy & Boch.

Clock stand with polychrome decoration. Fine ceramic, signed and dated, Jean Mathis 1807. Courtesy Villeroy & Boch.

Ceramic tea service, Mettlach, c. 1906. Courtesy Villeroy & Boch.

Luxembourg—wedding plate. Floral decor, c. 1829. Courtesy Villeroy & Boch.

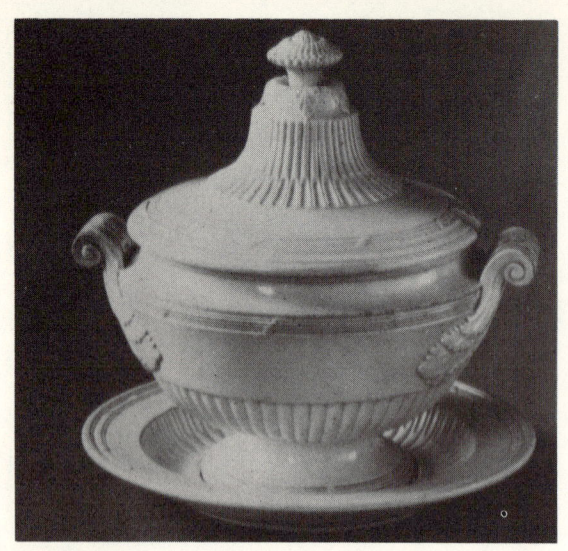

Soup tureen with cover and platter. Fine white ceramic, Empire form. Mettlach, 1820–25.

Magnificent large tureen, similar to silver shapes with molded panels, dolphin handle, and painted with Chinoiserie scenes in underglaze blue. The unglazed waster from Warmstry House exactly matches the handle and proves the tureen to have been made at Worcester. Period: Doctor Wall, c. 1755–58. Mark: Decorators marks only. Courtesy Dyson Perrins Museum, Worcester.

Beautiful group of Royal Worcester figures depicting Paul & Virginia modeled by James Hadley and decorated Raphaelesque colors on an ivory ground, c. 1865. Courtesy Royal Worcester Porcelain Company.

A large mug, painted in underglaze blue with the Gardener pattern, shown with an unglazed waster from the Warmstry House site with the same design but that has been painted by a different hand. Unglazed wasters allow a detailed examination of painting techniques that tend to blur when the piece has been glazed. Period: Doctor Wall, c. 1770–76. Mark: Open crescent.

80

Jug of Dr. Wall period fully decorated in the Mandarin style c. 1760. Courtesy The Worcester Porcelain Company.

Two cream boats. On the left Worcester and on the right Caughley. The Worcester boat carries the disguised Chinese numeral mark long thought to be Caughley but now known to be Worcester. Period: Davis/Flight, c. 1776–93. Mark: Disguised numeral on Worcester boat. S on Caughley boat. Courtesy Geoffrey Godden.

Punch bowl printed with the Fisherman pattern always thought to be the positive Caughley print. Attached to the inside of the bowl is an unglazed waster from Warmstry House which matches exactly and shows that the pattern is a much finer Worcester one. Period: Davis/Flight 1776–1793. Mark: Disguised Chinese numeral. Courtesy Geoffrey Godden.

A superb quality Derby porcelain-covered sauce tureen. The print panels by Thomas Steel, with magnificent gilding. Price Comparison: 1968 = 60 pounds sterling; 1978 = 120 pounds sterling. Courtesy Geoffrey Godden.

A scale blue ground Dr. Wall Worcester covered vase, c. 1760–65. Price comparison: 1973 = 180 pounds sterling; 1978 = 250 pounds sterling. Courtesy Geoffrey Godden.

A superb mint and large size Dr. Wall Worcester bell-shaped mug, c. 1760. Price Comparison: 1968 = 200 pounds sterling; 1978 = 360 pounds sterling. Courtesy Geoffrey Godden.

A fine quality John Ridgway porcelain plate, part of a dessert service shown by this firm at the 1851 Exhibition. Price Comparison: 1963 = 15 pounds sterling; 1978 = 85 pounds sterling. The reason for the dramatic price increase can be directly attributed to the increased interest in collecting Victoriana. Courtesy Geoffrey Godden.

A rare English Lowestoft soft-paste porcelain jug painted in underglaze-blue. Price Comparison: 1973 = 185 pounds sterling; 1978 = 275 pounds sterling. Courtesy Geoffrey Godden.

Coffeepot and cup, c. 1770. Zurich porcelain, painted in red camayeu with golden rim. The major part of Zurich porcelain manufacture is made up of coffee and tea sets. These services are particularly sober in form for the period and have a dainty ornamentation showing flowers and landscapes or, as here, birds painted in shades of one color. Gift of Heinrich Angst, 1903, Swiss Landesmuseum.

Spode dinnerware, Byron Views pattern. Various scenes taken from Findens landscape and portrait illustrations to the life and works of Lord Byron, published 1832–34. Dish, Bay of Naples. Dessert plate painted by Birbeck, c. 1882, Bay of Naples.

Spode, pattern number 2061, stone china and new stone. Only known breakfast set in stone china, although Cabbage pattern, based on Chinese tobacco leaf pattern, is not uncommon. Private collection.

Spode. Bone china, Bute shaped cup and saucer. Unmarked. Arms of the United States of America, with fourteen stars indicating a date after 1891. Courtesy Spode Museum. Gift of Thomas Cottnell, Jr.

Spode. Neo shape French Jar, bone china. Courtesy Spode Museum.

83

One of a set of four rare Chelsea botanical "Hans Sloane" dishes, c. 1755. 27 cms. wide. Courtesy Earle D. Vandelkar.

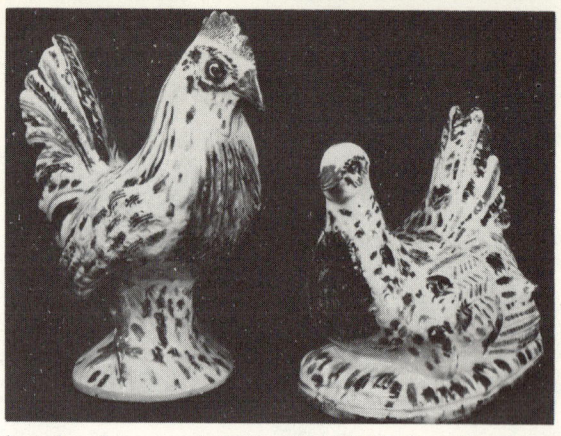

A pair of rare and interesting Whieldon English pottery figures of a cock and hen decorated in colored glazes, c. 1780. 18 cms. high. Courtesy Earle D. Vandelkar.

A large and exceptional Chinese porcelain dish finely decorated in *famille verte* enamels with birds and flowers. K'ang Hsi, c. 1700. 42 cms. diameter. Courtesy Earle D. Vandelkar.

A fine pair of Chamberlain's Worcester fruit coolers, covers, and liners decorated with *en grisaille* panels on both sides depicting Aesop's Fables, the body supported on three finely gilded dolphins, mermaid handles, and dolphin finial. c. 1796. 34 cms. high. Courtesy Earle D. Vandelkar.

An amusing large Chinese porcelain oval dish decorated in *famille rose* enamels with "Don Quixote." Chien Lung, c. 1770. 39 cms. wide. One of a pair. Courtesy Earle D. Vandelkar.

Punchbowl, 1973. Painted in colors by Finn Clausen, with sea fight representing battle of Copenhagen, 1801, and panel inscribed "Tilegnet O. Fischer og alle brave Danske Kiobenhavn 2.April 1801 af Roepstorff (dedicated to O. Fischer and all brave Danes, Copenhagen, 2.April 1801 by Roepstorff)". Roepstorff, wealthy patriot and former governor general of Danish Virgin Islands, ordered 21 copies painted in colors and 23 in grisaille as personal gifts to officers who had fought on April 2, 1801. The order was completed in 1807. The paintings were copied from a watercolor by C. A. Lorentsen. Diameter: 13½ in. Courtesy Royal Copenhagen Porcelain Factory.

...een Juliane Marie, 1970. Bust modeled by Carl Fred-...k Stanley, 1776. The model was bought by the factory... 1779. Height: 32 in. Courtesy Royal Copenhagen Por-...ain Factory.

Sèvres ewer and basin, 1763. Painted by Catrice. Marked interlaced L & K. Courtesy Victoria and Albert Museum.

St. Cloud, c. 1700. Teapot decorated with lambrequins in underglaze blue. Courtesy Victoria and Albert Museum.

...ried "Flora Danica" objects, 1973. The first service was ...ered by King Christian VII and delivered to the royal ...sehold in 1803. The decoration was copied from en-...vings in the botanial work Flora Danica (published ...1–99). A second service was made for Princess Alex-...ra for her marriage to Albert Edward, Prince of ...les, in 1863; thereafter the service was part of the ...tory's regular line. The decorations are still exactly ...ied from original engravings of the work completed ... 1883 with more than 3,000 plants. Courtesy Royal ...penhagen Porcelain Factory.

1. Wrotham Ware, 1649. 2. Decorated slipware mug. 3. Bristol puzzle jug, delft ware middle 18th century. Courtesy Victoria and Albert Museum.

85

Watch in watch stand, c. 1825. Pink luster and enamel colors of boy, girl, and long case clock. Courtesy Victoria and Albert Museum.

Pair of 19th-century Sèvres vases.

Teapot form of cauliflower color-glazed earthenware. Staffordshire, Burslem, c. 1763. Courtesy Victoria and Albert Museum.

Teakettle and stand. Delft, painted in blue GVS mark of G; 18th century. Courtesy Victoria and Albert Museum.

86

2 Collector's Plates

The limited-editions market is one of the fastest-growing investment possibilities in the world today. With over a half million people interested in the Christmas plate market alone, many false and misleading conceptions have developed related to the collection of these plates. Many forgeries have been produced, and careful attention should be paid to the details of each plate. Probably the best advice that any collector could receive would be to limit his collection to one manufacturer's plates alone. One of the biggest forgeries is to produce a plate that predates the original starting of a manufacturer's series. Therefore, the collector who is unfamiliar with all the various factories could easily make a very costly mistake. The following is a list of the major producers of Christmas plates and the dates when the various series were started.

Factory	Country	Dates Of Production
Bareuther	Germany	1967–Present
Berlin Design	Kaiser Alboth factory, West Germany	1970–Present
Bing & Grondahl	Denmark	1895–Present
Blue Delft Co.	Holland	1970–Present
Fenton	U.S.A.	1970–Present
Fürstenburg	Germany	1971–Present
Haviland	U.S.A. and Limoges, France	1970–Present
Hummel	Germany	1971–Present
Imperial	U.S.A.	1970–Present
Rorstrand	Sweden	1968–Present
Rosenthal	Germany	1910–70 open stock limited edition series started in 1971–Present
Royal Copenhagen	Denmark	1908–Present
Royal Delft	Holland	1915–41 1954–Present
Shenango	U.S.A.	1949–50 1952–61 1964–75
Spode	England	1970–Present

After evaluating the above, the intelligent collector now will refine his selection even further by selecting the factory plates that he wishes to collect. Perhaps two important points should be considered in making this selection:

(1) Collectors plates do not automatically become an antique because they are produced in limited editions. Great thought should be put into selecting plates that combine both quality of design and continuity of production.

(2) If the collection is being assembled for an investment potential, great emphasis should be placed on length of production. It should be noted that, although individual plates do increase in value over the years, a much greater return on investment can be realized from a complete connective range of collector's plates.

The following collection of photographs shows the entire range of Christmas plates produced by the Royal Copenhagen Porcelain factory of Denmark. It would be both challenging and financially rewarding to compile a complete collection of plates such as those illustrated. Of course, if you are only interested in the occasional collector's plate as a decorative accessory, you can safely buy almost any choice without fear of losing any money on your purchase.

88

89

90

91

92

93

94

95

96

97

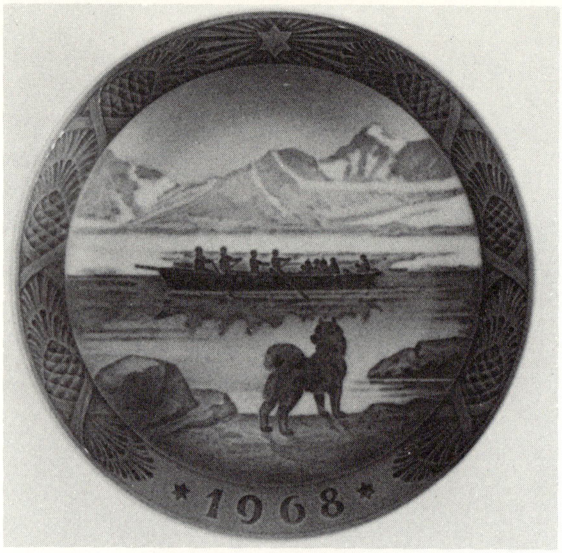
1968

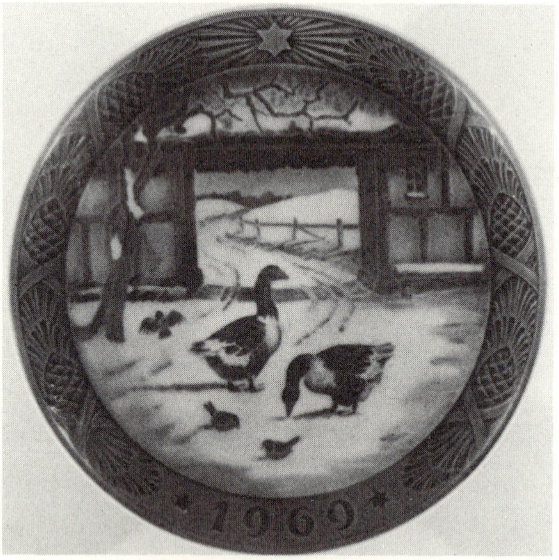
1969

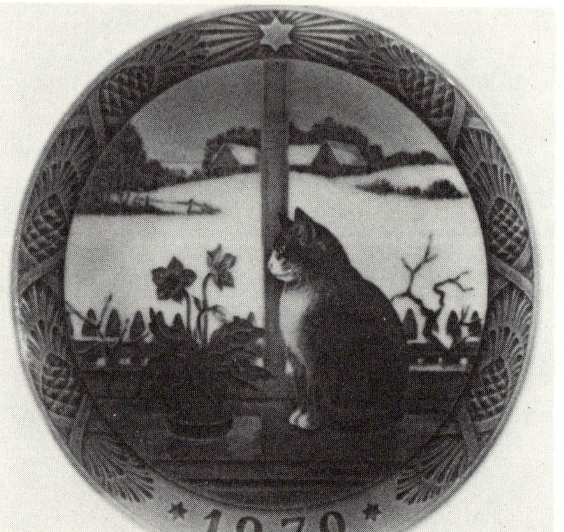
1970

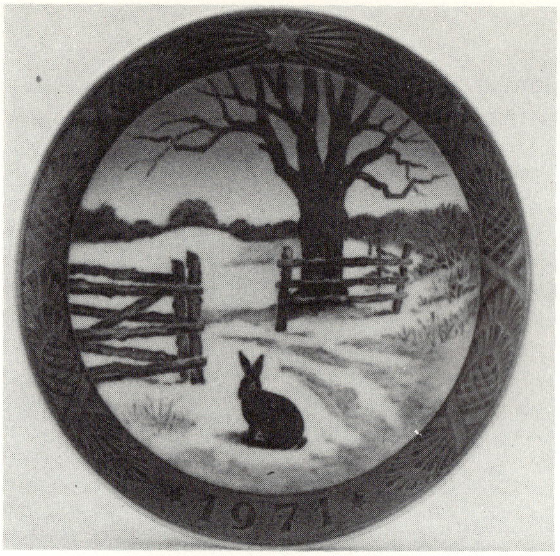
1971

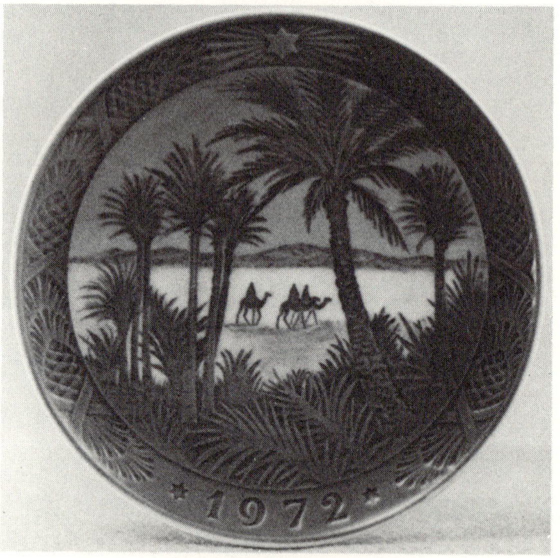
1972

1973

99

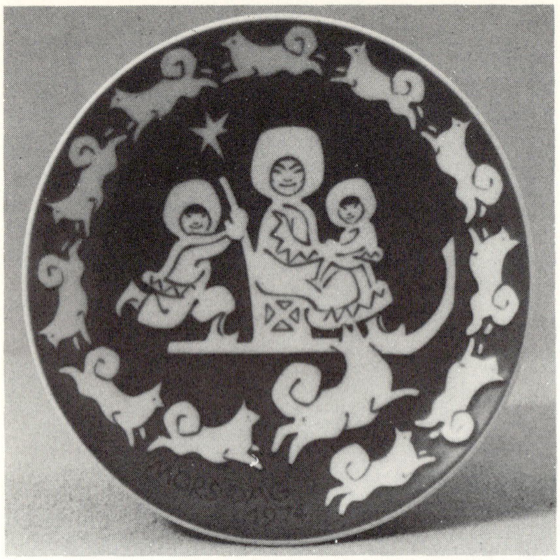
MORS DAG 1974

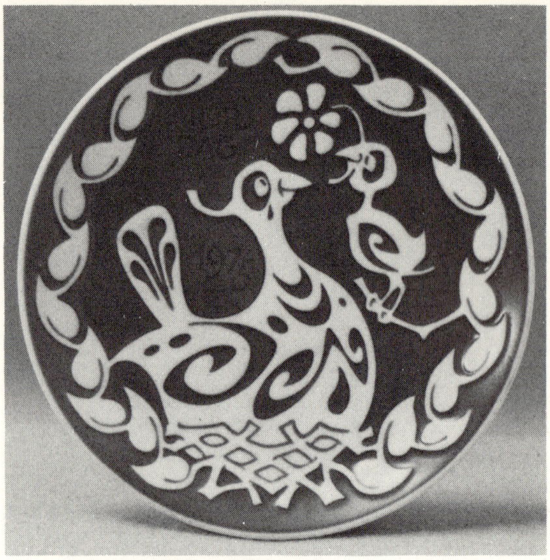

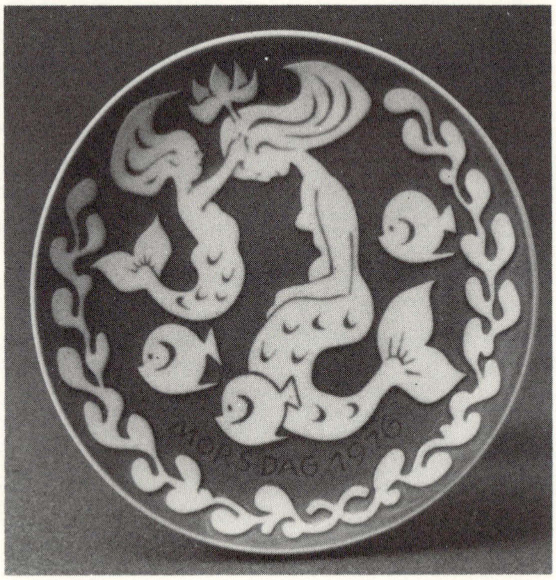
MORS DAG 1976

3 Enamels and Boxes

The decorative process of enameling, which is basically the fusing of a glass powder to a metal base, has been admired by collectors since before the Renaissance. It is very interesting to note that the art of enameling has developed throughout the centuries closely with the discovery and improvement of the glass industry. Enameling was originally developed as a method of decorating base metal-work of various types that attained immediate and long-lasting success throughout the world. Centers of enameling began to develop in the East, especially in China, during the late Sung dynasty and also in Persia beginning in the twelfth century. It was not until the eighteenth century that enameling was actively used in Europe, and both Limoges and Meissen became popular centers for enamel production. Also during the eighteenth century, England established a major area for the enameler's art, but styles as well as piece production were limited to the rococo, which was very popular during this period. While a very wide range of boxes and smaller decorative accessories were made, the limiting to rococo severely limited development of enameling in England. Throughout Europe enameling enjoyed an unparalleled success. France especially produced some very beautiful and extremely intricate examples of this art. Although the French enameling was exceptionally fine, it never quite attained the exquisite excellence of the Chinese.

Collectors today are mostly interested in securing examples of the very fine Chinese Cloisonné, as well as many fine pieces that were commissioned for export to the West, but retain the delicate Eastern designs. Also a favorite with collectors are both the printed as well as painted enamels of Battersea and Chelsea, England.

Enameling was very often used in decorating many different varieties of boxes such as snuff and patch boxes, which played an important part in the daily lives of people during the seventeenth and eighteenth centuries. Collectors during the past decade have renewed an increasing interest in enameled boxes. Up until this time, the majority of these boxes had remained in many of the original families. In this respect, they were accepted but very rarely appreciated for their delicacy and beauty.

Cosmetic boxes, although first produced toward the beginning of the fourteenth century, did not reach the height of their creativity until the end of the seventeenth century, when both jewelers and enamelers combined talents to outdo their competition. The design of each box was of paramount importance. People vied for status through the originality of their boxes. The famous Madame de Pompadour ordered a patch box in the shape of an enameled swan. Other favorite shapes included hearts, as well as the oval and triangle.

The decoration, as well as design shaping, played an ever-increasing role in the popularity of enameled boxes. Many of these designs were greatly influenced by political movements of the period and, therefore, were subject to rapid changes. Very often battles, war heroes, and rulers were emulated on the popular boxes of the period. Not all designers reproduced the intricate and very often austere battle scenes, and, therefore, many enameled boxes display delicate birds and flowers.

Perhaps the craftsmanship involved, especially the attention to the smallest details, best describes the enameler's art, and helps us to understand the decline of the process. It was not until the nineteenth century that the enameler's art was revived, but it was never spectacularly successful due to the amount of time involved in production. It is possible to find isolated enamels from this period that display excellent craftsmanship, but pieces are rare.

Vanity case in chased gold, wrought with enamels and pearls. On the base there is a watch and an automation with musical box. On the side of the case there is a landscape on enamel, attributed to the Geneva artist J. L. Richter (1766–1841); while on the front piece, above, cupid with quivers and torches. Courtesy Rolex.

Watch, c. 1680. Silver case, enameled. Diameter 35 mm. Work by Pierre II Huaud of Geneva (1647–ante 1698), who was official miniature painter to the Elector Frederick III of Brandenburg from 1691. The clockwork is signed by the Geneva watchmaker Jaques Joly (1622–94). The dial is of slightly later origin. Acquired in Lucerne in 1949. LM 23697. Courtesy Swiss Landesmuseum.

Top view of rectangular tortoiseshell snuff box with two enamel miniatures, one by Genevese S. G. Counis (1785–1859) of the Duchess deBerry, and the other by the Frenchman J. B. J. Duchesne (1770–1856) of the Duc de Berry. Courtesy Rolex.

4 Silver

AMERICAN SILVER

Unlike English silver, early American silver is readily available, at moderate prices to most collectors. Much of the American silver produced was closely patterned after its English prototype. The American silver industry was founded during the second half of the seventeenth century by emigrant English silversmiths. The majority of the earliest Colonial American silver was produced by these same emigrated English silversmiths who settled in Massachusetts. Toward the end of the seventeenth century Boston became the accredited capital of silver production. Between 1650 and 1700 many fine examples of Early American silver were produced. The Massachusetts Bay Colony soon developed into a highly industrial and professional area, which not only encouraged the development of the arts, but could well afford to patronize them.

Due to the fact that most of the Colonists were of English extraction, the styles of American silver were closely patterned after popular British designs of the period.

During the ensuing years, with differences in political doctrines developing between the Colonies and England, combined with the rising Puritan influence in the New World, styles began to differ. Silver designs in the Colonies were much simpler than the English, with very little ostentatious decorations with the key descriptive word being utilitarian. Much of the early silver produced in the Colonies has survived until today, and fine collections can be seen at the Philadelphia Museum of Art, and the Museum of Fine Arts in Boston.

John Hull and Robert Sanderson have been identified as the earliest silversmiths working in Boston. Other noted men of the period were Jeremiah Dummer, John Coney, and Edward Winslow, who were both talented as well as prolific craftsmen. Boston silversmiths during the seventeenth and eighteenth centuries became the symbol of elegance just as London makers were in England.

Newport, Rhode Island, quickly became a major export center, which was able to support local silversmiths during the eighteenth century. Some of the more important craftsmen of Newport were Daniel Russell, Samuel Vernon, Samuel Casup, and Arnold Collins. Unfortunately, the silversmiths of Newport operated under the auspices of their more famous Bostonian colleagues. It was still, regretfully, more prestigious to order your silver from Boston, regardless of the excellent native talent. As an important coastal port, Newport was gravely hurt by the Revolution, causing closing of most of the trade and seriously reducing the population. At this point the major silver work was being done now not in Newport, but in Providence.

It is interesting to note when studying silver produced in New York, that, besides the distinct English influence seen to date in Colonial American silver, the additional Dutch flair in design is clearly visible. The earliest pieces were brought directly from Holland by emigrant Dutch silversmiths. Prevalent designs included detailed engravings with floral motifs, which were very popular, and forms became more massive. Not only engraved designs were popular, but cast ornamentation and embossing were also used to decorate New York silver. Some of the more popular motifs seen on silver of this period are cherubs, festoons, fruit, cyphers, flowers, birds, and foliate scrolls. New York silver is also noted for beautifully engraved coats of arms. Some of the more famous silversmiths of early New York included Bartholomew Schoats, Peter Van Dyck, Jacobus Van der Spiegel, Jacob and Hendrik Boelen, Benjamin Wynkoop, Simeon Soumain, Charles, Bartholomew and John LeRoux, John and Kaenralt Ten Eyck.

The simplicity of the Quaker faith is predominant in the silver of Philadelphia. The earliest silver produced in Philadelphia dates from the end of the seventeenth century or beginning of the eighteenth century and shows definite design similarities with English silver of the same period. Philadelphia became famous for the domed-lid tankard with no finial. The early silversmiths of Philadelphia, Philip Syng, Joseph Richardson, Francis Richardson, William Vilant, Cesar Ghiselin, and John de Nys, were very talented, but unfortunately, the beginning economy of Philadelphia was unable to support their trade to the fullest of their ability. Later, as Philadelphia became the richest and politically most important city in Colonial America, the silversmiths enjoyed a greater patronage.

During the seventeenth century, the majority of American silver showed both architectural and cylindrical simplicity in lines of its design. It was not until the last half of the seventeenth century, about 1690, that these straight lines were replaced with the more genteel floral patterns and flowing curves. Silverpieces during this period became more massive and continued to be popular until about 1720, when a simplicity was returned to both form and design. It was not until the middle of the eighteenth century that surface ornamentation became popular, as well as repoussé work and engraving. Perhaps the most important silversmith of this period was Paul Revere.

For more than a quarter of a century, between 1775 and the early part of the 1800s, a gentle return to a more simplified silver design and ornamentation was seen. Between 1810 and 1840, designers of American silver became grander with definite Empire and Napoleonic influence.

HOW TO IDENTIFY EARLY AMERICAN SILVER

American silver collectors, unlike their British counterparts, are not quite as fortunate in authenticating pieces. Baltimore, Maryland, was the only city in the United States that registered silver at the assay office during the first quarter of the nineteenth century. American silver collectors must research the individual silversmiths, both birth, death, and working periods, in order to date silver pieces. Most silversmiths working during the nineteenth century dated their wares, and almost always American silver had either the initials or mark of the maker. Therefore, with a little ingenuity, the "working date" of the individual silversmith can be determined.

Between 1830 and 1860 the word *coin* was stamped on silver pieces. Although this word appearing does not guarantee that the article was produced from melted coin of the realm, it does guarantee that the piece is of an excellent quality. The word *sterling*, which is usually associated with quality, was not used until about 1850.

Famous Early American Silversmiths

1650–90

Timothy Dwight
John Hull
Robert Sanderson

1690–1720

Jurian Blanck, Jr.
Jeremiah Dummer
John Coney
Edward Winslow

1720–50

Peter Van Dyck
Nathaniel Morse
Jacob Hurd
Simeon Soumain

1750–1800

Paul Revere
Myer Myers
Joseph Richardson
Nathaniel Richardson
Joseph Richardson, Jr.

INVESTMENT POTENTIALS IN EARLY AMERICAN SILVER

Although Early American silver is readily available to the collector, prices vary drastically from period to period. Spoons at present, dating from the late eighteenth and early nineteenth centuries, are available to most collectors at prices ranging from five to ten dollars. Other tableware of the same period, such as pistol-handled knives, can be purchased for between thirty-five and fifty-five dollars, and forks can be readily found for twenty-five to thirty-five dollars. Sets of silverware are difficult to find and much more expensive than a combination of individually priced pieces. Tea sets made during the first part of the nineteenth century are readily available for beginning collectors with prices starting about eight hundred dollars and ranging to a high of one thousand, four hundred dollars. Not all Early American silver can be easily purchased. Noted silversmiths like Paul Revere's work demand prices well above the average collector's price range. Several years ago a sugar bowl with cover brought upwards of twenty thousand dollars at auction.

Silver produced between 1775 and 1810 has become a popular collector's period because it is much more moderately priced than earlier periods. Silver produced during the late eighteenth and early nineteenth centuries is considered to have both excellent design with noted simplicity, as well as being readily available at good silver shops and antique shows and fairs throughout the country. This combined availability at reasonable prices makes silver of this period a good investment, which should get progressively better in the future.

Another period in antique silver that collectors are finding considerably more interesting is the first half of the nineteenth century. Silver made during this period (1810–40) is fairly reasonable on today's silver market and has excellent potential for increasing in value during the near future and therefore is considered an excellent investment at present.

EARLY ENGLISH SILVER

As early as the fourteenth century it was required by law in England that all silverware bear an officially registered mark. Soon after this time London became the artistic center for English silver. Many provincial cities such as Chester, Exeter, York, and New Castle also produced beautifully crafted silverware.

Perhaps due to its intrinsic value as well as its versatility, silver has retained its popularity throughout the centuries. Silver was purchased during this period more for its monetary value than for its decorative assets: the sterling standard allowed either conversion to coin of the realm or a complete restyling by melting the plate and refashioning into the current mode.

Unfortunately, very little medieval sterling treasures are available today that predate the desecration of the churches by Henry VIII. Also, the royal treasury as well as private collections were heavily depleted to finance the Civil War of 1642–48 as well as for dowry and presentation gifts to visiting royalty. The preceding events, therefore, have made pre-Restoration sterling almost unattainable for the average collector. Therefore, due to the unavailability of silver of this period, many fakes have appeared on the market regardless of the stiff penalties for silver forgeries. Any buyer should be especially wary of silver of this period offered at sizable reductions in price.

The reign of Charles II beginning in 1660 started a long-needed period of economic prosperity. During the Restoration styles changed from the more sober lines of medieval and Tudor silver to the very extravagant and bold, if not gaudy. The returning exiled court brought many of these new styles from both Holland and France. Both countries were leaders in Continental silver production. Much of the European silver of this period was designed after both floral and wildlife motifs. Therefore, it is not unusual to see the more sober styles of English silver decorated with the more flamboyant Continental motifs that were gradually gaining popularity in England at that time. The most striking period pieces were the candle cups, posset pots, two-handled, cups and porringers. The majority of these wares were inspired by customers of the period, for example both posset and candle were very popular wine-flavored milk drinks that were drunk hot, which made the use of the two-handled cup very useful.

The Commonwealth period produced quantities of tankards that had a characteristic spread base or skirt foot. Later the rim foot replaced the former and remained almost the standard style until the beginning of the eighteenth century. The majority of tankards of the period were covered with usually flat-domed pieces or conversely sharp, pointed caps.

By the end of the seventeenth century, either to impress or influenced by the coronation of William III of Holland as King of England, the baroque style had arrived in full fashion. Basically, baroque styling was based on a somewhat more formal version of the naturalistic style that swept Holland during the first part of the seventeenth century. As well as the baroque style, which takes its inspiration from nature, another mode in English silver, chinoiserie, became popular during the last quarter of the seventeenth century. The derivation of this style is often misunderstood by collectors, who believe the silver pieces were produced in China for export to the English market instead of Chinese design inspired and made in England.

The last half of the seventeenth century saw the development of two new styles of silver vessels inspired by changing social customs. During the Charles II period casters for spices and sugar became popular. The majority of styles of casters of this period were characterized by cylinder shapes with straight sides and high-domed tops. Decoration was limited to pierced work.

The English industry greatly prospered during the last part of the seventeenth century. Many of the talented French craftsmen fled their own country after the king revoked the Edict of Nantes, which had until then protected the Protestants. Many of the fleeing Huguenots were noted designers and brought with them the closely guarded design books of the period. Within a very short time the meticulous decorative detail of the various French powers could be seen in the new designs of the British craftsmen. Perhaps it was this innovative influence that helped shape the British silver industry into the world leader during the eighteenth century. Not only were styles of decoration such as the shells, strapwork enclosing scrolls, foliage, husks, human head masks, and applied lions popular, but new forms derived from the baluster shape were introduced. Many of the old shapes were gracefully altered, such as the straight-sided flagon, which was turned in to a lever with a flying scroll handle and high, broad lip. Other important changes included the cast baluster candlestick, which gradually replaced the long-standing fluted columns, and the reshaping of the two-handled cup. This was done by adding height as well as a molded rib that extended around the body and either harp-shaped or scroll handles. These additions added an elegance not before associated with the cup.

Silversmiths progressed rapidly under the new design influences, which brought a new formality to silverwork. Pieces produced during the Huguenot period were usually well shaped with simple but graceful curved and beautifully detailed design work. From the beginning of the Huguenot emigration in 1685, England saw for the first time in silver history the emergence of two styles of production. Many of the older silver craftsmen refused the new French inspirational designs and kept producing wares in the traditional British baroque styles, but a certain faction of the market was greatly enamored of the lighter French styles and gradually broke away.

Due to increased interest in and demand for silver production, the British government passed an act in 1697 known as the "Britannia Standard," which greatly helped regulate the quality of silver used. All pieces that contained 3.3% more silver than previously used were punchmarked at the assay office with "the figure of a woman commonly called Britannia." Britannia silver, of a higher quality than sterling, was exceptionally plain in design despite the excellent texture of the metal for decoration. The beauty of Britannia silver lay in the simplicity of its design. The return to the sterling standard came in 1720, but several noted silversmiths continued to work with the more costly Britannia silver for many years because of the excellent qualities the ware displayed for decoration.

With the ascension of Anne to the throne, the more graceful Huguenot styles began to flourish. The teapot during the Queen Anne period underwent tremendous changes. The old wine-pot style was converted into a squat, pear-shaped design with a curved spout and dome cover. Although traditionally the form of silver coffeepots was unaffected by the new French influence, and remained a cylindrical straight-sided pot, during the Queen Anne period some design modifications were used. Basically, the straight-sided shape was unaffected, but both handles and spouts were designed with curving swanlike and scrolled shapes. Besides structural changes during the Queen Anne period, decorative designs were done by both engraving and applied detail work. Also during the first quarter of the eighteenth century there was a return to the more delicate, cut-card form of ornamentation as well as cast-applied detail work.

During the reign of George I (1714–27) exceptionally fine engraving was accomplished, and many fine dishes and salvers from the period have survived until today. Although much of the engraving was similar, the forms were readily changed, and in this respect variety was accomplished. Some favorite shapes of the period include the octagonal, hexagonal, square, circular, and multilobe.

Although silver plates had been made for years, King George popularized the silver dinner service. Now not only were there plates, but sauce boats, dining utensils, serving pieces, as well as soup tureens. Forks, a new innovation of the period, were either two- or three-pronged. Also during the first part of the seventeenth century, spoons underwent a basic design change with the shield top replacing the earlier formed end, and their stems becoming flatter with a distinct rail-tail extending down onto the back of the spoon bowl.

The French-inspired rococo style, which takes its form from symbols from nature, such as flowers, rocks, fish, scrolled vines, and leaping dolphins, touched the hearts of the English and retained its popularity through the centuries despite periodic revivals of other forms.

During the second half of the eighteenth century there was a distinct revival of Chinese influence on workmanship. About 1750 chinoiserie, together with pierced work and repoussé design, became vogue. Much of this chinoiserie-inspired silverware was limited to the tea table. It is interesting to note that, although the designs are altogether Chinese in origin, such as robed Oriental figures and pagodas, there still remains to be seen in the background and trim decoration a very distinct rococo influence.

During the 1760s English society was turning its interest to the lost classical civilizations. A young architect, Robert Adam, sensed the growing boredom with rococoism and brought back to England the neoclassical style of Greece. Restrained elegance characterized the decorations of scrolls, laurel wreaths, festoons, anthemion, and palmette. Despite the lack of metalware retrieved from archaeological excavations, silversmiths of the period copied the elegant stone vase and urn forms of past civilizations.

Robert Adam, with his simplistic but elegant neoclassic design, had a lasting impact on all forms of art. Bright-cut as well as fluting became popular for excavating the new designs in silver. Reeding and beading were used as popular border motifs. By the end of the eighteenth century, the simple and elegant styling was gradually being expanded to a grander version. Bold leafage, scrolls in relief, applied medallions, and festoons were being added to the previous simplistic Grecian styles. Perhaps the saddest misfortune of the period was the redecoration of earlier simple pieces into the "modern" styling.

By the first quarter of the nineteenth century, at both Sheffield and Birmingham, machine-made copies were being produced. Sheffield plate was readily accepted by the masses as a substitute for the much more expensive handmade silver. By 1840 the silversmiths were really feeling the competition when electroplating was developed. The age of mechanization was truly upon us.

Contrary to common belief, the Victorians tried to stimulate artistic freedom, not stifle it, but they were severely hampered by the economic situation of the country. Set was the age of the machine! Although very little new or innovative silver designs were produced during this period, the Victorians must be credited with the foundation of many art schools to further research.

By 1880 the period of art nouveau had dawned and influenced silver production of the time. In recent years collectors have begun investigating art nouveau silver, which promises to hold their interest.

Investing in English Silver

Georgian silver during the past decade has emerged as an excellent investment. Perhaps this can be best explained by the availability of purchasing Georgian silver, the wide range of prices involved that can be included in the budgets of various economic levels, as well as the steady increase in price observed since 1973.

The Georgian period encompasses the reign of George I (1714–27), George II (1727–60), and George III (1760–1820). The majority of silver produced during this period was centered on table service. For example, beautiful examples of Georgian design can be found in silverware, sauce boats, sugar bowls, coffee pots, tea pots, salvers, candlesticks, creamers, trays, and a large variety of service dishes.

Although London was primarily the center of Silver craftsmanship and pieces produced there have commanded higher prices, Georgian silver was mainly produced outside of the capital in many of the following cities: Newcastle, Chester, Edinburgh, Exeter, Norwich, Dublin, Glasgow, Norwich, York and Sheffield.

The identification of Georgian silver is relatively simple and accurate as to the make, date of production, as well as city of origin. Hallmarks, and not style, are perhaps the single most important factor in determining the value of English silver. Since the last part of the twelfth century, British law has required that silversmiths imprint their individual hallmarks, and during the fourteenth century the addition of a mark of city origin was included.

During the reign of George I, the hallmark on silver was divided into four separate parts.
1. Located on the farthest left was the symbol of Britannia, which indicated a 95.8% silver.
2. In 1719–20 the crowned leopard's head was used as representative of a London hallmark.
3. This mark indicates the year of manufacture, and can be easily translated when interpreted with a directory of silver marks.
4. This mark identifies the maker, with either his name or initials.

Another mark also found on Georgian Silver produced in London has the tax mark. This mark indicates that a tax was levied and paid on the piece. The tax law was in force from 1784 to 1890. Certain definite characteristics play an important role in determining the value of Georgian silver. *Age* plays perhaps the greatest role, with George I silver being more sought after and valuable than the following Georges in descending order of reign. The *condition* of both the piece of silver and the hallmark should be carefully scrutinized by the buyer. For any piece of English silver to come close to its appraised value, its hallmark must be undamaged. A slightly damaged hallmark can reduce the value by more than half. It is equally important for investment pieces of silver to be in perfect, unrepaired form. Damaged wares are worthless when being considered as an investment potential. Although many silversmiths produced Georgian silver, there are four important *makers* whose wares are steadily increasing in value:

1. Paul Storr, late eighteenth and early nineteenth century.
2. Hester Bateman, late eighteenth century.
3. Paul de Lamerie, early eighteenth century.
4. John Schofield, late eighteenth century.

Besides the craftsman, the quality of the silver work should be carefully studied. Although much Georgian silver was produced, many pieces lack good form and design. In evaluating designs, investors should be wary of elevated prices on pieces carrying family crests. Armoreal marks only add to the value when they are beautifully executed with fine, clear detail work. Extra value can also be estimated when either the crest or silver pieces can be *historically documented* or traced to royal ownership.

Forgeries

Although the hallmark system discouraged mass-market faking of silverware, nevertheless forging did occur. Earlier in the chapter we discussed the most common form of deception, grafting. Perhaps due to the enormous skill involved to produce a perfect product, other methods began to appear. The combination of two entirely different periods is quite common, which results in a price reduction of about fifty percent of what the pure Georgian piece would have been valued at. Perhaps the most blatant forgeries concern actual late-period Georgian silver pieces that have been both stamped with an earlier date and famous manufacturer's name. The latter addition of repoussé work on earlier Georgian pieces completely reduces any artistic value centered on the piece, and retains only the worth of the precious metal used in production. A lesser, but equally distinctive, technique was to add fine and sometimes intricate engravings to earlier plain silver pieces, which reduces the value of the piece involved anywhere from one-half to one-third.

The only valid approach to understanding and the eventual ability to spot forgeries is actual exposure. Dealers in Georgian silver are more than willing to explain these various techniques to the new collector.

Investment Trends

It is interesting to note when analyzing price trends in Georgian silver over the past two decades that its prices have fluctuated drastically, setting unprecedented highs as well as lows. During the late 1950s prices had decreased to a point where much inferior reproduction silver was being purchased for the same price as authentic Georgian silver. It took nearly ten years, until 1965, for prices to rise fifty percent from an all-time low. During the gradual increase in value of Georgian silver, the economic stability of the pound sterling was severely threatened by devaluation. Instead of reducing the value of silver, investors seeking a hike against inflation began to invest again, which caused the trebling of prices seen between 1965 and 1969. By 1970 prices had risen to unrealistic highs, and between further devaluation and uncertain economic conditions, Georgian silver prices took an unprecedented almost forty percent decline in price. The loss was quickly checked, and toward the last part of 1971 prices had begun to stabilize and should continue to rise during the next few years at a more realistic rate.

It is interesting to note that pieces of Georgian silver of museum quality were hardly affected by the economically stimulated price declines. The majority of pieces severely hurt were either at the top of the price range or at the opposite low end. Today as a general rule, the older the piece, the higher the price: a George I teapot would be worth considerably more than one from the George III era. Therefore, the majority of investors today are concentrating on collecting silver produced during the reign of George III, since such pieces are much more plentiful.

Since 1973 prices of Georgian silver have increased approximately twenty-five percent per year, and a continued increase in prices should parallel the price of silver bullion.

The majority of this investment chapter centers on the silver produced during the reign of George I, II, and III, mainly because it is felt that today this is perhaps the best investment in English Silver. Other periods such as George IV (1820–30), as well as William IV (1830–37), and Victoriana (1837–1901) are rapidly becoming excellent investment potentials. Victorian silver, although more ornate than previous Georgian styles, due to the majority of wares produced and moderate prices are producing a very interesting investment potential.

Understanding Hallmarks

Hallmarks have been in continual use for over six centuries and have provided an effective form of consumer protection in both the fields of gold and silver. The Hallmarking Act was extended as of January 1, 1975, for the first time to include platinum articles. By enforcing stiff penalties for both forgery and misrepresentation, both manufacturer and retailer take responsibility for the quality of the gold, silver, and platinum wares that they place for sale.

Due to the softness of pure silver, it is not easily adapted for either jewelry or various domestic articles that are easier produced from alloys with other metals. By alloying pure silver with other metals the intrinsic value is greatly reduced, plus it is almost impossible to determine without a detailed chemical analysis what proportion of silver was used in the mixture. Many amateur collectors feel that they can determine metal content by color alone, but even brass when plated with gold can look like solid gold.

A hallmark on a specific ware attests to the buyer that it has been officially tested for quality by the government's assay office.

Each hallmark tells either the sponsor or manufacturer of the ware. Every mark contains the initials of the firm or person that made the piece. If a manufacturer or craftsman had a duplication of initials, either type, style, or the surrounding shield design was altered.

The standard mark indicates that the ware produced conforms to the rigid purity laws enforced by the government. The following chart indicates the present legal standards for gold, silver, and platinum.

Gold	22 karat	916.6 parts gold in 1,000 or (22 in 24)
	18 karat	750 parts gold in 1,000 or (18 in 24)
	14 karat	585 parts gold in 1,000 or (14 in 24)
	9 karats	375 parts gold in 1,000 or (9 in 24)
Silver	Sterling	925 parts silver in 1,000
	Britannia	958.4 parts silver in 1,000
Platinum		950 parts platinum in 1,000

The assay office placed its individual mark on each piece, which assures that it was tested for purity. Today there are four assay offices, one each in London, Birmingham, Sheffield, and Edinburgh. Also added to this mark and an important part of the hallmark was the date letter, which indicates the year when the article was hallmarked.

The first hallmarking was started as early as 1300, and has been in continual use since that time. It is impossible to represent all the marks that have been registered since that time, but with the help of the assay office, in London the marks included will help the majority of English silver collectors.

Due to the strict monitoring of both the sterling standard and hallmark registration, the buyer of English silver can be relatively sure of what he is getting. Unfortunately, some faking of hallmarks did occur. To be precise, it was not a faking but grafting of genuine hallmarks from smaller items of very little importance onto larger unmarked pieces. Hallmark transfers, although very skillfully done, can usually be detected by identifying the trace adder marks left behind. These marks can be seen more clearly by breathing hard on the hallmark. Although this practice was rare, it should be known by collectors of antique silver.

The following addresses are of the assay offices of Great Britain, which are more than helpful with questions concerning their marking systems.

The Assay Office
Goldsmith Hall
Gutler Lane
London, EC 2V 8AQ

The Assay Office
Newhall St.
Birmingham, B3 15B

The Assay Office
137 Partobello St.
Sheffield, S1 4DR

The Assay Office
15 Queen St.
Edinburgh, EH 2 IJE

Further research can be done in several excellent books on silver and goldsmiths:

Pitcher, Howard. *Old Silver and Old Sheffield Plate*. New York: 1928 Doubleday.

Bradbury, *Bradbury's Book of Hallmarks*. Sheffield: 1930 J. W. Northend, Ltd.

Jackson, Sir Charles J. *English Goldsmiths and Their Marks*. London, 1905 Reprinted by Dauir Publications, Inc.

Assay Office Mark

British Articles

Prior to 1975	Assay Office	From 1975
gold & Sterling silver / Britannia silver	London	gold silver & platinum
gold / silver	Birmingham	gold & platinum / silver
gold / silver	Sheffield	gold & silver
gold & silver	Edinburgh	gold & silver

Notes – (i) Some variations in the surrounding shields are found before 1975. (ii) All Assay Offices mark Britannia silver, but only London (prior to 1975) had a special Assay Office mark for this standard.

Imported Articles

Prior to 1975	Assay Office	From 1975
gold / silver	London	gold & silver unchanged / platinum
	Birmingham	unchanged
	Sheffield	unchanged / —
	Edinburgh	unchanged / —

London

Year		Year		Year		Year		Year	
1678	a	1712	e	1744	i	1780	e	1815	U
1679	b	1713	f	1745	k	1781	f	1816	a
1680	c	1714	g	1746	l	1782	g	1817	b
1681	d	1715	h	1747	m	1783	h	1818	C
1682	e	1716	A	1748	n	1784	i	1819	d
1683	f	1717	B	1749	O	1785	k	1820	e
1684	g	1718	C	1750	P	1786	l	1821	f
1685	h	1719	D	1751	q	1787	m	1822	g
1686	i	1720	E	1752	r	1788	n	1823	h
1687	k	1721	F	1753	T	1789	O	1824	i
1688	l	1722	G	1754	t	1790	P	1825	k
1689	m	1723	H	1755	U	1791	q	1826	l
1690	n	1724	I	1756	A	1792	r	1827	m
1691	o	1725	K	1757	B	1793	S	1828	n
1692	p	1726	L	1758	C	1794	t	1829	o
1693	q	1727	M	1759	D	1795	u	1830	p
1694	r	1728	N	1760	E	1796	A	1831	q
1695	s	1729	O	1761	F	1797	B	1832	r
1696	t	1730	P	1762	G	1798	C	1833	s
1697	a	1731	Q	1763	H	1799	D	1834	t
1698		1732	R	1764	I	1800	E	1835	u
1699		1733	S	1765	K	1801	F	1836	
1700		1734	T	1766	L	1802	G	1837	
1701	ff	1735	V	1767	m	1803	H	1838	C
1702		1736	a	1768	n	1804	I	1839	
1703		1737	b	1769	O	1805	K	1840	e
1704		1738	c	1770	P	1806	L	1841	f
1705		1739	d	1771	Q	1807	M	1842	
1706		1739	d	1772	R	1808	N	1843	
1707		1740	e	1773	S	1809	O	1844	
1708		1741	f	1774	T	1810	P	1845	
1709		1742	g	1775	a	1811	Q	1846	
1710		1743	h	1776	a	1812	R	1847	
1711				1777	b	1813	S	1848	
				1778	C	1814	T	1849	
				1779	d				

110

Standard Mark

British Articles

Prior to 1975	Standard	From 1975
	22 carat gold Marked in England Marked in Scotland	
	18 carat gold Marked in England Marked in Scotland	
	14 carat gold	
	9 carat gold	
	Sterling silver Marked in England Marked in Scotland	
	Britannia silver	
—	Platinum	

Imported Articles

	22 carat gold	916
	18 carat gold	750
	14 carat gold	585
	9 carat gold	375
	Sterling silver	925
	Britannia silver	958
—	Platinum	950

The Standard Mark. The present legal standards of gold, silver and platinum are as follows:—

Gold	22 carat	916.6 parts gold in 1000 (or 22 in 24)
	18 carat	750 parts gold in 1000 (or 18 in 24)
	14 carat	585 parts gold in 1000 (or 14 in 24)
	9 carat	375 parts gold in 1000 (or 9 in 24)
Silver	Sterling	925 parts silver in 1000
	Britannia	958.4 parts silver in 1000
Platinum		950 parts platinum in 1000

The standard mark shows that the precious metal content of the alloy from which the article is made is not less than the standard indicated.

The Assay Office Mark identifies the particular office at which the article was tested and marked. There are now four Assay Offices – in London, Birmingham, Sheffield and Edinburgh. There were other Assay Offices in former times.

The Date Letter shows the year in which the article was hallmarked.

How can I recognise hallmarks? Hallmarking was first instituted as long ago as 1300. The designs of individual marks have changed from time to time and new marks have been added. It is impossible in a small booklet to show all the hallmarks which you may come across, but the illustrations on the following pages should help you to identify most of them.
After 1st January 1975 all four Assay Offices use the same date letter. To date earlier pieces you will first have to identify the Assay Office mark before turning to the appropriate list. Date letters for the existing Assay Offices are given in this booklet. The marks shown are those used on silver. The same letters are used on gold but before 1975 the surrounding shields on gold may sometimes differ. Earlier cycles of letters and those for Assay Offices which have closed can be found in the more comprehensive publications listed inside the back cover. Here is an example of a complete hallmark.

It shows the sponsor's mark, followed by the mark for sterling silver, the London Assay Office mark and the date letter for 1975.

London

Year	Mark	Year	Mark	Year	Mark	Year	Mark
1850	P	1888	N			1958	C
1851	Q	1889	O			1959	d
1852	R	1890	P	1923	h	1960	e
1853	S			1924	i	1961	f
1854	T	1891	Q	1925	k	1962	g
1855	U	1892	R	1926	l	1963	h
1856	a	1893	S	1927	m	1964	i
1857	b	1894	T	1928	n	1965	k
1858	c	1895	U	1929	o	1966	l
1859	d			1930	p	1967	m
1860	e	1896	a	1931	q	1968	n
1861	f	1897	b	1932	r	1969	o
1862	g	1898	c	1933	s	1970	p
1863	h	1899	d	1934	t	1971	q
1864	i	1900	e	1935	u	1972	r
1865	k	1901	f			1973	s
1866	l	1902	g	1936	A	1974	t
1867	m	1903	h	1937	B		
1868	n	1904	i	1938	C		
1869	o	1905	k	1939	D		
1870	p	1906	l	1940	E	1975	A
1871	q	1907	m	1941	F	1976	B
1872	r	1908	n	1942	G	1977	C
1873	s	1909	O	1943	H		
1874	t	1910	P	1944	I		
1875	u	1911	Q	1945	K		
1876	A	1912	R	1946	L		
1877	B	1913	S	1947	M		
1878	C	1914	T	1948	N		
1879	D	1915	U	1949	O		
1880	E			1950	P		
1881	F	1916	a	1951	Q		
1882	G	1917	b	1952	R		
1883	H	1918	c	1953	S		
1884	I	1919	d	1954	T		
1885	K	1920	e	1955	U		
1886	L	1921	f	1956	a		
1887	M	1922	g	1957	b		

Birmingham

Year	Mark	Year	Mark	Year	Mark	Year	Mark	Year	Mark
		1806	i	1841		1877	t	1912	n
		1807	j	1842		1878	d	1913	o
1773	A	1808	k	1843	U	1879	e	1914	o
1774	B	1809	l	1844	V	1880	f	1915	p
1775	C	1810	m	1845	W	1881	g	1916	q
1776	D	1811	n	1846	X	1882	h	1917	r
1777	E	1812	o	1847	Y	1883	i	1918	s
1778	F	1813	p	1848	Z	1884	k	1919	t
1779	G					1885	l	1920	u
1780	H	1814	q	1849	A	1886	m	1921	v
1781	I	1815	r	1850	B	1887	n	1922	w
1782	K	1816	s	1851	C	1888	o	1923	x
1783	L	1817	t	1852	D	1889	p	1924	y
		1818	u	1853	E	1890	q	1925	z
1784	M	1819	v	1854	F			1926	A
1785	N	1820	W	1855	G	1891	r	1927	B
		1821	X	1856	H	1892	s	1928	C
1786	O	1822	Y	1857	I	1893	t	1929	D
1787	P	1823	Z	1858	J	1894	u	1930	E
1788	Q	1824		1859	K	1895	v	1931	F
1789	R	1825	a	1860	L	1896	w	1932	G
1790	S	1826	b	1861	M	1897	x	1933	H
1791	T	1827	c	1862	N	1898	y	1934	J
1792	U	1828	d	1863	O	1899	z	1935	K
1793	V	1829	e	1864	P			1936	L
1794	W	1830	f	1865	Q	1900	a	1937	M
1795	X	1831	g	1866	R	1901	b	1938	N
1796	Y	1832	h	1867	S	1902	c	1939	O
1797	Z	1833	i	1868	T	1903	d	1940	P
				1869	U	1904	e	1941	Q
1798	a	1834	j	1870	V	1905	f	1942	R
1799	b	1835	k	1871	W	1906	g	1943	S
1800	c	1836	l	1872	X	1907	h	1944	T
1801	d	1837	m	1873	Y	1908	i	1945	U
1802	e			1874	Z	1909	k	1946	V
1803	f	1838	n			1910	l	1947	W
1804	h	1839	o	1875	a	1911	m	1948	X
1805	g	1840	p	1876	b				Y

Sheffield

Year	Mark	Year	Mark	Year	Mark	Year	Mark	Year	Mark
1773	E	1806	A	1840	U	1873	F	1907	p
1774	F	1807	P	1841	V	1874	G	1908	q
1775	D	1808	K	1842	X	1875	H	1909	r
1776	R	1809	L	1843	Z	1876	J	1910	s
1777	h	1810	C	1844	A	1877	K	1911	t
1778	S	1811	D	1845	B	1878	L	1912	u
1779	A	1812	R	1846	C	1879	M	1913	v
1780	T	1813	W	1847	D	1880	N	1914	w x
1781	X	1814	O	1848	E	1881	O	1915	
1782	G	1815	T	1849	F	1882	P	1916	y
1783	B	1816	X	1850	G	1883	Q	1917	z
1784	I	1817	I	1851	H	1884	R	1918	a
1785	V	1818	V	1852	I	1885	S	1919	b
1786	k	1819	Q	1853	K	1886	T	1920	c
1787	l	1820	Y	1854	L	1887	U	1921	d
1788	m	1821	Z	1855	M	1888	V	1922	e
1789	n	1822	U	1856	N	1889	W	1923	f
1790	L	1823	a	1857	O	1890	X	1924	g
1791	P	1824	b	1858	P	1891	Y	1925	h
1792	u	1825	c	1859	R	1892	Z	1926	i
1793	o	1826	d	1860	S	1893	a	1927	k
1794	m	1827	e	1861	T	1894	b	1928	l
1795	q	1828	f	1862	U	1895	c	1929	m
1796	Z	1829	g	1863	V	1896	d	1930	n
1797	X	1830	h	1864	W	1897	e	1931	o
1798	V	1831	k	1865	X	1898	f	1932	p
1799	E	1832	l	1866	Y	1899	g	1933	q
1800	N	1833		1867	Z	1900	h	1934	r
1801	H	1834	m	1868	A	1901	i	1935	s
1802	M	1835	p	1869	B	1902	k	1936	t
1803	F	1836	q	1870	C	1903	l	1937	u
1804	G	1837	r	1871	D	1904	m	1938	v
1805	B	1838	s	1872	E	1905	n	1939	w
		1839	t			1906	o	1940	x

Birmingham

Year	Mark
1949	Z
1950	A
1951	B
1952	C
1953	D
1954	E
1955	F
1956	G
1957	H
1958	J
1959	K
1960	L
1961	M
1962	N
1963	O
1964	P
1965	Q
1966	R
1967	S
1968	T
1969	U
1970	V
1971	W
1972	X
1973	Y
1974	Z
1975	A
1976	B
1977	C

113

Edinburgh

Year	Mark	Year	Mark	Year	Mark
1882	a	1918	N	1955	Z
1883	b	1919	O	1956	A
1884	c	1920	P	1957	B
1885	d	1921	Q	1958	C
1886	e	1922	R	1959	D
1887	f	1923	S	1960	E
1888	g	1924	T	1961	F
1889	h	1925	U	1962	G
1890	i	1926	V	1963	H
	(castle, thistle)	1927	W	1964	J
1891	k	1928	X	1965	K
1892	l	1929	Y	1966	L
1893	m	1930	Z	1967	M
1894	n	1931	A	1968	N
1895	o	1932	B	1969	O
1896	p	1933	C	1970	P
1897	q	1934	D	1971	Q
1898	r	1935	E	1972	R
1899	s	1936	F	1973-4	S
1900	t	1937	G	(castle, lion)	
1901	v	1938	H	1975	A
1902	w	1939	J	1976	B
1903	x	1940	K	1977	C
1904	y	1941	L		
1905	3	1942	M		
1906	A	1943	N		
1907	B	1944	O		
1908	C	1945	P		
1909	D	1946	Q		
1910	E	1947	R		
1911	F	1948	S		
1912	G	1949	T		
1913	H	1950	U		
1914	I	1951	V		
1915	K	1952	W		
1916	L	1953	X		
1917	M	1954	Y		

Other Marks

Here are some of the other marks which you may find on gold or silver articles.

Former Assay Office Marks Several of the larger provincial cities had Assay Offices which are now closed. Each had its distinctive mark, some of the more important of which are shown below. There is also an Assay Office in Dublin and marks struck there before 1st April 1923 are recognised as approved British hallmarks. The Dublin mark is a figure of Hibernia.

Chester   Dublin   Glasgow

Newcastle   Exeter

Duty Marks Between 1784 and 1890 an excise duty on gold and silver articles was collected by the Assay Offices and a mark depicting the Sovereign's head was struck to show that it had been paid. These are two examples.

George III   Victoria

Commemorative Marks There have been two other marks to commemorate special events, the Silver Jubilee of King George V and Queen Mary in 1935 and the Coronation of Queen Elizabeth II in 1953.

Silver Jubilee Mark   Coronation Mark

Marking in Other Countries Some countries besides Britain have hallmarking systems, but in many foreign countries the only marks used on precious metal articles are those struck by the manufacturer. These do not, of course, indicate the independent certification and consequent protection afforded by British hallmarks.

Sheffield

Year	Mark
1941	y
1942	Z
1943	A
1944	B
1945	C
1946	D
1947	E
1948	F
1949	G
1950	H
1951	I
1952	K
1953	L
1954	M
1955	N
1956	O
1957	P
1958	Q
1959	R
1960	S
1961	T
1962	U
1963	V
1964	W
1965	X
1966	Y
1967	Z
1968	A
1969	B
1970	C
1971	D
1972	E
1973	F
1974	G
1975	A
1976	B
1977	C

Between 1780 and 1853 the crown and date letter are sometimes enclosed in the same shield on small articles.

Edinburgh

Year	Mark	Year	Mark	Year	Mark	Year	Mark	Year	Mark
1705	A	1741	M	1777		1812	g	1847	
1706	B	1742	N	1778	z	1813	h	1848	R
1707	C	1743	O	1779		1814	i	1849	S
1708	D	1744	P	1780	A	1815	j	1850	T
1709	E	1745	Q	1781	B	1816	k	1851	
1710	F	1746	R	1782	C	1817	l	1852	
1711	G	1747	S	1783	D	1818	m	1853	
1712	H	1748		1784	E	1819	n	1854	
1713	I	1749	U	1785	F	1820	O	1855	
1714	K	1750	U	1786	G	1821	P	1856	Z
1715	L	1751	W	1787	G	1822	q	1857	A
1716	M	1752	x	1788	H	1823	r	1858	B
1717	N	1753	y	1789	IJ	1824	s	1859	C
1718	O	1754	z	1790	K	1825	t	1860	D
1719	P	1755	a	1791	L	1826	u	1861	E
1720	Q	1756	b	1792	M	1827	v	1862	F
1721	R	1757	c	1793	N	1828	w	1863	G
1722	S	1758	d	1794	O	1829	x	1864	H
1723	T	1759	e	1795	P	1830	y	1865	I
1724	U	1760	f	1796	Q	1831	z	1866	K
1725	V	1761	g	1797	R	1832	A	1867	L
1726	W	1762	h	1798	S	1833	B	1868	M
1727	X	1763	i	1799	T	1834	C	1869	N
1728	Y	1764	k	1800	U	1835	D	1870	O
1729	Z	1765	L	1801	V	1836	E	1871	P
1730	A	1766	M	1802	W	1837	F	1872	Q
1731	B	1767	N	1803	X	1838	G	1873	R
1732	C	1768	O	1804	Y	1839	H	1874	S
1733	D	1769	P	1805	Z	1840	J	1875	T
1734	E	1770	Q	1806	a	1841	K	1876	U
1735	F	1771	R	1807	b	1842	L	1877	V
1736	G	1772	S	1808	c	1843	M	1878	W
1737	H	1773	T	1809	d	1844	N	1879	X
1738	I	1774	U	1810	e	1845	O	1880	Y
1739	K	1775	V	1811	f	1846	P	1881	Z
1740	L	1776	X						

115

Silver gilt Wheatsheaf condiment set by Charles Edwards, c. 1877/78, 8.25 oz. 450 pounds. Courtesy Bloom & Sons Ltd., London.

5 Pewter

Pewter has been used for the production of household utensils as well as for various-sized plates and bowls since the Middle Ages. Perhaps the long-range popularity pewter has enjoyed as a substitute for silver and gold is primarily due to the much reduced expense required with pewter. Although pewter has always been popular, it has especially enjoyed a revival during the past decade. Experts credit this increased interest to the popular simple lines, subtle texture, and warm color of pewter pieces that accent today's more informal living style.

Pewter production can easily be traced back to the Bronze Age when it enjoyed worldwide appeal. The English derived the name for the new alloy, pewter, from the Italian word *petro*. Other countries named the new and nonstandardized alloy pewter, mainly after its main ingredient, tin. Holland and Germany call it *zinn*, France *étain*, but whatever it is called, pewter retains its popularity.

Throughout the centuries fashions in pewter have fluctuated greatly. Sometimes highly polished pewter, very similar to the patina of silver, was the height of fashion, and at other times the darker surface became popular. Very often this texture change can be directly attributed to the varying amounts of tin and lead used by the manufacturer. It should be understood that there is no standard rule to make identification easier. The earliest pieces, dating to the Roman Empire, combined both tin and lead, while later mixtures contained copper as well as bismuth and antimony. It was not until the beginning of the fifteenth century that regulatory action was taken to standardize production of pewter. For example, at this time England required pewter to be produced with tin as well as brass as the main ingredients. It is characteristic of pewter produced in England to be lead-free, while pewter of the same period made on the Continent reveals large lead deposits. This type of alloy combines to produce a very soft metal; therefore, very few utilitarian pewter pieces from earlier centuries have survived until today. Much of the worn-out plates and mugs were melted down and reshaped, but fortunately many early sixteenth- and seventeenth-century decorative pewter pieces have survived, which gives historians an excellent example of working techniques as well as styles of the various periods.

The pewter period that had enjoyed increased success from the Middle Ages began a decided decline toward the end of the eighteenth century and the beginning of the nineteenth. During this period, pewter was replaced with inexpensive ceramics. Pewter never regained its full previous everyday usage, but during the late 1860s once again it was revived as a decorative medium. During this period, many of the classical designs were reproduced that often are mistaken by collectors for original earlier pewter pieces.

MARKINGS

Each pewterer that established a firm was required to register his individual "touch" marking at either the Guild or Pewterer's Hall. Many of the very early touch marks of English pewterers were destroyed in the Great Fire of London, which ravaged the city in 1666. Fortunately, the remaining pewterers' touches were struck once again in 1668 after the fire, so not everything was destroyed by the blaze.

The individual "touch" was displayed by the producer as well as being stamped on the ware. In addition to the "touch" mark, several other noted marks were added to pewterware that could easily be compared to the various silver hallmarks. One of the most common of these marks is the rose and crown. This mark was applied to all wares that were of the finest quality. The crowned X mark was utilized mostly on Continental pewter to denote especially hard pewter representative of the alloy when ten parts tin to one part lead were utilized.

Touch marks are invaluable to the collector of antique pewter, since they can usually identify and authenticate most pieces. It should be noted that dates appearing within touch marks, represent the year the touch was registered and not the year the individual piece was produced. Unfortunately, determining the exact date of production of a specific piece of pewter is not simplified as with silver, which utilized the date-letter system. A very close estimate of the production date can be determined by finding both the first date the individual touch was registered and either the last year the pewterer worked or his death.

Shapes also play a very important part in establishing the age of pewter pieces. Pewter shapes classically followed earlier porcelain and silver designs. Over the years, the shapes gradually changed in relation to size but retained the majority of their prior characteristics. Perhaps the porringer can claim to be the only form produced in pewter that was not directly derived from silver shapes. Although the basic form of the porringer remained the same, handle shapes varied greatly not only in period styling, but in area of production as well. An interesting study can be made that affords beginning pewter collectors to familiarize themselves with both craftsmen and period pieces.

The production of porringers dates to the beginning of the seventeenth and early eighteenth centuries. Production in England was discontinued as early as 1750. Very few of the earliest examples are available to the collectors of today. The majority of porringers on the market were made after 1800. New England produced the majority of porringers until about 1825.

UNDERSTANDING BRITANNIA

There has been tremendous controversy over the definition of Britannia in relation to pewter. The experts agree that there is really no difference at all. Both pewter as well as Britannia were used to produce a reasonable substitute to silver for the everyday market. Toward the end of the eighteenth century, as pewter lost most of its market appeal, several very intelligent and market-oriented manufacturers saw the need for a replacement for everyday dishes and utensils. The new Englishware was named "Britannia."

The new formula took many years to perfect, even though the various amounts of copper, antimony, and tin as in pewter varied with each manufacturer. At first, Britannia was exported from England, but by 1808 the Meriden Britannia Company of the United States started production on a large scale. By the end of the nineteenth century, there were more than 120 independent factories producing Britannia within the United States. In fact, in 1898 seventeen of the original factories combined forces to incorporate their talents into the still-existing International Silver Company.

It was not until the middle of the nineteenth century that further developments in Britannia production, specifically the silver-plating of the metal, took place. At this time, nickel silver was substituted for Britannia metal, which, by 1879, caused the majority of independent factories to close their doors.

CARE OF ANTIQUE PEWTER

Older pieces of pewter that have been exposed to the elements over many years will have darkened in color mainly due to the oxidation of the various metal alloys. In most cases this condition is minor and affects only the surface of the piece, and with careful cleaning using a good quality metal polish the original texture of the metal can be regained. Unfortunately, very early pewter pieces, usually rare examples of utilitarian pieces that have not been used for generations, develop a severe and very damaging condition known as scale. This very hard, dark surface is almost impossible to remove without chemical assistance, which will almost certainly destroy the original surface of the soft pewter underneath. Experts recommend on such stubborn cases that as much of the scale as possible should be carefully removed with a mild metal polish followed by soap and water. In order to protect the piece from further deterioration the surface should be covered with a clear coat of paste furniture wax.

FORGERIES

It should be emphasized that pewter faking or forging has been in operation since the beginning of the 1900s and, therefore, many examples within several years will themselves qualify for the distinction of becoming antique. The main point here is that beginning collectors should *beware*.

Pewter has been blatantly forged to copy very old and rare pieces complete with the pewterer's touch marks. Many of these pieces are painstakingly aged to represent an oxidized finish. In other cases, original molds were used to reproduce parts that were especially noted by famous craftsmen.

Famous American Pewter Producers

Maker	State	City	Dates
Stephen Barnes	Connecticut	Wallingford	1791–1800
Luther Boardman	Connecticut	Chester & East Haddam	1839–70
Thomas Danforth Boardman	Connecticut	Hartford	1804–60
Thomas D. Boardman	Connecticut	Hartford	1810–50
Sherman Boardman			
I. Curtis	Connecticut	?	1818–25
Edward Danforth	Connecticut	Middletown	1765–1830
John Danforth	Connecticut	Norwich	1773–93
Joseph Danforth, Sr.	Connecticut	Middletown	1780–88
Josiah Danforth	Connecticut	Middletown	1803–72
Samuel Danforth	Connecticut	Hartford	1774–1816
Thomas Danforth I	Connecticut	Norwich	1733–75
Thomas Danforth II	Connecticut	Middletown	1731–82
Thomas Danforth III	Connecticut	Stepney	1777–1818
William Danforth	Connecticut	Middletown	1792–1820
Thomas S. Derby	Connecticut	Middletown	1786–1852
Fuller & Smith	Connecticut	New London County	1849–51
Ashbil Griswold	Connecticut	Meriden	1784–1853
Jehiel Johnson	Connecticut	Middletown	1784–1833
Isaac C. Lewis	Connecticut	Meriden	1834–52
William W. Lyman	Connecticut	Meriden	1844–52
Thomas Mix	Connecticut	Meriden	1826
H. B. Ward & Co.	Connecticut	Wallingford	1850
Jacob Whitmore	Connecticut	Middletown	1758–90
H. Yale & Co.	Connecticut	Wallingford	1822–31
William Yale	Connecticut	Meriden	1813–20
Samuel Yale			
Rufus Dunham	Maine	Westbrook	1837–60
Allen Porter	Maine	Westbrook	1830–40
Freeman/Porter	Maine	Westbrook	1835–65
Samuel Kilbourn	Maryland	Baltimore	1814–39
George Lightner	Maryland	Baltimore	1806–15
Nathaniel Austin	Massachusetts	Charlestown	1763–1807
Richard Austin	Massachusetts	Boston	1764–1817
Thomas Badger	Massachusetts	Boston	1787–1815
Roswell Gleason	Massachusetts	Dorchester	1821–71
Samuel Green	Massachusetts	Boston	1794–1834
David B. Morey	Massachusetts	Boston	1852–55
R. H. Ober			
Samuel Pierce	Massachusetts	Greenfield	1792–1830
James H. Putnam	Massachusetts	Malden	1830–55
George Richardson	Massachusetts	Boston	1818–28
Semper Eadem	Massachusetts	Boston	1725–72

John Skinner	Massachusetts	Boston	1760–90
Eben Smith	Massachusetts	Beverly	1814–56
L. B. Smith	Massachusetts	Boston	1847–49
Taunton Britannia Manufacturing Co.	Massachusetts	Taunton	1830–34
Israel Trask	Massachusetts	Beverly	1813–56
Oliver Trask	Massachusetts	Beverly	1832–39
J. B. Woodbury	Massachusetts	Beverly	1835–38
Francis Bassett I	New York	New York City	1718–58
Frederick Bassett	New York	New York City	1761–80
			1785–99
Boardman & Co.	New York	New York City	1825–27
Timothy Boardman & Company	New York	New York City	1822–25
Boardman & Hart	New York	New York City	1828–53
Timothy Brigden	New York	Albany	1816–19
Ephraum Capen George Malineux	New York	New York City	1848–54
Daniel Curtiss	New York	Albany	1822–40
William Ellsworth	New York	New York City	1767–98
Edmund Endicott William F. Sumner	New York	New York City	1746–1851
Gaius Fenn Jason Fenn	New York	New York City	1831–43
Henry Hopper	New York	New York City	1842–47
Charles Ostrander George Norris	New York	New York City	1848–50
Renton & Company	New York	New York City	1830s
Spencer Stafford	New York	Albany	1820–27
James Weekes	New York	New York City	1820–35
Thomas Wildes	New York	New York City	1833–40
Henry Will	New York	New York City	1761–75
Henry Yale Stephen Curtis	New York	New York City	1858–67
Peter Young	New York	New York City	1775–85
		Albany	1785–95
Blakeslee Barns	Pennsylvania	Philadelphia	1812–17
Parks Boyd	Pennsylvania	Philadelphia	1795–1819
Simon Edgell	Pennsylvania	Philadelphia	1713–42
Benjamin Harbeson Joseph Harbeson	Pennsylvania	Philadelphia	1793–1803
Louis Krueger	Pennsylvania	Philadelphia	1830s
William McQuilkin	Pennsylvania	Philadelphia	1839–53
John H. Palethorp Robert Palethorp, Jr.	Pennsylvania	Philadelphia	1817–45
William Will	Pennsylvania	Philadelphia	1764–98
Lorenzo L. Williams	Pennsylvania	Philadelphia	1838–42
Joseph Belcher Joseph Belcher, Jr.	Rhode Island	Newport	1764–84
William Billings	Rhode Island	Providence	1791–1806
William Calder	Rhode Island	Providence	1817–56
Samuel Hamlin	Rhode Island	Providence	1773–1801
Samuel E. Hamlin	Rhode Island	Providence	1801–56
Gershom Jones	Rhode Island	Providence	1774–1809
David Melville	Rhode Island	Newport	1776–93
Samuel Melville	Rhode Island	Newport	1793–96
Thomas Melville	Rhode Island	Newport	1793–96
Josiah Miller	Rhode Island or Connecticut		1725–75
Richard Lee, Sr.	Vermont	Springfield	1802–20
Richard Lee, Jr.	Vermont	Springfield	1795–1816
Joseph Danforth, Jr.	Virginia	Richmond	1807–12

Zurich, 1765.

SELECTED FAMOUS AMERICAN PEWTER TOUCH MARKS

Stephen Barnes.

Luther Boardman.

T.D. BOARDMAN

HARTFORD

Thomas Danforth Boardman.

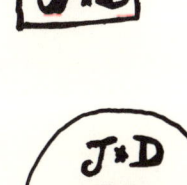

Joseph Danforth, Jr.

Samuel Danforth.

Thomas Danforth III.

William Danforth.

Ashbil Griswold.

Jehiel Johnson.

121

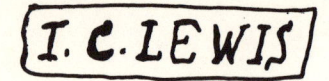

Isaac C. Lewis.

Jacob Whitmore.

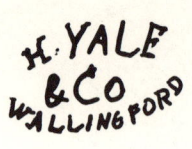

H. Yale & Co.

Samuel Kilbourn.

George Lightner.

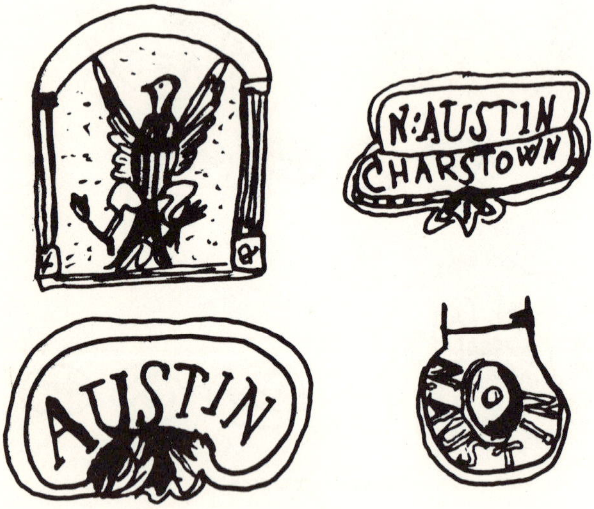

Nathaniel Austin.

Thomas Badger.

Richard Austin.

122

Roswell Gleason.

Samuel Green.

Samuel Pierce.

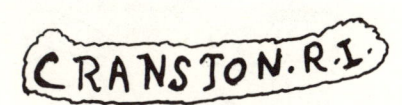

George Richardson.

John Skinner.

Oliver Trask.

Israel Trask.

Francis Bassett. Francis Bassett I.

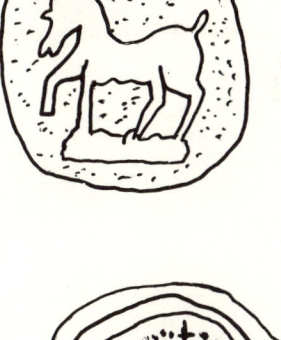

123

Francis Bassett II.

Timothy Brigden.

William Ellsworth.  **James Weekes.**

William Ellsworth.

Daniel Curtiss.

Thomas Wildes.

H. Yale & Co.

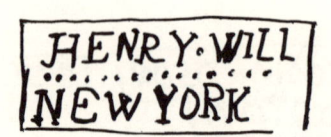

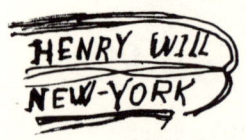

Henry Will.

Peter Young.

Blakslee Barns.

Parks Boyd.

124

Simon Edgell.

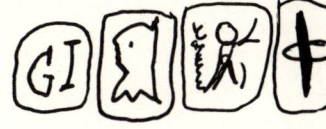

Gershom Jones.

David Melville.

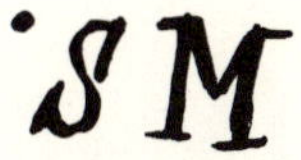

Samuel Melville.

Benjamin & Joseph Harbeson.

Thomas Melville.

John H. Palethorp.

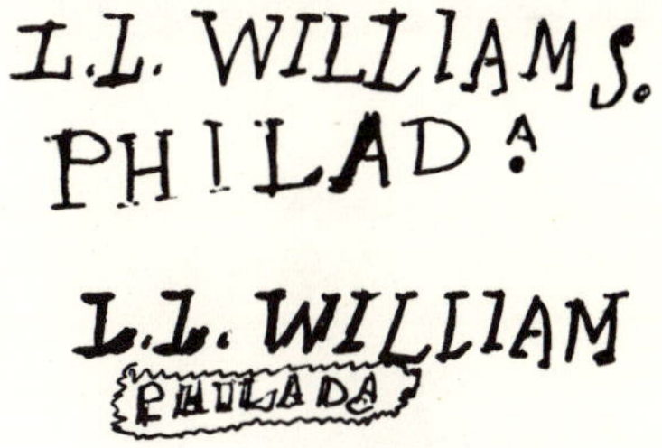

Lorenzo L. Williams.

Joseph Belcher.

William Calder.

125

Freeman Porter B. 1808 Westbrook, Maine. Active 1835–65. Mark on outside bottom, height 10¾ inches. Courtesy Boston Museum of Fine Arts.

Roswell Gleason, 1799–1887, Dorchester, Massachusetts. Pair of candlesticks with inserts. Mark on outside bottom, height 4¾ inches. Courtesy Boston Museum of Fine Arts.

Thomas D. Boardman, 1784–1873, and Sherman Boardman, 1787–1861, Hartford, Connecticut, 1810–50. Porringer, mark on handle top. H. 2 inches, d. of rim 5⅛ inch. Courtesy Boston Museum of Fine Arts.

Samuel Kilbourn, c. 1770–1839, active Baltimore, Maryland from 1814–39. Plate, height ⅞ inches, diameter of rim 9⅛ inches, width of rim 1⅛ inches. Courtesy Boston Museum of Fine Arts.

Oliver Trask (1792–1847), Beverly, Massachusetts, active 1832–39. Flagon with spout. Mark outside bottom. H. 11 inches, d. of rim 5⅛ inches, d. of base 5½ inches. Courtesy Boston Museum of Fine Arts.

Frederick Bassett, 1740–1800, New York City. Active 1761–80, Hartford, Connecticut, 1780–85; New York City, 1785–99. Quart tankard, mark on inside bottom. H. 5⅜ inches, d. of rim ⅜ inch, d. of base 5 inches. Courtesy Boston Museum of Fine Arts.

Samuel Danforth, 1774–1816, Hartford, Connecticut. Active 1795–1816. Flagon marks on outside bottom. H. 11½ inches, d. of rim 4 inches, d. of base 6½ inches. Courtesy Boston Museum of Fine Arts.

Pewter jug, c. 1600 with iron handle. The town arms of Baden, Switzerland (Canton Aargau), are soldered on both sides. Inside the lid is a medallion with the arms and name of Caspar Falk, a magistrate of Baden who died in 1611. Courtesy Swiss Landesmuseum.

6 Brass and Copper

Brass has been used by craftsmen since before the birth of Christ, but the Romans with their artistic gifts perhaps were the first people who worked with the substance we know as brass today. Due to their widespread geographic influence, many examples of this craft were left in various countries.

The first widespread use of brass was seen in England during the Middle Ages when the earlier stone tombs were replaced with brass ones to eulogize noted statesmen and noblemen. Unfortunately, many of the earliest thirteenth-century hard brasses were destroyed for purely monetary gain. In recent years, a renewed interest in discovering and making rubbings of these ancient brasses has become a very popular hobby. Many collectors try hard to find original brass rubbings that were done during the turn of the century. Prices on these earlier rubbings have more than doubled during the past few years with the renewed interest in brass rubbing.

England is not the only country in which original brasses for rubbing can be found. Germany has retained her fame for ornamental brasses since the Middle Ages, and excellent examples from the thirteenth century can be found. Unfortunately, the beautiful brasses of France were almost totally destroyed during the Reign of Terror.

THE IMPORTANCE OF BRASS

Brass through the centuries has played an ever-increasing part in everyday life. As early as the Middle Ages, the almost indispensable pin was made from brass. By the early eighteenth century England became a well-known center for brass production. Both Bristol and Birmingham by the first quarter of the eighteenth century had become the main exporters of both pins and needles to the New World.

The majority of brass products made during the seventeenth–nineteenth centuries were made in Birmingham, England, which was fast becoming the number one industrial city in the world. Unfortunately, very few brass pieces were ever marked, so that establishing the maker and exact date of production is almost impossible.

Brass was important and found its place in almost every room in the home. In the earliest periods when life in the home was centered around the focal point of existence, the fireplace, brass adapted to the challenge and useful utensils were produced. Beautiful brass fenders, shovels, tongs, and andirons were made, as well as intricate fire clogs and stoking sets. It was not just in the fireplace that brass was utilized, but irons, lamps, candlesticks, foot warmers, and kettles of every size made life in the home a little easier.

Brassware became a treasured possession and was very often passed from generation to generation in wills.

America began the local production of utilitarian brass pieces during its Colonial period, but more elaborate pieces were almost always imported from Europe. Holland, as well as England, also produced large quantities of brassware as early as the seventeenth century, and even today remains a leader in decorative brass accessories. In fact, a Dutchman is credited with the discovery of the thimble during the

Majolica vases, 1878, with applied decoration.

Majolica ware. Jug and plate from late 19th century.

Black basalt vase, 1775.

Portraits of Mistress Ford and Sir John Falstaff. Late 19th century.

Majolica ware. Dolphin, about 1870.

Enamel plaque by Thomas Allen, about 1890.

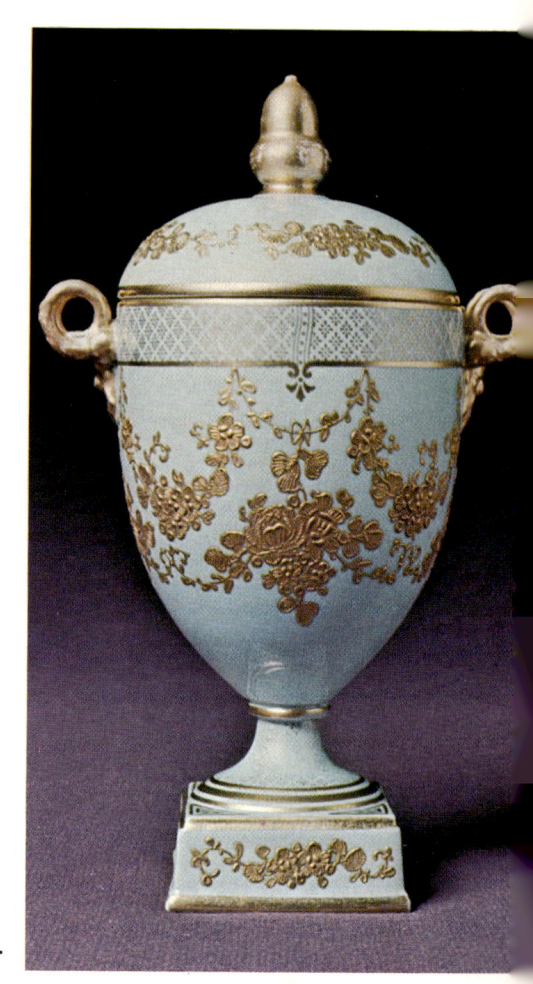

Second Period bone china vase, about 1880.

last part of the seventeenth century. At first, thimbles were almost exclusively made from brass, and not until many years later, as their credibility was gradually established with the upper class, did society demand thimbles to be made from more expensive materials such as silver, gold, mother-of-pearl, and glass. Not all thimbles were made in Europe, because Colonial America began to produce this small but indispensable article by such notable craftsmen as Paul Revere.

Chandeliers were a major source of decorative as well as utilitarian fixtures in early homes. As with early cutwork the Colonial housewife was admired by her choice of design, and chandeliers displayed the affluence of the home. The first English-produced chandeliers were introduced toward the end of the seventeenth century, but the majority of brass chandeliers from this time until about the end of the eighteenth century were made in Holland.

Lighting devices were very important in early homes, and the candlestick played an important role as the fixed lighting device. The earliest brass candlesticks, which were made about 1700, were usually produced from solid cast brass. The stems of these candlesticks were hollow with sliding knobs that could adjust the candle.

Brass beds, which have enjoyed such a successful comeback during the last ten years, were originally developed around the turn of the twentieth century. These beds remained popular for only fifteen to twenty years, and all evidence predicts that their revival will last for a longer period than the actual production.

Horse brasses have only recently become a much-sought-after collector's item and, when restored to their glowing brilliance and warmth, are now proudly displayed by collectors on walls and fireplaces. Very few people realize the long and very ancient history these brasses command, some tracing their lineage back almost two thousand years.

It was not until about the middle of the nineteenth century that horse brasses as we know them today returned to popularity when it became the custom to use more than one brass to decorate a horse's harness. By 1860, horse brasses became so popular that more than three hundred different patterns of horse brasses were readily available and marketed through pattern books of the period.

Victorian horse brass producers enriched their motifs by designing brasses that denoted specific occupations. For example, the windmill was a very popular design that millers ordered, especially popular in Lincolnshire, England.

The following chart shows how horse brasses can be divided into chronological collecting groups, which hopefully will help the collector to understand criteria for collectors.

Period of Production	Type of Brass	Identifying Characteristics	Historic Significance
1750–1800	Hand-worked	Made from very hard textured latten brass	Used mostly for Georgian sun flashes
Until 1860 First Period	Cast brass	Noticeable pits in surface; not as highly polished	Very rare
Second Period 1800–1850	Hand-worked from rolled brass	Soft texture with dull surface; very few pits in surface	Sun flashes were often made from this type of brass
1830–60	Cast brass alloy	More expensive, but achieves higher reliefs; attained reddish golden texture by heat-and-acid polish process	Most brasses of this period were cast into heraldic designs
1860–1900	Cast brass, file-finished	"ets" on the back of each piece; early examples removed, but later examples were crudely finished	Poorly finished; pieces denote souvenir pieces

1865–1900	Stamped brass	Backs filled with lead; almost half the weight of contemporary pieces; much cheaper to produce	Stamped brasses are very often confused with much earlier pieces
1920 onward	Reproduction of previous horse brass types	Designs either of contemporary motifs or copies of earlier designs	Many brasses are reproductions sold purely for souvenirs, but some are hand finished to deliberately fake earlier models

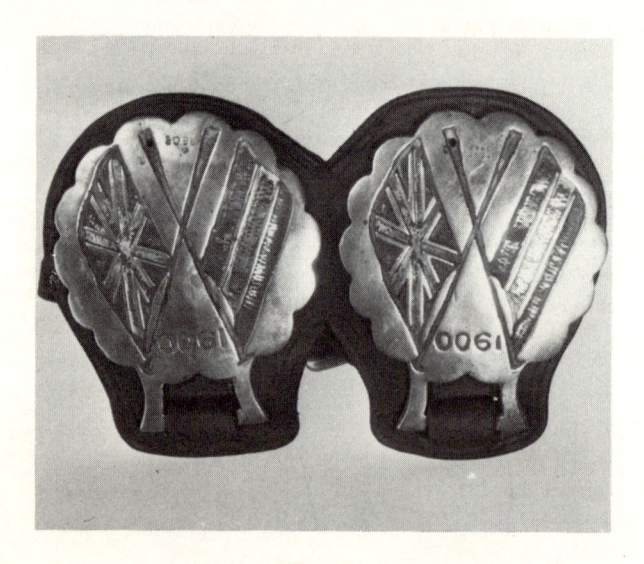

Examples of interesting horse brasses from the 18th and and 19th centuries. Courtesy Museum of English Rural Life, University of Reading.

7 Clocks

THE INTERNATIONAL MOVEMENT

American Clocks

The first settlers to the New World built their towns much like the ones left behind in Europe. The basic plan during the early seventeenth century centered around a square with perhaps the most important structure being the bell tower, which tolled the hours for the entire town. Fortunately for the development of the clock industry in America, many of the new settlers brought their prize clocks with them from all over Europe. Therefore, the new clockmakers had a very wide variety of designs from England, France, Holland, Germany, and Switzerland to pattern their clocks after. Perhaps the most prevalent clock at this time in the Colonies was either the eight-day grandfather clock or the popular lantern clock.

Early American clockmakers were the masters of ingenuity. New production methods were developed in order to adapt to the crude and often nonexistent tools and materials in the Colonies. Nevertheless, the trade improved, and although still very expensive, more clocks were being made during the eighteenth century. At this time, mostly in the Metropolitan areas such as Philadelphia and Boston, more sophisticated examples of grandfather clocks were produced. These examples combined the best of both clock and cabinetmakers' expertise. Unfortunately, the revolutionary war brought an abrupt end to the newly prosperous clock industry. The valuable metals and tools used by the skilled clockmakers were almost overnight turned into the tools of the gunsmith.

After the war the clockmakers returned to civilian status and began to rebuild their industry, but found that it was not possible to continue producing the more elegant clocks that had become popular before the war because of the enormous shortages of almost everything throughout the Colonies. But the spirit and determination that won them the War of Independence helped create new styles that could be made during this period of reconstruction. Consequently, clocks became smaller, and wood, which was readily available and inexpensive, was used whenever possible. In fact, a Connecticut clockmaker, Gideon Roberts, made a wag-on-wall clock entirely from wood that started a new trend of thought in clock production. With the new clocks prices were drastically reduced, and therefore more people were able to afford timepieces. This increased production, combined with simplified styling, allowed clockmakers to mass-produce these less expensive clocks, which began a new era in the American clock industry.

The beginning of the nineteenth century saw the development of the clock industry in the New England state of Connecticut. Both Eli Terry and Seth Thomas produced mass-market clocks for the expanding American market. At this time the war of 1812 helped instead of restricted the growing clock industry by limiting imports from England, where there still existed strong cultural ties despite political convictions.

Dwarf tallcase clock: B. Youngs, Watervliet, New York, c. 1812. Courtesy Greenfield Village and Henry Ford Museum.

Ogee shelf clock: Waterbury Clock Company, Waterbury, Connecticut, c. 1870. Courtesy Greenfield Village and Henry Ford Museum.

Octagon wall clock: possibly by Atkins, Whiting, and Company, Bristol, Connecticut, 1850–65. Courtesy Greenfield Village and Henry Ford Museum.

Dwarf tallcase clock: B. S. Youngs, Schenectady, New York, c. 1800. Courtesy Greenfield Village and Henry Ford Museum.

Shelf clock: American Clock Company, New York. New York, c. 1850. Clock made from cast iron. Courtesy Greenfield Village and Henry Ford Museum.

Double steeple shelf clock: Birge and Fuller, Bristol, Connecticut, 1844–48. Courtesy Greenfield Village and Henry Ford Museum.

Shelf lyre clock: Lemuel Curtis, Concord, Massachusetts, c. 1830. Courtesy Greenfield Village and Henry Ford Museum.

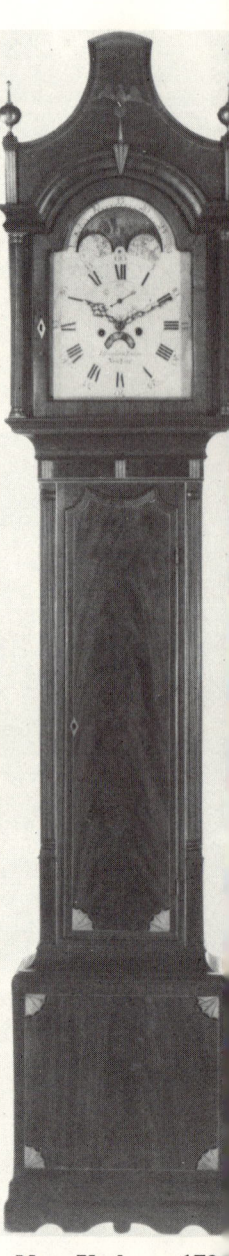

Tallcase clock: Effengham Embree, New York, c. 179
Courtesy Greenfield Village and Henry Ford Museum

Acorn shelf clock: Jonathan Clarli Brown, Forestville Manufacturing Company, Bristol, Connecticut, 1847–50. Courtesy Greenfield Village and Henry Ford Museum.

Dwarf tallcase clock: David Studley, Hanover, Massachusetts, c. 1830. Courtesy Greenfield Village and Henry Ford Museum.

Ithaca parlor calendar clock: Pendulum engraved ICC (Ithaca Calendar Clock Co.), Ithaca, New York. Patent of H. B. Horton, c. 1875. Courtesy Greenfield Village and Henry Ford Museum.

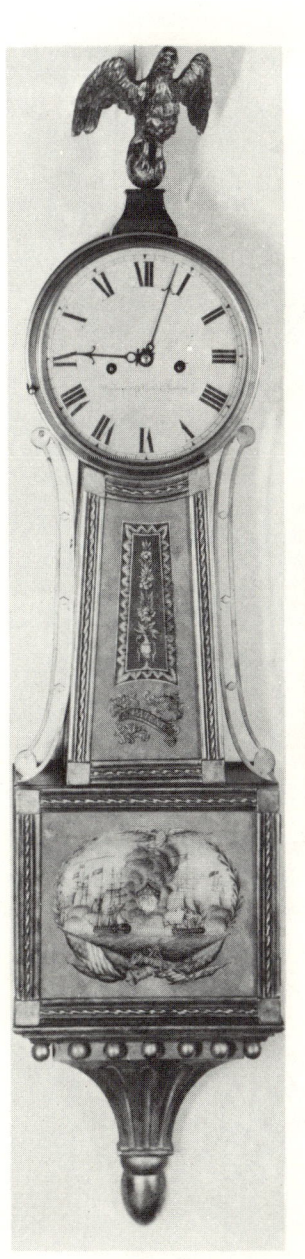

Banjo wall clock: Curtis and Dunning, Concord, Massachusetts, c. 1815. Courtesy Greenfield Village and Henry Ford Museum.

135

Shelf clock: Welch Spring and Company, Bristol, Connecticut, c. 1890. Courtesy Greenfield Village and Henry Ford Museum.

Shelf clock: William L. Gilbert Clock Co., Winstead, Connecticut, c. 1880. Courtesy Greenfield Village and Henry Ford Museum.

Shelf clock: New Haven Clock Co., New Haven, Connecticut, c. 1890. Courtesy Greenfield Village and Henry Ford Museum.

Ogee shelf clock: E. N. Welch Manufacturing Company, Forestville, Connecticut, c. 1860. Courtesy Greenfield Village and Henry Ford Museum.

Shelf clock: Ansonia Clock Company, Ansonia, New York, c. 1890. Courtesy Greenfield Village and Henry Ford Museum.

Mirror wall clock: Benjamin Morrell, Boscawen, New Hampshire, c. 1830. Courtesy Greenfield Village and Henry Ford Museum.

Shelf clock: Eli Terry Jr. and Company, Terrysville, Connecticut, c. 1835. Courtesy Greenfield Village and Henry Ford Museum.

Pillar and Scroll shelf clock: Eli Terry, Plymouth, Connecticut, c. 1820. Clock has outside escapement. Courtesy Greenfield Village and Henry Ford Museum.

THE EARLIEST CLOCKS

The first known mechanical clocks were produced about 1300, mainly by blacksmiths. Commonly called turret clocks, because of their elevated positions in towers, these clocks recorded time by a system of striking bells. The most famous turret clock and perhaps the oldest (c. 1386) and still in working condition is at the Salisbury Cathedral in England. This clock predates both the clock dial and pendulum, which was invented much later in 1656.

The chamber or domestic clock replaced the larger turret clocks for individual home use about 1470. These clocks were made along much the same lines as the turret clocks, but supplemented a dial for recording time instead of the larger bells used on previous clocks. Chamber clocks were usually made from iron with no structural case, and were weight driven. Chamber clocks were very popular in the Germanic areas of Europe, and were widely produced until some time during the mid-seventeenth century, when the pendulum was developed.

With the development of the pendulum clock, design progressed rapidly and became much more sophisticated. Many variations of the domestic clock were produced with some fairly good examples made in brass instead of the more base iron that was usually used. These advances in design were limited, since the domestic clock was naturally of the pre-pendulum period and was eventually replaced by new developments.

The middle of the seventeenth century in England, about 1660–75, saw the development of the grandfather or long-case clock. During this period both the technology of the movements plus the styling of cases were very much improved. The long-case clock was accepted with great enthusiasm. At first the cases of these clocks closely resembled much of the very severe architectural styling of this period, with an ebony finish that blended well with this type of design. It was not until later that marquetry was introduced on the cases along with lacquering, which definitely demonstrates a more elegant and lighter decorating motif representing the tastes of the society of the day. Walnut never became as popular in the production of clock cases as mahogany, which was first used about 1730 and remained in favor until the last half of the nineteenth century. But there are isolated exceptions to every rule, and the use of mahogany can be seen as early as 1709, when the celebrated Thomas Topion presented the Pumproom in Bath with a grandfather clock made from mahogany.

In fact, as technology improved and the styles of cases became more refined, instead of decreasing in overall size, clocks, especially grandfather clocks, increased. There are two reasons for this development. The first explains the structural elongation of the case to accommodate a longer drop by the weights in order to allow the clocks to operate for a longer period of time, but the second reason deals with the social importance clocks played in the household. Grandfather-clock ownership showed social prestige. Therefore the increased size of the clocks only added to the importance clocks demanded in the home.

The next development in horology was prompted by the increased size that clocks had attained to this point. Neither the domestic nor grandfather clocks lent themselves easily to be moved; therefore the bracket clock was developed to fit the various needs of the changing society. These clocks were basically spring-driven with a pendulum, designed on a verge escapement to allow easy transportation.

Some of the basic structural changes in clock design can be very helpful in determining not only the maker, but the place and date of production.

EUROPEAN STYLING

As early as the fourteenth century weight-driven chamber clocks were made throughout Europe, especially in the Germanic areas, as well as in France and Northern Italy. At this time England played almost no part in developing styles in the clock industry and continued her silent observance until sometime during the fifteenth century.

This century saw definite advancement both in technology and size so that clocks became more portable; but the real advancements did not occur until almost one hundred years later during the middle of the sixteenth century. By this time brass had replaced wood, screws had replaced wedges, and the development of the pendulum greatly advanced the fast-growing clock industry. The Dutch must be credited with the invention and development of the pendulum, which was widely exported throughout Europe as well as to England. This design became so popular as a method of keeping time that it was widely copied and improved upon, developing individual country styling, but never varying very much from the basic principles.

The beginning of the eighteenth century saw once again the erection of country borders in relation to clock design, which greatly aided the development of national styles. Austria became rated for the Vienna

139

regulator, England for the grandfather clock, and the French admired for their elegant and gay society-developed clocks that displayed very ornate decorations. We are very fortunate that the clock industry closed ranks during the late seventeenth century, because today many very beautiful native clocks exist that help us to understand the culture of the various periods throughout European history.

Austria

Austria, capital of the Holy Roman Empire, also during the seventeenth century became the center of both cultural and technological advancements. The English influence on design was very pronounced from about the end of the seventeenth century until almost one hundred years later. The majority of styles of the period successfully combined both the simple elegance of the English with the popular baroque influence of the Austrian. Although the long pendulum clock was popular in Austria it was not until about 1780 that the regulator clock was developed and attained national acclaim. The regulator was designed to hang on the wall and was only about four feet in height. Also popular at this time were the bracket clocks, which were also known as *Stockurhr* or short clocks.

The quality of clocks produced was extremely high with constant improvements being made in technology.

Germany and the Black Forest

The Germans living in the southern part of Germany, better known as the Black Forest, began producing clocks during the middle of the seventeenth century. The majority of these typically regional clocks were made from wood for primarily two reasons, the first being the availability of workable woods in the Black Forest area, and the second that one of the major industries of the area was woodworking.

The entire clock was carefully made from wood by these skilled expert carvers substituting metal only for such parts as the metal pins and the verge. This type of clock was produced until about 1730, when further advancements such as the pendulum and a striking device were added. After this time the industrious Germans developed the cuckoo to be added to the striking mechanism, and it has attained almost as much acclaim worldwide as if it had been officially declared the national bird.

Holland

The Dutch must claim credit for several important discoveries in the growing clock industry. The native son Christian Huygens developed both the balance spring and pendulum, which have since greatly altered horology.

Clock production throughout Holland was very national-style-oriented, the Friesland and Zaandam being the two most noted examples.

Friesland Timepieces

These clocks were first produced during the first part of the eighteenth century. This timekeeper is termed a timepiece and not a clock because it has no striking mechanism. Following Huygens's pendulum invention of 1656, pendulum clocks and timepieces were soon put into production by clockmakers in Holland, and various characteristic types became established. One of these the Dutch described as a *Stoelklok*, but it is generally known in the United Kingdom as a Friesland clock, from the area of Holland in which it was most usually made. Its hood is a modern reconstruction. A typical Friesland clock or timepiece is weight-driven and mounted on a bracket attached to a wall. It is surmounted by a hood, and usually has simple decorative side-pieces on either side of the dial. It has a short, light pendulum that swings through a considerable arc and is linked with a verge escapement. The striking hammer is inside the bell and rotates about a vertical axis.

Zaandam Clocks

Zaandam clocks were first produced in Zaanland during the last half of the seventeenth century. These clocks are weight-driven and set on the wall with a large bracket case that accommodates the pendulum. One of the most striking aspects of these clocks is their large, pear-shaped weights, which are suspended on ropes instead of chains.

ENGLAND

The development of the pendulum in Holland influenced clockmaking history but perhaps benefitted the English horology industry the most. By 1680 England had taken her place as the world leader in clock production as well as craftsmanship. Great workmen such as Thomas Tompion continued the research begun in Holland, and both the technology and casework continued to improve over the next century. The majority of production during this period centered on both bracket and grandfather clocks.

During the beginning of the eighteenth century the thirty-hour movement became popular in the more rural areas. These long-case clocks were usually very simple, with the cases made from either oak or other local woods. At this time the dials of the thirty-hour clocks were square and retained the single hour hand. Many of these clocks were made at large clock shops and ordered by the smaller tradesmen in rural areas, who then supplied the cases. Toward the middle of the eighteenth century the provincial thirty-hour movement was supplemented by a second hand, and unfortunately many of the earlier examples of single hour hands were converted during this period.

By the nineteenth century, although the thirty-hour clock was still being produced, it was gradually being replaced by the eight-day movement, which had been produced in the larger towns since the early eighteenth century.

The English Parliament passed an act in 1797 that deeply affected the English clock industry. This legislation levied a tax on clock and watch ownership and thereby almost crippled the clockmakers. Fortunately, the act was repealed by the next year. The majority of clocks that were produced during this year were extremely large and intended for church or hall usage to benefit a large majority of people. These clocks were very distinctive, with black dials, brass hands, and gilt numerals. The cases were usually patterned after Chinese motifs with impressive lacquer work popular at this time.

During the last half of the eighteenth century smaller versions of these clocks were produced and gained their full popularity with the development of the railroad system throughout the country as station clocks.

The English clock industry flourished, and today examples of the various styles are some of the most sought after in the world.

During the eighteenth century fashionable society wanted clocks incorporated into furniture. The Weeks cabinet is an excellent example of a style that was instituted in France. Courtesy Temple Newsam House, Leeds.

A calendar clock by Whillian Dutton, c. 1780–90. Courtesy Fitzwilliam Museum, Cambridge.

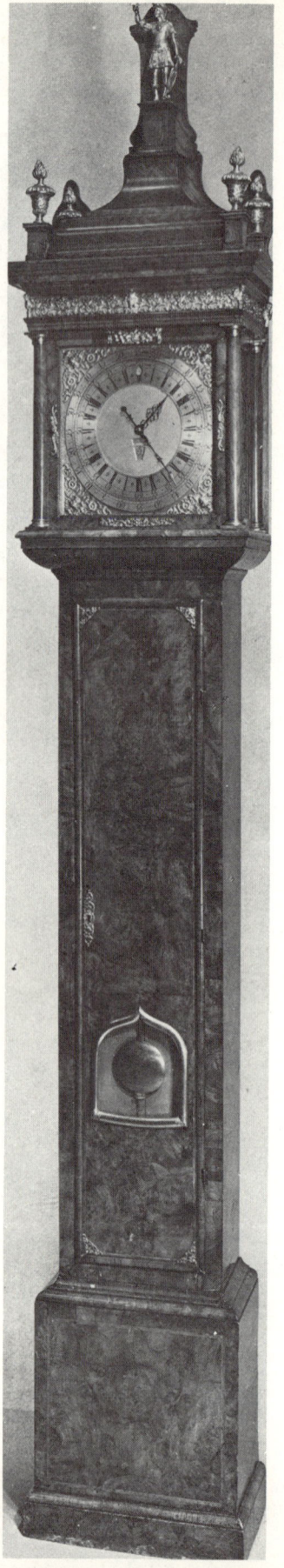

Close-up of the intricate workmanship of a clockface by Thomas Tompion. Courtesy Fitzwilliam Museum, Cambridge.

Table clock by John Ellecott, English, 1760–72. Courtesy White Boniface.

Longcase clocks by the famous Thomas Tompion. Courtesy Fitzwilliam Museum, Cambridge.

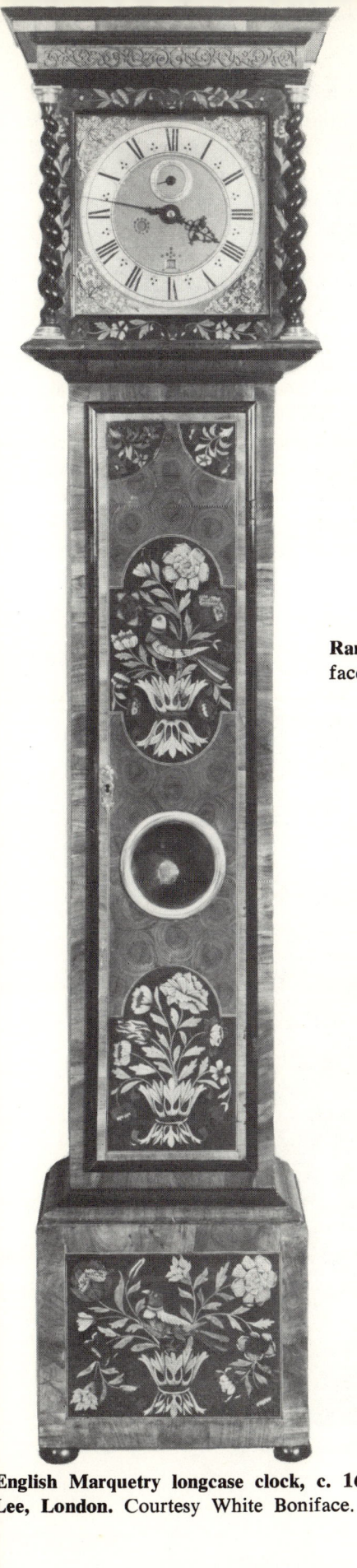

Very rare bracket clock c. 1690 by Thomas Tompion. Price: 18,000 pounds sterling. Courtesy White Boniface.

Rare 17th-century lantern clock. Courtesy White Boniface.

English Marquetry longcase clock, c. 1690 by Cuthbert Lee, London. Courtesy White Boniface.

FRANCE

French styles were greatly influenced by the reigning monarchs of the time, the most noted period being during the reigns of Louis the XIV, XV, and XVI. The French were noted and copied throughout the world for their elegance of style. In France this styling became as important, if not more so, than the quality of workmanship in the movement. During the middle of the eighteenth century both the cabinetmaker and movement producer stamped their individual names on each clock. This is a unique situation, because in most cases throughout Europe and especially in England, only the clock movement was signed by the maker. Both the quality of the movements and the cases were of excellent design and technical expertise.

Before the development of the pendulum, the French industry was at a very low point, but the pendulum gave the clockmakers an entirely new concept with which to work. Inspirations flourished and new styles were produced. During the beginning years of production the industry adapted its styles from the Dutch, but during the reign of Louis XV the designers turned to Rome and then with Louis XVI to Greece, which enjoyed enormous success.

Perhaps the bronze mantel clock in the rococo style was one of the most successful ever produced in France. Very often these clocks were also put in porcelain cases made at either the famous Vincennes or Meissen factories. Also, popular during the reign of Louis XV was the animal-motif clock. These clocks were fashioned in the shapes of various animals, such as lions, horses, and camels.

By the beginning of Louis XVI's reign, most clock cases were molded from metal, not wood as was previously used. During this period, toward the end of the eighteenth century, the clock industry improved greatly in France and entered into what was to be known as the "Golden Age of French Clock Production."

Traveling clock and case belonging to Gaston d'Orleans Petit Palais.

Ormolu band clock, French, late 18th century. Courtesy Fitzwilliam Museum, Cambridge.

Longcase clock, French, by deRabors. Courtesy Fitzwilliam Museum, Cambridge.

SWITZERLAND

Switzerland, noted for her clock and watch industry throughout the world, did not have a typical national style. Geneva became the center of the watch and clock industry during the sixteenth century, but the styles of this period were mainly influenced by the French. The workmanship was excellent on these pieces, and slowly over the years Switzerland emerged as a leader in the clock industry, a title that she has never relinquished.

The photograph on page 145 shows a small, lyre-shaped clock of the French Empire period. It is wrought and chased gold with enamels and pearls, and on the back there is a medallion-shaped painting on enamel. The Geneva movement winds the hours and the quarters. The base pedestal has a separate musical box.

Swiss Domestic Clock, 1669

This clock, made probably in Davos, Switzerland, is of special interest in that it is made almost entirely of wood. Its timekeeping is controlled by a verge escapement with a wooden balance wheel, and it is

Small, lyre-shaped clock of the French Empire period. Wrought and chased gold with enamels and pearls. On the back there is a medallion-shaped painting on enamel. The Geneva movement sounds the hours and the quarters. The base pedestal has a separate musical box. Courtesy Rolex, Geneva.

145

provided with two hands moving over separate dials. The upper hand indicates hours in the usual way, while the lower hand, which is attached to the shaft of the great wheel of the clock, rotates once per hour, its dial being divided to indicate quarter hours. As with the Knifton lantern clock, the only means of regulating the clock is by increasing or decreasing the driving weight according to whether the clock is losing or gaining.

The upper dial is provided with an alarm plate with holes into which a peg can be inserted to actuate the alarm.

The framework, wheels, pinions, and shafts are made of wood, and the great wheels of both going and striking trams have wooden pivots. The other wheels have steel pivots that are formed of wire passing through the wooden shafts, and they run in brass bushes in the wooden frames. The escape wheel is a wooden disk into which inclined iron teeth are driven; these engage with an iron verge.

COLLECTING ANTIQUE CLOCKS

The interest in clock-collecting has increased rapidly during the past few years Not only in the United States, but abroad clocks have become an integral part of a room's decor. More and more dealers, decorators, and auction houses are offering clocks for sale, but very few of these sources understand what is valued in purchasing a clock. Perhaps the best investment a beginning collector can make is to find an antique dealer who specializes in clocks and deal exclusively with him until a thorough understanding of this vast and very technical field is fully understood. It is interesting to note that prices are much more realistic in these specialty shops, plus you have the added insurance that most clock dealers either repair their wares themselves or have access to reputable repairmen, who are becoming harder and harder to find. Not only do these clock shops usually offer a good selection for comparative shopping in both quality and price, but their owners will be experts in their field and, more importantly, stand behind their clocks.

After your introduction into the field of horology and a basic knowledge of the various types of clocks available today has been gained, the next step is to venture into the vast marketplace specializing in clocks with a specific plan to start a worthwhile collection. Besides the clock shop, both auctions and antique fairs supply the widest variety of clocks. A subscription to specialty catalogues issued by the various auction dealers is an invaluable reference aid. Names and addresses of these auction houses can be found in the international section of this book. But careful study and pricing trends should be studied and analyzed before bidding at auction, because the spirited atmosphere stimulated at these sessions can very often carry prices over realistic market value.

As your knowledge grows, good quality pieces can be found at antique fairs, which are growing in popularity. Due to the low overhead of most of these dealers, combined with limited capital for investment, very often good prices can be secured. The antique fair dealer is usually especially susceptible during the closing hours on the last day of the fair, when he is faced with the return transportation of his merchandise. Since a large collection of clocks is harder to transport safely without damages, he will usually willingly take a much lower return on his investment in order to realize any type of profit for available reinvestment. Be sure to get a signed and dated certificate that accurately describes your purchase. Many of these dealers have no permanent shop, so it is always wise and to your advantage for future contacts to get the dealer's actual business address or home.

If knowledge places first in importance when embarking on collecting in a specific field, quality must come in a close second. It is far better to purchase only one fine example of a specific clock that is entirely original than several bastardized comglomerations with reproduction parts. Quality antique clocks will always increase in value, while lesser examples may only claim worth as decorative accessories and operable timepieces.

Books are very important to the collector. The following list has been compiled to help the interested horologist to both expand his reference library and gain valuable knowledge.

Baillie, G. H. *Watchmakers and Clockmakers of the World*, London, 1963
Clocks and Watches
Britten, F. J. *Old Clocks and Watches and Their Makers*, London and New York, 1933
Edey, N. *French Clocks*, New York, 1967; London, 1968
Bruton, F. *The Long Case Clock*, London, 1964; New York, 1968
Clocks and Watches, London, 1968
Daniels, G. *English and American Watches*, New York, 1967
Drepperd, C. W. *American Clocks and Clockmakers*, New York, 1947

Palmer, B. *A Treasury of American Clocks*, New York, 1967

A Book of American Clocks, New York, 1968

Edwardes, E. L. *The Grandfather Clock*, Altrinchan, 1971

Lloyd, A. H. *The Collector's Dictionary of Clocks*, London, 1964

Old Clocks, London, 1970

Tyler, E. J. *European Clocks*, London, 1968; New York, 1969

Museum collections are an excellent way to gain first-hand knowledge of the many varied styles of clocks. For the readers who may have the advantage of visiting the British Museum in London, a special grant established the Ilbert room, which displays the extensive Ilbert Clock and Watch Collection. A student's room has been set aside where the actual clocks and watches may be examined. This is an educational experience that should be taken advantage of if at all possible.

Of course, if the British Museum is not accessible, there are many other extensive collections that can give you a broad range of clocks.

America

American Clock and Watch Museum, Mystic Seaport, Connecticut
Henry Ford Museum, Dearborn, Michigan
Franklin Institute, Philadelphia, Pennsylvania
Metropolitan Museum of Art, New York, New York
Smithsonian Institution, Washington, D. C.

England

Museum of the History of Science, Oxford
Fitzwilliam Museum, Cambridge
British Museum, London
Science Museum, London
Wallace Collection, London
Victoria and Albert Museum, London

HISTORICAL COLLECTOR'S NOTES

The following is a basic listing, chronologically, of distinguishing characteristics that may help date various clocks.

Date	Salient feature
1600	Hour hand divides dial in quarters
1660	Portico top introduced on cases
1670	Flat top introduced on cases
1670	Maker's name added to dial
1675	Domed top introduced on cases
1675	Basket top introduced on cases
1675	Addition of second hand on grandfather clocks
1690	Addition of name on dial
1700	Important styling change on moldings under the hood of grandfathers clocks; before 1700 the moldings were noticeably convex, while after the above date the moldings gradually changed to become more concave
1700	Bracket clocks with both inverted bell top and double basket tops
1720	Curved door tops on grandfather clocks
1720	Grandfather clocks hoods with arched styling
1720	Addition of square dials in brass
1725	Grandfather and bracket clocks with arched dials in brass
1725	Addition of minute timing on both bracket and grandfather clocks
1730	Introduction of mahogany in clockcase production, many with bell tops
1750	Painted dials
1760	Silvered dials
1785	Round dials
1795	Addition of second hand on bracket clocks

Very often the style in which the clock is produced can be a very important indicator to where it was made. For example, clocks made in regional areas usually display calendar openings that are curved, and instead of glassed side panels, solid panels were mostly used. While in comparison, London-made clocks are usually more elegant in styling, with square calendar openings and glass side panels used on the hoods of grandfather clocks. The above are only a few of the styling indicators that can help you at a glance to identify the age of various clocks. Very often you may find one special characteristic that will help you in identifying various clocks, so it is best to develop your own list, perhaps based on some of the above facts.

DEVELOPMENT OF THE WATCH INDUSTRY

Germany

Peter Henlein has been credited with the development of the first watch about 1500. In actuality the Henlein watch was a small portable clock that was suspended from the waist with a belt. The watches produced during this period were either spherical or drum-shaped with cases made from gold or silver that were very often elaborately decorated. The edges of these watchcases were very often pierced to accept both the alarm and striking mechanisms.

Two unique features of German watches of the sixteenth century is their raised hour digits that enabled easy reading of the watch even in total darkness, since often they were left on the nightstand, and the peculiarity of the number two, which closely resembled the letter Z. The greatest care was taken with the decoration of the dials, which was very often enameled, and the hour hands were skillfully and delicately fashioned.

The great period of German watch production ended during the seventeenth century, when the country was almost crippled by the Thirty Years War. After the devastation of this war (1618–48) Germany never regained its former place of honor in the watch industry.

France

The French, noted as craftsmen throughout the civilized world at this period, took over where the Germans left off during the Thirty Years War. The watchmaking industry in France began in the town of Blois, but rapidly spread throughout the country. Many believe that the first French watch was made as early as 1519, but the first documentation was not made until much later in 1551 by Jacques de la Garde.

Very little German influence can be seen in the French styling. Most watches during the sixteenth century in France were oval or spherical, with straight sides and elaborately decorated cases.

The French watch industry continued to prosper, but the greatest period of production took place during the end of the sixteenth and beginning of the seventeenth centuries, when both the craftsmanship of the cases and mechanisms were of the highest quality.

England

The English watch industry did not develop until the sixteenth century, and merely copied both the French and German watches that had been perfected by this time. It was not until the following century that any specific national style can be attributed to the English. During the seventeenth century great technological advancements were made in England that changed the direction of the clockmaking industry. It is during this period that the watch actually attained the size that would permit it being worn in the pocket. By the end of this century the English watchmaker had indeed become the undisputed leader in watch production.

A silver decimal watch, made by Berthoud Freres, Paris, during the French Revolution. It follows the Republican calendar, which had twelve months of thirty days and divided the day into ten hours of 100 minutes. Toward the bottom of the dial there is a small traditional dial. The Republican decimal system lasted only a year (1793–94). Courtesy Rolex, Geneva.

A watch signed Bordier, Geneva (1796–97). The enamel miniature of General Bonaparte, found on the inside, is of a higher quality than the watch and attributed to one of the finest enamelists of the period, J. A. Lissignal. Courtesy Rolex, Geneva.

Watch and chatelaine by Thuilet, London. Courtesy Fitzwilliam Museum, Cambridge.

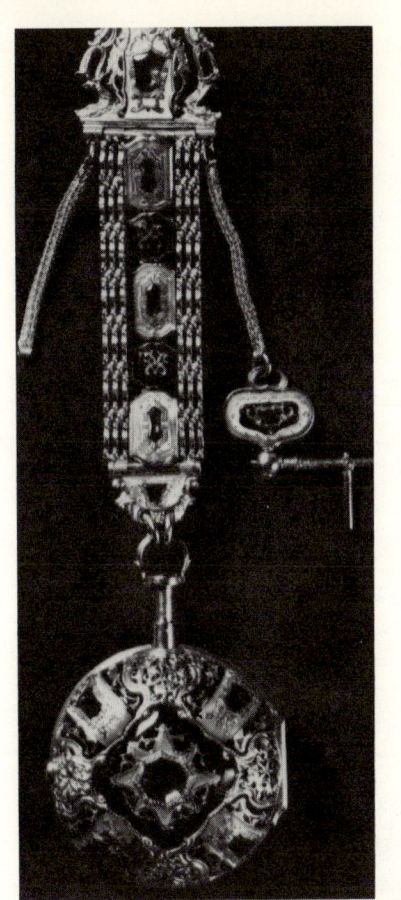

Watch and chatelaine by Jas. Rowe, 1758. Courtesy Fitzwilliam Museum, Cambridge.

Watch and chatelaine: The right side by Peregal, London, 1790–. The left side by Peregal, London, 1760–70. Courtesy Fitzwilliam Museum, Cambridge.

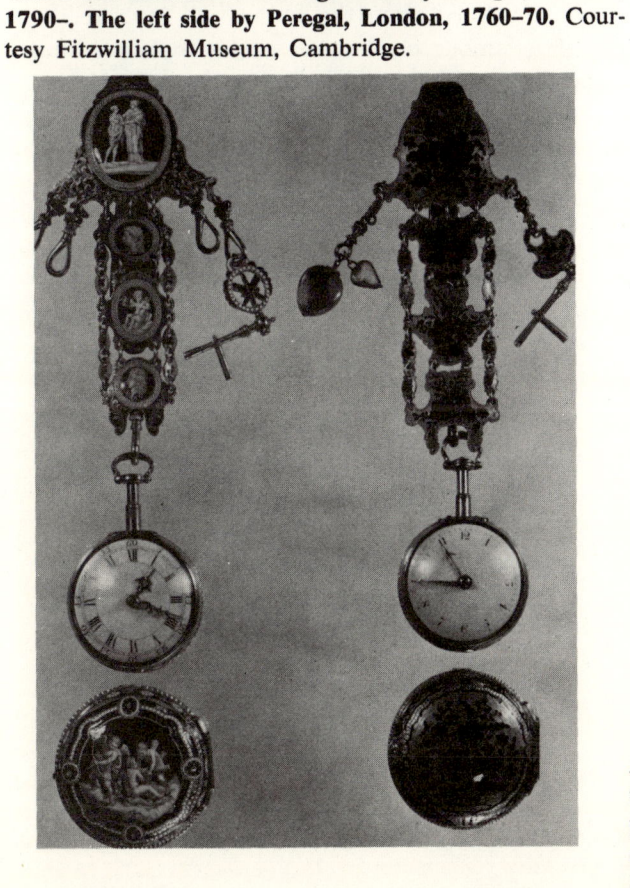

A watch signed Bordier, Geneva (1796–97). The inside of the watch contains the enamel miniature of General Bonaparte, which is of a higher quality than the watch, and is attributed to one of the finest enamelists of the period, J. A. Lissignal. Courtesy Rolex, Geneva.

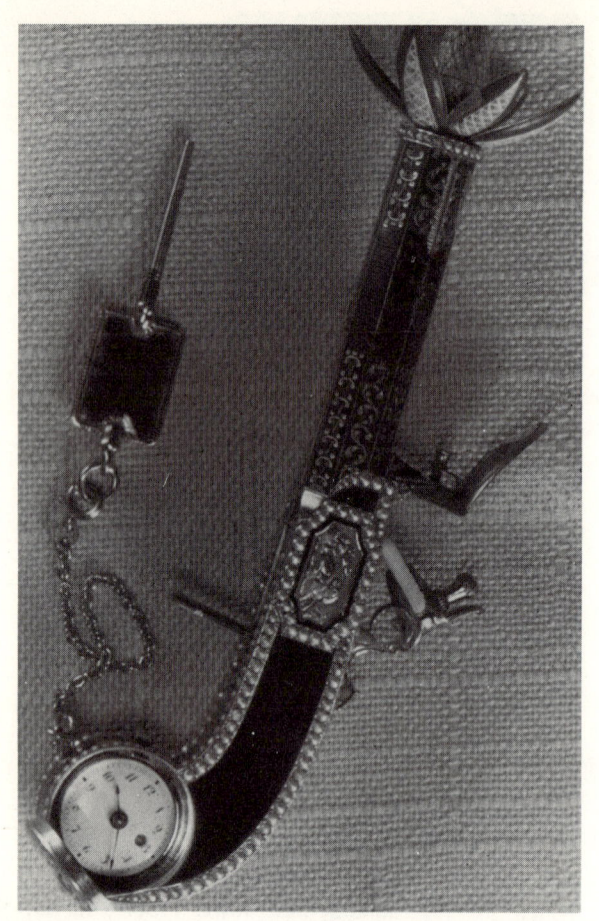

Pistol-watch of the French Restoration period. By pressing on the trigger, a flower comes out of the end of the barrel and acts as a perfume spray. Watch concealed in the butt. Movement and enamel both of Geneva. Courtesy Rolex, Geneva.

UNDERSTANDING CLOCK AND WATCH FORGERIES

Toward the end of the seventeenth century many of the most famous English clockmakers were being copiously forged throughout Europe Although each country produced its own special types of forgery, the most specialized and organized centers for this work took place in either Holland or Switzerland. Many collectors find these forged period pieces of as much interest as the originals they copied. And although the copies do not command as high prices as the originals, good forgeries from the period made by skilled craftsmen are becoming much sought after and are rapidly increasing in price.

The beginning collector should be careful that the original seventeenth-century clock he is purchasing is not in reality a modern-day forgery. Forgers of today are extremely skilled and clever in their work. Much time and money is invested to reconstruct and age a clock authentically, and primarily only very expensive clocks are worth the forger's time. Therefore, it is usually worthwhile to deal with reputable dealers who will stand behind their sales for authenticity.

One of the most popular forms of forgery today is the dial change. Smaller clock and watchmaker's names are erased from the original dial and replaced with famous makers of the various periods. Since this is a relatively inexpensive change to make, it is fairly common. The only way in which to help protect yourself is to study and thoroughly understand styles and periods. Very often the forger will inscribe the name of a famous clockmaker not operating during the specific period the clock was made.

8 Folk Art

During the past decade there has been a definite increase in the popularity of folk art throughout the world. This renewed interest in the national art forms of our forebears closely parallels both the growth of the antique market and the return to a more simplified life-style, together with a greater interest in the home and its decoration.

The peasants of the Middle Ages, originators of the rustic cultural artifacts that today are categorized as folk art, were guided by prevailing economic conditions and utilized primarily wood in making both household furniture and utensils. Perhaps wood was the favorite medium used because of its local availability plus durability. Designs of this period were basically utilitarian, and it was not until after the Reformation that designs became freer and more inspired to parallel the feelings of the times. Although folk art has always been accepted as a part of our culture, it was not until the middle of the eighteenth century that it was accepted as a form of art in itself. This new awareness affected every aspect of the culture, and exciting designs were developed in each art form from the textile industry to the local woodcarver.

One of the most popular design innovations of this period, c. 1750, was the introduction of painted furniture. Each country evolved its own specific style, such as the *Bauernmaleri* of the Germanic countries, the *Rosemaling* of Scandinavia, and the hex designs of the Pennsylvania Dutch. Painted decoration or ornamentation gave the furniture produced during this period distinct characteristics. The majority of painted furniture was made from softwoods such as pine, poplar, and tulipwood, and decorated with symbolic designs in strong colors, such as reddish brown, green, blue, and yellow. The designs were carefully painted, using such popular motifs as birds, animals, stars, flowers, and hearts. Many of the paintings tell stories of the time, and it is relatively simple to interpret the designs by reading the symbols. The following list may help you understand the symbolic painting of our ancestors.

Heart: happiness
Star: luck
Mounted horseman: chivalry
Turtledove: peace
Rampant unicorns: maidenly virtue
Birds: spiritualization
Flowers: spring and beauty
The single rose: perfection
Tree: inexhaustible life
Pine tree: immortality
Pansy: thought
Leaf: happiness; when leaves are grouped together they represent people
Grapes: fertility
Fruit: the origin of earthly desire
Fox: the Devil
Dog: faithfulness
Child: the future
Old man: the past
Bell: creative power

Besides the symbolic designs, most of the painted furniture was dated, and in the case of dower chests and wardrobes intended for a wedding, usually included both the initials or name of the bride and the date of the marriage.

Although much of this stylized painting was done in the home and was in fact one of the first forms of interior decoration, not all families were artistically talented. Therefore, traveling painters went from village to village to decorate furniture in exchange for room and board.

Today, with the renewed interest in folk art, people are once again learning the craft of stylized painting, but the last original work was done during the late eighteenth and early nineteenth centuries.

It was not just the larger pieces of furniture that were intricately carved or decorated, but a good variety of everyday household wooden articles. Salt cellars, as well as spoon racks, pitchers, and boxes, were beautifully decorated. Boxes were very important in the household, and in many alpine regions delicately carved and decorated small caskets were given as a token of love, a custom that traces its origin to the Middle Ages, and could be the forerunner of the modern day hope chest.

Folk pottery or earthenware was not generally decorated until the seventeenth century. At this time, raised decorations, mostly depicting regional motifs on the reddish-brown pottery, became popular. Although the designs were usually locally inspired and primitive in execution, the shapes were expanded to copy both the popular porcelain and faience pieces of the period.

Redware has become extremely popular within the last few years and commands ever-increasing prices. The majority of the pottery being collected at this time dated from the early eighteenth and nineteenth centuries. During this period the Pennsylvania Dutch produced a glazed earthenware using the Old World potter's wheel method of pottery production. Designs were usually scratched into the glaze and depicted either animals, birds, or flowers, with special emphasis placed on stylized flowers such as the tulip and the native American eagle. The Colonial plates produced in Pennsylvania are very rare and expensive, with a pie plate in excellent condition costing upwards of two thousand dollars.

Fortunately for the collector, European examples of redware are much more numerous and considerably less expensive. A comparable size pie plate would cost not more than six dollars for a nineteenth-century piece, but considerable attention should be paid to authenticity, since many of these plates are readily forged today.

Tinware or tole, as it is more commonly called, is an interesting field for collectors, both throughout the United States and Europe. Basically tinware is grouped in two categories: the first, gray work, was usually decorated with punchwork patterns, and the second favored primitive painted designs. Although produced as early as the eighteenth century, the majority of toleware pieces on the market date from the latter part of the nineteenth century.

The Continental tinware is much more sophisticated in design than its more primitive American counterpart. England, especially, became a noted center for tinware production during the late eighteenth century. A great variety of pieces were made at this time, with Chinese designs painted on solid-colored backgrounds in either yellow, black, brown, red, or green. Unfortunately, the industry became more mechanized toward the last half of the nineteenth century, and tinware gradually became stamped or cast with a marked simplification of design. Many of the designs, like the Alpine stylized paintings, were copied from the popular pottery motifs.

Prices for tinware vary greatly as to preferred styled. Early European designs, although not as elaborate as the sought-after French Empire toleware, will bring more money due to their rarity, but generally the prices are geared quite closely to the quality of decoration. American work generally is much less expensive than European tinware, with prices starting as low as twenty to thirty dollars for a simple piece from the early nineteenth century, while a European piece from the same period may bring upwards of twenty to thirty percent more. Not all prices are in this low range, and a truly original coffeepot or tray may carry a price tag of more than five hundred dollars.

Needlework played an important part in the lives of our ancestors. All classes of society participated in the craft, from the smallest child to the wealthiest ladies—some for pleasure, since needlework was considered a very genteel pursuit, and a lady of generations past was judged accomplished by the quality of her stitches, while others relied on needlework for their clothes and linens they used daily.

The majority of needlework pictures that survive today were produced by the middle and upper classes of the eighteenth and nineteenth centuries. Subject matter for such pictures was strictly influenced by the morals of the time. Dutiful damsels during this period produced such lovely pictures as mourning scenes that emulate a departed loved one or reproduce various scenes from the Bible. Unfortunately, the majority of this work is uninspired, although technically perfect. Early eighteenth-century Colonial samplers produced by children are quite interesting and eagerly sought after for their insight into the individual life-styles of the period. It is always interesting to find a sampler where one letter has been reworked many times to attain perfection—simple things like this make lasting and appealing keepsakes for the future.

Stumpwork, or relief embroidery, was popular during the seventeenth century, especially throughout Europe, and due to the exquisite detail displayed in these pieces, equally high prices are being demanded on today's market. Not very much stumpwork was seen in the Colonies due to the expense of the silks required to finish projects, but the wealthier American Colonists perhaps imported such extravagant wares from England. This outline needlework, which accentuates figures, was done in a much more simplified form in the rural and alpine regions. Often entire pastoral scenes were cut from a dark paper and silhouetted against a much lighter paper, which created a very dramatic effect. These designs could well have been the forerunners of today's needlework patterns, and were popular in rural areas where decoration with needlework was considered a luxury that could not be afforded. Fortunately, much of this work has survived in its original form and was eventually supplemented and outlined with embroidery, which only added to the primitive charm of these pieces.

Patchwork, although considered a national American folk-art form due to the emphasis placed upon the quilt within the last few years as a medium of decoration, in reality has been used for centuries throughout the world as an economical and practical method of conserving textiles in the home.

The detailed and very colorful mosaic, as well as appliqué, designs used in quilting have endured the centuries and have become much more versatile than their originally intended use as bed coverings. Many women, perhaps out of necessity, wore patchwork petticoats, and in the colonies tablecloths and linen were appealingly patched together to double for curtains. Since textiles were very scarce and expensive, every inch was utilized in as many ways as possible until it was completely worn out.

Although it is sometimes very difficult to determine both age and origin of quilts there are a few guidelines that may help with your identification:

- Quilts made before 1790 very often still have the seeds in the cotton that had not been removed by ginning.
- Early American quilts, produced before the end of the first quarter of the nineteenth century, contained mostly imported fabric; after this period cotton was introduced into American quilt production.
- European quilts were commonly sewn with the backstitch, while the American housewife, due to economy and to conserve on thread, used a very simple running stitch.

Design and material are also an excellent determining factor in establishing period of production.

- Quilts produced during the eighteenth century usually had motifs that were symmetrical from top to bottom, while during the following century quilt designs became larger, more formal, and were usually centered in the middle of the quilt. It was not until after 1825 that the individual square method of production was begun.
- Woolen quilts were made between 1800 and 1850.
- The famous crazy quilts were produced much later (1870–80).
- Perhaps one of the most appealing quilts, better known as the friendship or signature quilt, was produced between 1840 and 1860.

Quilts have greatly escalated in price during the past few years. This dramatic increase can be attributed to two basic factors: first, a much greater interest in decorating the home, and second, the American Bicentennial has stimulated an awareness of our ancestors and the way they lived. While several years ago a very good example of an early eighteenth- or nineteenth-century quilt could be found in the price range of seventy to four hundred dollars, today prices have nearly doubled. Although prices have increased greatly, quilts are still a wise investment. Due to the stimulated interest in early quilts, more and more excellent quilts are being discovered across the country.

In addition, quilts up until now have rarely been forged due to the amount of detailed hand needlework involved in their construction. After 1850 some quilts were machine produced, but these were not copies of earlier quilts, just a simplification of the time-consuming method of quilt construction.

BUYING FOLK ART

The field of folk art is one of the most diversified for collectors at present. Very little information on pieces available or comparative prices has been made available during the past few years, but as interest has been stimulated in the crafts of our oncestors, more sophisticated collector's guides have slowly begun to appear.

Unfortunately, the pursuit of folk art is a long and painstaking process, but more often the experience becomes a rewarding education. Many folk museums have been established throughout the world, which greatly helps more people understand the crafts of our ancestors as well as preserve an important and past way of life.

Folk art has had a long, hard climb in order to become a recognized art form. Having been produced by peasants, the pieces made were considered more utilitarian than artistic. But as more people became interested in antiques the boundaries were expanded to include less formal aspects of the trade. It was not until the last ten years that there was a worldwide interest in collecting and decorating with folk art, and prices began rising dramatically. The period for bargains in the folk-art field has long past. At one time it was possible to exchange or barter throughout the countryside for excellent pieces of native folk art. Unfortunately, due to the public demand and price increases over the past few years, much of the market has understandably been flooded with forgeries and very poor copies that carry very high price tags. But with careful research and diligent attention to flea markets and auctions, many interesting pieces can still be found.

Although all forms of folk art are popular today, perhaps furniture has experienced the largest increase in sales and returns the greatest profit on an investment. Clocks and ceramics are becoming equally popular and demanding higher and higher prices every year. Even the most unpredicted field of European painted and decorated houses are being eagerly sought after and sometimes dismantled and shipped to various destinations throughout the world.

Porcelain-headed doll with leather body dressed in piqué dress, c. 1870. Courtesy Schweizerisches Museum fur Volkskunde, Basel.

Miniature logging camp, hand-carved from wood toward the end of the 19th century. Courtesy Schweizerisches Museum fur Volkskunde, Basel.

Miniature dolls' kitchen, c. 1890. The individual pieces were made in Germany, Italy, Spain, and Switzerland. Courtesy Schweizerisches Museum fur Volkskunde, Basel.

The marketplace, hand-carved in Germany and Yugoslavia about 1910. Courtesy Schweizerisches Museum fur Volkskunde, Basel.

The small salon—a dollhouse from the Wurttembergerhof, Basel, Switzerland, c. 1872. Courtesy Schweizerisches Museum fur Volkskunde, Basel.

Alpine procession by Johannes Muller, 1806–97; oil on cardboard, 1865. Courtesy Schweizerisches Museum fur Volkskunde, Basel.

Flight to Egypt; reverse painting on glass, c. 1800. Courtesy Schweizerisches Museum fur Volkskunde, Basel.

Love letter printed and hand colored with text and three pictures from the 18th century. Courtesy Schweizerisches Museum fur Volkskunde, Basel.

Wall decoration "The Wedding Procession"; oil on linen. Swedish, toward the end of the 18th century. Courtesy Schweizerisches Museum fur Volkskunde, Basel.

Bride's shoes from Yugoslavia. Made from hand-carved wood in a geometric pattern with mother-of-pearl inlay. Courtesy Schweizerisches Museum fur Volkskunde, Basel.

Silhouette (1808–71). Courtesy Schweizerisches Museum fur Volkskunde, Basel.

Procession in Pays d'Enfant, Switzerland (Louis Saugy, 1871–1953). Silhouette about 1900. Courtesy Schweizerisches Museum fur Volkskunde, Basel.

Hand-carved wooden figures from Israel. Courtesy Schweizerisches Museum fur Volkskunde, Basel.

Charming Czechoslovakian wedding cake made from varied shades of paper, c. 1940–50. Courtesy Schweizerisches Museum fur Volkskunde, Basel.

Protestant nurse in uniform; Niklaus Stoecklin; Basel, Switzerland, 1892. Courtesy Schweizerisches Museum fur Volkskunde, Basel.

Memento of the Holy Lands, 1960, Jerusalem. Courtesy Schweizerisches Museum fur Volkskunde, Basel.

Ceramic Christmas figures, Vienna, Austria, 1930. Courtesy Schweizerisches Museum fur Volkskunde, Basel.

Scene from the Old Testament in wood, Berlin, 1965 (Harry Brauer). Courtesy Schweizerisches Museum fur Volkskunde, Basel.

Wooden statue, Austria, 18th century. Courtesy Schweizerisches Museum fur Volkskunde, Basel.

Ceramic jug, Thuringer, Germany. Courtesy Schweizerisches Museum fur Volkskunde, Basel.

Goose egg decorated in Solothurn, Switzerland. Courtesy Schweizerisches Museum fur Volkskunde, Basel.

Wedding jug, Oboga, Rumania-glazed earthenware, 1970. Courtesy Schweizerisches Museum fur Volkskunde, Basel.

Decorated religious relic about 1750, CSSR, Prague. Courtesy Schweizerisches Museum fur Volkskunde, Basel.

Pilgrimage medallion, 18th century. Courtesy Schweizerisches Museum fur Volkskunde, Basel.

Various alpine painted furniture.

Easter eggs decorated, Czechoslovakia. Courtesy Schweizerisches Museum fur Volkskunde, Basel.

Painted alpine schrank, c. 1748.

Easter eggs with multicolored decorations, Moldau, Rumania. Courtesy Schweizerisches Museum fur Volkskunde, Basel.

Early Baroque schrank.

Glass rolling-pin, Nailsea, early 19th century. Courtesy Museum of English Rural Life, University of Reading.

Needlework with painted inscription, England, 1842; "The Father's Grave." Courtesy Museum of English Rural Life, University of Reading.

English hanging corner cupboard about 1800. Picture shows cupboard closed as well as inside decorations on doors. Courtesy Museum of English Rural Life, University of Reading.

Glass rolling pin, Nailsea, early 19th century. Courtesy Museum of English Rural Life, University of Reading.

160

English paintings on glass, early 19th century. 1. The Agony in the Garden. **2.** The Lord's Supper. **3.** Scenes in the Life of Queen Caroline. **4.** Scenes in the Life of Queen Caroline. Courtesy Museum of English Rural Life, University of Reading.

Early embroidered dress with smocking. Courtesy Museum of English Rural Life, University of Reading.

161

Hand-carved English wooden nutcracker. Courtesy Museum of English Rural Life, University of Reading.

Interesting early Hawaiian quilt. The dramatic bold designs show the beautiful art of appliqué. Courtesy Kauai Museum.

9 *Fraktur*

Manuscripts painted and decorated by hand played a very important part in the lives of our ancestors. Great care and pride was taken with the preparation of these personal and family certificates, and due to careful preservation many of these beautiful illuminated manuscripts have survived until today. The origin of these works dates to the Middle Ages, when the characteristic illuminated capital letters were introduced. From this period, each culture added its own influences, which make each document an individual comment on the society of the time.

One of the most sought after periods is the Fraktur of the Pennsylvania Dutch. The word *Fraktur* is derived from the German *Frakturschrift*, lettering used during the sixteenth century in Germany. The majority of these manuscripts date from the eighteenth and nineteenth centuries and are intricately decorated with hand-drawn lettering in water colors of the period. Some of the more popular motifs used in these manuscripts were the heart, deer, dove, lamb, butterfly, various flowers, as well as angels. Although Fraktur illuminations were used to decorate plaques and wall hangings, primarily these decorations beautified baptism, marriage, and birth certificates.

It was not until the last half of the nineteenth century, about 1860, that many of the more popular designs were preprinted. Collectors are not so much concerned with this latter period of production as with the more creative illuminated certificates made before the preprinted 1860 period. Unfortunately, intact examples are becoming increasingly rare and command very high prices. Perhaps due to the scarcity of good Fraktur manuscripts, combined with the increased demand, there has been an increase in the fakes on today's market. The collector in this market should be doubly aware of the ingenious twentieth-century fakes. In fact, many of these forgers were so talented that their work has become very well known and sought after for specialized collections.

Interesting 18th- and 19th-century illuminated manuscripts. Courtesy Schweizerisches Museum fur Volkskunde, Basel.

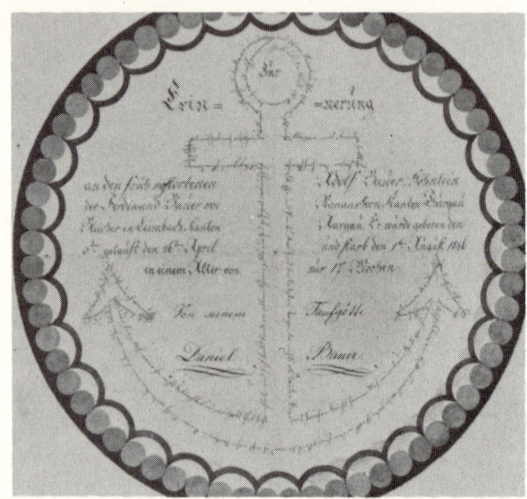

164

10 Packaging Collectibles

The twentieth century we live in is an age of packaging. Everything we use comes to us prepackaged in some form from the manufacturer. In our grandparents' time the local merchant individually wrapped and weighed each order on request. It was not until the beginning of the nineteenth century that manufacturers' packing was introduced as a form of advertising.

Due to technical advancements in mass production, multiunit packaging became a reality. At first it was reluctantly used, but then the individual manufacturers began to see the great advantages to be gained from package advertisement. In effect an advertising war erupted during the nineteenth century between companies in order to produce the most unusual boxes for their products. One of the prime concerns was versatility of styling. The successful box of this period not only promoted its product, but became a useful part of the household after the contents were finished. Boxes of the late nineteenth century were not only colorful, but unusual. Many had intricately designed transfer-prints depicting various holiday scenes, especially Christmas. Special-shaped boxes became very popular during the late 1880s. Some of the more unusual types were made to resemble ships, dolls, houses, and even the product itself, such as cookies.

The surprising success this new form of collecting has achieved can only be attributed to the availability of items in this field as well as reasonable prices. Most boxes and tins also are not fragile and can easily be utilized in everyday living, and make excellent decorative accessories.

OUR
MOTHER'S
PURE
ALL OCCASION
COCOA
NET WEIGHT 1 LB.
E. & A. OPLER, INC.

MONARCH
TEA
MONARCH
COCOA
BOSTON

QUAKER
ROLLED
WHITE OATS
The Quaker Oats Company

CLUSTER
RAISINS
1 POUND

CHOICE
BOTANIC DRUGS
PRESSED
MANUFACTURING
CHEMISTS

167

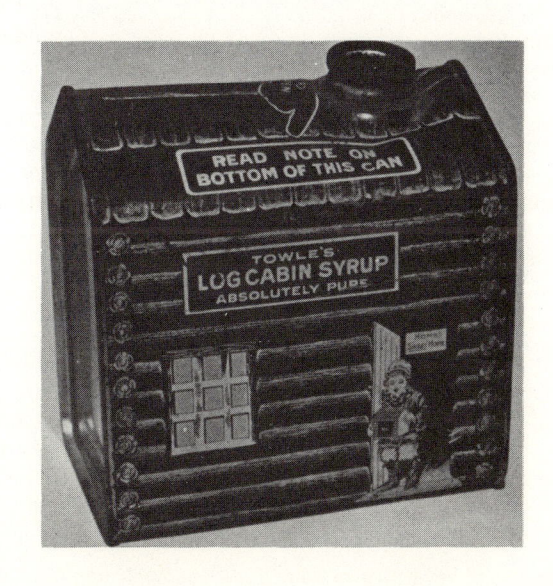

11 Furniture

FURNITURE PERIODS

Tudor Period	1485–1603
Elizabethan Period	1558–1603
Inego Jones	1572–1652
Jacobean Period	1603–88
Stuart Period	1603–1714
A. C. Boulle	1642–1732
Louis XIV Period	1643–1715
Grinling Gibbons	1648–1726
Cromwellian Period	1649–60
Carolean Period	1660–85
William Kent	1684–1748
William & Mary Period	1689–1702
Queen Anne Period	1702–14
Georgian Period	1714–1820
T. Chippendale	1715–62
Louis XV Period	1723–74
G. Hepplewhite	1727–88
Adam Period	1728–92
Angelica Kaufmann	1741–1807
T. Sheraton	1751–1806
Louis XVI	1774–93
T. Shearer	1780
Regency Period	1800–1830
Empire Period	1804–15
Victorian Period	1830–1901
Edwardian Period	1901–10

ENGLISH MONARCHS

Henry IV	1399–1413
Henry V	1413–22
Henry VI	1422–61
Edward IV	1461–83
Edward V	1483–83
Richard III	1483–85
Henry VII	1485–1509
Henry VIII	1509–47
Edward VI	1547–53
Mary	1553–58
Elizabeth	1558–1603
James I	1603–25
Charles I	1625–49
Commonwealth	1649–60
Charles II	1660–85
James II	1685–89
William & Mary	1689–95
William III	1695–1702
Anne	1702–14
George I	1714–27
George II	1727–60
George III	1760–1820
George IV	1820–30
William IV	1830–37
Victoria	1837–1901
Edward VII	1901–10

It is impossible in one short chapter of this book to describe everything in the broad field of furniture collecting. Understanding furniture, especially pieces purchased for investment, requires years of specialized study, because furniture, more than any other field of antique collecting, has been outrageously forged and copied through the centuries. In fact, many of these ingenious forgeries are collector's items themselves today. Therefore the collector of antique furniture must work hard to uncover all the facts, but in addition he must strive to develop an astute second sense to help aid him in the detection of clever frauds. The beginning collector should make an intense study of the various furniture styles so that he can better identify an original piece. Experts in the field call this getting to know the *feel* of a piece of furniture.

A noted authority of antique English furniture once told me that, after examining a Queen Anne chair that was listed at a country auction, he decided not to bid on the piece even though he had traveled over two hundred miles to the sale at the expressed wish of a client, because even though the style of the chair was perfect the feel was missing and he felt that the chair was a clever forgery. His instincts were proved correct years later, when the chair was eventually donated to a national museum and the staff appraiser verified a forgery!

Of the vast quantities of antiques collected throughout the world, perhaps no other field except furniture has through the centuries given more enjoyment. Craftsmen have expressed their artistic talents through the medium of wood, each trying to surpass the other in quality and originality of design. If the number one concern of most collectors had to be evaluated, it would more than likely be originality, or to be more precise, the authentication of an acquisition. Such expert forgeries are produced today that many of the experts are fooled themselves. "Antique factories" exist where exact replicas are turned out by the hundreds. Italy is notorious in this field, producing fabulous Louis XIV furniture and art objects by the famous Fabergé. The rule here is "to the buyer beware," be suspicious of a real find by one of the old masters. Although it could happen, the chances are badly stacked against you.

Also due to the enormous interest stimulated in antique furniture during the past several decades, combined with excellent restoration work, very few pieces of authentic old furniture have been overlooked. Bargains are realistically scarce, but this problem has been compensated by the drastic increase in prices during the past few years. The high prices paid in today's market are the "bargains" of tomorrow.

The following is a brief but complete listing of the various furniture styles as well as transitional periods through the centuries. History and the everyday living habits of our ancestors whose possessions we are collecting is very important, if not vital, if we are ever to grasp the true feel of the furniture of the past.

GOTHIC

Furniture of the Middle Ages was basically functional. Artisans of this period expressed themselves in gold, silver, and tapestries, as well as oils. It wasn't until late in the fifteenth century that furniture began to be seen as a status symbol. Up until this time furniture styles were basically boxlike and extremely simple, with very few pieces adorning even the wealthiest homes, and chairs especially being reserved for the honored few. The keynote for furniture of the fifteenth century was durability, with oak being the favored wood because of its strength.

As furniture became more popular and a symbol of wealth, the style rapidly changed, with carved decorations becoming popular, and walnut was substituted for the plainer oak as the chosen wood. The Gothic style, which was adopted during this period, remained popular on and off for several centuries in northern Europe. Motifs of this period favored pointed arches with naturalistic embellishments such as various leaf designs. Also popular was the linen-fold, or "outline design," favored by tapestries of the period. These carvings are seen mostly on large areas such as screens, sides of cupboards, and backs of high chairs.

Even at the height of its popularity, Gothic furniture was produced in limited quantities. Therefore original examples of this period are rarely found by today's collector. The style did exist until the twentieth century, and it is usually these latter pieces that find their way into today's market. Therefore, the best way for a student of furniture to study the Gothic period is in a museum, where most of the best pieces can be seen.

The Gothic style was revived during the middle of the nineteenth century in England to follow the original principle of form and function, but designers of the period quickly expanded on the basic form to include intricate decorations and carvings that were popular during this period. The Gothic revival style spread rapidly to both the United States and Europe, where unusual examples of design were always actively sought.

RENAISSANCE

Unlike the Gothic period, which was basically a functional art of the people, the Renaissance brought a return of both Roman and Greek classical beauty. Although the Renaissance began in Italy during the beginning of the fourteenth century, little evidence can be seen of its dramatic style change until the following century.

Artisans of the fifteenth century experienced an

intellectual reawakening that was seen as a new design form reshaping everything from furniture to entire buildings. Furniture of the fifteenth century became exquisitely painted works of art. Shapes of furniture changed from the more mundane and heavier style to reflect the classical splendor, taking on gracefully and richly decorated motifs. Rich materials were incorporated into the new style. Tooled leathers, fine silks, rich velvets, and jewels were all used to produce opulent furniture designs.

The height of the Renaissance took place in Florence, where a sophistication of classical design was developed unmatched elsewhere in the Western world. Although Florence reigned supreme, each small Italian town produced its own interpretation of the Renaissance style. It is easy to understand why the classical form was revived in Italy, where the people lived surrounded daily with the ruined splendor of Ancient Rome. This, combined with their desire for a more comfortable and graceful mode of living, made an easy transition for the revival of the classical styles of the past.

Although Renaissance furniture is rare, it is still possible to find superb examples of furniture of the period.

The influence of the Renaissance was not limited to Italy alone, and therefore during the sixteenth century Germany, Spain, France, and England began their own cultural revolution.

In France, styles paralleled closely the Italian form with a lot of surface decoration, which sometimes makes identifying furniture from the two countries difficult. The majority of furniture of this period was made from oak or walnut.

It wasn't until almost a century later with the ascension of James I to the throne that England began to adopt the classical design in furniture. This style became known as Jacobean, after King James. Although the famous designer Inigo Jones became a major force in the classical movement in England, basically architecture was affected and not individual furniture, as in other countries.

BAROQUE

The baroque style began in Italy during the sixteenth century. Furniture as a form of art and decoration began to take on new meaning. The decorators added movement to their designs, and draping, turns, curves, and swirls became popular. Embellishment became the prime motivation in furniture construction of this period. In other words, as the decoration increased, the quality of the initial workmanship decreased. During the seventeenth century the quality of workmanship reached an all-time low, with the elaborate carvings and decorations masking much of the flawed construction.

The furniture of this period is extremely busy, being the fantasy of its creator. Styles throughout Italy ran wild, and little refinement was seen late in the seventeenth century, when French cabinetmakers adapted versions of the Italian baroque for the court of Louis XIV. Under French domination the baroque style acquired an elegance that was widely copied throughout Europe.

LOUIS XIV

Due to the considerable influence that King Louis XIV exerted over styles of the period, the elaborate baroque style became synonymous with the name. Louis XIV, better known as the Sun King, surrounded himself with the finest forms of the decorative arts. His palace of Versailles was widely copied throughout Europe as the pinnacle of elegance of the period. The Sun King left a legacy in his palaces of Versailles, Fontainebleau, Saint Cloud, Saint Germain, and Trianon that shows history how his life-style affected the style of the period, baroque.

Due to the grandeur of these palaces, furniture was naturally built on a large scale. The basic shape of the period was rectangular, softened by both gentle curves and carved decorations, as well as by gilt ornamentation. Ormolu was first introduced as surface decoration during this period. Other innovative decorative styles included boulle and exotic wood inlays, as well as the use of precious metals such as silver, brass, and pewter in the inlaid decoration.

All artisans of the period sought through their work to glorify the king. New woods were used to create more unusual workmanship, and chestnut, ebony, and sycamore were to replace the more standard oak and walnut normally used by the French. Some of the more famous craftsmen even used silver alone to create masterpieces of furniture for the king, but this drastically depleted the national treasury, which required the funds for national defense, and the furniture was then remelted.

IMPORTANT FURNITURE OF THE LOUIS XIV PERIOD

Furniture	Descriptive Remarks
High-backed armchairs	Backs of chairs during this period extended high enough to protect the

	powdered wigs gentlemen wore, and were excessively wide to accommodate the width of ladies' gowns; distinctive architectural features are the clown-scrolling arms, as well as the baluster, pedestal, or scrolled legs
Canapé	An unusual sofa with wing sides
Bergère	A solid-sided upholstered wing chair
Tabaret	An upholstered stool
Banquette	An upholstered bench
Carreaux	Flat floor cushions for additional seating
Chaffeuse	An upholstered sidechair on short legs
Bureau Plat	Flat-topped writing table
Bureau à Gradin	Writing table with a storage unit consisting of drawers and pigeonholes located on top to the rear of the writing surface
Cabaret à Café	Small, two-tiered serving table for either chocolate or coffee
Consoles	During this period consoles became an important piece of furniture; with increased decoration of individual consoles, they alone became the focal point of decoration in a room
Suites of furniture	It is during this period that entire groups of furniture appear for the first time, a practice that has survived until the present time

ENGLAND

The sober English were never greatly influenced by the French baroque style, although furniture of this period shows a definite influence of the modified baroque that was popular on the Continent, especially in Holland.

England during this period was extremely slow to respond to new style trends. Still deep in the Middle Ages, as far as originality, she needed to experience her own Renaissance before developing any further in the decorative arts.

It was not until the reign of William and Mary when Dutch furniture-makers began to emigrate to England that a transitional period was established. Although the true French baroque was never to take hold in England, a modified version was imposed upon the solid, traditional English styles. Perhaps the first concession was the addition of the scroll, as well as metal inlays and marquetry. Marquetry quickly became very popular. It was often done in contrasting colored woods as well as floral and bird designs. Other popular decorative techniques employed during this period were ivory inlay, parquetry, and veneering.

Lacquered cabinets became popular during the reign of Charles II, when a definite Oriental influence was introduced. But it was not until William and Mary ascended the throne that both lacquering and japanning reached the height of popularity. Large quantities of this furniture were made at this time and bring increasingly high prices on today's market.

Besides decorative finishes, detailed carving became popular during the late seventeenth and early eighteenth centuries. The master Grinling Gibbons made such styles as delicate swirls and pierced foliage the vogue.

During the Carolingian period, minor influences of the French court can be seen, especially in the chair design of the period. Cane was employed for seats and backs of chairs, but more elegantly upholstered armchairs in the Louis XIV style came into use as well. Dining rooms became a focal point under the reign of Charles II, with both round and oval tables with gatelegs being popular.

The baluster leg with tall or teardrop-shaped feet became popular under the reign of William and Mary. Furniture during this period is lighter and simpler in design.

China cabinets filled with beautifully decorated porcelain of the era became a symbol of wealth. Tea tables, as well as dressing tables, became popular during this period.

FRANCE

Régence (1715–23)

The Régence period is basically a transitional period. The Sun King's power had set, and Philippe II, duc d'Orléans, had become regent for Louis XV. The distinctive characteristics of this period are the overpowering ornamentation with excessive ormolu appliqués.

Fauteuils, commodes, and escritoires were popular during the Régence period, but it was not until later that furniture styles were modified to accept the increase in surface ornamentation. Much of the work done during this period is inspired. Beautiful painted decorations with an unusual blend of both East and West adorn commodes and chests.

The expanding China trade was excitingly translated into furniture decoration. The most noted artist of this period, Antoine Watteau, created delicate Oriental scenes that are masterpieces of workmanship.

Régence furniture, especially chairs, was smaller and lighter in design with beautiful surface designs. Legs are slimmer, curved with scroll feet, while arms have padded centers.

Furniture of this period is popular and prices are high, especially original French pieces. Continental furniture of the same vintage retails in today's market at a much reduced rate.

Louis XV or Rococo (1720–60)

The cabinetmakers of this period reached a new height of fantasy and imagination. The word *rococo* is derived from the French *rocaille*, which means a certain kind of shell. Perhaps the best examples of rococo furniture were done during the first quarter of the eighteenth century before Louis XV came to the throne.

The scale of this furniture was smaller, more elegant than previous styles, with a definite effeminate influence. The freedom of the court of Louis XV, the social decadence of the period, as well as the tastes of Madame de Pompadour, the king's mistress, all were translated into the furniture style of this period. The senses were glorified in every medium available to the artisan. The old rectilinear lines of both Louis XIV and the Régence periods were now replaced by graceful curves and bombé, as well as by decorative motifs such as the shell, scroll, leaf, and garland. Although the majority of pieces from the more noted craftsmen were usually signed with their stamp somewhere on the underside of the frame, many experts would prefer to judge a piece on the quality of the design. This is because fraudulent names were often added to furniture produced at a later period. During the eighteenth century the central motif of the flower, shell, or leaf was the entire design and gave the effect of generalization, but later period furniture shows designs to be clear and very realistic.

The French cabinetmakers of this period were master craftsmen who supplied the aristocracy with furniture that in reality was a realization of their sensual fantasies. As the period progressed, decoration increased with vivid colors as well as with totally painted surfaces being extremely common. The wood gradually became encased in metal ornamentation. Therefore, it is the designs executed during the beginning of the rococo period up until about 1760 that are most largely sought.

IMPORTANT FURNITURE OF THE LOUIS XV PERIOD

Furniture	Descriptive Remarks
Bergère	Although this chair first appeared about 1720, it is considered as an important upholstered armchair of the Louis XV period, and remained popular in various versions for several centuries
Canapés or Tête-à-tête	A settee for two people, although various styles can be found to accommodate three people
Daybeds	The custom of the period allowed women to recline on daybeds to receive guests in their bedrooms
Ambulante	A small table with two tiers and side handles for easy transport
Table à ouvrage	A small worktable to accommodate needlework
Serre-bijoux	A small jewelbox
Dressing tables	Beautiful toilet tables were designed during this period, many having a wide variety of French porcelain scent bottles
Chiffonières	Tables used for storage of sewing supplies
Tables de nuit	Bedside or night tables
Tric-tracs and Bouillottes	Game tables and especially backgammon tables
Secrétaire à abattant	Fall-front desk
Bas d'armoire	A cupboard designed especially to be placed under either windows or between two doorways
Commodes	Commodes of the Louis XV period are considered important collector's pieces, with beautiful designs that show the total treatment that is characteristic of this era

French Provincial

The term *French provincial* refers to the furniture produced for the country or château during the eighteenth century. It makes a definite distinction between pieces made by the master craftsmen working in

Paris at this time. It does mean country or rustic furniture and definitely does not refer to a reduction in the quality of workmanship. French provincial furniture is in reality a less formal approach to furniture of the period than was normally requisitioned to furnish the châteaux that dotted the French countryside during the eighteenth century. Life in the country, far from the glitter of the court, was geared more to the pleasures of the country, but was definitely not lacking in comfort or quality. Therefore the furniture of this period was just more relaxed in order to accommodate this life-style.

Perhaps the most prized piece of furniture of the eighteenth century was the armoire. The pride of brides, armoires were cherished pieces that passed from generation to generation and remain popular even today. These pieces were produced in quantity and are easily found on today's market.

The decoration of this period was often simple with painted surfaces that offered an easy method of designing as well as protection for the piece. Fruitwoods were mainly used in construction, with the shell motif one of the favorite decorative influences. Chairs of this period were adaptations of earlier slat-back designs, with their backs delicately carved in either a neoclassical or rococo motif. Low chests with curved fronts and heavily carved skirts were popular during this period. Furniture of eighteenth-century France is large in scale, the provincial styles often being larger than pieces made in Paris during the same period.

Although Provincial furniture has always been popular, during the past decade an increased interest in more informal life-styles has stimulated the provincial furniture market. Prices are rising, but new pieces that had up until now graced barns and storage rooms are gratefully being brought onto the market.

Louis XVI

Louis XVI and his queen, Marie Antoinette, came to the throne in 1774. France at this time was in the middle of social, political, and religious turmoil. The state was nearly bankrupt from the extravagances of Louis XV, and taxation was increasing throughout the country.

The new monarchs, young and immature, began their reign oblivious to the dire social circumstances of their subjects. The fantasy of their lives helped shape a new decorative style that was greatly influenced by the archeological discoveries of Pompeii. Gone were the curves of the rococo style, replaced with a classical approach to furniture design. This more refined classical design was skillfully modeled by the cabinetmakers into beautiful examples of quiet elegance.

The lines of the Louis XVI period were much lighter, and for the first time in many decades, straight, which gave the furniture a feeling of being delicate. Beauty and grain of wood became important, and therefore mahogany regained its popularity during this period. Surface ornamentation at this time was more refined in its application and was definitely used in all forms throughout the reign of Louis XVI. Porcelain plaques with classical motifs adorn the panels of many works.

The keys to this period are the straight lines and the quiet elegance of the Greco-Roman era. Legs and forms such as the cabriole are gradually straightened, which also influenced the entire structure of chairs of the period to be more angular and have straighter lines. The only curves remaining in furniture design seem to be on chair backs, where the medallion form can be seen. Perhaps the most noted structural change is the return of the stretcher, which was needed to join the now in-vogue straight chair legs as well as lyre-shaped table supports.

Inlay work gained in popularity during the reign of Louis XVI and favored floral motifs. Ormolu work was used in restrained quantities throughout most of the period, but was used in richer designs towards the end of the period.

Furniture of this period is not quite so much in demand as Louis XV furniture, but still has an ever-increasing following.

Directoire (1790–1804)

The Directoire style is basically a transitional period between the neoclassical styles of Louis XVI and the Empire period. In France following the Reign of Terror, a new spirit of patriotism emerged. Fine furniture that was once the expression of the aristocrats' wealth began to be produced by mechanical methods for the new and powerful middle class. The name of the style itself, Directoire, is derived from the governmental board of directors that ruled France during this period.

The furniture of this period shows innovative styles that characterize the internal struggle of the country. Due to the methods of construction and perhaps the newer element for which the furniture was being produced, designs are failing in elegance and display a coarseness of design not seen before the Revolution. There was a definite trend toward the classics, with both Greek and Egyptian motifs playing an important part in the ornamentation of this period. Etruscan, Egyptian, and Greek motifs abound, with hawks and sphinxes being favored in detailed ornamentation. It was a period where the true classics were embellished. The carved Greek or Egyptian head was a favored emblem that appeared at either the top of arms or legs of chairs. Furniture feet of this period resembled either animalistic or human forms. Vibrant colors were used, especially scarlet, white, and blue, which were the colors of the new republic's flag.

It was a nationalistic period when France was trying to recover from the Revolution and prove that the guillotine had totally killed the decorative arts.

ENGLAND

Queen Anne (1702–14)

Although this period bears the name of the English monarch, she was not in the least influential in the style that developed, a style that furniture designers admit to being one of the most beautiful and graceful ever to be developed.

England during the beginning of the eighteenth century was just emerging from the influences of the Stuarts. The baroque style, with its curves, was retained but modified and refined. The cabinetmakers of the Queen Anne period were concerned with translating comfort as well as elegant and graceful design into their furniture. The key note of the period is simplicity in decoration, with designs being shaped to conform more to the structure of the body. With comfort being of prime concern upholstered furniture as well as settees became very popular.

Fine woods were used in furniture construction with delicate carvings and special attention paid to detail work. Chairs were an important piece of furniture during this period. The original fiddleback splat chair underwent design changes during the Queen Anne period. The splats were eventually pierced and delicate motifs (for example, the shell) were used as carvings on the sides and legs for ornamentation. The most noted structural change in chairs of the Queen Anne period is the missing stretcher.

Besides chairs, game tables became an important piece of furniture during the eighteenth century. Elaborate designs were developed, with reversible lap tables becoming very popular. Game tables are increasing in value in today's market with the renewed interest stimulated by such games as backgammon.

The Queen Anne period chronologically ended in 1714 with her death, but design influence continued well into the reign of George I.

Georgian

The term *Georgian* when applied to furniture design is a broad phrase spanning well over a century. Up until about 1780, English furniture displayed both elegance of design as well as utility. But during the early years of the eighteenth century, English cabinetmakers showed a profound interest in the classics, taking their designs from the sixteenth-century Italian Renaissance. This period of architecture in England is known as the Palladian style. Palladino was a noted architect in Verona, Venice, and Vincenza during the sixteenth century. Large scrolls and garlands of heavy design were used as surface ornamentation during this period. It was not only furniture that was embellished during the Palladian era, but fireplaces and doorways as well as other forms of architecture, primarily for the large homes of this time.

It was not only to the classics that Georgian England turned for architectural inspiration, but also to the Orient, which had always had a lure of the romantic since the first clipper ships established trade centuries before. Lacquer was improved and new design forms were created with lighter approaches to chairs of the period.

Mahogany began to regain popularity during the second quarter of the eighteenth century, and continued to grow in usage throughout the Georgian period.

One interesting style that developed during this period was the corner chair, which remains today of increasing interest to collectors. The chair remained of great importance throughout the Georgian period, with special interest being placed on increased decoration of the typical Queen Anne chair. The seat, as well as the legs, was widened and decorated with shell or acanthus carvings. Also, the splat was pierced and eventually carved with a variety of motifs. Carved surface ornamentation was the key note of the period, with the Indian headdress, mask, or lion's face being the most popular motifs.

Storage furniture, as well as secretaries, increased in popularity. Desks, especially, were in demand during the Georgian era. Dining tables, as well as sideboards, were heavily used. Marble tops became popular, as well as small tables, used for serving.

Chippendale

Thomas Chippendale was born in 1718 and lived

until 1779. He operated a cabinetwork shop in London and published some of his original designs, as well as other cabinetmaker's works, in a book titled *The Gentleman and Cabinet-Maker's Directory*. This book was much respected during the period as a representative collection of the highest style of the times, and perhaps accounts for the reason Chippendale's name was associated with the most stylish furniture.

The period of Thomas Chippendale marks the combination of the exotic and classical, a merging of styles.

The Chinese influence in England, although popular before, was re-created under Chippendale. During previous periods, Oriental design had been limited to surface decoration. Now, not only carvings, but furniture shapes, were being influenced. Pagoda tops became popular, as well as motifs like the Chinese bell, bird, dragon, and bamboo, which were incorporated into a variety of forms.

Perhaps the Chippendale period could best be described as the closest the English ever came to the fantasy of the rococo style. Chippendale tried to carry through his fantasies with such light pieces of furniture as riotous foliage used to adorn china cabinets, the cabriole legs, and swan-necked pediments, as well as the ribbon-backed chairs. Unfortunately, the rococo style used in England was not as effective as the French, although small decorative pieces such as mirrors are more harmonious. The rococo period only accounts for one aspect of Chippendale designs between 1740 and 1780.

Chippendale's Gothic period is best described as being dominated by ornamentation. It is hard to specify one particular style at this time, because cabinetmakers of the eighteenth century liberally combined architectural details of the rococo, Gothic, and Chinese styles.

Sofas and settees of this period show a very definite French influence. In fact there is an underlying French feeling throughout the furniture of this period. Perhaps Chippendale was trying to translate the more elegant life-style of the French into English furniture. This can certainly be seen in the dining-room furniture. More intimate dining habits were instituted, and therefore gone were the large banquet suites of furniture of previous periods. Tilt-top tables, as well as dumbwaiters, were the ultimate design outcome of the mode of living change. Tables of the period were smaller, but also round, square, or oval in shape. Bookcases, as well as secretaries, became very popular furniture pieces in eighteenth-century England. Excellent examples can be found with elaborate Chinese fret-work or pierced Gothic facades.

The library became an important room of the house at this time, and therefore furniture was designed to accommodate the need. Designs for the period were ornate, and the library tables followed the custom with heavily carved ornamentation. Desks were also heavy and large in scale, especially partner's desks, although some smaller kneehole desks were made, and these are largely sought on today's market due to their light design.

Thomas Chippendale, perhaps the most famous name in furniture design in history, was a master marketing mind. It is readily acknowledged that his hand did not create the wonders that bear his name, but he is fully responsible for their success by selling their advantages to the nobility of the period. The quality of workmanship and excellence of design have made his work as popular today with collectors throughout the world as it was during the eighteenth century.

Adam

Robert Adam was an architect who brought his neoclassical ideas back to England after extensive studies and travel throughout Italy. He believed in the theory of total design and wanted not only to design homes, but all the furniture and furnishings that went into them.

England during the last half of the eighteenth century was ready for a change. George III had taken the throne in 1760, and the Chippendale styles in furniture had reigned supreme through most of the century, so perhaps a little bored, England sought a new protégé.

The excavations in Italy, especially at Pompeii, brought excitement into the staid life of the British. It became the vogue to be interested in the digs, and the wealthy actually went abroad to finance excavations on their own.

Adam was an individualist: his designs were unique to England and wholly independent of French design of the period. Ornamentation during the neoclassical period included such distinctive shapes as the winged sphinx, lyre-back chair, honeysuckle border, ram-headed capital, as well as swags with foliage, vases, and urns. One of Adam's designs, the sideboard, was developed to the extent that we use this piece today.

Unfortunately, much of Adam's original furniture was originally designed with the entire room in mind and is very large in scale and not practical for today's lifestyle.

Adam's style continued long after his death in 1792 and was gradually adapted by other cabinetmakers.

Hepplewhite

George Hepplewhite has become known not as an innovator of furniture design during the eighteenth century, but rather as promoter of the French-influenced version of Adam's designs. Hepplewhite used satinwood in his furniture designs, as well as a variety of painted decorations, among which the most noted was the insignia of the Prince of Wales, the three feathers. This design form became a popular chair back of the period. Little of original Hepplewhite furniture has survived until today due to its delicate construction.

Perhaps the most noted of Hepplewhite furniture is the shield-backed chair. In addition to his chairs, which can also be found with oval and heart-shaped backs, he favored the Pembroke table. Bookcases and chests, as well as secretaries, were important pieces of furniture during the eighteenth century in England. Hepplewhite decorated his designs with satinwood inlays, as well as with various veneers, but the majority of his work was made from soft woods (for example, rosewood and satinwood), which greatly contributed to its lack of durability.

The sideboard popularized during the Adam period continued to remain in vogue in various forms. Beautiful examples of serpentine, bowed, and straight-fronted sideboards were made in smaller sizes during the Hepplewhite period.

George Hepplewhite left his furniture designs for the benefit of other cabinetmakers in a book, *The Cabinet-Maker and Upholsterer's Guide*, which was published posthumously in 1788.

Sheraton

Thomas Sheraton, like Chippendale and Hepplewhite, influenced cabinetmakers of the day mostly through his book, *The Cabinet-Maker and Upholsterer's Drawing Book*. Unlike Chippendale and Hepplewhite, Thomas Sheraton was an author and designer alone, never having a cabinet shop of his own.

Sheraton, like his predecessor, Hepplewhite, used painted decorations in his designs, as well as classical motifs, columns, and medallions. Chairs of the Sheraton period have rectangular backs, although the splats do contain delicate urn and heart designs. One of the most popular chair designs of the period was the lyre-back motif.

The French influence is evident in Sheraton's designs. Painted decorations almost always followed a floral motif, although mahogany and satinwood were also used in construction. Furniture was elegant during the Sheraton period, with a French influence that gradually reduced the proportions. Small tables, many having lyre supports, were very popular and served a variety of uses in the drawing room. Desks increased in popularity during the Sheraton period, and some truly fine examples of exquisite workmanship can be found.

Thomas Sheraton left a legacy through his writings that influenced not only England, but the Colonies as well, to continue the refinement of furniture design.

Victorian

Queen Victoria took the British throne in 1837 and reigned until 1901. The furniture that has become known by her name started to be produced several years before she ascended the throne and continued several years after her death.

It is interesting to note that it is only in the past several years that any interest has been shown in this period of furniture production. Scholars and historians of the great furniture periods all readily admit that, as a whole, Victorian furniture is large, overdecorated, and offensive to the eye. Perhaps the initial interest shown in Victorian furniture should be traced to two motives: first, it was in great supply and, secondly, it was cheap.

Comparing this style with the other greats of furniture history would clearly be an insult, and I shall basically evaluate the style on its own. Perhaps in several hundred years, future generations will be more qualified to expound on the quality of design when compared to present periods.

Basically, Victorian furniture is not antique, but because of the large demand for items of this period, plus the fact that they are sold as antiques in today's market, the period will be dealt with in this chapter.

There are three basic types of Victorian furniture:
1. *Very Large and Ornately Decorated Furniture*
These pieces are not readily available because either they were designed as part of a particular Victorian room, remain or are too large to move, and therefore would have no place in today's smaller homes or apartments.
2. *Highly Carved, but Smaller Furniture*
These smaller pieces of Victorian furniture, which display tasteful carved decorations, are readily finding a market in today's antique stores and auction houses. This style of Victorian furniture is showing the greatest area of growth and promises to continue as the market for Victorian furniture grows.
3. *Undecorated Victorian Furniture*
The furniture that falls under this classification

has made up the major source of Victorian export furniture.

Few purists recognize any furniture made after 1800, which to them signals the beginning of the decline in quality. The Industrial Revolution began in England about 1795 and was in full force by 1815. Furniture of the Victorian era was basically a product of the Industrial Revolution. The first "mass-produced" furniture designs began at this time, which resulted in simpler forms as well as standardized decorations. Unfortunately, designs did not remain plain. Machines were developed that could carve, and overdecoration ensued.

Although Victorian furniture, when compared to the finest furniture of the eighteenth century, does not compare favorably, when its good qualities are considered on their own and in light of the prices asked, Victorian furniture has a definite market.

Child's wainscot chair; made prior to 1700, possibly Swedish. Courtesy The Smithsonian Institution.

Oak and yellow pine Hartford chest, dated 1680–1700. Courtesy The Smithsonian Institution.

Turned, three-corner chair. Paneled seat. Earliest type of chair, the design derived from ancient and medieval form of undetermined 16th- or early 17th-century origin. Probably brought to America by first settlers. Used in Topsfield, Massachusetts. Courtesy The Smithsonian Institution.

Maple desk on Frame American interpretation of the Queen Anne style made in Marlborough, Massachusetts prior to 1750.

American chest of drawers, c. 17th century. Courtesy The Smithsonian Institution.

Seven-paneled oak chest, New England, c. 1680–1700. Courtesy The Smithsonian Institution.

Turned table; Sudbury, Massachusetts. Courtesy The Smithsonian Institution.

Banister-back armchair painted black with gold at turnings, probably follows original paint scheme. Essex County, Massachusetts, c. 1700. Courtesy The Smithsonian Institution.

Windsor armchair brown shellac over brown paint over brick-orange-red paint of thick buttermilk type. Branded on the bottom I BURDEN, Joseph Burden, Philadelphia, Pa. working 1793–1833. Courtesy The Smithsonian Institution.

Maple side chair, stained mahogany, New England, c. 1760–70. Courtesy The Smithsonian Institution.

16th-century Spanish chest with polychrome bone inlay, on hutch stand with molded panels. Courtesy The Smithsonian Institution.

Desk on turned frame, locality Sudbury, Massachusetts. Courtesy The Smithsonian Institution.

Marquetry commode, style of Robert Adams. Courtesy Fitzwillian Museum.

179

Chippendale chair. Courtesy Fitzwilliam Museum.

French traveling toilet case; marked M. G. Paris; 19th century.

Vitrine in two parts, Dutch, 8th century.

Beautifully inlaid chest, Germany, 17th century.

Finely inlaid Dutch table, c. 1770.

Mahogany bureau with veneers of walnut and yew, England, c. 1710. Courtesy Victoria and Albert Museum.

Inside view of desk. Courtesy Victoria and Albert Museum.

Commode inlaid in Adams style, late 18th century. Courtesy Victoria and Albert Museum.

Drop-front secretaire; David Roentgen, c. 1770. Courtesy Victoria and Albert Museum.

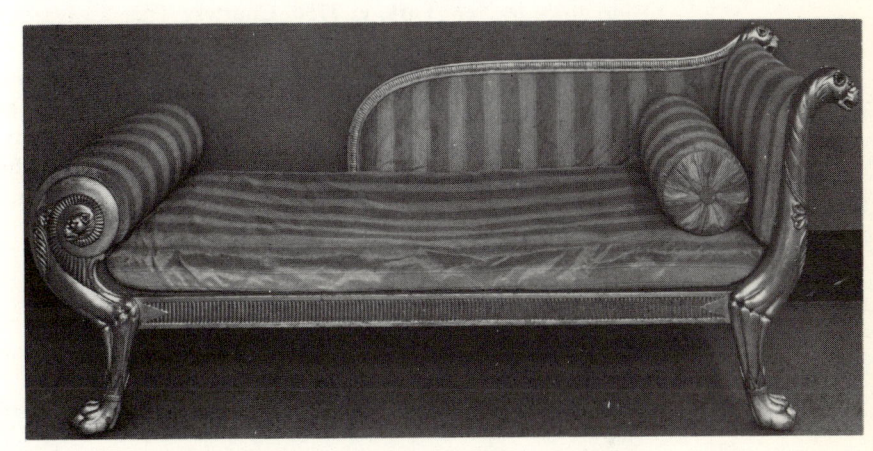

Soft, carved and gilt beechwood made by Gillow, England, c. 1805. Courtesy Victoria and Albert Museum.

Top of writing table with colored inlay by David Roentgen, c. 1770–80. Courtesy Victoria and Albert Museum.

Queen Anne side chair with Chippendale claw and ball feet. Probably made in New York, c. 1750. Courtesy The Smithsonian Institution.

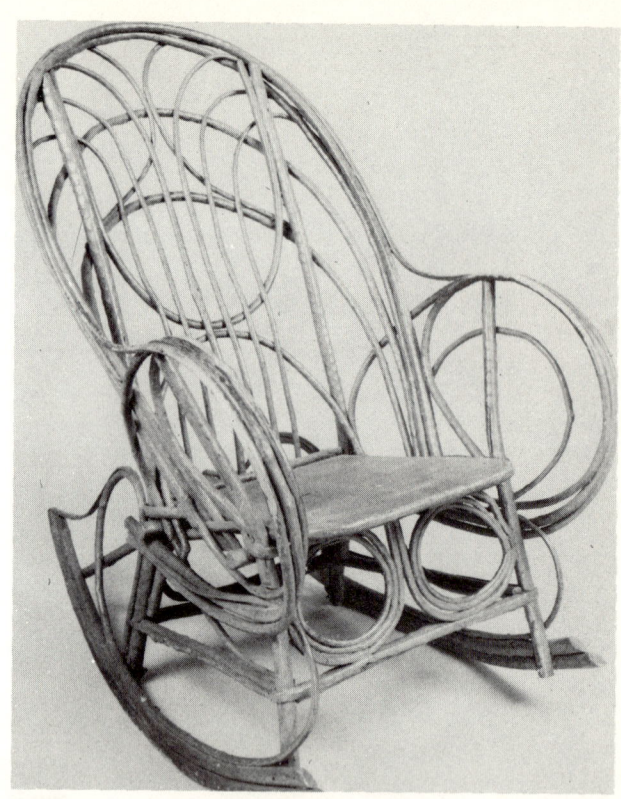

Rocking chair of soaked bent willow has been painted dark green, light green, then beige. Made in Mendoave County, California, 19th century, called a Gypsy chair in the Shenandoah Valley of Virginia. Courtesy The Smithsonian Institution.

Turned banister-back side chair. New England, first half, 18th century. The seat is coarse homespun linen or tow. Courtesy The Smithsonian Institution.

Lowboy of mahogany with accompanying bill of sale made by George J. Kilguss for Dr. C. N. Williams, Providence, Rhode Island, c. 1817. Courtesy The Smithsonian Institution.

Child's Windsor chair. Courtesy The Smithsonian Institution.

Rush-seat chair, black over original gilt decoration, probably made in New England or Ohio c. 1815. Courtesy The Smithsonian Institution.

Hepplewhite side chair with upholstered seat and painted surfaces of a type of beechwood in Philadelphia, c. 1795. Courtesy The Smithsonian Institution.

Mahogany and pine sideboard with single-string inlay. Two drawers above double cupboard with convex doors are flanked by single drawer above cupboard with single concave door. Handles of stampled brass are not original. Courtesy The Smithsonian Institution.

Scottish Pollard oak center table, c. 1840. Courtesy Portmeirion Antiques.

Chippendale style mahogany, c. 1775. Courtesy The Smithsonian Institution.

Regency rosewood brass inlaid library/games table. Courtesy W. R. Harvey, Co., Ltd.

Center table with cartouche-shaped top (left), table with oval top (right). Part of a parlor set consisting of a sofa, arm, and matching side chair, two open-back side chairs, center table, and table. Courtesy The Smithsonian Institution.

High chest, American, Framingham, Massachusetts, c. 1730-60. Courtesy The Smithsonian Institution.

Highboy in the Philadelphia manner. In three sections: (1) removable top, (2) upper case section, (3) base. This piece embodies both typical and atypical features of Philadelphia school of about 1760–1800. The absence of a projecting molding or cornice around the top of the lower section is not duplicated in the illustrated literature on highboys of this class. The pediment, though unusual, has counterparts on other Philadelphia pieces, while the carving is characteristic of the Philadelphia school. Courtesy The Smithsonian Institution.

Cottage furniture painted shades of green with trim. The name Lily painted on top in floral cartouche is that of the original owner. Courtesy Smithsonian Institution.

Pine dower chest. Floral motifs in three painted panels, one foot restored. Courtesy The Smithsonian Institution.

185

Child's side chair from Roux and Company, New York, 1888. Exposed wood frame, upholstery of cream and yellow floral stripe most likely dates from about 1920. Courtesy The Smithsonian Institution.

Black-painted tripod table, American, c. 1800. Courtesy The Smithsonian Institution.

Corner chair, Newport, Rhode Island, c. 1750. Courtesy The Smithsonian Institution.

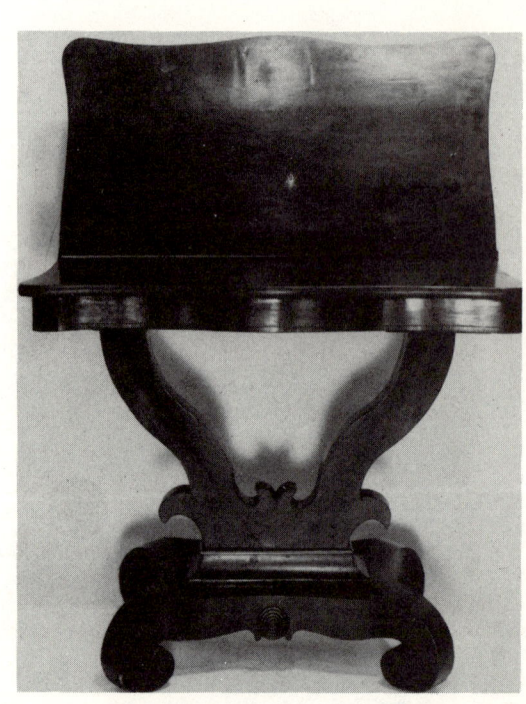

Late Empire card table, American, c. 1850. Courtesy The Smithsonian Institution.

Federal style, mahogany, Philadelphia, c. 1800. Courtesy The Smithsonian Institution.

Ladder-back chair, 18th century or early 19th century. Height 40½ inches and 41½ inches. Courtesy The Smithsonian Institution.

American desk made by Donn & Co., Washington, D.C., c. 1837–43. Courtesy The Smithsonian Institution.

Turnpet-and-cup front legs and sabre rear legs, oil on castors, support horseshoe-shaped seat and high back of the set of side chairs. The backs are created with a carved urn supported by sphinxes. Upholstered in red silk damask, c. 1876. Attributed to Allen and Brothers Philadelphia. Courtesy The Smithsonian Institution.

Pembroke type table of cherry wood made by Samuel S. Noyes, East Sudbury, Massachusetts. Courtesy The Smithsonian Institution.

12 Glass

ANCIENT GLASSMAKING

The earliest man-made glass has been documented to be in Egypt about six thousand years ago, which consisted of a thin glaze covering a stone and clay vessel. But it was not until the reign of Thotmes III (1501–1449 B.C.) in Egypt that the first hollow glass vessels were produced. Although earlier solid glass beads and ornaments were made prior to 1500 B.C., nothing of any consequence was produced during this period.

Three basic techniques were used in making glass before the first century B.C.
1. Core-forming (Sand-core method)
2. Mold pressing
3. Cutting (abrasion)

CORE-FORMING

This process was used almost exclusively on all Egyptian glassware made from 1500 B.C. to 100 B.C. The core was made from either clay or sand and sometimes held together by fibers and put at the end of a rod. This enabled the core to be dipped into the molten glass. The resulting mass was then rotated quickly on a flat, hard surface and attained both form and smoothness. After this procedure, the mass was reheated, and threaded decorations, feet, and handles were added. Now, the object was complete, and when cooled both the core and rod were removed. Core-forming remained the major method of glass production until the beginning of the Christian era when the discovery of the blowpipe made it obsolete.

MOLD-PRESSING

The earliest hollow glass vessels were produced by mold-pressing. In this method molten glass is poured directly into the mold, and then manipulated with a plunger in order to form the various objects. In fact, many versions of mold-pressing are still used today.

CUTTING

The process of cutting glass to produce vessels dates back to 1500 B.C. By this laborious task, glass ingots were carefully scraped by hand and shaped into the desired shape.

ROMAN DOMINATION, 100 B.C.–A.D. 400

Although the Egyptians in Alexandria have been credited with the development of advanced glass techniques, in reality they only adopted existing Syrian methods. The Syrians were accomplished in the production of both mold-blown and free-blown objects Such procedures as cased-cameo, millefiori, painted decorations, and mosaic were developed during this period and perfected by the skillful

Syrian craftsmen. In fact, some of these early pieces even have the maker's signature skillfully incorporated into the mold-blown design.

ROMAN BLOWN GLASS, A.D. 1-400

The discovery of the glass blowpipe at the beginning of the Christian era completely revolutionized glassmaking. It was now possible not only to produce more quantities of glass, but to vary shapes and sizes, too. The glass industry did not see another significant development until the nineteenth century, when bottle and glass-pressing machines were discovered.

ROMAN GLASSMAKING TECHNIQUES, A.D. 300-600

The craftsmen of the Roman Empire profoundly influenced both decoration and glassmaking techniques. Artisans of this period perfected such techniques as engraving, mold-blowing, cameo, gilding, enameling, threading, cutting, and millefiori. Examples of this period served as guidelines for craftsmen of the future.

THE ISLAMIC PERIOD, A.D. 600-1200

It was not until the seventh century that the glassmaking industry began a comeback following its decline after the fall of the Roman Empire. Glassmaking centered in the Middle East began to flourish again during this period in Syria, Egypt, Persia, and Mesopotania, although works of this time show strong Islamic influences. Luster staining became a well-known decoration process during the Islamic period, as well as pressing, mold-blowing, free-blowing, and new cutting techniques. Islamic craftsmen were noted for their elaborate decorations, tooling, and threading, and became highly respected for their quality of workmanship. Perhaps they are most noted for their elaborate gilding and enameling techniques. But the famous Islamic mosque lamps that display such beautiful craftsmanship combining both the enamelers' and gilders' arts came at a much later period, in the late thirteenth and fourteenth centuries.

VENETIAN GLASS

Invention and creativity were inborn traits of the Venetians. It seems incongruous that a nation that traces its origins from fishermen should excel in the arts. Glassmaking became a very important Italian industry quite early. Some of the first glass was produced as early as the fifth century in Italy, but Venice is not credited with any glass production until much later in the eleventh century. During that time, the glass industry was located on the mainland, but in 1291 the furnaces were transferred to the island of Murano by order of the Grand Council. Unfortunately, none of this early glass is known to exist today. It was not until the fifteenth century that Venetian glass attained the perfection that we associate with the name.

Venetian glassware was not always lovely and fragile art. Practical glass was produced from the very beginning. The first glass was made for the mosaic makers, and later in the fourteenth century production was geared to light houses and lanterns for galleys.

With the development of eyeglasses in the thirteenth century by Salvino d'Amato, glass was then made by the block for the various spectacle makers. During the fifteenth century, the famous colored Venetian glass was perfected. Later in the fifteenth and sixteenth centuries, enameling and gilding were popular, while it was not until the seventeenth century that marbled and variegated glass and vitro di trina were introduced. Millefiori was produced during the entire history of Venetian glassmaking, but the enameled glass of the sixteenth century shows some of Venetian craftsmen's finest work. Beautiful imitations of agate, chalcedony, and jasper ware were skillfully reproduced.

VENETIAN TECHNIQUES

Venetian craftsmen were very interested in the work of the early Romans and perfected many of their techniques to complement their own glasswares. The two most favored processes were:
1. Vitro di trina and latticinio: In this method, threads of either colored or opaque white glass were worked into a decoration.
2. Millefiori: Here, small pieces of glass are fused together to produce a mosaic design and are embedded in clear glass.

Venetian mirrors have been revered throughout the world. Many craftsmen have tried unsuccessfully to reproduce their beauty. During the fifteenth and sixteenth centuries, mirrors were small due to the fact that the process for making large sheets of glass had not been discovered. Venetian frames became works of art, richly adorned with jewels and gold or ornately carved and carefully inlaid with tortoiseshell. Production of these artistic masterpieces lasted well into the eighteenth century, when England developed a method to produce such mirrors in larger quantities, taking much of the trade away from Venice.

The once prosperous artistic island of Murano suffered drastically during the fall of the republic, from which it never fully recovered. Today, one of the greatest artistic colonies of the world still flourishes, but produces glassware primarily for the tourist and export trades.

GERMAN GLASS

Throughout the centuries, the Germans have contributed greatly to the advancement of glassmaking. During the fifteenth century, four new forms were developed that helped expand the designer's art:
1. Römer (rummer)
2. Stangenglas (Pole-glass)
3. Krautstrunk (Cabbage stem)
4. Humpen (large tumbler)

There is a definite Venetian influence noted in German glass of the sixteenth and seventeenth centuries, when profuse enameling was used. It was not until late in the seventeenth and eighteenth centuries that German glassware exhibits the engraving and cut work for which it is well known.

EARLY BOHEMIAN GLASS

The glass industry began in Bohemia during the thirteenth century and was a direct result of production in Venice. Bohemia was very fortunate to have excellent natural resources where the glass industry could flourish. Natural minerals were abundant in the mountain regions where the factories were built and still exist today.

Bohemia produced its best glass during the seventeenth century under the protection of Emperor Ferdinand III. This ware, far different from the stereotyped glass crystal exported during the eighteenth and nineteenth centuries, revealed the Venetian glass of the period in both artistic form and quality.

Bohemian glass became best known for its cutting. Contrary to common belief, not all Bohemian glass was blown. Much of the heavier pieces, especially when deep cutting was involved, were molded in wooden molds.

It was not until the last half of the seventeenth century that the famous ruby glass was produced.

Bohemian glass is characteristically very heavy. This was necessary to accommodate both the ornate style of decoration and the deep cutting. Decoration of the period centered around a main subject, which was usually a picture of a town, portrait, or even a geometric design. Also popular were naturalistic subjects, such as large bunches of flowers or fruit.

Kalligraphen ornamente, which was elegant and delicate scrollwork used together with a conventional decoration to cover the entire piece, was introduced during the late eighteenth century It was an immediate success and spread rapidly throughout Europe. The tremendous success of Bohemian glass almost ruined the Venetian glass industry, whose craftsmen up until this point had been considered masters of the art.

Late in the eighteenth century an additional new style was introduced called *Doppelwandglas*. In this form, two layers of glass were used to encase the decoration, which was held firmly between. The decorations were often etched in either silver or gold leaf. During this period, as with Venice, Bohemia was beginning to feel the competition from England and the introduction of the popular flint glass. Therefore, the Bohemian glass industry began developing novelty glass in hopes of romancing back the market. Some interesting forms of silhouette glass, milk glass, and enameling were tried.

NINETEENTH-CENTURY BOHEMIAN GLASS

It was not until the nineteenth century that Bohemia once again found a profitable market. The United States readily accepted the elaborately decorated Bohemian glass. Cased glass was popular, but yellow and ruby stains were then introduced to imitate the more expensive cased blass with the patterns cut through the stain.

FRENCH GLASS

The French were pioneers in the field of glassware. As early as the sixth century, glass dishes were used at the table. But it was not until the fifteenth and sixteenth centuries that immigrant Italian glassworkers from L'Altare and Venice established glass houses in France. Very little of this early glass exists today.

In 1688 Louis de Nehou invented a method to cast glass slates, which greatly expanded production at his father's factory, the Manufactoire Royale. Some small, ornamental glass was produced, as well as decorative plates, toys, and figurines, at several factories located at Marseilles, Paris, Nevers, Bordeaux, and Rouen, but the majority of glassware used during this period was imported from Germany, Bohemia, and England.

A Frenchman, M. Petitjean, in 1855 discovered a new method of plating mirrors by silvering the back of the glass. This process greatly increased trade in the glass mirror industry. But it wasn't until the mid-nineteenth century that the French began to look to a group of new glass artists for world-wide recognition in the glass industry. By 1900, art nouveau glass and the names of Emile Galle, Joseph Brocord, Daum Freres, and Eugene Rousseau were synonymous. A new generation of craftsmen was born and breathing life into the glass industry. By the twentieth century, Rene Lalique, François Decorcemont, Jean Sala, and Maurice Marinot had already established themselves as top craftsmen in the art glass profession, creating masterpieces in both the United States and Europe. This group of men were dedicated to the development of the art as well as new decorative techniques in which to express themselves.

GLASS AS AN INVESTMENT

Glass collecting is steadily increasing in popularity, perhaps due to the wide range of possibilities it offers collectors. The "something for everybody" concept in this field spans centuries, dating back to the early Romans up to the modern art glass of today. An interested collector can still amass a worthwhile collection that fits his individual budget. Very few antique specialties offer this possibility in today's ever-increasing market.

The addition of a piece of ancient Roman glass to any collection would be a definite asset, if not solely for the monetary value, then for the sheer mystique of owning a piece of the earliest glass ever made, but today more collectors are centering on a newer type of glassware: art nouveau. More of an art form, art nouveau was first produced during the last part of the nineteenth century and was enormously successful until the mid 1930s and early 1940s, when design trends turned to functionalism, making the ornate design of art nouveau obsolete. During this period, art nouveau glass hit an all-time low in price. One foresighted collector purchased a beautiful Tiffany table lamp for $5.00. Since this period of disfavor and today, the same lamp would be valued at upwards of $15,000. Most of the extensive collections of today were amassed over the twenty-five-year period between 1940 and 1965, when prices were low and little interest was stimulated in the art world by art nouveau. After 1966, interest increased, and prices began to skyrocket. Comparatively, prices have more than quadrupled since the late 1960s, even on commercial-grade glass, and prices should continue a gradual increase over the next several years.

UNDERSTANDING THE FORM

Art nouveau glass is purely decorative, and value is determined as in other art forms by two criteria:
1. Quality of artistry.
2. Quantity or rarity.

The majority of art nouveau glass forms were adapted from nature with botanical forms, with the vine, flower, stem, leaf, and bud being the most popular. Glass of this type was very often patterned after ancient glass and emulated precious materials of the period, such as gold, silver, onyx, mother-of-pearl, jade, and ceramic. It is characterized by being either opaque or translucent, with surface ornamentation either in the form of an insert or a simple glass on glass overlay. Surface textures were obtained by grinding, carving, or application of an acid, which produced an unusual effect.

TIFFANY

Perhaps the best-known name associated with art nouveau in the United States was Louis Comfort Tiffany, who was the son of the founder of Tiffany and Company in New York City. Tiffany lived from 1848 to 1933 and was a noted decorator and artist. He became interested in the works of the William Morris group in London during one of his many trips abroad and tried to emulate their work of reproducing the art of stained-glass windows at his own Tiffany Glass Company, which was started in 1885. Later, in 1893, Tiffany founded a second glass company, this time in Corona, New York, to produce only decorative glass, which is known as Favrile. This production was greatly influenced by a previous trip to Paris, where he met and admired the ornamental works of a contemporary, Emile Galle.

Comparing the two works, Tiffany glass had much less surface decoration than Galle, with its artistic qualities being portrayed through the density, color, and design of the individual pieces. Perhaps the most noted characteristic of Favrile glass is its iridescent colors. Favrile glass was widely copied, and collectors should carefully look for identifying signatures before purchasing. All large and medium-sized pieces were signed "Louis C. Tiffany" or "L. C. Tiffany-Favrile," while the smaller pieces merely bear the initials L.C.T.

In today's market, the leaded lampshade has become the most sought-after piece by collectors. The following is a comparative price list for various examples of Tiffany shades.

1970   *Price*

1. Lotus form carmel shade with orange and green $ 640.00
2. Crocus form shade, green and yellow $ 725.00
3. Acorn motif shade, mated green and gold $ 400.00
4. Bell-shaped shade, bronze and gold $ 300.00

1975   *Price*

1. Dragonfly dome $7,200.00
2. Lily shape, light shade bronze, amber, blue $2,000.00
3. Tulip shape $ 550.00
4. Grape shape, shade, green, red, and purple $ 450.00

1978   *Price*

1. Turtle back lamp, green $4,750.00
2. Lamp, cranberry to camphor shade $1,000.00
3. Lamp, ivy leaf, olive green, mottled $1,600.00
4. Lamp, dragonfly dome $8,500.00

Tiffany glass, in comparison with other art glass of the period, has shown the greatest increase in price and should continue to do so in the future. Prices in some areas have increased more than ten times since the late 1960s.

GALLÉ

Emile Gallé lived from 1846 to 1904 and is considered one of the greatest artisans of the late nineteenth century. The son of a glassmaker, Gallé started his career early designing glass in his father's shop, and by the age of twenty-nine he had founded his own factory in Nancy in 1878.

Gallé was fortunate to be working in a time in which there was rebellion against the stagnation caused by the Industrial Revolution. Art forms were looking back toward the Renaissance for inspiration. Eventually, designs turned to nature for freshness, originality and, above all, artistry.

By 1900, when his work was shown at the Paris International Exposition, Emile Gallé had become known as the creator of the most famous glassware school of the time within Europe.

Gallé's Four Periods: First Period

Gallé founded his factory in his home town of Nancy in 1874. During this period only transparent glass was used and colored either green or brown. Ornamental forms such as gilt and enameling were placed over the existing transparent glass. Very few innovative pieces were produced during this period, with many forms being influenced by the classics.

Second Period, 1878–84

During this period, Gallé produced some of his finest work. His work is more inspired, freer, with nature forms being his prime motif. Gallé was a master craftsman and continually experimented in his medium, glass. He eventually developed his own enameling, cutting, and engraving process that made his wares unique. Gallé's famous signature became part of the decoration.

Third Period, 1884–1904

This period is known as Gallé's colored or opaque period and his finest period of work. During this time, he developed "Moonlight" glass, a special formula where cobalt oxide is added to molten glass. As the demand for his wares grew, a new method of cutting was needed to reduce production time. Therefore, he developed "quick cutting," where acid replaced the old grinding wheel. Although this process greatly helped to reduce production time, Gallé was forced to repeat designs during the third period to keep up with the demand for his wares. Basically, during this time his wares consisted of an opaque body overlaid with various layers of translucent glass. The design was created by cutting back the various layers of glass. The colors of the third period were mostly purple, pale mauve, and varying shades of green. Signatures were placed only on plain surfaces, with some displaying a definite Oriental influence. Contrary to common belief, Gallé did not sign all of his pieces.

Fourth Period, 1904–35

After Emile Gallé died in 1904, the factory was taken over by Victor Prouvé. Although his glass was not as highly sought after by purest collectors, the factory ran successfully until 1935. During this period, a star appears just before the signature.

THE GALLÉ STYLE

Due to the popularity of Gallé's glass throughout the world, his works were readily copied. In 1900 Antonin and Auguste Daum began producing glass in the Gallé style. Both brothers were associates of Gallé at the Ecole de Nancy. All pieces made by the brothers Daum are clearly marked "Daum Nancy" and in today's market hold their own in comparison with Gallé glass of this period. Other famous glassmakers operating in the Gallé style were Joseph Brocard, who tried to revive the art of enameling, and Eugène Rousseau, who, like Brocard, attempted the revival of enameling but in the Oriental style.

During the first quarter of the twentieth century, several other Gallé-influenced workshops began to flourish. Perhaps the most productive were DeVez and Walter, whose works are readily available in today's market. But collectors agree that the best work of this period was done by G. Argy-Rousseau. At present, glass made by DeGuy is moderately priced for signed pieces, and $150 will be adequate for a good piece.

It is interesting to note that, while Gallé's first period is generally considered to have produced his lesser work, pieces for this period are not much lower than for his later works. Rarity is directly responsible for the high prices that works of the first period command. Therefore, it is easier to understand why. Signed works of Gallé's contemporaries who produced on a larger scale are worthless in today's market.

Noted Art Nouveau Artist Glass Makers

Louis Comfort Tiffany	New York	1848–1933
Karl Koepping	Dresden/Berlin	1848–1914
Auguste Daum	Nancy	1853–1909
Victor Prouvé	Nancy	1858–1943
Rene Jules Lalique	Paris	1860–1945
Emile Gallé	Nancy	1864–1904
Antonin Daum	Nancy	1864–1930
Josef Emil Schneckendorf	Darmstadt	1865–1949
Otto Vittali	Munich/Frankfurt	1872–
Val St. Lambert	Belgium	1872–

COLLECTING ART NOUVEAU GLASS

Any collector of art glass should not be unduly intimidated by the name of the great masters Gallé and Tiffany. Works by these men are readily available in today's market, and serious collectors should concentrate on purchasing these pieces while they are still financially a good investment. While staggering prices are quoted for Tiffany wisteria lamps at $30,000 by Sotheby Parke Bernet, astute collectors can still find smaller items for around $100. By comparison, the lesser-known makers' works are demanding almost as high prices as Gallé and Tiffany.

It is wise to select a respectable dealer who is familiar with the art glass market and deal exclusively through him. Also, the auction catalogs on glass issued by Sotheby Parke Bernet, Christie's, and Sotheby's are invaluable tools by which to chart the market. It should be emphasized that demand, not scarcity, seems to be greatly influencing the art glass market today.

It is also interesting to note the price difference between the European and American market for Nancy pieces. Interested collectors should establish themselves with a noted Paris dealer, since the prices are more competitive and the selection is much broader.

As with any collection, selection of the individual piece is ultimately up to the discretion of the buyer, but impulse purchasing should be avoided when pieces are being acquired for investment purposes. In the art glass market, no piece should be bought if it has been damaged in any form. Collectors should make a careful study of the forms and styles of each artist, because clever grinding methods have been used over the years to conceal prior chips and breaks. Today's market demands perfect pieces, and the collector should be forewarned.

EARLY ENGLISH GLASS

The first glass production in England dates back to the thirteenth century, when the first furnace was built near Chiddenfold on the border between Sussex and Surry. Almost three hundred years later, Jean Carré of Lorraine founded a glass factory in London at Crutched Frears. It was not until his death that Jacopo Verzelini, a native Venetian, took charge of the factory. In 1575, Verzelini received a government license to produce glass in the "Venetian style." Unfortunately, only a few authenticated pieces from this period exist today. Verzelini died in 1606, but several years previous, Jerome Bowes had taken over the management of the factory. The works remained open until 1641, but only one piece and many small fragments are its legacy.

It was not until the latter part of the sixteenth century that glass was used successfully for domestic purposes. During this time, many refugees left France due to religious problems and settled in England. Many of these people were from glassmaking families and brought with them their industry and talent. In 1664, several of these men joined together to form the Glass Sellers Company, whose charter was granted the same year in order to help promote English glass products. In 1673, George Rovenscroft established a glass factory in London and perfected the formula for leaded glass about 1685. Despite this significant breakthrough, soda glass continued to be used for basic household pieces, as well as for less expensive decorative items.

The majority of the eighteenth-century English glassware that survives today is centered on the wineglass. As the method of production became more sophisticated, varying styles were developed. Shapes of both stems and bowls changed rapidly. Of the two, stem styles were the more stable, with the baluster stem predominating in both the seventeenth and eighteenth centuries. After the baluster came the drawn, air twist, white twist, and cut stems. It is very difficult to affix an exact date, since each style overlapped the other. For example, cut stems were seen as early as 1765, but also prevalent were plain and twisted stems.

The air twist or tear is characterized by the pear-shaped air bubble within the stem. The configuration of the individual tears change according to the maker, with some being squat and fat or long and thin, as well as having their points turned either up or down. Air twist stems were popular until the last decade of the eighteenth century. About 1780 the colored twist gained popularity. It should be noted that in authentic twisted stem glasses the pontil mark is never smoothed off. Many excellent forgeries of a recent vintage have the mark completely smoothed away.

In most old glass, the pontil mark is an immediate authentication of age. Rough pontil marks always existed until the emergence of the cut stem, but even then a telltale circular depressed mark was left on the bottom of the vessel.

Toward the end of the eighteenth century cutting began to be used on stems with the majority of production occurring between 1775 and 1800. Many design modifications started to be seen, with colored bowls being mounted on clear stems as well as fluting and a beautiful color combination of two greens used for a unique bowl.

During this period, the wheel was used to create the finest surface decoration. The glass was hard, lustrous, and clear, a combination that produced beautiful end results. Pontil marks were carefully erased, leaving smooth, circular spots.

The variety of glasses was vast, and besides the wineglass form collectors can choose from ale glasses, goblets, dram glasses, rummers, ciders, and mugs. Unfortunately, the American market has little of the great variety to offer collectors of early English glasses. Therefore, selection of an English dealer is imperative for the serious collector.

Beautiful candlesticks were made out of clear glass with their shape patterned after the stems of wineglasses. Many outstanding objects were made in clear glass, for example, sugar basins, sweetmeat glasses, covered cups, pitchers, and salt cellars.

Gin glasses are avidly sought by collectors today. These small-bowled, thick-glass receptacles were made between 1736 and 1743 when the tax levied on gin was extremely high and the smallest amount of the liquor was expensive.

English glass production was not merely restricted to wineglasses. Many beautiful and richly cut glass objects were made. Many were mounted in silver or Sheffield plate. Especially beautiful were the tea caddies, with their heavy cutting and silver handles. Punch bowls of varying shapes and sizes were also produced in fairly large quantities.

Large quantities of English glass were exported to the Colonies as early as 1719. Many plainer wineglasses were sent, as well as tumblers, scent bottles, salts, scalloped, flowered, and plain decanters, mugs salvers, jugs, and finger basins. Also popular in the Colonies were punch bowls, tazzas, sugar bowls, fruit baskets, vases, butter pots, weather glasses, holy-water vessels, doorstops, and paperweights. Especially important were sets of glasses. During the Adam period, elegant chandeliers as well as wall lights were produced.

Despite its variety, a serious collector can indeed become a connoisseur of English glass.

BRISTOL GLASS

The settlement of Bristol began in about the year 1000 at the junction of the rivers Avon and Frome. It was basically a merchant community with flourishing wool, wine, and tanning industries. By the sixteenth century, Bristol began trafficking slaves to the Colonies. More than two centuries later, the traffic in slaves was still flourishing, as well as additional industries such as copper, tin, brass, and iron.

By 1696, there were nine glass houses in Bristol, and by 1761 the number had grown to fifteen. Many of these factories were confined to produce only wine bottles for export.

Besides its bottles, Bristol made a fine-quality table glass, both transparent and in beautiful colors, such as red, blue, purple, and greenish blue. Bristol red glass is characterized by its ruby hue, which was softer than the products of Bohemia. The glass was mostly decorated in gold with floral designs, which had a tendency to wear off with constant handling. Other products of interest produced by the Bristol factories were rolling pins, witch balls, flasks, mugs, pipes, scent bottles, jugs, and small, decorative objects.

Painting on glass became popular between 1762 and 1788. Much of this opaque white glass is decorated in the Chinese style and avidly sought by collectors on the Continent. American collectors of Bristol glass seem more interested in the blue glass production. Noted by its vivid royal blue color, much of the glass was decorated with white spirals. The richness of Bristol blue glass is due to the high quantities of antimony, which gives the product both its brilliance and deep rich color. Pieces of blue glass are best displayed against the light to show off their color to advantage.

The influence of the Bristol glass producers was very far-reaching. Steigel is said to have produced objects in a transparent blue glass following the Bristol tradition.

WATERFORD GLASS

Glass production in the city of Waterford was started in 1729 and stopped in 1851. Joseph Harris first started a glass house there during the first quarter of the eighteenth century, and then in 1783 George and William Penrose began their own works. In 1799, they sold their factory to Ambrose Barcroft, James Ramsey, and Jonathan Gatchell. In 1811, Gatchell became sole owner, and he continued the works until 1823, when the factory became known as Gatchell and Walpole. The firm was dissolved in 1835. In 1835, production was started under the name George Gatchell and Co. and continued until 1848. It was begun again but finally closed in 1851.

A vast amount, numbering in the hundreds of thousands, of pieces of glass were exported to the United States beginning in 1786. This quantity export lasted until about 1822.

Waterford, noted for its drinking glasses, manufactured many varied products, for example, candlesticks, cruets, baskets, cans, cream ewers, egg cups, dishes, jelly glasses, pickle jars, sugar basins, tumblers, smelling bottles, rummers, and various bowls.

Many decanters were made during the late eighteenth and early nineteenth centuries. More of these pieces are available today due to the special care they received, and provide a very interesting statement on the customs and manners of the times. They are characterized by globular bodies with ringed necks and decorative stoppers. The rings are interesting because they provided a place to grab the decanter and pour without dropping. Not all the rings were plain. Many were beautifully cut in the diamond pattern, square cut, or triangular cut. Nineteenth century decanters are basically characterized by their ribbed necks.

Not all production was for export, and many special orders were done for the nobility. This is the reason that it is possible to find undecorated pieces of Waterford, since they were made for future decoration to cover breakage in the special order services.

Much of the early glass was extremely heavy, which was needed to accept the deep cutting. The edges of these pieces were not plain and therefore displayed either the scalloped, saw-toothed or fan-shaped decoration. It is also interesting to note that much of the cutting was done outside the actual glass factories, which allowed for greater freedom in design. As with the cutting, gilding was done by traveling journeymen, although little gilding is found on eighteenth-century Waterford glass.

AMERICAN GLASS

The first settlers of the New World were forced, due to their primitive surroundings, to use pewter, leather, or wood for their drinking and domestic vessels. As the Colonies started to prosper, experimentation with glass began.

As early as 1607, the first glass furnace was begun in Jamestown, but production was limited to bottles, which were desperately needed by the infant colonies. Later production was expanded to beads, which were used for barter with the Indians.

Throughout the seventeenth century, various factories began to emerge in different Colonies. Window glass became the prime production of these factories, to replace the wooden panels and oiled paper that was presently being used instead of glass.

Much of the Colonial production was patterned after the European factories. By 1739, Casper Wistar, with his son Richard, started a factory in New Jersey that made color-striped glass in the Nailsia manner.

195

The second important name in American glass history is Henry William Stiegel who came to America from Germany and produced wares for the American market that closely imitated the large European factories. Other important names in American glass were John Frederick Amelung and Albert Gallatin. Amelung founded his New Bremen Glass works in 1774 near Frederick, Maryland, and made glass that displayed high artistic quality until 1795. Albert Gallatin established his first factory in 1797 at New Geneva, Pennsylvania, and his second factory at Greensboro, Pennsylvania, in 1807.

Fine glass was also produced during the eighteenth and early nineteenth centuries in Baltimore, Philadelphia, and Pittsburgh. The first cut glass produced in the United States was made about 1810 by a Pittsburgh firm, Bakewel & Co.

STIEGEL GLASS

William Henry Stiegel built two glass factories at Manheim, Pennsylvania, in 1765. At first production was limited to bottles, and it was not until the second factory began production in 1770 that a larger and varied glass line was made. By 1772, a large variety of wares were produced that included decanters, vinegar glasses, salt cellars, tumblers, wine glasses, cream pots, covered sugar dishes, and jelly glasses, to name only a few of the styles available.

In 1772, Stiegel changed the name of his works to "The American Flint Glass Factory." Stiegel glass was readily available in stores, and advertisement was heavily employed by the factory. Despite his heavy production and marketing practices, his finances failed and the business was sold in 1774 to a nephew of Stiegel's, George. Stiegel, a great and creative glassmaker, died a bankrupt and broken man in 1785, at the age of fifty-six.

Much of the Stiegel colored glass was produced in the "Bristol tradition." Drinking glasses were a favored production at the Manheim factory, some displaying interesting decorations. Engraving done by the Stiegel factory was accomplished by the aid of the copper wheel and diamond method.

Colored glass production ranged from "Stiegel blue" to two shades of green, one brilliant and the other very pale. The purple used varied from a bluish hue to a deep reddish. Also popular in production was a warm brown, mostly used in the early bottles, as well as a beautiful amber.

Stiegel spent his life working to produce beautiful pieces of glass that displayed artistic designs but were cheaper than the imported wares that daily flooded the American market.

CUT GLASS

Brilliant Period, 1880–1915

Designs of the brilliant period were adapted from variations and combinations of existing basic patterns. These cuts were usually applied to colorless, heavy, clear lead-glass pieces. The following basic cuts were

A. A Rhenish "Kuttrolf," of pale green color, the bulbous body with a tall neck attached by four tributaries with globular top, high kick-in base, 8½ inches. 9th century.

B. A Venetian rosewater spray, the pale yellow globular body with a divided stem and spreading U-shaped half top with horizontal ribbing and turnover edging, the reverse with a spout, high kick-in base, 9 inches. Italian, 17th century.

C. A Venetian rosewater spray, the globular body with high kick-in base, set with a divided spiral stem and spreading U-shaped neck, horizontally ribbed neck on the upper half, translucent blue edging and two crossover translucent blue tubes on the reverse, 10⅛ inches. Italian, 17th century.

D. A Venetian rosewater spray, the globular body with high kick-in base, set with a spiral divided stem below a spreading U-shaped neck on the upper half, horizontally ribbed with translucent blue edging, the reverse with a long spout, 9¾ inches. Italian, 17 century. Courtesy Alan Tilman Antiques.

the most popular: bull's-eyes, diamonds, facets, miter cuts, and flutings. Many times these basic cuts were combined to form varied motifs, and these combinations also became popular, such as the pinwheel, star, block, fan star, hobnail, vesica, and other varieties.

It is very difficult if not impossible to identify the production of any specific factory, since they all cut the same design with only minor deviations. In fact, many cutting factories bought "blanks" from European as well as American manufacturers. Therefore the same design or slightly modified version might be cut by the same shop onto blanks from many different factories.

A. A miniature Venetian ewer, the conical body flared rim with a vertical loop spout, small C-scroll handle, and a translucent blue applied ring, high kick-in base, 3 inches high. Italian, first quarter 16th century.

B. A Venetian beaker, the squat, flared body applied with two horizontal three-ply latticinio tapes, high kick-in base, 3 inches in diameter. Italian, first quarter 16th century.

C. A Venetian latticinio vase, the waisted clear body inlaid with evenly spaced vertical latticinio threads and everted rim in clear glass, inset with evenly spaced latticinio threads, high kick-in base, 3¾ inches. Italian, 16th century. Courtesy Alan Tilman Antiques.

A large Venetian tazza, the wide circular top with slightly everted rim applied with a translucent blue chain garland contained within two applied milled trailings set on a spreading turnover foot applied with a trailed band, 13½ inches in diameter, 4 inches high. Italian, early 17th century. Courtesy Alan Tilman Antiques.

A. A Venetian decanter bottle, the fluted, spreading body applied with a translucent blue vermicular collar below the angular neck and flared rim with pouring spout, set on a short, turnover foot, 6½ inches. Italian, 16th century.

B. A double-handled Venetian vase, the bulbous body waisted and pulled in, applied with alternating white latticinio vertical tapes and multispiral latticinio threads on three-quarters of the body, the shoulder applied with two horizontal rings of latticinio threads and tapes; the loop handles containing latticinio threads and applied with clear glass molded masks set on a short stem of a cushion knop and conical foot with turnover rim composed of fine latticinio threads, the knop between two collars, 8½ inches. Italian, last quarter 16th century. It is extremely rare to find this form of trailing on latticinio pieces, the complex design was called "Vetro de Trina."

C. A Venetian double-winged vase, the fluted spreading body waisted with an applied vermicular collar, set with two translucent blue scroll handles with outer clear glass pincer work, set on either side with a well-defined molded mask, terminating with a turnover circular foot, 5¼ inches. Italian, mid-16th century. Courtesy Alan Tilman Antiques.

A Venetian latticinio bowl, the shallow fluted body inset with white latticinio flattened tapes alternating with spiral five-ply tapes and multispiral opaque threads below turnover rim and radiating to the center of the short conical foot, slightly kick-in base, 10½ inches in diameter, 3½ inches high. Italian, mid-16th century. Courtesy Alan Tilman Antiques.

A. An unrecorded teapot of silver form, the bulbous body applied with loop handle with kick terminal and a long spout, set on three large lion's mask pawfeet, the domed cover surmounted by an air-beaded acorn knop, 6¼ inches. English, c. 1720. Compare with another teapot but with no feet exhibited at the Glass Exhibition, Victoria and Albert Museum, 1962. No other teapot appears to be recorded with lion's mask feet.

B. A 17th-century decanter bottle and stopper, the bulbous body with a tall, tapering neck applied with a collar and a thick strap handle with thumb rest and kick terminal, the body set with a vertical spout with short loop, high kick-in base surmounted by a teared double knopped stopper, 12 inches high, stopper chipped. English, c. 1685. Courtesy Alan Tilman Antiques.

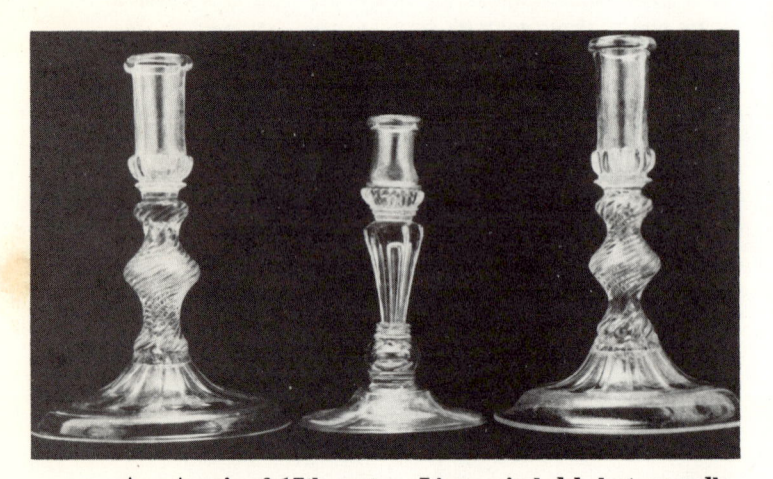

A. A pair of 17th-century Liege crizzled baluster candlesticks, each with a deep cylindrical nozzle, slightly flared rim, and gadrooned base, set on a collar over a knopped, incised baluster stem, terminating in a domed and petal-molded foot, 9 inches high. Belgium, c. 1680.

B. A baluster candlestick, the waisted nozzle with turned-in rim and gadrooned base set on a hollow, six-sided Silesian stem between triple collars and large, hollow base ball knop, terminating in a domed and panel molded foot, 8¼ inches. Soda, English, 1710. Courtesy Alan Tilman Antiques.

A. A baluster champagne glass, the ogee bowl wheel engraved with a continuous band of fruiting vine, set on a stem composed of two thin collars over a teared acorn knop and base ball knop terminating in a domed and terraced foot, 5½ inches. English, c. 1710. Formerly in the Walter Smith Collection.

B. An engraved wine glass, the deep, pan-topped bowl wheel engraved and polished with four different flower heads divided by bunches of fruit, namely two apples, grapes, and pears, set on a centrally swelling stem containing multispiral airtwist threads, terminating in a wide conical foot, 6⅞ inches. English, c. 1745.

C. A mixed twist goblet, the waisted, round funnel bowl wheel engraved with a wide band scrolling flowers and leaves below the rim set on a stem containing a corkscrew air twist cable entwined with an opaque white spiral tape, terminating in a conical foot, 7¼ inches. English, c. 1755.

D. An engraved goblet, the round funnel bowl wheel and acid engraved with a hunting scene, the riders and hounds pursuing a stag in the forefront and a village in the rear, set on a faceted stem composed on interlocking diamonds and terminating in a wide, conical foot, 7⅝ inches. English, c. 1770. Courtesy Alan Tilman Antiques.

A. A baluster goblet, the flared, drawn trumpet bowl solid at the base, set on a stem containing two angular knobs terminating in a folded conical foot, 7⅛ inches. English, 1710.

B. A massive punch bowl, the flared, ovoid body set on an inverted baluster stem containing two rows of air beads terminating in a domed foot; the bowl engraved in diamond point with the coat of arms composed of baroque and C-scrolls, among floral sprays, enclosing a stork surmounted by a crown, 9 inches. English, 1710.

C. A baluster goblet, the large, flared, round funnel bowl set on a stem composed of an annulated section over a short, true baluster and base ball knop terminating in a domed and folded foot, 8 inches. English, c. 1710. Courtesy Alan Tilman Antiques.

A. A Newcastle goblet, the flared, round funnel bowl, wheel engraved with a wine master holding a goblet and decanter bottle among barrels, below the inscription "Hansie. In. De. Kelder." enclosed on either side by continuous garland of fruiting vine, set on a stem composed on annulated knop over a teared true baluster and a base ball knop, 7⅜ inches. English, c. 1730.

B. A continental engraved goblet, the flared, round funnel bowl wheel engraved with two gentlemen shaking hands, below the inscription "Vivat Tollerantia" also engraved with two flowering trees set on a stem composed of a faceted baluster section containing red spiral threads between two faceted knops terminating in a domed and folded foot, 7 inches. Bohemian, c. 1740.

C. An Irish trade wine glass, the flared, round funnel bowl engraved with "Success to the City of Dublin" below a flowering spray set on a plain stem terminating in a folded conical foot, 6 inches, repaired stem. Irish, c. 1740. This glass appears to be unrecorded.

D. A Newcastle friendship light baluster wine glass, the flared, round funnel bowl superbly wheel-engraved with two hands shaking, set on a stem composed on a cushion knop over a long, air-beaded inverted baluster section and base ball knop terminating in a conical foot, 7¼ inches. English, c. 1730. Courtesy Alan Tilman Antiques.

A. French paperweights, c. 1850.

B. A Stevens & Williams cameo vase, by Joshua Hodgetts, the bulbous white body with an everted rim and short foot, glazed on the inside and superbly overlaid and carved in black with two birds of paradise perched in scrolling, flowering prunus branches within formal borders, 4½ inches high. English, c. 1890.

C. A Baccarat newell post dated B1848, the massive, circular body enclosing a ground of evenly spaced color millefiori canes including green shamrock, red arrowhead, yellow honeycomb, green and yellow whorl canes, these further enclosing large silhouettes of a swan, a goat, a cockerel, a goose, a dog, a horse, a man with a gun, a reindeer, a pheasant, two peahen, and a butterfly, set on a baluster stem with metal mount, 5½ inches in diameter, 9½ inches high. French. Exhibited at the C.I.N.O.A. International Art Treasures Exhibition, Bath 1973, No. 436. Reputably the largest overall antique millefiori paperweight recorded. Largest diameter recorded for a millefiori paperweight is 4¼ inches, classified as a magnum.

D. French paperweights, c. 1850.

E. A Tiffany paperweight vase, the globular, gold, iridescent body inset with green water lilies below the short neck, 2⅜ inches, signed "L. C. Tiffany Favrile—H.848." American, c. 1885. Courtesy Alan Tilman Antiques.

200

A. A Webb cameo vase, the baluster frosted body overlaid and carved with blue and white flowers growing from long stalks with large leaves within blue and white ringed borders, 6 inches high, impressed mark. Thos. Webb & Sons. Cameo. English, c. 1890.

B. A Webb cameo plaque, the translucent, raisin-colored body finely overlaid and carved in superb contrasting depth with apples growing from a flowering branch enclosed by a continuous leaf rim, 9½ inches in diameter. English, c. 1890.

C. A Webb cameo scent bottle, the globular red body overlaid and carved with a flowering rose branch in white silver, silver stopper, 4 inches high. English, c. 1890.

D. An opaque, enameled baluster goblet, the thistle bowl and double knopped stem terminating in a domed and folded foot, the bowl decorated in colored enamels, predominantly iron red, blue, and yellow with a circular panel of a man blowing a horn with a landscape, the reverse with a wide formal border and above a continuous floral garland, also reproduced on the foot, 6 inches. Dutch, c. 1770.

E. A color twist wine glass, the bell bowl set on a stem containing two entwined opaque white spiral tapes each edged in a deep maroon color, terminating in a conical foot, 6½ inches. English, c. 1755. This color appears to be unrecorded.

F. An engraved decanter and stopper dated 1836, the globular body and tall neck set with a molded handle below the pinched spout and set on a frosted, circular foot, the body engraved with two crests above initials and encircled by continuous garlands of flowering branches; the neck with three rows of fruiting vine and the inscription "Lord Arthur Hill to I. Lushington Reilly Esq.," 10⅜ inches. English, 19th century. Courtesy Alan Tilman Antiques.

A. A Clichy swirl, set with alternating swirling deep purple and white tapes centered by florette of blue whorl and red and white star canes, 3¼ inches.

B. A Clichy close millefiori, the evenly spaced ground composed of brightly colored pastrymould florettes, including many pink roses and moss canes, contained in a basket of alternating pink and white staves, 3¼ inches.

C. A Clichy pansy, set with two large, purple petals above three pale yellow ones with purple veining and green center, growing from a green stalk with five leaves and a bud set on a swirling white latticinio ground, 3 inches.

D. A Clichy turquoise-color ground, set with a quartrefoil garland of alternating pale pink and green and pink pastrymould florettes, the loops divided by larger burgundy red, pink, and white pastrymould florettes centered by a large, white rose, 3⅜ inches.

E. A Clichy chequer, set with two circles of brightly colored pastrymould florettes centered by a large, pink rose, and divided by short lengths of white latticinio tubing, 3⅜ inches.

F. A large Clichy chequer, set with two rows of large pastrymould florettes centered by a large, pink rose and divided by short lengths of white latticinio tubing, 3⅜ inches. Courtesy Alan Tilman Antiques.

A. A St. Louis fruit, set with two pears, one unripe, an apple, and four cherries, among green leaves set on a swirling, white latticinio basket, 2⅝ inches.

B. A Baccarat butterfly over a flower, the faunae with colored marbled wings, translucent amethyst body, black head, blue eyes, and deep blue antennae hovering over a large double white clematis with pointed veined petals and yellow honeycomb center growing from a pale green stalk with six green leaves and a bud, star-cut base, 3⅛ inches.

C. A Baccarat pear, the naturalistically modeled fruit growing from a green branch with three green leaves and set in clear glass, 2⅝ inches.

D. A St. Louis vegetable, set with two turnips, a carrot, a radish, and two beetroots, set on a double swirling latticinio ground, 3 inches.

E. A large Baccarat primrose, the flower with five recessed white petals, with red interiors centered by two rows of white stars and a pink whorl, growing from a deep green stalk with eleven leaves, star-cut base, 3¼ inches.

F. A Baccarat apple, the large, shaded, pink fruit growing from a short, green stalk, with six leaves in clear glass, 2⅝ inches. Courtesy Alan Tilman Antiques.

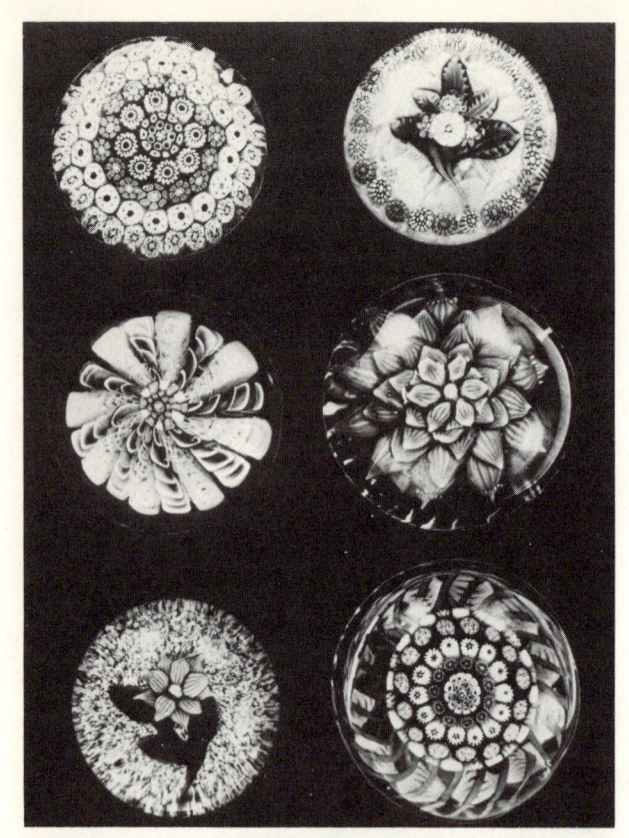

A. A St. Louis concentric millefiori, inscribed S.L.1848, set with five rows of colored canes, predominantly in blue, pink, and white with arrowhead canes, and a green hollow cogwheel center, 2⅝ inches.

B. A St. Louis crown, set with alternating red and white twisted tapes with white edging divided by white latticinio spiral threads, centered by pink, white, and green canes, 2⅞ inches.

C. A St. Louis double pink clematis, the pointed, striped pink petals with yellow center growing from a green stalk with three leaves set on a green and white jasper ground, 2¼ inches.

D. A St. Louis flat bouquet, set with four colored, stylized flowers, set on five green leaves enclosed by a garland of alternating blue and white and pink, white and blue canes, the whole set on a white latticinio ground, 2⅝ inches.

E. A St. Louis dahlia, set with the five rows of pink and mauve petals with blue veining centered by a blue, white, and orange cogwheel center, with five green leaves at the edges, star-cut base, 3 inches. It is rare to find a dahlia with this color combination.

F. A St. Louis mushroom, the evenly spaced tuft composed of four rows of color canes, centered by pink and white and green hollow tubes, encircled around the base by royal blue spiral tapes, star-cut base, 3 inches. Courtesy Alan Tilman Antiques.

A. A St. Louis red bouquet, set with a large, red, five-petaled clematis with a similar blue, white, and yellow one enclosed by green leaves encircled around the base with a thick, pink, solid cable enclosed by a white latticinio multiple tape, star-cut base, 2¾ inches. It is rare to find a cable of this form.

B. A Baccarat white wheatflower, set with two rows of pointed petals with blue spots centered by a circle of red and white stars enclosing blue and red arrowhead canes, growing from a short, green stalk with seven green leaves, star-cut base, 2⅝ inches.

C. A Baccarat faceted buttercup, the yellow flower with interlocking petals growing from a short, green stalk with yellow bud and six leaves encircled by a garland of white stars and pink whorls, alternating with blue and white canes, the sides cut with three rows of angular facets, star-cut base, 2⅜ inches, cut down.

D. A Baccarat tulip bouquet, set with three white tulips and two deep pink ones growing from three green stalks with four leaves, star-cut base, 3 inches.

E. A Clichy pansy, set with two large, purple petals above three smaller, yellow ones with markings growing from a green stalk with a large, purple bud and numerous leaves in clear glass, 2¾ inches.

F. A Baccarat white camomile, the flower with interlocking petals and yellow stamen center with two large buds growing from a short, green stalk with five leaves encircled by a garland of pink and white with blue and white canes, star-cut base, 2⅝ inches. Courtesy Alan Tilman Antiques.

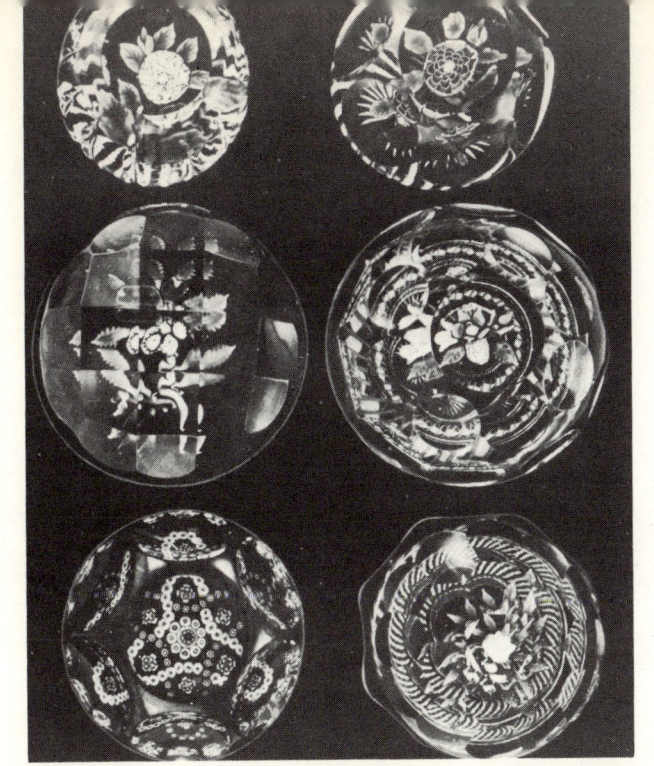

A. A Baccarat two-colored camomile, the flower with interlocking blue and white petals with yellow stamen center growing from a short, green stalk with six leaves and red buds, the sides with vertical shaped cutting, star-cut base, 2½ inches, recut.

B. An unrecorded St. Louis Pansy, set with two large, purple petals above small, blue and white ones with arrowheads centered by an orange, blue, and white cogwheel, growing from a green stalk with eight leaves and a deep purple bud, the sides cut with eight circular windows and the top with interlocking squares, 3¼ inches. This flower in some ways resembles an early Baccarat pansy.

C. A Baccarat translucent green overlay, set with two entwined trefoil garlands, one of white stars and green whorls, the other red and white pastry mold florettes enclosing blue, green, and red arrowhead canes, the sides cut with six circular windows above continuous thumb flutes and a large, circular top window, 3⅛ inches.

D. A Baccarat rust-red camomile, the interlocking petals with yellow stamen center growing from a short, green stalk with six green leaves and a red bud, the sides cut with six circular windows and a larger top window, star-cut base, 2¾ inches.

E. A St. Louis upright bouquet, set with a red, white, and blue flower and two florettes enclosed by green leaves enclosed by blue spiral threads, the sides cut with three rows of circular windows, 2⅜ inches.

F. A St. Louis faceted upright bouquet, set with a central double white clematis surrounded by blue, orange, and red flowers with three florettes and numerous green leaves encircled by a translucent pink and opaque white multi-ply spiral cable, the sides cut with eight circular windows and the top with interlocking facets, 3 inches. Courtesy Alan Tilman Antiques.

A. A continental two-colored beaker, the flared, translucent amber body, with a faceted pink knopped lower half, star-cut base, 3⅞ inches. Bohemian, c. 1860.

B. A Lithyalin tazza, by Friedrich Egermann, the fluted circular top set on a waisted, faceted baluster stem terminating in a circular, faceted foot, the whole composed of marbled green and brown glass, 3½ inches. Bohemian, c. 1830.

C. An enameled beaker, painted in the manner of Anton Kothgasser, the clear glass flared body painted with a cupid in a cage on a green, grassy mound, with broken trophies of war; namely arrows, a bow, and sheaf between gilt and amber borders, the solid base with a continuous cut band amber flash and star-cut base, 4¾ inches, c. 1840.

D. A Lithyalin scent bottle and stopper, by Friedrich Egermann, the faceted body of mushroom form with a waisted, faceted neck and stopper set on a multisided foot, the whole of brown and purple marbled glass applied with gilt bands, 3¾ inches. Bohemian, c. 1830. Courtesy Alan Tilman Antiques.

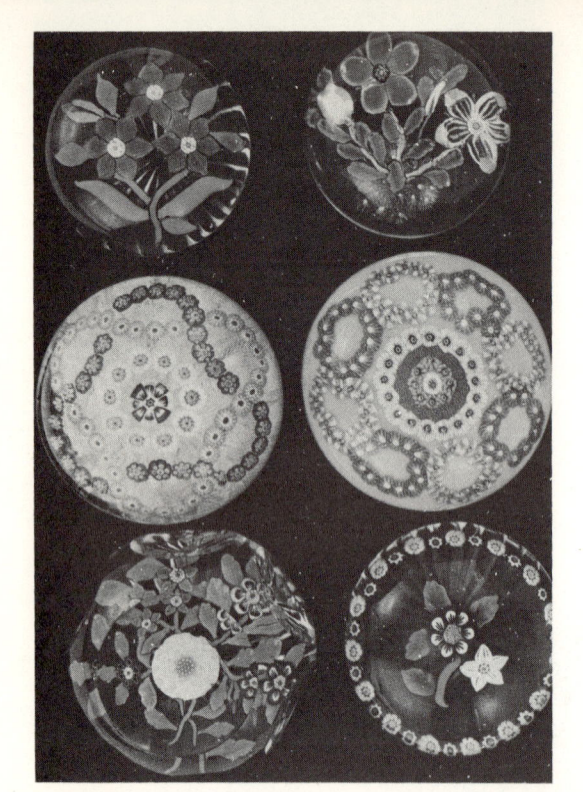

A. A Stevens & Williams vase, designed by W. Northwood and carved by B. Fenn, the tapering turquoise body with a tall neck containing an angular knop and flared rim, overlaid and carved in white with two large flowers among branches and leaves; the reverse with long fern leaves, the knop carved with flower heads between white rims, 11½ inches, impressed mark Stevens & Williams Stourbridge Art Glass. English, c. 1887.

B. A Stevens & Williams cameo oil lamp, the tapering, cylindrical body in translucent yellow overlaid and carved with flowering rose branches and leaves, the reverse with a thrush perched in a short, flowering branch, set on a small, circular foot carved with a formal border, gilt metal base and fittings, 13½ inches high. English, c. 1890.

C. A Stevens & Williams cameo bowl, the squat, angular, translucent pink body superbly overlaid and carved with two peaches and two apples on flowering branches, formal border around the rim, and with a thick yellow leaf band around the top rim, 3¼ inches high, 4⅛ inches in diameter. English, c. 1885.

D. A Webb cameo vase, the bulbous turquoise vase with short neck and flared rim, overlaid and carved in white scrolling flowering prunus within white borders, 6½ inches. English c. 1890.

E. A Stevens & Williams cameo vase, the translucent lime green conical body overlaid and carved with a large poppy among leaves, stalks, and four buds, the reverse with a butterfly and dragonfly set on a short, circular foot, 12¼ inches, impressed mark, Stevens & Williams, Stourbridge Art Glass. English, c. 1890. Courtesy Alan Tilman Antiques.

204

A. A Baccarat clematis bouquet weight, set with three single, six-pointed, petaled blue flowers centered by two rows of white stars with a green whorl, growing from green stalks with numerous leaves and a bud, star-cut base, 2¾ inches. French, c. 1850.

B. A Baccarat patterned millefiori, set with two entwined trefoil garlands, one red, white, and blue canes, the other green, white, and red, enclosing a circle on pink and white canes and centered by a large florette of red and green arrowheads set on a domed ground of white latticinio, 2¾ inches. French, c. 1850.

C. A Baccarat faceted bouquet, set with a large central white pompon, the interlocking petals centered by yellow and white stamen surrounded in a horseshoe arrangement with a red and blue imaginary flower, two mauve single clematis, a blue and white early pansy, and a blue and white flower with red arrowheads and a blue bud growing from a green stalk with numerous green leaves, the sides cut with six oval windows and a large circular one on the top, star-cut base, 3⅝ inches. French, c. 1850.

D. An unrecorded Clichy bouquet, set with a large white rose, a pink daisy with five pointed petals centered with a red, green, and white pastrymould florette and an imaginary flower, the five pointed petals with red stripes and yellow tips, centered by white and pink canes, the flowers growing from green stalks with numerous green leaves with a clump of moss canes at the base, set in clear glass, 2¾ inches. French, c. 1850.

E. A Clichy color ground, set with alternating, irregular circles on green and white canes and pink, white, and green ones, enclosing three concentric rows of red, white, and blue canes, the whole set on a rich turquoise ground, 3⅝ inches. French, c. 1850.

F. A Baccarat bouquet, set with a white flower the seven rounded petals with red edging and large, blue arrowheads with a yellow honeycomb center growing from a green stalk with four green leaves, set to one side of a white single clematis with pointed petals with yellow and red star centered cane encircled with an alternating garland of red and white, green and white, and red pastry molds, star-cut base, 3 inches. French, c. 1850. Courtesy Alan Tilman Antiques.

A massive engraved goblet, by James Couper & Sons, the large, cup-shaped bowl wheel engraved and polished with a view of ships passing under a bridge with buildings on either bank within a rectangular frame and above the inspection "Flow On River Majestic," the reverse with the inspection "Presented to G.S. 1876" set within a floral garland; the bowl cut with a wide band of interlocking flat diamonds and set on a hollow faceted stem terminating in a circular, star-cut base, 12¾ inches. English.

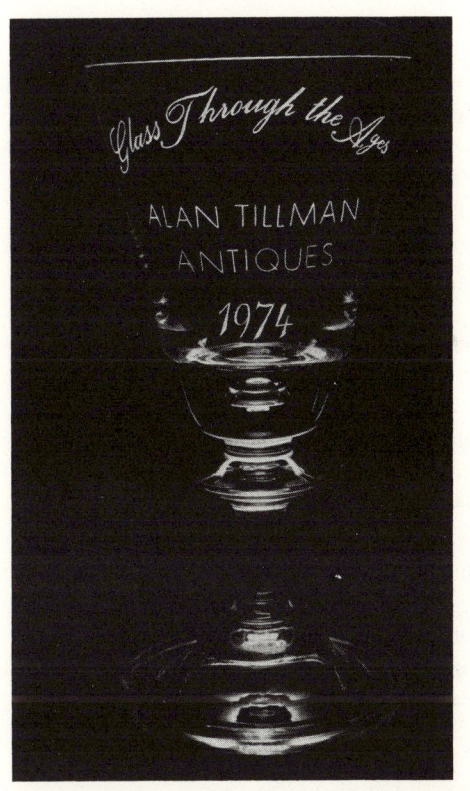

A Hadeland baluster goblet, signed and dated "Michael Conway 1974," the flared, round funnel bowl teared and solid at the base set on a stem composed of a wide, angular knop, over a straight section, the bowl engraved in diamond point "Glass Through the Ages," Alan Tilman Antiques, 1974, terminating in a domed foot, 6¾ inches. Norwegian, c. 1974.

13 Paperweights

GLASS PAPERWEIGHTS: A COMBINATION OF ART AND GLASS

The Egyptians have been credited with the discovery, development, and initial design of the glass paperweight. The designs of this period, mainly decorative and religious, demonstrated the role paperweights played in their culture. The initial construction required a simple, clear-glass magnifying lens placed above a glass design to round out the construction of a paperweight.

Toward the end of the seventeenth century with the development of lead glass by Ravenscroft more intricate designs were used in the manufacture of paperweights. Designers realized that various motifs were enhanced and made more intricate by the magnifying and light-refracting properties of the thicker glass lens. Continued refinements in the development of the glass paperweight have been traced throughout Europe in the middle of the nineteenth century.

The most noted period in paperweight production began in southern Europe, especially Venice, around 1842 and is better known as the classical period. The next ten years saw the development of the art in Bohemia and France around 1851. The American cycle began and ended within the next ten years.

The flourish of the classical period is followed by a period of decline both in the quantity and quality of the paperweights that were produced. The beginning of the 1870s saw a revival in the art with the production of the three-dimensional form. Since this time there has been a fluctuation at various times in the worldwide production of paperweights.

The paperweight industry has been in a current worldwide revival since World War II. The current success being enjoyed by the industry is due to a revival by glass artists who have brought back the flat millefiore designs of the classical period combined with the three-dimensional flora and fauna of the postclassical period.

For centuries collectors have been recuring paperweights from neglected household objects. The first noted collectors were members of royalty. Some of the more noted collections were made by the Empress Eugenie, Empress Carlotta of Mexico, and King Farouk of Egypt. The famous French crystal factories at Baccarat, Clichy, and St. Louis are noted for their paperweight production. Many factories such as Bacchus in England, the Bast of Sandwich Company, and the new England Glass Company produced special lines of paperweights, but most other factories produced paperweights made by glassworkers in their spare time.

Hamp working refers to the production and styling of the leaves and additional small parts that make up the integral parts of the designs from rods of glass. They are assembled by the aid of a torch or Bunsen burner. A worker would assemble the floral motif at home and reserve it until it could be reheated and eventually enclosed in glass at the factory.

"Off-hand" paperweights, not officially produced by the factory, were often made by the glassworkers as anniversary or wedding presents. This method of production was very often sanctioned by the factory as a method of development of skills during prosperous times. As management saw declining profits from its paperweight sales, the "off-hand" production was stopped because it used the expensive colored glass of the factory.

It takes several months to make a millefiore paperweight from the first bundling of the rods to making the first cane through the final annealing. The famous Baccarat factory in France reports that it takes between three and four months to produce a stock of canes sufficient to make 150 millefiore paperweights. Each weight contains between 180 to 200 canes. The actual construction of one weight took seven hours, and these were simple, close millefiore paperweights.

Historically, glassmaking has been done in secrecy. The medieval glassmakers of Venice were housed ilke princes on the island of Murano, and forbidden to leave their seclusion or tell their secrets on pain of death. Today, the average tourist is encouraged to view the glassblowing practices on Murano, but the formulas are still carefully guarded. Paperweight-making is perhaps the most secretive section of the glass industry.

The most striking aspect about paperweights of the classical period is the process of alternate diminution and enlargement. The canes are begun large, then pulled out to minute cross section. This is again enlarged by a convex lens of the crown and reduced by the concave curvature which produces a series of reverse transformation resulting in increasing mystification of the eye.

What is the inside mystery surrounding the paperweight? The answer of colored glass hardly satisfies anyone. The interior mystery continues and is enhanced by the continuity of the single refractive index. As we look into the center trying to determine the true dimension and composition we are unable to rely on our senses.

Over fifty thousand paperweights of collector's quality have been produced, but not more than one-third have survived. Museums and private collections now house most of the best examples. Collecting trends indicate that within the next several years most of the best examples of paperweights will be off the market. Today paperweight collecting has become a symbol of status.

NINETEENTH-CENTURY VENETIAN MILLEFIORE PAPERWEIGHTS

The first paperweights of this period are described as the Venetian ball. This design can be compared as waste filigree, canes, and aventurine, which has been picked up with a gather of clear glass and eventually covered with a thin glass coating.

The production of these paperweights started in 1843 and ran less than a decade, and the level of sophistication was never comparable to the contemporary French or Bohemian factories.

The major distinguishing feature of paperweights from other millefiore production is the magnifying crown, which is made of clear glass and covers the inside material. The crown focuses the design and adds to the mystery.

Venetian scrambled weights are made from soda-lime glass, which is unclear, tinted, and often can look wet or watery. The designs often were placed very near the surface, which is rough and mottled. A study of the surface of these weights shows that Venetians of this period did not fully realize the effect they were trying to create. Many experts cite this failure to discredit the Venetians with the discovery of the classic paperweight, although it is agreed that the revival of the millefiore production must be credited to the Venetian Renaissance.

BOHEMIAN PAPERWEIGHTS

The subject of Bohemian paperweight-making has been largely neglected, because many examples have been difficult to distinguish from the Venetian production.

Paperweights from Bohemia are classified to be contemporary to the Venetian and French works of the classic period. Glass scholars of today studying the production from this area feel the designs are much closer to the French than the Venetian work of the period.

Bohemian paperweights, as all glass produced in this country, which is known as the present-day Czechoslovakia, are noted for excellent design as well as charm and the highest workmanship.

BOHEMIAN-SILESIAN MILLEFIORE PAPERWEIGHTS

Although the first dated paperweights did not appear until 1848, there is reason to believe that Bohemian production was started several years earlier. By 1846 there were excellent French examples to copy, and Bohemian style has always emulated these designs. Glass scholars still argue over the theory of who influenced whom. It is impossible as yet to determine in which direction the initial ideas and innovations in the paperweight industry were being channeled either between France and Bohemia or the reverse, although the great French crystal factories of this period were noted for their foreign interpretations and adaptations to fit the French trade of the time.

Bohemian paperweights are distinguished by two individual shapes. Both basic shapes have a flat base rim with a shallow concavity. It must also be noted that some overlays display flat bottoms. The glass used in production is lime-potash, which is harder and lighter than true lead glass. Lead glass, when used, can often remain slightly yellowish.

The millefiore production of this period was relatively simple. The basic construction was centered around six or more rods centered about a relatively larger rod. The characteristic rods of this period were shaped like tiny flower petals. Another popular motif was crimped or plain tubes, star-centered or marked in the Baccarat method with a small arrow.

The colors used in the millefiore canes is extensive and of a softer tone than used by the Venetians. Although a full range of colors were used in Bohemia at this time, in comparison to the French their production colors were slightly less brilliant. Important colors of the period were pink, scarlet, and a deep wine red, dark green, light and cobalt blue, pale yellow, lavender, and various pale hues. It should be noted that, where reds and greens were used, they are frequently dense in comparison to the application of the other colors, which was very often very lightly applied.

FRENCH PAPERWEIGHT MANUFACTURE

It is not surprising that the French, famous for centuries for their excellence in crystal and glass design and production, became the world's leading paperweight producers between 1843 and 1848.

These manufacturers took the original Bohemian models, perfected them, expanded them, and introduced such new designs as lampwork flora and fauna.

The French classical period has contributed an enormous selection of designs, which far exceeds the amount of designs produced by other countries at this time. The silhouette and millefiore canework was more delicately produced, and the new flowerwork was, in fact, a native art that at this time had no foreign counterpart. Although many flowers were used in the decorative arts of France during the nineteenth century only two basic flowers can be seen regularly in French paperweights—the pansy and the famous symbolic Clichy rose. This lack of variety in the flowers seen in paperweight production when many different flowers can be seen in the decorative history of the country may be attributed to the difficulties in the growth of the new paperweight industry in France.

Baccarat

This world-famous French crystal factory had its origins as a small glassworks that was established in 1764. For the next several years, until 1815, the mainstay of its production centered around industrial glass. The small factory underwent some struggles between management and existing economic conditions to emerge in 1822 as a well-established producer of first-quality glassware. Baccarat's reputation grew through the enthusiastic acceptance of new and innovative designs at the Paris exhibitions. The entire paperweight era lasted barely a decade, from 1845 to 1855. Unfortunately, little is known about their public acceptance, since paperweights were considered a very small part of the glass production of the factory. In fact, the only production records that remain seem to be the dated paperweights.

As with all paperweight manufacturing, great secrecy has always surrounded their production, and Baccarat is no exception. In fact, revival of the craft seems to coincide with the old masters' deaths, who very often took their secrets to the grave with them, and a renewed interest showed by the public. New blood with fresh ideas seemed to keep the old craft alive through the centuries. For example, late in October 1951, a dated Baccarat paperweight was found imbedded in the cornerstone of a church bombed during World War II. This discovery spurred renewed interest in paperweight production.

Markings

Less than one half of all Baccarat paperweights are either signed or dated. Most dated weights are also topped with the letter B. The dates most common to the production were 1846, 1847, 1848, 1849, 1853, 1858; these were usually marked in either blue, green, or red and appear at the end of the opaque white rods that have been fused together. The B stands for the factory name, Baccarat, since individual artists were not allowed to sign or date company-produced paperweights.

It is possible to find a Baccarat paperweight that is only dated and does not carry the factory mark B, although these examples are the exception to the rule.

Millefiore Canes

Due to the extensive variety of the colors and forms used in the Baccarat canes, it is very difficult to make any general characterization. If a Clichy and Baccarat-close millefiore paperweight were compared, it would be noted that they displayed great similarities in both cane parts. Perhaps the only dissimilarity would be seen in the coloring. The Clichy weight would show a warmer tone and the Baccarat would appear to be cooler.

Baccarat is famous for such rods as the arrowhead, star, trefoil, honeycomb, and quatrefoil. The star, perhaps the most famous of the Baccarat rods, shows a great deal of sophistication in both color and size.

Silhouette Canes

Silhouette canes seemed to be popular at Baccarat, and among the most successfully produced were the squirrel, dog, horse, elephant, goat, monkey, rooster, dove, crane, pheasant, swan, and pelican. Also popular were the butterfly or moth, dancing devil, hunter with a gun, and assorted flowers.

The most popular colors used were plum, white and blue, and red, but black was almost never executed.

St. Louis

St. Louis and Baccarat have, since their foundation, remained arch rivals in the field of paperweight production. St Louis was established in 1767, only three years after Baccarat. Essentially, the factory gained its reputation by winning the French Academy of Sciences prize for crystal that equaled the quality being produced at the time by both England and Bohemia under the patronage of the king. By 1788 the factory had become successful and employed more than seventy workers. The factory's name was officially changed to Compagnie des Crestallerus de Saint-Louis in 1829, as the production became more specialized. With the introduction of multicolored, overlaid glass in 1830 was the first production of paperweights. Although the first dated cane is 1845, glass experts feel that experimental production was started around 1830. St. Louis, like its arch rival, Baccarat, expanded its reputation by exhibiting at the famous Paris expositions of 1834, 1839, 1844, where paperweight manufacturers were displaying their production. St. Louis has continuously made a line of paperweights, but the post-World War II prosperity saw a very successful revival of the art.

It is difficult to stereotype St. Louis shapes because they show a lot of variation, but many resemble Clichy paperweights. The basal rim thickness tends to vary from a wide to fairly thin edge, and this variation is also seen in the basal depth. St. Louis is famous for the glass used in its weights. The main characteristics are its very clear appearance, extreme heaviness, and high refractive index. The bases are usually cut with bouquets, floral groupings, and the favorite mushroom. Very little distortion is noted in these paperweights, since the designs are usually set very low, which also allows viewing from a variety of angles.

Markings

The most common marks of the St. Louis production are from 1848 and were done in cobalt blue, red, deep purple, and a mauve. They were marked with the letters "S.L." in either blue or black, located just above the figures. Several of the more popular weights that were dated were the mushroom, center silhouette canes, and concentrics. It is very often that you may find some concentrics that have been marked with the "S.L." but that are not dated.

Canes

The variety of canes produced by the St. Louis manufacturers were far less than those made by its arch rivals, Clichy and Baccarat, which makes classification of the paperweights much easier. The rods are usually composed of tubes, stars, or a variation of the star, called a crimp, which is a blossom resembling a six-petaled rod.

Perhaps the best-known trademark of the St. Louis production is the crimped, coglike cane.

Silhouette production was making use of such fauna as a dog, either an unshorn poodle or mutt, the walking duck with duckling, or the rubber-kneed camel, just to mention several of the most popular motifs used, as well as the much-produced stylized flower. Some additional canes that were used showed two dancing girls or a dancing couple. One of the most dramatic motifs was of the skating red devil.

Coloring

The most notable thing about the colors over the opaque white base color in the St. Louis weights is that they are defined, clean, and extremely luminous. Perhaps this harmonious use of both color and design have kept the production from the St. Louis factory at the top of the craft.

Clichy

The factory at Clichy, a suburb of Paris, was founded around 1837 and was the newcomer compared to the firms of St. Louis and Baccarat, which were both founded in the eighteenth century. The almost immediate acceptance of the Clichy products at the Paris exhibitions caused alarm at the older, more established houses of Baccarat and St. Louis. With these houses paperweight production was only a small part of their line, and most experts feel that by 1849 the new factory at Clichy had become the number one producer of paperweights in France. In fact, the almost overnight success at Clichy caused expansion at the factory in order to accommodate sales potential.

1849 saw the invention of a new type of glass at Clichy, called boracic glass, which was to become a competitor to lead-based crystal. The properties of the new glass, which was soda-based with zinc oxide in which boric acid was used as a flux, were superior, and finished product was the clearest glass that had yet been produced.

Many Clichy weights are characterized by the manner in which the curve ends abruptly. These weights have basically a very shallow, but at the same time wide, basal concavity. It may often look frosted, an effect that has often been unscrupulously used to simulate antique paperweights of the period. Another similar feature Clichy weights possess is a ring that is slightly depressed near the base. This depression can be felt by rubbing the fingers along the base, which very often coincides with the ground edge. Perhaps it could best be compared with a previous mold mark that was overlooked during the finishing process. Clichy weights are noted for their extremely clear glass, which is noticeably lighter than works by either Baccarat or St. Louis.

The Clichy Rose

The Clichy factory has become famous for its paperweights with rose motifs, which appear in perhaps more than thirty percent of production. The Clichy rose is merely a cane whose petals are made of flattened tubes that have been bundled together around a core of thin rods. These rods are placed to symbolize the pistil and anthers of the rose.

The centers of the first Clichy roses are made up of cylinders, cross-sections of which resemble lemon slices. Later production was dominated by pale green and yellow rods, which are called "whorls." The most predominant colors used in making the roses were many hues of red from the palest to a very deep rose red. White was very often seen framed with rows of wine red, green, amethyst, lilac, and especially pale yellow and aquamarine.

Canes

The canes of Clichy show a variety similar to production at Baccarat, but surpass that of the St. Louis factory. The most popular cane is that of the pastry mold, or floret. This cane is best described as having an outer casing that is deeply ruffled. The diameter is very similar to other French-produced canes of the period, but these often seem larger. Perhaps the second most popular cane produced at Clichy are the whorls, stars, and crimped rods. A direct comparison between the whorls produced at Baccarat and those of Clichy reveals that the Baccarat resemble scrolls that have both a beginning and end; the ones Clichy produced were made out of concentric tubing. Although the coloring of the canes are very similar to Baccarat and St. Louis, it should be noted that cobalt blue was not often used in production, although deep aquamarine, pink, a medium blue, green, lilac, ivory, and deep cherry red are very often used in Clichy paperweight production. Clichy paperweights, because of the brilliant colors used, appear to be in a constant glow.

Unfortunately, most weights were not dated or, as often as not, signed. If they were signed, it appears as an opaque white rod that comprises the cane center marked with the famous "C." The letter is often in the shape of a horseshoe done in either green, black, or red.

ENGLISH PRODUCTION

Although English glass production was well established as producers of lead glass as early as 1700, unfortunately 1745 saw the establishment of the Glass Excise Duty, a law that taxed glass by weight. The repercussions of this act were felt throughout the industry, but especially hurt were the producers of heavy glass, for example flint or lead. In effect, the act virtually stopped heavy glass production throughout the country, and England had to relinquish its position as a leading producer of glass to France, Bohemia, and Ireland. The tyranny of this tax lasted one hundred years until its repeal in 1845.

The English glass industry flourished over the next several years and especially in paperweight production. The English paperweight industry was centered around the factories at Birmingham and London.

Although England did not enter into the industry

until much later than the Continental makers, the production of millefiore paperweights of the classic period is styled and greatly influenced by the famous French factories at Baccarat and St. Louis. Not all English production was patterned after the French. In fact, the first nonmillefiore paperweights were of English origin. These weights, which were usually produced from green glass, date from around 1829 and were usually made by bottle factories. This specific type of weight remained in production until about 1930.

Bacchus

The original factory was started in 1818 by George Bacchus, but for the next several decades underwent several name changes and reorganizations. George Bacchus died in 1840, but production from this factory has always been known by the name Bacchus regardless of company name.

The following is a chronological listing of the Bacchus factory ownership:

    1818   Bacchus, Green & Green
    1833   George Bacchus & Co
    1841   George Bacchus & Sons
    1858   Bacchus & Sons
    1860   Stone, Fawdry & Stone
               Late George Bacchus & Sons

When the glass taxation was finally repealed in 1845 there was an immediate increase in imports from the Continent. Therefore, a direct comparison should be made between the production of English paperweights of this period and imports from France and Bohemia.

The Bacchus factory was mainly a producer of domestic glass. With the repeal of the Glass Act and increased imports, Bacchus began experimenting with various glass forms. At one period, the production was heavily influenced by the Venetians. Although many factories discouraged free-lance experimentation, Bacchus favored this method for discovery of new glass design. This part-time experimentation was known as friggering or whimsy, and often paperweights produced in this manner are referred to as friggers. Although much experimentation was encouraged, it is estimated that perhaps only around four hundred paperweights were produced by the Bacchus factory.

Although Bacchus paperweights are heavy to the touch, they display a medium index of refraction. The distinctive profile is distinguished by the gentle curve that starts at the top and becomes more obvious as it descends. It should be noted that the basal cavity of these weights is very shallow, and while the glass consistency often appears quite sugary, the glass used in the crown is always clear and brilliant. The motifs of the Bacchus paperweights can be most accurately described as a cushion resembling a hassock centered on the concave base. The size of the cushion is either one-half to two-thirds the height of the weight. Perhaps the most distinguishing characteristic of Bacchus paperweights is an outer sheath of canes that is predominently cup-shaped.

Canes

The crimp, cog, ruffle, and star represent the four basic cane motifs. Often the hollow tube is used as a frame for the various other canes.

Bacchus weights make use of most of the primary colors, although there seems to be a definite tendency to use pale colors including tourmaline greens, pink, aquamarine, lilac, and white, which seems to be favored as a basic color modifier.

Whitefriars

The factory derives its name from the monastery of Whitefriars, which stood on the same location during the sixteenth century. During the early 1680s the first factory was built and specialized mostly in producing decanters and tableware, especially glasses.

Although changing ownership quite often, the Whitefriars factory was able to supply, during the nineteenth century, both the growing domestic and foreign markets quite adequately. A diversification of production was seen during the beginning of the nineteenth century, when stained-glass windows were produced.

In 1835 James Powell, a glassmaker from Bristol, purchased Whitefriars, and the factory flourished. Experimentation was encouraged, and the repeal of the Glass Excise Duty increased the production of lead glass forms. The factory followed this course until 1853, when, under the direction of H. J. Powell, blown glass was reintroduced. After Powell's death in 1922, the factory transferred from its original site in London to Wealdstone, Middlesex, where it still operates under the name Whitefriars Glass Ltd.

Due to poor record-keeping, there is no way to estimate the number of weights produced by the factory since 1848, since paperweight production at this time was classified as a sideline to the normal production of tablewares, stained glass, and decanters. Accurate experimental production accounting is impossible, but commemorative paperweights began being produced during the middle of the twentieth century. For example, more than six hundred weights were made for the coronation of Queen Elizabeth II in 1953.

Colors and Composition

Although Whitefriars produced several different shapes in the basic weight, the canes they used were either tubes, tubes enclosing single rods, or single rods. Although only a limited number of cane types were used, the vast color spectrum gave the illusion of multiciplicity of design.

BELGIUM FACTORIES

Paperweights were produced extensively in Belgium during the middle of the nineteenth century, and the paperweights produced at the famous Val St. Lambert factory are perhaps the most famous.

Val St. Lambert

The factory was founded in 1825 near Liège, and produced the largest amount of paperweights in the country. Due to expert management that was able to accurately anticipate market trends, Val St. Lambert flourished.

Shapes and Characteristics

It must be noted that the lightness of the glass is very characteristic of these weights where very little lead is used in production. Some weights can be identified by a slight sugary texture, which at times can be impregnated with bubbles or foreign particles. One of the other distinguishing marks is that at times the glass appears to have either a yellow or gray tone.

Canes

The most distinctive cane types used were various pastry molds, star rods, and crimped canes, The brilliancy of the colors used is quite distinctive, with various colors being used in either combination or side by side. Two of the most original cane designs that make recognition simplified are the barber-pole and the bow, while the former was used extensively, the latter is still to be found. The bow, which is produced by lace rods that have been placed to give the illusion of bows and ribbons, and the barber-pole, made up of rods that have been twisted and comprised of several vivid colors, truly typified the production at Val St. Lambert.

AMERICAN PRODUCTION

Interest in paperweight production in America began shortly after the Great Exhibition of 1851, which took place in London, and was stimulated further during the exhibition in 1853 at the Crystal Palace in New York.

American styles were greatly influenced by European production. As the interest in paperweights grew in America, the glass factories hired men from Europe who were trained in the craft and, therefore, instructed the factory workers with a very Continental approach. As hard as the European professionals tried to impose their standards on the American factories, they basically only instructed on how to start paperweight production in America and, as always, the Americans shaped and produced paperweights that, although showing their European origins, were basically unusual and represented American ingenuity and customs.

The New England Glass Company

The factory was founded in 1817 at Cambridge, Massachusetts, and incorporated the following year under the name of the New England Glass Company. The majority of production during the first few years centered around cut glass, chandeliers, and domestic glass, which was sold in the United States as well as exported to both South America and West Indies.

Paperweight Production

Paperweights were produced at the New England Glass Company during roughly a thirty-year period from 1850 to 1880. During this period great originality was shown in the production, which can be totally attributed to the talent of the workers at the factory.

Paperweights were made at the factory during the 1850s and 1860s as part of the normal company production, and received great praise for both style and form at the Franklin Institute exhibition in 1856. This nationwide recognition caused the factory to successfully continue paperweight production through the next decade, when this form of glassmaking was stopped around 1874. The New England Glass Company continued the production of various glass forms for many more years but, due to economic conditions, was forced to close its doors in 1888.

Although there is really not an established profile of the weights from the New England Glass Company, these weights generally have broad bases with irregular basal rims that look like a jelly-glass bottom. Paperweights produced at this factory have the deepest basal concavity of additional paperweight production. Another notable characteristic is a low profile that rises steeply to accommodate a high crown. The lead glass is heavier than that of other factories (for example, production from Sandwich) and, although mostly clear, often displays either a pink or gray tint that can at times be sugary.

Canes

In close examination of the cane work it is obvious that the design fundamentals are of European origin, with the bases of the canes being either cog rods in tubes or the star rod.

The coloring of the weights produced are distinctive in that each weight displays a specific color tone. Several colors that were popular and used often in production were salmon, crimson, peppermint pink, several yellows, apple, dark ink blue, black, and white, which is often opaque.

Figure canes were often used and represent mostly animals, such as the running rabbit with the pink eye, bee, eagle, and dog.

Boston and Sandwich Glass Company

This factory was started in 1825 by one of the original founders of the New England Glass factory, Deming Jarvis. The new factory, located in Sandwich, Massachusetts, produced rival wares such as tablewares, chandeliers, lamps, and glasses to its arch competitor, the New England Glass Company.

1828 saw the development and patenting of a new method of pressed glass that forever linked the names of the Boston and Sandwich Glass Company with pressed glass.

Most paperweight production was started around 1852, but certain dated weights have been found bearing the date 1825, which more than likely refers to the founding of the factory and not the dating of the weight. In 1869, Nicholas Luty came to Sandwich and made paperweights until the factory closed in 1888. His weights, although decidedly French at the onset, with many canes being imported from France, changed rapidly, and the majority of his production centered on fruit and flower paperweights. After the closing of Sandwich, Luty worked at the Mt. Washington Glass factory in New Bedford, and then in 1895 he moved to the Union Glass factory at Somerville, where he worked until he died.

Basically, these weights have very low profiles with a surprisingly high-rising curvature that rises directly from the base to a fairly flat crown. Very often a clue to Sandwich identification can be noted in the form of either a cowlick or whorl, which can be seen very clearly near the crown apex. This mark was usually either caused by cutting away the tail of glass or weight rotation, at this point on the weight. Sandwich paperweights are comparably light to the touch, caused by the low amount of lead used in their production.

Cane Characteristics

It should be noted that the canes produced at Sandwich bear a marked resemblance to the one produced by its arch rival, the New England Glass Company. The most striking dissimilarities are the lightness of the weights and the decided French flair, which, although present, is decidedly less predominant than at other factories.

Typical figure canes that appear in Sandwich production are the rabbit, which is either black, inky blue, or white, having one red eye, and the heart, bee, Greek cross, which usually appears quite thick, and the eagle. The color production is quite beautiful, with many predominant hues such as crimson, salmon, orange, yellows, apple, various shades of green, royal as well as dark blue, lavender, black, and opaque peppermint pink being used in production. One of the most interesting characteristics is the continual use of white, which is not seen in Continental production.

PAPERWEIGHTS AS AN INVESTMENT

More and more collectors have begun to realize recently that artistic glassware offers a broad field for both collectors and serious investors. One of the most rapidly growing fields recently has been paperweights, especially ones made during the nineteenth century in France. French craftsmen surpassed themselves when creating these tiny jewels of ornamental glassware.

Perhaps the renewed interest in paperweights can be accounted for by both social and economic conditions. Due to the time-consuming method of production, few paperweights were forged; therefore, it is easy for a collector in a relatively short period of time to become familiar with paperweights. Paperweight collecting appeals to the connoisseur who enjoys these beautiful decorative pieces that are not only easy to store because of their small size, but extremely decorative as well.

Of all antiques, paperweight prices seem to fluctuate the most. This is perhaps due to the limited number of paperweights produced during the peak collecting years of the mid-nineteenth century. Therefore, since there are relatively few pieces available, any increase in the demand for a certain paperweight tends to immediately drive the price upwards.

WHAT IS IT WORTH?

Many beginning collectors are so impressed with the beauty of paperweights that the three basic criteria that determine the value of a particular weight are completely overshadowed by its look. The following characteristics are listed in order of importance relating to the value of an individual paperweight:
1. Rarity
2. Workmanship
3. Condition of the piece

The greatest increase in price has been seen in French paperweights. Since the beginning of the twentieth century, when a dated Baccarat weight could be purchased for under $50, prices have soared to today's incredible highs with a Clichy lily-of-the-valley weight with translucent pink ground selling for $22,000.

Prices on French paperweights showed their greatest increase during the mid 1960s, when they reached unprecedented highs, but as demand lessened toward the end of the decade, prices dropped drastically and have only begun to recover in the mid 1970s. Since continued interest has been established in the field of paperweight collecting, prices should continue to increase at a more stable rate.

Collectors should note that only the best-quality weights retained their value during the last decade's price decrease and were the first to show an immediate increase in value when the market took an upward turn during the mid 1970s. Many of the more common weights decreased in value a surprising fifty to sixty percent, proving the fact that rarity is the most important factor to consider in collecting paperweights as an investment.

14 Bottles

Bottle-collecting has suddenly become one of the most popular hobbies throughout the world. The field is so broad that the lover of antiquity can limit his acquisitions to the intricate and very colorful bottles of ancient Rome, while the lesser collector needs very little to start a most interesting eighteenth- or nineteenth-century whiskey-bottle collection.

Bottles throughout history have always been saved for economic purposes because of the expense involved in their production, but it was not until the middle of the nineteenth century that bottle-collecting as a hobby and potential investment possibility was officially recognized. The beginning collector can still begin a worthwhile collection, especially if he concentrates on bottles produced during the last part of the nineteenth and beginning of the twentieth century.

Bottle-collecting covers a broad range of interests and specialties. Many collectors concentrate on nostalgic productions such as those made by the Avon and Jim Beam companies. As a selected specialty these are a wise investment, because due to limited production they will certainly appreciate in value, but unfortunately they do not reflect the social aspects of the period.

Historic-figure bottles and flasks dating from the end of the nineteenth century have become very popular collectibles during the last few years. A wide variety of these bottles are available both in the United States and throughout Europe and seem to be a much safer investment than the very popular patriotic relief bottles that have been mass-reproduced since their production during the first half of the nineteenth century. The only expert way to identify and judge authenticity of these bottles is by close examination of the motif. Recent imitations have less ornate rims, and the motif, which often regulates the price, is usually clear and very pronounced, while on the original bottles these motifs tend to be slightly fuzzy, perhaps due to more primitive production techniques that were used at the time. Unfortunately the majority of bottle collectors limit their collections severely by age. The beautiful bottles of ancient Rome are almost always automatically overlooked as unaffordable by the average collector. The museum quality and price syndrome these bottles of antiquity have attained has needlessly locked out many bottle collectors from expanding their collections to include ancient glass bottles. Many good-quality bottles from the early Roman Empire can be purchased for well under one hundred dollars. Perhaps the best source for obtaining ancient bottles is through specialty auction houses where experts can advise you on the best bottles to expand your collection.

Beginning a bottle collection usually requires very little capital, and knowledge can be easily acquired from some of the excellent specialty books on the market as well as from the many eager and interested bottle collectors throughout the world.

UNDERSTANDING AND EVALUATING BOTTLES

There are four basic qualifications that help to evaluate a bottle:
1. Age
2. Color
3. Labeling
4. Shape

Age

There are many interesting characteristics that help to determine the age of bottles. The following chronological list may help you in the identification process, but the only reliable method is by continual examination with actual bottles. Perhaps the lip of a bottle can be the most revealing part, since it has undergone more variations throughout the centuries than any other part.

Lip Characteristics	Date
Screw threads on outside	early 18th century
Applied lip	early to middle 1800s
Ground	19th century
Tooled lip	1820–c. 1860
Sheared lip	commonly used until middle of 19th century
Flared lip	used until 1840
Folded lip	used until 1840
Screw thread outside	from 1857
Screw thread inside	c. 1860
Crown top	late 19th century
"Biob" or soda bottle top	c. 1880

There are, of course, other characteristics such as stopper types and marks found on bottle bottoms, but lip types are so varied that they seem more reliable to gauge the time of production.

Color

Color plays a very important part in determining the age of various bottles. Perhaps the most sought-after for beauty are the amber and dark green bottles that were made during the eighteenth century. Dark purple and cobalt blue are also valued by collectors for the richness of their color. Many collections are comprised of only original and beautifully shaped milk-glass bottles. The above colors are perhaps the most sought after by bottle collectors. Some of the more common colors, but still collected, are limited to the browns and greens.

Labeling

An original, intact label on most any bottle of the past century will make it of extreme interest to the collector. Bottles that are contained in the original boxes and labeled, especially poison, patented medicine, and original shaped bottles from the nineteenth century have greatly increased in value and are most eagerly sought after by collectors today.

Labels of the period give an insight into the lives of our ancestors and are perhaps sought for more sentimental value than artistic merit, but nevertheless bottles that have their original labels are valuable to the collector. Perhaps the most valuable labeled bottles are the ones that were hand-blown, but since intact bottles are difficult to find, many collectors eagerly seek the next best version, the raised-lettered bottle. Machine-produced bottles with labels are very common and as yet not much sought after by collectors.

Shape

Perhaps the shape is the one most important factor that influences the bottle collector. There have been some very unusual-shaped bottles produced throughout the centuries, and every collector hopes to enrich his collection with at least one. The most sought-after shape at present is the bottle made after people and famous places. Ingenious shapes will always be valued, but there are many good bottles worthy of collectors that are basically plain, and this is where the three other factors, age, color, and labeling, are considered in establishing value.

The following price comparison will illustrate the dramatic increases seen during the past few years in the field of bottle collecting. A very rare, dark olive De Witt Clinton whiskey flask (top shelf, center figure 1), American 19th century, was sold for $650 in November 1974. Then barely two years later an equally rare American Eagle flask, 19th century, was sold for $6,500 in January, 1976, Figure 2. Courtesy Parke Bernet Inc.

Imported Bottle, 7 oz., made in Italy. Courtesy Museum of Packaging.

Very old Imperial whiskey decanter. Courtesy Museum of Packaging.

217

Gilt-edge whiskey bottle with stopper. Courtesy Museum of Packaging.

Lacey, ribbed bottle with stopper. Courtesy Museum of Packaging.

Buffalo Lithia water bottle. Light green fully embossed with lady. Courtesy Museum of Packaging.

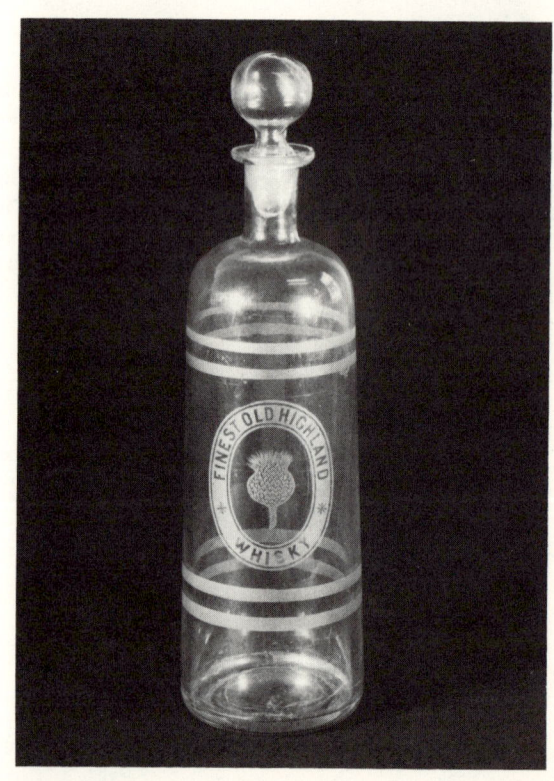

Finest Old Highland whiskey bottle. Courtesy Museum of Packaging.

A very scarce light-aqua half-pint flask. Courtesy Museum of Packaging.

Blown glass bottle, cobalt, 7¾ inches. Courtesy Museum of Packaging.

Mason jar, patented November 30, 1858, quart. Courtesy Museum of Packaging.

Figural bottle, bulldog, screw-head closure. Courtesy Museum of Packaging.

Ribbed clamshell bottle with original screw-on top cap and paint. Patented 1892. Courtesy Museum of Packaging.

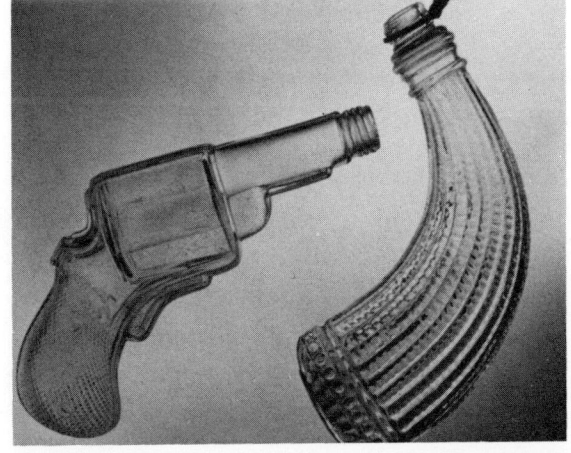

Commemorative bottle gun series. Courtesy Museum of Packaging.

219

Free-blown amber glass carafe. Courtesy Museum of Packaging.

An aqua masonic calabash flask, the reverse with American eagle and shield. Courtesy Museum of Packaging.

One-pint, Evansville, milk bottle. Courtesy Museum of Packaging.

Part II

Investing in Antiques:
An International Price Guide

This part of the book is divided into two sections: (1) price comparison tables, and (2) pictorial pricing studies. The tables have been designed to show price trends over a seven-year period from 1971 to 1978, with financial predictions to 1984. The following example illustrates how to interpret the price tables in this section and use them to your best advantage.

	1971	1975	1978	AVERAGE ANNUAL INCREASE	FINANCIAL OUTLOOK 1978–84
Maple schoolmaster's desk c. 1800	$70	$180	$240	19%	2

Numerous pieces were analyzed to develop a reliable and representative price guide. Dealers around the world submitted price data to develop the tables. The average annual increase is the compounded growth rate, or percent at which the piece increased each year. The column marked "Financial Outlook 1978–84" evaluates whether or not the antique is a stable investment for the future:

1 = Excellent investment potential
2 = Good investment with buyer interest increasing
3 = Average investment potential with no significant increase expected
4 = Poor risk

The smart collector can use this information to figure general price increases over the next several years. For example, if the above-mentioned schoolmaster's desk is worth $240 in 1978, then extrapolating an average annual increase of 19% the price in 1982 should be about $480. This investment guide should be considered a workbook to help collectors and dealers become more familiar with price increases and fully understand them.

The pictorial section of the book essentially does the same as the charts but gives the reader an individual note column, which should help increase the worth of the investment guide as additional information is added.

15 Price Guide to England

VALUE GROWTH CHART

SILVER

PRICES QUOTED IN POUNDS STERLING

ARTICLE	1971	1975	1978	Average Annual Increase	Financial Outlook 1978-84
Pr. Georgian candlesticks, c. 1785	59	150	325	27%	2
Pr. Georgian candlesticks, c. 1805	120	170	250	11%	1
Pr. George III candlesticks, 10" high	550	675	790	5%	3
George III sweetmeat basket	110	200	290	15%	2
Pedestal sugar basket, 1810	80	110	148	9%	3
Oval bread basket, 1765	165	240	310	9%	3
Boat-shaped sugar basket, 1790	100	150	250	14%	1
Pr. George III wine coasters	145	255	300	11%	2
Pr. fluted side wine coasters, 1830	60	85	110	9%	3
George II cylindrical coffeepot	450	595	750	7%	3
George II coffeepot w/wooden handle	375	645	720	10%	2
Pear-shaped coffeepot, 1845	155	260	300	10%	2
Pear-shaped coffeepot, London, 1775	300	430	560	9%	3
Pear-shaped coffeepot, circular foot, 1825	135	200	250	9%	3
Fluted, pear-shaped coffeepot, 1810	275	340	400	5%	3
Set of 4 salts, c. 1750	89	115	190	11%	2
Set of George III circular salt cellar	75	155	295	22%	2
George III drum mustard pot, 1765	90	140	210	13%	2
13 pcs. pistol handle Georgian knife set	72	240	300	23%	1
Victorian wine ewer	52	160	275	27%	1
Urn-shaped hot-water jug, 1792	250	340	450	9%	2

VALUE GROWTH CHART

SILVER

PRICES QUOTED IN POUNDS STERLING

ARTICLE	1971	1975	1978	Average Annual Increase	Financial Outlook 1978-84
George II ale jug w/cover	100	220	375	21%	1
George II helmut-shaped creamer	52	65	90	8%	3
Engraved oval creamer, 1800	65	95	145	12%	2
George II baluster cream jug	30	69	125	22%	1
George III, 3-foot sauce boat	90	140	290	18%	1
Victorian circular salver, 1765	140	200	295	11%	1
Pie crust molded salver, 1765	275	360	495	9%	3
Victorian salver, bead edge	115	210	260	12%	2
George III bulbous water jug	110	155	295	15%	1
George III sauceboat, waved rim	90	120	165	9%	3
Pr. fruit spoons, embossed, c. 1780	20	49	64	18%	2
Apostle spoon, 1614	52	79	135	14%	2
George III punch ladle, engraved	10	25	45	24%	1
George II marrow spoon, engraved	16	26	39	13%	2
George I marrow spoon, engraved	20	39	55	15%	2
Seal-top spoon, c. 1612	50	89	190	21%	1
George I, rat-tail gravy spoon	61	95	155	14%	2
George III engraved tea caddy	90	145	200	12%	2
George III scrolled hanale tankard	120	375	500	22%	1
William IV crested teapot	78	145	210	15%	2
William IV engraved small teapot	54	120	180	19%	1
George III oblong engraved teapot	52	179	215	22%	1
Victorian teapot w/flowers	60	90	125	11%	1
George III oval teapot, engraved	85	100	178	11%	1
George IV half-fluted teapot	100	165	275	15%	1
Victorian vinaigrette, oval	30	55	79	15%	2
George III vinaigrette, reeded and gilt	25	60	90	20%	1
George II waiter, shell border	94	130	189	10%	3
Pr. George II waiter, shell border	125	200	265	11%	2
3 ps. Georgian fluted tea set	165	240	320	10%	2
Victorian 4 ps tea & coffee set	150	265	300	10%	2
George IV, 3 ps embossed tea set	110	179	295	15%	1
William IV tea service	310	650	760	14%	1
Victorian snuffbox, c. 1895	21	32	49	13%	2
Oval snuffbox, c. 1798, engraved	22	43	66	17%	2
Victorian plated gallery tray	10	26	44	24%	1
19th C. plated 3-bottle decanter se	30	52	78	15%	2
Edwardian plated toast bar rack	2	6	14	32%	1
Silver wine label, c. 1840	6	13	19	18%	2
Victorian engraved match case	3	8	13	23%	1
Victorian button hook	1	4	8	34%	1

VALUE GROWTH CHART

CLOCKS

PRICES QUOTED IN POUNDS STERLING

ARTICLE	1971	1975	1978	Average Annual Increase	Financial Outlook 1978-84
Acorn clock, c. 1850 (U.S.A.)	50	60	70	5%	3
Act of Parliament, c. 1797	50-190	150-325	250-475	26-14%	2
Altar clock, c. 1660	100	375	550	28%	2
Arch-top clock, c. 1790	75	150	200	15%	3
Architectural top clock, c. 1650	1,500	3,000	6,000	22%	2
Astrolabe Clock, c. 1690	1,500	3,000	5,500	20%	2
Automatic clock, c. 1750	350	1,500	3,500	39%	1
Ball & tape clock, c. 1675	550	1,500	2,000	20%	2
Balloon clock, c. 1750	250	450	600	13%	3
Banjo clocks, c. 1802	150	300	550	20%	1
Basket-top clock, c. 1700	750	2,000	3,500	25%	?
Bell-top clock, c. 1720	650	1,500	3,200	26%	1
Birdcage clock, c. 1775	2,000	3,200	4,000	10%	3
Boudoir clock, c. 1860	100	325	500	26%	1
Boulle clock, 1641 & 1722	750	1,500	2,200	17%	2
Box chronometer, c. 1760-70	100	375	500	26%	2
Brequet clock, c. 1795	3,000	9,000	12,000	22%	1
Broken-arch clock, c. 1780	100	250	375	21%	2
Bull clock, c. 1750	700	1,500	2,000	16%	2
Cartel clock, c. 1750	750	1,750	2,250	17%	2
Chaise clock, c. 1750	150	575	950	30%	1
Chamber clock, 1400-1500	500	1,700	2,200	23%	2
Chamber tap clock, c. 1810	100	175	225	12%	2
Chiming clock, c. 1700	700	1,500	3,000	23%	1
Column clock, c. 1700	500	1,900	2,700	27%	1
Congreve clock, c. 1808	250	750	1,500	29%	1
Conical pendulum, c. 1667	100	175	225	12%	3
Cottage clock, c. 1790	35	50	100	16%	2
Crucifix clock, c. 1625	200	550	800	22%	3
Dial clock, c. 1875	35	50	150	23%	2

WALL & MANTEL CLOCKS

	1971	1975	1978		
18th C. Cartel clock, ormolu work	9,200	16,000	17,800	10%	3
19th C. gilt sunburst wall clock	10	22	56	28%	2
Victorian regulator in mahogany	37	60	90	13%	2
19th C. mahogany-framed regulator	30	42	57	10%	2
Victorian 7-day regulator	51	70	110	11%	2
19th C. Act of Parliament	127	169	220	8%	3
8-day wall clock with brass case	12	16	32	15%	1
19th C. papier-mâché clock w/mother-of-pearl inlay	34	50	85	14%	2
Japanese pillar clock, c. 1800	175	310	540	17%	2
Victorian brass skeleton clock	90	150	210	13%	1
Brass lantern, c. 1675	325	690	845	15%	2
19th C. brass skeleton under glass dome	12	20	37	17%	2
Victorian mantel clock, mahogany	10	21	39	21%	1
19th C. French Ormolu mantel clock	85	127	195	12%	2
Edwardian 8-day in oak case	3	8	16	27%	1
19th C. mahogany-cased mantel clock	2	4	11	28%	1

VALUE GROWTH CHART

CLOCKS **PRICES QUOTED IN POUNDS STERLING**

ARTICLE	1971	1975	1978	Average Annual Increase	Financial Outlook 1978-84
WALL & MANTEL CLOCKS					
Regency mahogany 8-day mantel	30	65	95	18%	1
Boulle ebonized bracket clock	110	169	210	10%	2
French bronze ormolu, c. 1810	120	340	500	23%	1
Regency rosewood bracket clock	70	115	185	15%	1
Louis XV signed ormolu mantel clock	250	560	825	18%	2
19th C. sevres & ormolu French mantel	165	269	490	17%	2
French exhibition clock, c. 1851	650	1,150	1,450	12%	3
19th C. Dresden figure mantel clock	450	890	1,350	17%	2
Empire clock w/ormolu decoration	85	160	230	15%	2
Victorian walnut domed mantel	6	13	22	20%	1
Victorian reproduction brass lantern	19	34	49	14%	3
19th C. picture clock	21	37	59	16%	1
Victorian regulator w/carved eagle on top	50	72	42	9%	1
Victorian mahogany round school clock	12	22	42	19%	2
Ebonized balloon clock, c. 1772	225	400	625	16%	1
Directoire clock, c. 1795	150	350	750	26%	1
Double-basket top, c. 1750	350	600	1,000	16%	2
Dresden clock, c. 1830	400	900	1,500	21%	1
Dressing-case clock, c. 1875	25	39	55	12%	3
Drumhead clock, c. 1865	35	79	150	23%	2
Dutch clock, c. 1700	75	250	500	31%	1
Elephant clock, c. 1765	750	1,500	2,500	19%	3
Empire clock, 1799-1815	750	1,500	2,000	15%	2
Engine clock, c. 1850	50	75	100	10%	3
English flour-glass clock, 1850	100	150	225	12%	2
Regulator clock, c. 1750	75	800	1,000	45%	1
Eureka clock, c. 1906	25	50	150	29%	2
Fan clock, c. 1650	500	1,000	2,000	22%	1
Fountain clock, c. 1845	750	1,500	2,200	17%	2
French 4-glass regulator, 1850	50	125	250	26%	2
French regulator, c. 1750	750	1,500	2,700	20%	2
Friesland clock, 1700	150	250	400	15%	2
Gothic clock, c. 1450	500	1,500	3,000	29%	2
Grande sonnerie, 1700	17,000	25,000	30,000	8%	4
Inclined plane, c. 1690	1,000	1,500	2,000	10%	4
Lamp clock, c. 1600	35	75	200	28%	1
Lancet-top clock, c. 1800	75	100	225	17%	2
Lantern clock, 1620-1700	200	500	1,000	26%	1
Light house clock, c. 1850	10	25	100	39%	1
Lion clock, c. 1765	750	1,500	2,000	15%	3
Lyre clock, c. 1785	350	1,500	3,000	36%	1
Marble clock, c. 1885	300	500	790	15%	2
Minute repeating clock, c. 1870	100	250	550	27%	1
Monstrance clock, c. 1600	500	1,500	3,000	29%	1
Morbier clock, c. 1750	100	250	500	26%	2
Musical clock, c. 1750	550	1,500	2,500	24%	2
Mystery clock, c. 1850	100	150	300	17%	3
Nef clock, c. 1875	750	1,000	2,000	15%	3

VALUE GROWTH CHART

CLOCKS

PRICES QUOTED IN POUNDS STERLING

ARTICLE	1971	1975	1978	Average Annual Increase	Financial Outlook 1978-84
Negro clock, c. 1890	15	25	35	13%	2
Negro clocks, French	2,000	4,000	4,000	14%	2
Night clock, c. 1685	1,500	3,000	5,000	19%	3
One-wheel clock, c. 1750	1,000	2,000	5,000	26%	2
Organ clock, c. 1750	1,500	2,200	3,000	10%	4
Orrery clock, c. 1715	1,000	2,500	4,000	22%	2
Picture clock, c. 1750	70	125	250	20%	1
Pillar clock, c. 1590	350	1,500	2,200	30%	1
Religieuse clock, 1680-1700	125	275	500	22%	2
Sedan clock, c. 1750	25	50	100	22%	2
Sevres clock	1,200	1,800	2,500	11%	2
Shelf clock, c. 1800	50	150	220	23%	2
Skeleton clock, c. 1860	50	100	250	26%	1
Stagecoach clock, 1760	50	190	400	35%	1
Sunray clocks, 1860	45	125	200	24%	2
Swing clock, c. 1890	35	75	150	23%	2
Table clocks, c. 1500	1,000	2,200	3,200	18%	3
Term clock, c. 1720	375	1,200	2,000	27%	1
Urn clock, c. 1750	750	1,250	2,500	19%	3
Vernis Martin clock, 1730	500	900	1,600	18%	3
Vertical table clock, 1530	250	750	2,000	34%	2
Vienna regulator, 1875	150	200	350	13%	1
Wagon-spring clock, 1825	150	300	525	19%	2
Zaandam clock, 1600	50	200	450	37%	2

VALUE GROWTH CHART

FURNITURE

PRICES QUOTED IN POUNDS STERLING

ARTICLE	1971	1975	1978	Average Annual Increase	Financial Outlook 1978-84
Marble-top washstands	2	4	12.50	30%	1
(V) Cabriole leg chairs (6)	60	180	350	28%	1
(V) Burr walnut card tables	35	75	150	23%	1
(V) Burr walnut loo tables	50	100	300	30%	1
(V) Burr walnut davenports	50	150	30	30%	1
(E) Chippendale chairs (6)	100	200	400	22%	2
(E) Parlor sets (9)	15	40	100	31%	2
(G) Bureaux, 3-foot	80	125	300	17%	3
(G) Bookcases, breakfronts	500	800	1,250	14%	3
(G) Chest of drawers	20	30	50	14%	3
17th C. oak dresser	600	800	1,000	7%	4
17 C. refectory table	750	1,500	1,250	7%	4
16th C. refectory table	800	3,500	4,000	26%	2
17th C. chest of drawers	80	150	200	15%	3

VALUE GROWTH CHART

FURNITURE PRICES QUOTED IN POUNDS STERLING

ARTICLE	1971	1975	1978	Average Annual Increase	Financial Outlook 1978-84
18th C. dresser	200	350	400	10%	3
Gothic 15/16th C. cupboard	800	2,000	2,500	17.5%	2
Enclosed 17th C. corner cupboard	400	800	1,600	14%	4
18th C. tridoon	300	800	1,000	17%	3
Large 17 C. gate-leg table	500	700	1,000	11%	3
Good 17th C. side tables	100	100	120	3%	4
17th C. credener table	250	800	1,000	22%	2
18th C. settee	25	100	120	25%	2
17th C. carved settee	120	250	300	14%	3
Jacobean chair	40	60	70	8%	4
Yorkshire chair	50	150	200	22%	2
Jacobean carved armchair	120	400	500	22%	2
Elizabethan carved armchair	150	500	500	27%	1
17th C. open buffet	250	500	800	18%	1
18th enclosed buffet	500	1,000	1,200	14%	2
17th C. closed presses	80	200	300	20%	3
Dresser base 6' wide, c. 1680	250	700	800	18%	2
Chest on stand, elm, c. 1710	500	900	1,500	17%	2
18th C. Oak Table, 6' x 2'7"	100	400	600	30%	1
Oak chest of drawers, c. 1680	75	400	675	37%	1
Oak child's chair, c. 1670	28	80	140	26%	1
Walnut bureau, c. 1730	700	1,500	1,800	14%	3
Walnut kneehole desk, c. 1720	310	500	700	12%	3
Oak dresser, c. 1700	195	400	900	25%	2
18th C. elm dresser	100	300	450	24%	2
17th C. Spanish walnut table	95	200	300	17%	3
18th C. yew wheelback Windsor	60	125	145	13%	3
Walnut corner chair, c. 1720	65	160	170	14%	3
George I, olivewood bookcase	350	450	590	8%	3
Georgian mahogany bureau	170	300	450	15%	2
Regency mahogany dwarf bookcase	120	250	500	23%	2
19th C. bureau-bookcase	170	275	400	13%	3
William & Mary walnut bookcase	180	325	600	19%	2
George III double-door bureau	240	340	575	13%	3
Victorian secretaire bookcase	100	175	300	17%	2
Regency inlaid book cabinet	240	375	540	12%	3
19th C. bookcase, 13 pane doors	165	325	600	20%	1
Sheraton-style inlaid bookcase	100	275	450	24%	1
Georgian mahogany bookcase	85	320	400	25%	1
George II double-dome lacquer bureau	120	275	500	23%	1
William & Mary walnut desk	95	400	600	30%	1
Late Georgian mahogany bureau	50	175	300	29%	1
Chippendale mahogany bureau	160	275	400	14%	2
Edwardian inlaid bureau	100	200	375	21%	2
Late Sheraton bureau-cabinet	170	275	500	17%	2
Queen Anne-style walnut bureau	275	375	600	12%	3
Mahogany display cabinet	110	250	400	20%	2
Mahogany display case, Queen Anne	100	225	375	21%	2
William IV music canterbury	50	150	200	22%	2
Georgian mahogany canterbury	70	175	230	18%	2

VALUE GROWTH CHART

FURNITURE

PRICES QUOTED IN POUNDS STERLING

ARTICLE	1971	1975	1978	Average Annual Increase	Financial Outlook 1978-84
Queen Anne-style dwarf cabinet	80	140	275	19%	2
Pr. Hepplewhite style armchairs	25	60	100	22%	1
Sheraton open armchair	100	190	225	12%	3
Sheraton oval-back chair	45	65	75	7%	3
Chippendale mahogany armchair	50	250	325	31%	1
12 Hepplewhite-design dining chairs	600	900	1,200	10%	2
8 Chippendale-style dining chairs	400	625	900	12%	2
18-19th C. mahogany dining chairs	150	275	450	17%	2
4 William IV sabreleg chairs	55	225	300	27%	1
6 Sheraton mahogany chairs	120	200	300	14%	2
8 Georgian-style carved chairs	80	140	225	16%	2
6 country Chippendale-style chairs	49	170	250	26%	1
8 Mahogany Chippendale-style chairs	120	250	375	18%	2
8 George I-style fiddle splat chairs	150	320	400	15%	2
6 Hepplewhite square-back chairs	275	400	595	12%	2
6 George II red walnut, carved chairs	300	525	700	13%	2
Victorian sabre leg, mahogany chair	8	20	35	23%	1
Pr. Regency mahogany hall chairs	55	95	150	15%	2
Pr. Hepplewhite shield-back chairs	145	275	350	13%	2
Pr. Regency ebonized cane-seat chairs	30	75	120	22%	1
Chippendale mahogany wing chair	400	900	1,200	17%	2
Georgian wing fireside chair	92	140	270	17%	2
William IV bergère armchair	25	40	80	18%	2
George III mahogany partner's desk	250	375	600	13%	2
Chippendale-style Mahogany desk	100	225	350	19%	1
Sheraton satinwood-inlaid desk	100	150	170	8%	2
Mahogany corner cupboard	85	110	150	8%	2
18th C. mahogany hanging corner cupboard	60	90	120	10%	3
Oak corner cupboard	14	35	55	21%	1
18th C. oak dresser	75	225	350	25%	1
Mahogany kitchen dresser	60	100	175	16%	2
19th C. oak dresser	55	200	300	27%	1
Oak Welsh dresser, 6' 8" (h & w)	110	450	600	27%	1
Elm dresser, carved, 5' 10" (height)	70	225	400	28%	1
Queen Anne walnut chest	125	200	350	16%	2
William & Mary marquetry chest	290	450	600	11%	3
George II serpentine chest	250	390	500	10%	3
18th C. banded walnut chest	135	200	250	9%	3
Georgian inlaid mahogany table	130	225	300	13%	2
Sheraton tulipwood card table	43	70	100	13%	2
Sheraton card table, inlaid	110	190	250	12%	2
Georgian mahogany card table	56	95	170	17%	2
18th C. satinwood table	66	200	450	31%	1
George III mahogany dining table	260	375	550	11%	2
19th C. mahogany oval gateleg table	56	175	290	26%	1
Victorian inlaid burr dining table	190	350	590	17%	2
George III two-pillar dining table	265	560	900	19%	2
Sheraton mahogany dining table	220	390	590	15%	2
Rosewood inlaid occasional table	15	35	60	22%	1
Sheraton satinwood pembroke table	165	290	350	11%	3

VALUE GROWTH CHART

FURNITURE

PRICES QUOTED IN POUNDS STERLING

ARTICLE	1971	1975	1978	Average Annual Increase	Financial Outlook 1978-84
17th C. oak refectory table	290	600	675	13%	3
18th C. walnut side table	179	450	625	20%	1
Georgian mahogany wine table	110	225	350	18%	1
Pr. Georgian mahogany tea tables	165	290	400	13%	2
Hepplewhite tea table	82	175	325	22%	1
Regency rosewood sofa table	210	325	475	12%	2
Regency sofa table on lyre ends	500	690	900	9%	3
19th C. mahogany sofa table	200	475	650	18%	2
Regency mahogany writing table	129	250	375	16%	2
Queen Anne-style walnut kneehole desk	280	490	600	11%	3
17th C. carved oak armchair	100	250	500	26%	2
Side chair, carved oak, c. 1649	35	60	100	16%	2
17th C. country oak armchair	40	180	250	30%	2
Cromwellian chair, 1660	50	190	275	27%	2
Cromwellian straight-back chair	35	85	125	20%	2
Charles II carved chair, c. 1675	60	100	175	16%	3
Carved oak armchair, c. 1685	70	100	150	11%	3
17th C. turned straight-back chair	35	75	100	16%	2
Pr. 17th C. oak straight-back chairs	70	150	275	21%	2
Upholstered 17th C. straight chair, carved legs	150	250	375	14%	2
William & Mary walnut armchair	120	225	360	17%	3
William & Mary cane-back chair	190	270	410	12%	3
Queen Anne walnut chair w/splat back	75	110	165	12%	3
Ornate walnut armchair, c. 1725	410	620	875	11%	4
Walnut chair, rush seat, c. 1710	60	65	100	14%	3
Pr. Queen Anne oak side chair	60	90	120	10%	2
Queen Anne walnut corner chair	150	300	450	17%	2
George II carved mahogany chair	85	100	150	8%	3
Walnut cabriole leg chair, 1740	40	100	155	21%	1
Walnut square leg chair, 1750-55	20	40	65	18%	2
Scroll-back mahogany chair, 1755	22	49	78	20%	2
Chippendale armchair, 1760	250	400	600	13%	2
Carved Chippendale armchair, 1760	190	290	520	15%	2
Chippendale side chair, 1760	50	75	125	14%	2
Chippendale Ribbon back chair, 1765	180	250	375	11%	3
Country Chippendale armchair, 1770	35	60	85	13%	3
Chippendale armchair, elm, 1770	30	70	105	19%	2
Ladder-back chair, 1765	45	60	85	9%	3
Country Chippendale, scroll back, 1760	25	50	72	16%	2
Mahogany Chippendale chair, c. 1770	25	40	75	17%	2
Hepplewhite hooped back arm, 1790	50	90	125	14%	1
Hepplewhite, carved back, c. 1790	40	59	80	10%	2
Hepplewhite armchair, c. 1790	50	85	125	14%	2
Hepplewhite single chair, c. 1790	30	50	72	13%	3
Country Hepplewhite, elm, c. 1795	9	20	29	18%	2
Pr. Hepplewhite shield-back arm, 1790	150	200	275	9%	4
Hepplewhite shield-back, 1790	100	150	210	11%	3
Mahogany carved back, c. 1795	200	320	400	10%	2
Carved Sheraton armchair, c. 1795	190	275	450	13%	3

VALUE GROWTH CHART

FURNITURE

PRICES QUOTED IN POUNDS STERLING

ARTICLE	1971	1975	1978	Average Annual Increase	Financial Outlook 1978-84
Georgian chair, arm, c. 1805	45	59	95	11%	3
Sheraton-type armchair, c. 1795	40	65	95	13%	2
Country Sheraton-type, single c. 1815	8	17	20	14%	3
Set Sheraton-type chairs (6), c. 1800	325	550	900	16%	2
Gothic Sheraton-type chair, c. 1800	25	49	62	14%	2
Mahogany armchairs, c. 1800	35	65	83	13%	3
Finely carved mahogany armchair, 1800	55	79	115	11%	3
Georgian mahogany armchair, 1810	45	69	110	14%	2
Country Sheraton armchair, c. 1815	25	42	60	15%	2
Country Sheraton single chair, 1815	8	15	21	15%	2
19th C. oak spindle-back chairs	15	55	80	27%	1
Regency period armchair, 1820	80	92	125	7%	4
Regency chair, rope-twist back, 1825	55	75	110	10%	3
Regency armchair, c. 1825	65	95	125	10%	3
Regency lyre back, c. 1825	40	75	115	16%	2
Pr. Regency lyre back, c. 1825	100	190	265	15%	2
Pr. Regency reeded side chairs, 1830	55	110	165	17%	2
Regency sabre-leg chair, 1830	25	49	62	14%	2
Regency library chair, 1830	250	365	500	10%	3
Regency curled armchair, 1835	32	59	75	13%	3
Regency rosewood chair, 1835	12	15	22	9%	4
Country Regency armchair, 1835	25	49	70	16%	1
Upholstered mahogany chair, 1845	12	19	32	15%	1
Victorian ballon-back, walnut, 1850	12	16	22	9%	2
Side chair, needlework, c. 1850	13	26	47	20%	2
Victorian mahogany side chair	8	13	21	15%	2
Carved Victorian chair	14	24	42	17%	3
Leather wing chair, cabriole legs, 1720	230	550	780	19%	2
George II upholstered side chair	200	325	420	11%	2
George III upholstered wing chair	95	125	295	17%	3
George III leather wing chair	320	450	620	10%	2
Chinese mahogany armchair, 1760	410	620	950	13%	3
18th C. mahogany armchair	115	235	360	18%	2
Giltwood armchair, c. 1762	400	550	925	13%	2
George III open armchair	320	525	820	14%	2
18th C. open armchair, French	550	800	1,000	9%	4
Bergère caned rosewood, 1830	40	75	115	16%	2
Victorian Bergère chair, 1855	69	120	240	19%	2
Victorian open armchair, walnut	65	140	210	18%	3
Button-back armchair, 1850	60	100	165	15%	2
Button-back ladies chair, 1850	55	100	145	15%	2
Victorian upholstered armchair	50	90	125	12%	3
Bentwood rocker, 1850	30	65	95	18%	2
Mahogany armchair, c. 1895	35	59	85	13%	3
Mahogany chaise lounge, 1820	25	45	95	21%	1
Walnut Chaise Lounge, 1865	50	110	145	16%	2
Windsor chair, c. 1762	65	140	325	26%	1
Comb-back Windsor, c. 1782	45	69	110	14%	3
18th C. elm Windsor chair	42	59	96	13%	2

VALUE GROWTH CHART

FURNITURE

PRICES QUOTED IN POUNDS STERLING

ARTICLE	1971	1975	1978	Average Annual Increase	Financial Outlook 1978-84
Low-backed Windsor, c. 1760	60	120	169	16%	2
19th C. Windsor chair	40	69	80	10%	3
Child's Windsor, c. 1765	60	100	140	13%	2
Ornate 19th C. Windsor chair	20	35	55	15%	2
19th C. smoker's bow chair	9	20	37	22%	1

TABLES

ARTICLE	1971	1975	1978	Average Annual Increase	Financial Outlook 1978-84
Oak refectory, c. 1600	250	900	1,250	26%	1
17th C. turned-leg, oak	145	325	600	22%	1
Oak gate-leg table, 1690	85	125	185	12%	3
Small oak gate-leg table, 1675	85	150	225	15%	3
Walnut gate-leg table, c. 1695	150	425	610	22%	2
Mahogany drop-leaf, c. 1725	275	425	600	12%	2
Sabre drop-leaf, George III	200	325	475	13%	2
Oak gate-leg, George III	65	200	345	27%	3
Georgian drop-leaf, c. 1760	65	98	160	14%	2
Mahogany gate-leg drop-flap, 1770	55	95	125	12%	3
Mahogany dining, c. 1800	700	1,200	1,600	13%	3
2-column Regency dining, 1815	500	790	1,250	14%	2
Finely turned Regency dining	550	780	1,100	10%	3
Mahogany breakfast table, 1820	325	565	750	13%	3
Carved base Regency breakfast Table	140	275	400	16%	2
Extendable Regency dining, 1835	100	250	450	24%	1
Rosewood circular table, c. 1830	225	400	620	15%	2
Regency pedestal table, c. 1825	65	220	325	26%	1
Victorian circular table, c. 1850	85	200	300	20%	1
Edwardian dining, c. 1870	35	95	165	25%	1
Victorian mahogany dining	20	49	75	21%	1
Oak side table, c. 1650	145	225	320	12%	3
Oak side table, c. 1680	95	125	200	11%	3
Restoration walnut table, 1685	400	565	750	9%	4
William & Mary fruitwood table	95	250	335	20%	3
William & Mary walnut side table	325	525	750	13%	2
William & Mary carved side table	220	375	550	14%	2
William III inlaid side table	525	750	1,000	10%	4
Carved period gilt table, 1690	200	310	420	11%	3
William III walnut card table, 1700	1,000	1,500	2,200	12%	3
Queen Anne card table, c. 1710	950	1,500	2,300	13%	3
18th C. walnut card table	850	1,250	1,900	12%	3
George I mahogany card table	200	440	720	20%	1
George II mahogany card table	185	350	600	18%	2
Walnut folding table, c. 1720	140	325	575	22%	1
George I oak occasional table	125	200	310	14%	2
George II mahogany game table	225	350	550	14%	3
George II carved side table	600	820	1,000	8%	4
Folding table, mahogany, 1740	125	290	420	19%	1
Tea table, mahogany, c. 1760	185	300	520	16%	1
Folding mahogany tea cart, 1770	190	300	500	15%	1

VALUE GROWTH CHART

FURNITURE   PRICES QUOTED IN POUNDS
                                    STERLING

ARTICLE	1971	1975	1978	Average Annual Increase	Financial Outlook 1978-84
Walnut side table, 1760	50	70	105	11%	3
Chippendale card table, 1775	300	475	610	11%	3
Mahogany circular folding, 1795	150	235	345	13%	2
Mahogany card table, 1765	175	275	425	14%	2
George III satinwood card table	800	975	1,250	7%	4
Sheraton satinwood table, 1800	200	325	500	14%	3
Serpentine front side table, 1800	75	120	160	11%	4
Regency mahogany table, 1820	65	110	185	16%	2
Rosewood card table, 1820	145	250	390	15%	2
Pedestal Regency card table	95	125	185	10%	3
Victorian mahogany card table	35	55	92	15%	2
Folding walnut card table, 1855	45	95	165	20%	1
William & Mary walnut dressing table	450	690	900	10%	3
Dressing table & mirror set, 1710	550	725	925	8%	4
Queen Anne walnut dressing table	490	675	850	8%	4
George fruitwood dressing table	175	320	500	16%	3
Oak dressing table, c. 1745	125	275	360	16%	2
Country dressing table, c. 1775	85	170	200	13%	3
Mahogany dressing table, c. 1770	65	100	155	13%	3
Georgian dressing table, c. 1785	75	165	220	17%	2
Mahogany dressing table, c. 1825	55	110	165	17%	2
Mahogany pembroke table, c. 1785	50	75	110	12%	3
Detailed pembroke table, c. 1790	135	245	340	14%	3
Sheraton pembroke table, c. 1810	250	420	590	13%	2
18th C. sofa table, c. 1790	450	780	1,000	12%	3
Georgian sofa table, mahogany	475	700	865	9%	4
Regency sofa table, c. 1810	425	675	925	12%	3
Regency sofa table, c. 1825	245	400	625	14%	2
Regency rosewood sofa table	300	450	700	13%	3
Regency writing table, mahogany	95	140	200	11%	4
Regency rosewood library table	500	750	960	10%	4
Regency rent table, c. 1810	550	700	1,000	9%	4
Victorian library table, 1850	75	140	245	18%	1
Mahogany writing table, c. 1820	65	115	170	15%	3
Walnut candle stand, c. 1675	175	325	520	17%	2
Walnut tripod, c. 1720	150	300	455	17%	2
Mahogany tripod, c. 1760	55	72	90	7%	4
Piecrust tripod table, c. 1765	550	675	750	5%	4
Simple tripod table, mahogany, 18th C.	30	50	65	12%	3
Mahogany tripod table, c. 1790	25	35	55	12%	3
Mahogany tripod w/"bird-cage," 1765	75	90	125	8%	4
Georgian mahogany dumbwaiter	175	290	450	14%	2
Georgian dumbwaiter, c. 1790	125	270	345	16%	2
Fruitwood tripod, c. 1800	35	65	92	15%	2
Georgian tripod, c. 1810	30	55	75	14%	2
19th C. country tripod table	15	25	39	15%	2
Rectangular-top tripod, c. 1850	75	145	225	17%	1
19th C. tripod table	8	15	30	21%	1
Painted papier-mâché table, 1850	55	68	90	7%	4
Mahogany tripod table, c. 1850	9	20	35	21%	1
Oak cricket table, c. 1795	35	55	90	14%	2

VALUE GROWTH CHART

FURNITURE ARTICLE	1971	1975	1978	Average Annual Increase	Financial Outlook 1978-84
CHESTS					
16th C. carved chest	55	110	185	19%	2
3-Panel carved oak chest, 1635	75	190	245	18%	2
Paneled top & sides carved, c. 1655	85	145	255	17%	2
4-panel plain oak chest, c. 1655	45	95	150	19%	2
17th C. oak chest w/drawer	65	125	250	21%	1
18th C. oak mule chest	45	90	135	17%	2
Inlaid walnut chest w/handles, 18th C.	145	275	360	14%	3
Elm country chest, plank 1755	20	30	49	14%	3
Paneled chest of drawers, c. 1675	110	240	340	17%	2
Oak chest of drawers, c. 1685	120	175	240	10%	4
17th C. simple oak chest of drawers	95	140	225	13%	4
William & Mary chest on stand	300	525	820	15%	3
Oyster & Marquetry chest, 1690	950	1,400	1,700	9%	4
Oak chest on stand, c. 1695	175	320	590	19%	1
William & Mary inlaid chest	300	550	820	15%	2
Walnut chest, inlaid, c. 1710	200	325	450	12%	3
Queen Anne chest on stand	175	375	590	19%	1
Queen Anne chest on stand, walnut	300	570	895	17%	2
Walnut chest on chest, c. 1735	450	675	1,100	14%	2
George I chest on chest, c. 1710	400	570	820	11%	3
Country chest on stand, c. 1720	200	420	610	17%	2
Bachelor chest, walnut, c. 1725	875	1,400	1,800	11%	3
Bachelor chest, walnut, c. 1745	900	1,500	1,750	10%	3
Plain bachelor chest, c. 1755	420	625	940	12%	3
Walnut chest, inlaid, c. 1745	165	270	410	14%	2
Country walnut chest, c. 1755	100	225	365	20%	1
Mahogany chest, bracket feet, c. 1760	75	120	155	11%	3
18th C. mahogany chest of drawers	85	135	210	14%	3
Chest of drawers, mahogany, 1765	175	325	600	19%	2
Serpentine-front chest, c. 1760	450	670	875	10%	3
Mahogany tallboy, c. 1765	75	220	360	25%	1
Detailed mahogany tallboy, 1775	225	450	620	15%	2
Plain mahogany clothes press, 1765	35	55	95	15%	2
Mahogany reeded tallboy, 1770	125	240	310	14%	3
Serpentine mahogany lowboy, 1795	75	135	190	14%	3
18th C. bow-front chest, mahogany	170	240	300	8%	4
18th C. bow-front mahogany chest	125	180	295	13%	3
Bow-front mahogany chest, c. 1800	65	90	125	10%	3
Bow-front mahogany chest, c. 1810	55	80	110	10%	3
Mahogany wardrobe, c. 1800	50	90	140	16%	2
Military chest, c. 1825	80	120	225	16%	2
Mahogany military chest, c. 1825	125	250	365	17%	2
Regency bow-front chest	95	140	195	11%	3
Victorian bow-front chest	11	20	50	24%	1
Specimen chest, c. 1855	35	100	150	23%	1
Victorian chest, mahogany, c. 1860	9	21	42	25%	1

VALUE GROWTH CHART

FURNITURE

PRICES QUOTED IN POUNDS STERLING

ARTICLE	1971	1975	1978	Average Annual Increase	Financial Outlook 1978-84
DESKS					
William & Mary walnut desk, 1695	1,500	2,400	3,100	11%	3
Oak bureau, c. 1685	175	275	520	17%	2
Fine walnut bureau, c. 1695	450	670	950	11%	3
William & Mary walnut bureau	525	750	1,050	10%	3
Queen Anne walnut bureau bookcase	2,500	4,200	6,575	15%	2
Burr walnut bureau bookcase, 1725	4,200	6,500	8,500	11%	3
Fall-front secretaire walnut, 1695	550	875	1,400	14%	2
George I walnut bureau bookcase	2,500	4,750	7,200	16%	2
Kneehole desk, Queen Anne, c. 1715	825	975	1,250	6%	4
George I secretaire tallboy	400	765	950	13%	3
Bureau, walnut, c. 1740	200	400	620	18%	1
Walnut bureau, c. 1735	150	320	550	20%	1
Stepped-inside bureau, c. 1735	450	675	1,000	12%	3
Queen Anne bureau on stand	300	640	825	16%	2
Oak bureau, c. 1745	200	325	475	13%	3
Oak bureau, c. 1770	75	225	350	25%	1
Mahogany kneehole desk. c. 1745	450	675	900	10%	2
Mahogany bureau, c. 1750	150	290	450	17%	2
Simple 18th C. mahogany bureau	75	255	375	26%	1
Oak bureau, c. 1755	85	275	355	23%	1
Mahogany bureau-bookcase, c. 1755	475	675	1,200	14%	3
Mahogany kneehole desk, c. 1765	800	1,000	1,300	7%	4
Ladies mahogany bureau, c. 1770	275	425	690	14%	2
Hepplewhite bureau-bookcase	2,500	3,000	3,700	6%	4
Sheraton secretaire, c. 1795	350	850	1,250	12%	3
Mahogany bureau, c. 1825	100	160	260	15%	3
Partner's desk, leather top, 1795	375	600	875	13%	3
Regency davenport, mahogany	95	160	265	16%	2
Davenport, c. 1800	170	375	550	18%	2
Victorian burr walnut davenport	65	145	225	19%	2
Regency secretaire, c. 1835	125	250	365	17%	2
Pedestal desk, leather top, 1845	65	95	139	11%	3
DRESSERS					
Small oak dresser, c. 1675	550	750	1,250	12%	3
Large oak dresser, c. 1675	400	675	950	13%	3
Fruitwood dresser, c. 1725	250	375	550	12%	3
Country oak dresser, c. 1730	150	300	450	17%	2
Oak dresser & shelves, c. 1725	275	325	475	8%	4
Oak dresser, c. 1735	175	255	400	13%	2
Country oak dresser, c. 1740	100	220	325	18%	2
Elegant oak dresser, c. 1765	220	340	500	12%	2
Oak dresser top w/cornice, 1760	300	550	875	17%	3
18th C. country oak dresser & top	220	375	650	17%	2
18th C. oak cupboard	225	400	575	14%	3
18th C. Welsh oak dresser	145	400	560	21%	1
Oak court cupboard, 17th C.	135	270	420	18%	2

VALUE GROWTH CHART

FURNITURE		PRICES QUOTED IN POUNDS STERLING				
ARTICLE		1971	1975	1978	Average Annual Increase	Financial Outlook 1978-84
Oak cupboard, plain, 18th C.		135	265	565	23%	1
Mahogany sideboard, inlaid, 1775		450	575	800	9%	4
Ornate inlaid sideboard, 1785		650	825	1,000	6%	4
Serpentine front sideboard, 1795		600	800	925	8%	4
Georgian serpentine sideboard		400	625	775	10%	3
Regency walnut sideboard		200	290	375	9%	4
Mahogany sideboard, c. 1820		75	150	270	20%	1
Mahogany chiffonier, c. 1825		150	225	380	14%	3
Regency mahogany chiffonier		140	250	345	14%	3
Victorian mahogany chiffonier		55	95	135	14%	1
Ornate mahogany chiffonier, 1865		40	100	150	21%	1
Walnut corner cupboard, 1725		95	140	260	15%	3
Walnut glassed cupboard, 1730		275	325	410	6%	4
Paneled oak corner cupboard, 1750		75	125	195	15%	2
Bow-front corner cupboard, 1745		65	125	195	17%	2
Mahogany corner cupboard, 1745		75	140	160	11%	3
18th C. oak bow-front cupboard		60	95	150	14%	3
18th C. oak corner cupboard		45	80	130	16%	2
Inlaid mahogany cupboard, 1795		50	85	120	13%	3

SMALL TABLES, NIGHT STANDS

Paneled mahogany table, 1795		55	75	90	7%	4
18th C. mahogany night table		70	95	125	9%	4
Mahogany night stand, c. 1810		65	79	90	5%	4
Detailed mahogany table, c. 1790		70	90	115	7%	4
Victorian night stand, c. 1865		5	10	15	17%	3
Victorian circular stand, 1850		20	35	55	16%	2
Walnut worktable, 1830		95	120	140	6%	4
Regency mahogany worktable		100	145	210	11%	3
Yewwood worktable, c. 1825		130	225	320	14%	2
Victorian mahogany table, 1845		65	100	135	11%	3
Georgian mahogany worktable		85	120	165	10%	3
Victorian mahogany worktable		50	65	80	7%	4
Regency tripod mahogany table		110	150	175	7%	4
Regency mahogany worktable		125	180	250	10%	3
Japanned & painted table, 1845		80	125	165	11%	3
Victorian walnut worktable		30	65	95	18%	2
Regency rosewood teatable		65	115	145	12%	3
Victorian rosewood teapoy		45	65	90	10%	4
Georgian mahogany washstand		55	80	100	9%	4
Georgian mahogany wine cooler		155	210	300	10%	3
18th C. fruitwood bread box		35	65	95	15%	3
Regency whatnot		55	95	140	14%	2
Victorian whatnot		35	55	70	10%	3
18th C. mahogany knife box		35	65	80	13%	3

MIRRORS

18th C. mahogany toilet mirror		60	85	120	10%	3

VALUE GROWTH CHART

FURNITURE

PRICES QUOTED IN POUNDS STERLING

ARTICLE	1971	1975	1978	Average Annual Increase	Financial Outlook 1978-84
Inlaid dressing glass, 1745	250	350	460	9%	4
Mahogany cheval glass, 1785	10	20	35	20%	1
18th C. cheval glass, plain	10	20	25	14%	2
Mahogany toilet mirror, 1785	30	65	90	17%	2
Oval inlaid hepplewhite mirror	45	70	120	15%	2
Georgian mahogany mirror	30	50	75	14%	2

VALUE GROWTH CHART

RUSTIC ANTIQUES

PRICES QUOTED IN POUNDS STERLING

ARTICLE	1971	1975	1978	Average Annual Increase	Financial Outlook 1978-84
Pulpit candleholder	4	6	12	17%	2
Round wooden bowl	5	7	10	10%	3
Steel saucepans, 3 pcs.	7	10	14	11%	3
Wooden salting bowl	12	16	22	9%	3
Carbide bicycle lamp	2	6	9	24%	1
Steel tea urn	6	9	12	10%	3
Cheese press	3	5	9	17%	2
18th C. trivet	6	12	14	13%	3
Oval steel stockpot	3	7	12	22%	1
17th C. wrought-iron lark spit	23	45	80	19.5%	1
Victorian oak coffer, bun feet	5	15	35	32%	1
19th C. metal & mahogany silver chest	7	15	45	30%	1
17th C. iron-bound Armada chest	100	320	475	25%	1
15th C. child's oak coffer	275	525	675	14%	2
Early iron & brass flatiron	6	12	14	13%	2
George III iron door key	4	14	20	26%	1
Iron rush-light holder, 1710	56	80	110	10%	4
19th C. tun "bulls-eye" lamp	5	10	17	19%	2
Queen Anne brass & horn lantern	17	39	62	20%	1
Victorian copper ship's lamp	4	18	27	31%	1
19th C. brass carriage lamp	12	25	42	19%	2
Victorian brass carriage lamp	6	16	39	30%	1
Victorian brass student's lamp	3	8	18	29%	1
Victorian brass table lamp	10	27	39	21%	1
19th C. mangle	2	8	14	32%	1
19th C. mahogany bootrack	12	30	64	27%	1

TAVERN SIGNS

	1971	1975	1978		
Coat of arms, lions	12	50	69	28%	1

VALUE GROWTH CHART

RUSTIC ANTIQUES

PRICES QUOTED IN POUNDS STERLING

ARTICLE	1971	1975	1975	Average Annual Increase	Financial Outlook 1978-84
Portrait of Henry VIII, wood	49	100	169	46%	1
19th C. fishmonger's shop sign	69	150	225	18%	2
Portrait, Duke of Marlborough	35	100	150	23%	2
Brass, Lloyds insurance	10	32	69	31%	1
Wood, The Three Lambs Inn	32	70	140	23%	1
Double, The Bull, on wood	25	62	89	20%	1
Silhouette metal, The Beehive	22	40	95	23%	1
Carved figure, Tobacconists	95	250	450	25%	1
Wood, The Red Lion	35	70	92	15%	2

SPINNING WHEELS

ARTICLE	1971	1975	1975	Average Annual Increase	Financial Outlook 1978-84
George III, oak & elm	26	45	80	18%	2
18th C. oak, working order	20	40	62	17%	3
18th C. fruitwood, dated 1795	25	50	95	21%	1
17th C. oak, ivory finials	32	69	120	21%	1
19th C. beechwood, small	52	115	149	16%	3
19th C. beechwood, steel wheel	26	57	74	16%	3
18th C. woolwinder	6	14	25	23%	1
18th C. elm woolwinder	9	17	29	18%	2

WEATHER VANES

ARTICLE	1971	1975	1975	Average Annual Increase	Financial Outlook 1978-84
Copper & brass weathercock	100	240	375	21%	1
18th C. copper & iron fox	56	115	145	15%	2
18th C. copper & iron wolf	59	140	195	19%	2
19th C. iron w/copper ball	69	110	185	15%	3
17th C. copper ship	65	125	200	17%	3
Victorian copper arrow	9	22	39	23%	1
Victorian copper hen	12	25	42	20%	1

VALUE GROWTH CHART

BRASS, COPPER, PEWTER

PRICES QUOTED IN POUNDS STERLING

ARTICLE	1971	1975	1978	Average Annual Increase	Financial Outlook 1978-84
Brass tavern tobacco box, 1840	47	82	96	11%	3
19th C. brass birdcage	30	59	72	13%	3
19th C. bronzed brass vase, 12" tall	3	8	14	25%	1
Pr. 19th C. cast brass doorstop	19	32	45	13%	2

VALUE GROWTH CHART

PRICES QUOTED IN POUNDS STERLING

ARTICLE	1971	1975	1978	Average Annual Increase	Financial Outlook 1978-84
Pr. 19th C. brass candlesticks	12	25	36	17%	3
Pr. embossed bronze candlesticks	10	20	33	19%	2
19th C. large brass candlesticks	9	23	36	22%	1
19th C. 6-branch candelabrum	16	32	45	16%	3
Pr. 18th C. brass candlesticks, 20"	40	62	84	11%	3
Pr. George II brass candlesticks, 10"	12	26	39	18%	2
19th C. brass-center, candelabrum	18	30	46	14%	3
Pr. 18th C. brass candlesticks, 20"	39	72	95	14%	3
Pr. 19th C. ornate metal candlesticks	6	14	20	19%	2
Pr. 19th C. cylindrical candlesticks	19	46	64	19%	2
Pr. 17th C. bell-metal candlesticks	38	64	79	11%	3
Pr. Regency ormolu candlesticks	82	127	145	8%	4
Pr. 19th C. brass altarsticks	16	32	67	23%	1
Iron cauldron, c. 1800	12	23	37	17%	3
18th C. copper coal helmet	19	34	47	14%	3
19th C. brass coal helmet	9	20	39	23%	1
19th C. copper coal skuttle	8	17	29	20%	1
19th C. copper coal skuttle	7	14	30	23%	1
French ormolu coal skuttle, 17th C.	38	76	87	13%	2
Edwardian mahogany coal cabinet	6	12	24	22%	1
Regency brass coal box w/crest	12	26	39	18%	2
19th C. circular brass bucket	9	16	32	20%	1
Edwardian oak coal box	2	4	9	24%	1
18th C. oval copper skuttle	12	38	62	26%	1
19th C. brass log box	26	59	84	18%	2
Edwardian walnut coal cabinet	4	10	18	24%	1
19th C. mahogany coal box	5	12	28	28%	1
Brass candlesticks	3	5	12.50	17%	3
Brass fenders	2	5	10	26%	1
Brass footmen trivets	10	25	50	26%	1
Pr. Queen Anne candelsticks	38	90	140	20%	1
Queen Anne copper chocolate pot	20	37	56	16%	2
18th C. lead tobacco jar	11	27	40	20%	1
Brass scales	12	17	32	16%	2
Apothecary's box	10	15	24	13.5%	3
Pr. 19th C. Russian candleholders	22	35	47	11%	3
George III copper measure	7	12	19	15%	3
Steel fire irons, c. 1895	32	44	56	8%	4
George III copper teakettle	9	19	27	17%	2
18th C. copper kettle w/stand	19	32	53	16%	2
19th C. brass spirit kettle	10	25	38	21%	1
19th C. copper samovar	25	40	62	14%	2
Victorian pierced brass fender	6	12	22	20%	1
Victorian plated samovar	14	23	39	16%	3
19th C. copper samovar w/crest	22	45	59	15%	3
George III copper tea urn	16	35	49	17%	2
19th C. copper plaque, 16" x 8"	20	36	47	13%	2
Copper wine flagon, c. 1720	27	50	64	13%	3

VALUE GROWTH CHART

PRICES QUOTED IN POUNDS STERLING

ARTICLE	1971	1975	1978	Average Annual Increase	Financial Outlook 1978-84
19th C. copper saucepan	2	5	12	29%	1
19th C. martingale of 6 brasses	7	18	29	23%	1
15th C. copper luster dish	72	126	159	12%	3
Victorian copper jelly mold	5	12	20	22%	1
19th C. brass footman	20	32	46	13%	2
Pr. brass candlesticks, 1765	40	60	87	12%	2
19th C. copper warming pan	9	16	24	15%	3
Copper & brass hot punchbowl, 1850	36	65	86	13%	3
19th C. copper preserving pan	12	20	34	16%	2
19th C. copper kettle	6	13	24	22%	1
22" pewter charger, 1715, signed	94	165	225	13%	3
15" pewter charger, 18th C.	12	29	64	27%	1
17th C. French 16" crested plate	140	290	425	17%	2
12 signed 18th C. octagon plates	245	650	900	20%	1
19th C. half-pint measure	6	15	29	25%	1
18th C. pewter chalice	19	40	69	20%	1
19th C. ornate coffeepot, 1870	5	12	20	22%	1
17th C. tankard w/lid	55	100	165	17%	3
Domed lid measure, qt., 1800	60	100	140	13%	2

PEWTER

ARTICLE					
7 graduated spirit measures	45	70	95	11%	3
19th engraved half-pint tankard	6	17	35	29%	1
19th C. quart tankard	12	20	50	23%	1
½ gal. measure, c. 1825	49	95	160	18%	3
19th C. pewter teapot	4	12	18	24%	1
18th C. German baluster pitcher	65	200	325	26%	1
18th C. German wine flagon	145	300	495	19%	2
Swiss 10 lidded flagon, 1820	44	80	160	20%	2
18th C. Swiss wine pitcher	140	250	500	20%	1
17th C. wine flagon, 14" tall	250	560	800	18%	2
German 18th C. 7-peg tankard	90	165	245	15%	2
English cider pitcher	32	62	94	17%	3
17th C. Swiss wine flagon	90	179	320	20%	1
Pr. 18th C. 16" candlesticks	60	140	195	18%	2
18th C. quark tankard	12	25	59	25%	1
Dutch, 18th C. pewter jug	49	100	250	26%	1
19th C. hot-water dish	7	20	39	28%	1
18th C. German tureen & cover	120	250	500	23%	1
19th C. tulip tankard	14	20	52	21%	1
18th C. bulbous measure	92	185	320	19%	2
19th C. Saxon candlestick	72	125	200	16%	3
17th C. cylindrical tankard	220	400	760	19%	2

VALUE GROWTH CHART

CHINA   PRICES QUOTED IN POUNDS
                                        STERLING

ARTICLE	1971	1975	1978	Average Annual Increase	Financial Outlook 1978-84
Flow blue jug & basins	3	5	20	31%	1
Ralph Wood bust, c. 1754	100	175	275	16%	3
Derby pigeon tureen, c. 1760	175	300	450	16%	2
Swanseau cup & saucer, c. 1820	50	150	200	22%	1
Rockingham plate, c. 1830	20	50	75	21%	1
1st period Worchester plate, c. 1770	75	125	175	13%	3
Chelsea teapot, c. 1750	1,250	2,400	3,250	15%	3
Pr. 19th C. Chelsea Derby candlesticks	84	135	200	13%	2
19th C. Copeland spade teapot	2	6	12	29%	1
19th C. Copeland toilet jug	4	10	22	28%	1
Pr. 19th C. Copeland 2-handled vases	12	32	65	27%	1
Copeland tazza, ornate, 19th C.	20	49	78	21%	1
18th C. Dutch ship tile	1	4	9	37%	1
Pr. 18th C. Dutch floral tiles	10	26	38	21%	1
17th C. Dutch picture tile	3	10	17	28%	1
17th C. Dutch portrait tile	2	9	19	38%	1
18th C. Dutch bird tile	1	5	9	37%	1
17th C. Dutch cavalier tile	2	8	22	41%	1
17th C. pr. Delft drug jars	54	125	169	18%	2
18th C. Dutch drug jar	19	45	67	20%	1
19th C. Delft windmill vase	6	16	25	23%	1
Derby woman figure, 12", 1770	69	155	249	20%	1
1775 Derby putto	12	24	49	22%	1
Derby, Venus figure candlestick	120	240	540	24%	1
Derby vase, 6" with medallion	70	125	195	16%	3
Derby cake dish w/handle, 1820	7	12	25	20%	1
19th C. Derby cavilier figure	21	50	96	24%	1
19th C. Derby desk & inkstand	12	39	86	32%	1
18th C. Derby tankard, 5" tall	95	200	420	24%	1
Royal Doulton jardiniere	5	16	32	30%	1
19th C. Royal Doulton jug & basin	2	10	22	41%	1
Royal Doulton floral toilet jug	2	6	14	32%	1
Lambeth Doulton salt glaze jug	4	10	19	25%	1
Lambeth Doulton jubilee jug, 19th C.	6	14	27	24%	1
Royal Doulton floral vase, 19th C.	12	20	38	18%	2
19th C. Royal Doulton vase, 7"	6	16	34	28%	1
Pr. Doulton Lambeth vases	70	132	195	16%	2
19th C. Dresden comport	12	22	49	22%	1
19th C. Dresden floral plate	6	14	38	30%	1
19th C. Dresden floral mirror	12	25	59	25%	1
19th C. covered floral Dresden bowl	9	15	44	25%	1
19th C. Dresden figure group	86	175	269	18%	2
Dresden coffee urn w/flowers, 1820	125	350	550	24%	1
19th C. Dresden of Bacchus	69	150	290	23%	1
19th C. Dresden flower clock, 16"	89	200	435	25%	1
4-19th C. Dresden seasonal figurines	125	245	500	22%	1
Victorian alabaster peep show	6	16	32	27%	1
Victorian floral jug, c. 1860	3	8	19	30%	1
Victorian fruit bowl	4	10	20	26%	1
Salad bowl & spoons, c. 1860	5	9	24	25%	1

VALUE GROWTH CHART

CHINA

PRICES QUOTED IN POUNDS STERLING

ARTICLE	1971	1975	1978	Average Annual Increase	Financial Outlook 1978-84
Fruit bowl pedestal, c. 1860	4	15	28	32%	1
19th C. commemorative jug	1	4	9	37%	1
Pr. floral Victorian vases, 16"	6	14	27	24%	1
19th C. Swansea coronation mug	45	125	240	27%	1
19th C. cheese dish w/cover	22	30	69	18%	2
Newhall luster C & S, floral, 1815	5	12	20	22%	2
Exeter pottery vase, floral	1	4	12	43%	1
Hanley teapot, c. 1805	19	40	59	18%	2
19th C. Fishley toad plate	4	10	20	26%	1
19th C. parian figures w/glass dome	10	37	68	32%	1
Toby jug, c. 1901	3	9	14	25%	1
18th C. floral pottery plate	5	13	29	29%	1
Enoch wood bust, 15"	69	145	210	17%	2
Sunderland luster plate, 8"	8	20	38	25%	1
Victorian bust of lady, unglazed	2	5	12	29%	1
Spode pearlware dish, c. 1840	4	12	20	26%	1
12 Ps. 19th C. floral spode dishes	95	250	445	25%	1
8 octagon davenport plates, c. 1860	30	70	110	20%	1
19th C. Mason ironstone mug	12	25	38	18%	2
Victorian floral toilet pail	3	9	14	25%	1
Victorian vase, floral, 12"	1	4	9	37%	1
19th C. jug, portrait Princess Victoria	19	38	64	19%	1
Pr. Victorian figures, 14"	4	12	20	26%	1
Pr. Exeter flower urn, 19"	5	16	29	28%	1
Longton Hall coffee cup, c. 1760	12	30	58	25%	1
Bow putto, enameled, c. 1775	8	22	49	29%	1
Pr. alabaster ewers, 14"	2	10	19	38%	1
Victorian porcelain plaque, 12"	12	40	59	26%	1
Victorian floral jug & basin	1	5	12	43%	1
Large Victorian floral jug & basin	2	7	16	34%	1
Victorian potpourri vase	2	6	16	35%	1
Pr. Victorian square vases	2	5	15	33%	1
19th C. decorated scenic vase	1	4	10	39%	1
Victorian statue, woman, 6'	2	4	12	29%	1
Victorian chamber pot	50	2	9	51%	1
Enoch Wood mustard pot, c. 1835	4	12	22	27%	1
Victorian vase, urn type	3	7	14	25%	1
Pr. Oriental Victorian figures, 6"	2	7	17	36%	1
Victorian unglazed figure group	29	60	89	17%	2
Victorian 6 ps. porcelain tea service	100	225	350	19%	2
Pr. neoclassic Berlin vases	95	200	450	25%	1
Pr. 19th C. man & woman figures	19	42	69	20%	1
17th C. Bellamine jug, 18"	14	39	58	22%	1
19th C. bisque porcelain bust	20	48	69	19%	2
Early Rosenthal eagle on iron c. 1900	13	32	68	27%	1
Pr. Royal Dux figures, 18" high	12	58	92	34%	1
Art Deco figure of dancer	60	190	300	26%	1
19th C. sculptured Berlin cup & saucer	19	52	98	26%	1
19th C. Meissen figure of spring	50	80	125	14%	2

VALUE GROWTH CHART

PRICES QUOTED IN POUNDS STERLING

ARTICLE	1971	1975	1978	Average Annual Increase	Financial Outlook 1978-84
Pr. of Meissen rabbits	55	130	210	21%	1
19th C. Meissen teapot, German flowers	20	52	110	27%	1
Meissen hen on a nest	32	86	120	21%	1
Pr. of Meissen goldfinches	300	550	895	17%	2
Meissen musical group, c. 1765	159	375	690	23%	1
19th C. figure group	42	80	149	20%	1
19th C. Oriental stick stand, floral	14	30	76	27%	2
Oriental vase with cover	65	145	225	19%	2
Imari vase, 15"	12	28	64	27%	1
19th C. Oriental bottle vase	12	50	36	17%	2
19th C. Satsuma crackleware vase	3	9	22	33%	1
K'ang Hsi, blue & white saucer dish	10	39	65	31%	1
Nankin serving dish w/cover	39	80	140	20%	1
Ch'ien Lung, famille rose large dish	125	345	625	26%	1
Pr. K'ang Hsi pear-shaped vases, 8"	100	250	550	28%	1
Chinese stem cup, 5", transitional	34	94	149	23%	1
K'ang Hsi onion-shaped bottle, 11"	69	200	345	26%	1
19th C. Satsuma figure on stand	19	40	76	22%	1
19th C. Satsuma 2-handled vase	12	30	76	30%	1
19th C. bulbous bronze, cloisonne vase	5	18	32	30%	1
Pr. 19th C. Cloisonne vase, 2 handles	19	50	82	23%	1
Crackleware vase w/imperial dragon	16	48	72	24%	1
19th C. Satsuma pail, 12" with flowers	12	25	47	21%	1
17th C. Chinese vase, w/dragon	295	525	720	14%	2
19th C. Satsuma ginger jar	2	9	26	44%	1
19th C. Minton parian figure	19	48	72	25%	1
19th C. Minton crested tureen	16	45	78	25%	1
19th C. Jasperware, Minton cheese dish	29	59	86	17%	2
Minton floral comport	2	6	14	32%	1
Pr. 19th C. Minton vases, 16" on bases	110	295	490	24%	1
19th C. Minton sucrier	12	20	36	17%	2
19th C. Minton parian figure group	3	16	34	41%	1
19th C. Minton little flower plate	2	5	9	24%	1
19th C. Rockingham covered dish	6	13	22	20%	1
6" Rockingham shepherd dress	140	235	400	16%	2
Prattware plate w/border	14	36	62	24%	1
19th C. Saltglaze puzzle jug	11	26	39	20%	1
Saltglaze Lord Nelson Toby jug	20	50	70	19%	2
19th C. Seires ornate tureen	90	160	360	22%	1
Pr. 19th C. 2 handled Sèvres vases	240	600	925	21%	1
Sèvres pierced oval fruit dish, 1810	21	39	58	16%	2
Sèvres globe w/cupid decor	69	195	345	26%	1
19th C. Vienna floral plate	2	9	16	34%	2
12 Ps. 19th C. Vienna tea service	62	140	259	23%	1
Pr. 2-handled Vienna vase on base	12	38	72	29%	1
Victorian Staffordshire bowl and vase	4	10	18	24%	1
19th C. Staffordshire castle model	6	20	29	25%	1
19th C. Staffordshire figure glove, 8"	3	9	14	25%	1
Staffordshire figure, Duke of Edinburgh	12	22	39	18%	2

VALUE GROWTH CHART

PRICES QUOTED IN POUNDS STERLING

ARTICLE	1971	1975	1978	Average Annual Increase	Financial Outlook 1978-84
Staffordshire figure, Duke of Clarence	10	20	36	20%	1
Staffordshire figure, 2 figures, 14"	14	24	50	19%	2
Staffordshire dog group, 9"	2	9	18	37%	1
Staffordshire figure group, 19th C.	4	12	32	34%	1
Staffordshire figure, dancing, c. 1850	6	16	30	26%	1
19th C. Staffordshire clay jug, 9"	5	12	19	21%	1
19th C. figure of Prince Albert	12	20	42	19%	2
Staffordshire figure Queen Victoria	14	32	54	21%	1
Figure of Princess Royal, c. 1858	12	30	59	25%	1
Statue Emperor Napoleon, 1846	10	29	52	26%	1
19th C. Staffordshire dalmation	5	20	36	32%	1
19th C. Staffordshire figure, "Winter"	9	23	42	25%	1
Staffordshire statue, Albert & Victoria	14	34	48	19%	2
Staffordshire figure, Shakespeare	11	30	52	25%	1
Hollow-based Staffordshire, sailor, 1835	14	33	56	22%	1
Late 19th C. Staffordshire, lady, 5"	2	9	16	35%	1
19th C. Staffordshire figure group	3	14	26	36%	1
Pr. 19th C. Staffordshire figures	20	42	68	19%	2
Staffordshire figure of Justice, 1790	22	38	46	11%	3
19th C. Staffordshire hen on nest	20	36	54	15%	2
Pr. Staffordshire pug dogs, c. 1870	20	50	92	24%	1
Staffordshire Dog, 13", c. 1870	9	20	36	22%	1
19th C. small Staffordshire vase	6	15	30	26%	1
Pr. Staffordshire luster spaniels, 1850	16	32	60	21%	1
Staffordshire leech jar, 30", c. 1835	160	345	475	17%	2
Pr. 19th C. Staffordshire pugs	18	50	79	24%	2
Staffordshire figure of Don Quixote	48	96	120	14%	3
Porcelain cottage lift lid, c. 1840	15	35	59	22%	1
Pr. Staffordshire horse statues, c. 1845	10	25	62	30%	1
19th C. Martinware "monk" bird	320	675	825	14%	2
Martinware stoneware pitcher	19	42	68	20%	2
Martinware vase, c. 1902	20	34	64	18%	3
Royal Worcester 2-handled pot and cover	14	30	59	23%	1
1st period Worcester floral jug	18	42	79	24%	1
Chamberlain Worcester meat plate, 1800	30	62	120	22%	1
Pr. Grainger sauce tureens, c. 1810	29	60	98	19%	2
Dr. Wall coffeepot, 1st period, floral	175	300	485	16%	3
1st period Dr. Wall coffee cup and saucer	48	94	155	18%	2
Pr. Grainger sauce tureens, 1810	39	60	110	16%	2
1st period Worcester plate w/crest	42	98	138	19%	2
1st period Dr. Wall teapot, floral	32	72	110	19%	3
Pr. Royal Worcester Persian vases, 1878	140	300	525	21%	1
Royal Worcester fish plate, c. 1870	6	15	38	30%	1
1st period Worcester sauceboat	18	42	74	22%	1
Dr. Wall Worcester bowl, floral, 1770	5,200	9,250	12,000	13%	2
Royal Worcester jug, 5", c. 1891	7	16	32	24%	1
Royal Worcester white leaf design pot	4	12	23	28%	1
Pr. Royal Worcester statues, 1825	39	87	125	20%	1

VALUE GROWTH CHART

PRICES QUOTED IN POUNDS
STERLING

ARTICLE	1971	1975	1978	Average Annual Increase	Financial Outlook 1978-84
19th C. Wedgwood biscuit barrel	16	32	59	20%	1
19th C. Wedgwood pagoda dish	5	19	39	34%	1
Wedgewood paper biscuit barrel	18	42	69	21%	1
19th C. green Wedgwood serving plate	2	6	12	29%	1
18th C. green Wedgwood fern plate	9	14	32	20%	1
19th C. black basalt female figure	36	96	142	22%	1
Wedgewood black basalt bust, 18"	64	125	196	17%	2

Miniature bracket Clock, strike repeat, by Joseph Knibb.

Profit Record
1971: PS 7,000
1978: PS 15,000

Individual Notes

Investment Predictions
1979–84

This bracket clock over the past 7 years increased in value 114%, which is a compounded growth rate of 11.5% per year. Bracket clocks have always commanded high prices and should continue to appreciate at a similar rate.

Various Victorian clocks, by Thomas Cole, gilt and decorative.

Profit Record
1971: PS 900
1978: PS 3,000

Individual Notes

Investment Predictions
1979–84

These Victorian clocks increased in value over the past 7 years 233%, which is a compounded growth rate of 18.6% per year. Clocks of this period that are attractively engraved and decorated are at present much in demand and should continue to appreciate at a stable rate for many years to come, while lesser Victorian clocks may only remain the same.

Orrery clock by Riango Paris; 24 inches high.

Profit Record
1971: PS 6,000
1978: PS 12,000

Individual Notes

Investment Predictions
1979–84

This clock over the past 7 years increased in value 100%, which is a compounded growth rate of 10.5% per year. The originality of this piece will help sustain a continued appreciation.

French carriage clock, automatic, striking and repeating Dentent escapement.

Profit Record
1971: PS 2,000
1978: PS 6,000

Individual Notes

Investment Predictions
1979–84

The above clock over the past 7 years increased in value 200%, which is a compounded growth rate of 17% per year. Continued appreciation is expected in clocks of this quality and period.

French calendar clock by Henrie Marc, who is a famous Paris maker. Pinwheel escapement, moon dial.

Profit Record
1971: PS 400
1978: PS 1,000

Individual Notes

Investment Predictions
1979–84

The above French clock increased in value 150% over the past 7 years, which is a compounded growth rate of 14% per year. Clocks of this period are in continuous demand and will continue to appreciate at a stable rate over the next few years.

Tortoiseshell clock, striking and repeating, by D. Quare. 9½" high.

Profit Record
1971: PS 24,000
1978: PS 30,000

Individual Notes

Investment Predictions
1979–84

This Tortoiseshell clock increased in value 25% over the past 7 years, which is a compounded growth rate of 3.3% per year. Prices in this range tend to increase much slower, but remain very stable and are considered solid investments.

INVESTING IN COUNTRY FURNITURE

Due to the fluctuating economic situations in both the United States and England, prices have more than accurately followed economic trends within each country. There has been an appreciable reduction of sales throughout the United Kingdom, which can be directly attributed to the reduced sales experienced by American dealers. Therefore, prices have begun to level off after the drastic increases experienced in the United Kingdom during the 1972/73 period. In fact, where unprecedented price increases were experienced during this period, some antique groups have actually begun to decline in prices.

Furniture, especially useful pieces, are becoming increasingly more popular. The buying public has begun to demand antiques that combine both investment possibilities with useful furniture that enables them to furnish their homes with a touch of the past. Only the privileged few today have a cash flow that enables purely investment purchasing of antiques. Dealers report that prices are increasing faster and at a more stable rate in the smaller antique furniture group, which complements today's smaller homes. "Low-end" antiques are enjoying a surprising success, especially decorative accessories, and many dealers who before specialized in purely period pieces have added lines of lower-cost smaller pieces to ensure a continual cash flow.

Buyers from the Continent were less severely affected by the economic depression than the American dealers; therefore, the more general antique dealers that catered to the European trade have been able to maintain more stabilized prices. In general, prices in the United Kingdom, after the dramatic increases experienced between 1972 and 1973, have begun to decline gradually and are expected to stabilize at a level that would reflect the price under normal inflation since 1972. The recent 1976 devaluation of the pound is not expected to bring a repeat of the 1972–73 price increases, but will hopefully accelerate the stabilization of the previous inflated prices and help stimulate waning sales.

Although the low-end antiques over the past few years have perhaps shown the most dramatic increases in prices, the middle-range antiques, especially the smaller and more useful items, have experienced not only more volume of sales, but greater stability in prices, which is predicted to continue for many years to come. The larger and more expensive "top of the line" antiques have been severely hurt by not only the unstable economic situation, but by changing life-styles, which puts severe size restrictions on many buyers to accommodate smaller homes and apartments. Therefore it is quite possible to find an extremely tall grandfather clock, of excellent quality and craftsmanship, selling for the same if not less than last year's price, and often substantial price reductions can be realized from a dealer who wants to get rid of this specialized piece in order to free his capital for additional investment. At this time excellent buys can be found in slightly damaged furniture. This has resulted in the higher cost of top-quality restoration, which cannot be justified in periods of tight money and reduced sales.

BUYERS' TRENDS

With the reduction of American buyers, England has turned toward the Continent for sales. The Continental dealers, more than enthusiastic with the American trade removed from competition, largely increased their purchasing throughout the United Kingdom. Continental buyers tend to be much more cautious in their purchasing than most American dealers, who look to England as their only European source. Europe for many American dealers poses additional problems in cultural, monetary, and language adjustments that they are not willing to make, unfortunately. The Germans, Dutch, and Swiss are, at present, the most prominent Continental dealers, with the majority of interest centered on country furniture.

GOOD BUYS IN TODAY'S MARKET

Perhaps one of the most frequent questions asked both dealers and appraisers is, "Did I get a good buy?" A "good buy" as applied to antique country furniture is difficult to define, but as a very knowledgeable dealer once told me, "Consider anything a good buy if you pay less than the price of a comparable new piece."

Country furniture is a very expansive field due to the sheer volume of the original pieces. Therefore many areas could be designated as good investment potentials that are undervalued at present. For example, the following pieces could be considered undervalued in today's market and be recommended as good buys:

- Queen Anne single chairs   £90–120
- 18th-century corner cupboards   £65–75
- 18th-century side tables   £70–85
- oak cricket tables   £55–69

... dresser base, c. 1740.

...fit Record
1: PS 150
8: PS 450

...vidual Notes

**Investment Predictions
1979–84**

This 18th-century dresser, which is 4 ft. 8 in. wide, increased in value over the past 7 years 200%, which is a compounded growth rate of 17% per year. Furniture of both this period and size is very popular at present and will continue to appreciate in value in the near future.

18th-century oak dresser with excellent lines and color.

Profit Record	Investment Predictions 1978–84
1970: PS 100	
1974: PS 400	
1977: PS 600	

Individual Notes

The oak dresser over the past 7 years increased in value 500%, which is a compounded growth rate of 30% per year. Prices have begun to stabilize for this type of early oak furniture, but prices will continue to appreciate yearly at a slightly lesser rate.

Walnut bureau with well and stepped interior, c. 1720.

Profit Record
1970: PS 120
1974: PS 450
1977: PS 700

Individual Notes

Investment Predictions
1979–84

The above walnut desk has over the past 7 years increased 483%, which is a compounded growth rate of 29% per year. Desks of this type will continue to increase due to the demand for useful furniture with excellent lines.

Early oak sideboard, c. 1700.

Profit Record
1969: PS 150
1971: PS 300
1973: PS 600
1974: PS 800
1977: PS 900

Individual Notes

Investment Predictions
1978–84

This early oak sideboard over the past 8 years increased in value 500%, which is a compounded growth rate of 30% per year. Useful pieces of furniture such as this will continue to appreciate, but at a slightly reduced rate.

Early cupboard, oak, made before 1700.

Profit Record
1969: PS 150
1971: PS 200
1974: PS 400
1977: PS 590

Individual Notes

Investment Predictions
1978–84

The early oak cupboard over the past 8 years increased in value 293%, which is a compounded growth rate of 22% per year. Although the largest increases have in the past few years been realized, prices should stabilize.

Superb quality Queen Anne period walnut kneehole desk of small proportions, c. 1710.

Profit Record
1971: PS 1,350
1978: PS 2,250

Individual Notes

Investment Predictions 1979–84

This beautiful Queen Anne kneehole desk increased in value 66%, which is a compounded growth rate of 7% per year. Fine quality walnut appears to be coming back into fashion after a period where mahogany has predominated and oak and pine have surged up and down.

Joined or "coffin" stools.

Profit Record
1969: PS 100
1973: PS 200
1977: PS 300

Individual Notes

Investment Predictions 1979–84

Over the past 8 years these early stools increased in value 200%, which is a compounded growth rate of 17%. These stools are rare and highly sought after. Prices should remain fairly stable in this area.

Gothic chair, made from oak.

Profit Record
1969: PS 200
1971: PS 400
1974: PS 700
1977: PS 2,000

Individual Notes

Investment Predictions 1979–84

This early Gothic chair over the past 8 years has increased in value about 900%, which is a compounded growth rate of 39% per year. Recent interest in early oak has caused this surprising appreciation, but prices in this range are beginning to stabilize.

Sheraton period mahogany tambour top lady's writing table with satinwood interior, c. 1780.

Profit Record
1971: PS 1,000
1978: PS 1,500

Individual Notes

Investment Predictions
1979–84

This lady's writing table over the past 7 years increased in value 50%, which is a compounded growth rate of 7%. Since individual wealth has increased considerably faster than the prices of antiques have risen, many people are now in a position to be able to purchase one fine quality piece for their homes, and this is typical of such items. Increases in such prices will continue a slow but steady appreciation.

Chippendale period mahogany long case clock, c. 1770.

Profit Record
1971: PS 1,100
1978: PS 1,700

Individual Notes

Investment Predictions
1979–84

This long case clock over the past 7 years increased in value 54%, which is a compounded growth rate of 6.5%. Clocks like this, by good London makers, with simple lines have always been popular, and will continue steady appreciation.

Regency period rosewood library/games table with brass inlay to the drawer ends and feet, the center panel of the top reversing for chess and removing for backgammon, c. 1810.

Profit Record
1971: PS 1,000
1978: PS 1,500

Individual Notes

Investment Predictions
1979–84

This Regency game table over the past 7 years increased in value 50%, which is a compounded growth rate of 6% per year. With the return of interest in games such as backgammon, pieces of this kind have risen steeply in price.

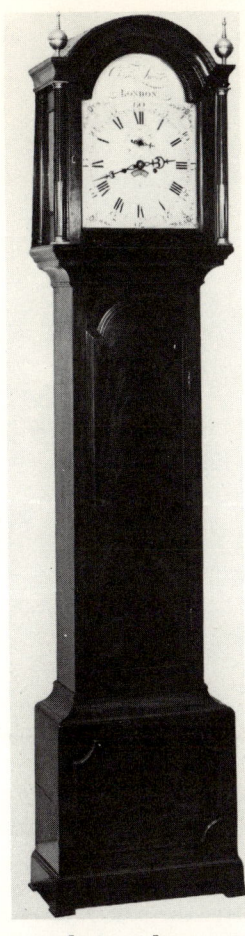

Late 18th-century mahogany long case clock with painted dial by Charles Storer of London, c. 1800.

Profit Record
1971: PS 300
1978: PS 750

Individual Notes

**Investment Predictions
1979–84**

This long case clock over the past 7 years increased in value 150%, which is a compounded growth rate of 18% per year. As the finer clocks have moved up in price so pieces like this have come in at the bottom of the market to fill a gap and are now rising.

Late 18th-century mahogany long case clock by James Ivory of Dundee, c. 1790.

Profit Record
1971: PS 400
1978: PS 1,050

Individual Notes

**Investment Predictions
1979–84**

Over the past 7 years this long case clock increased in value 162%, which is a compounded growth rate of 14.7% per year. While not so many years ago one would not have given this clock a second look, it is indicative of current trends in the clock field. This item now commands a good price and will continue to do so for many years to come.

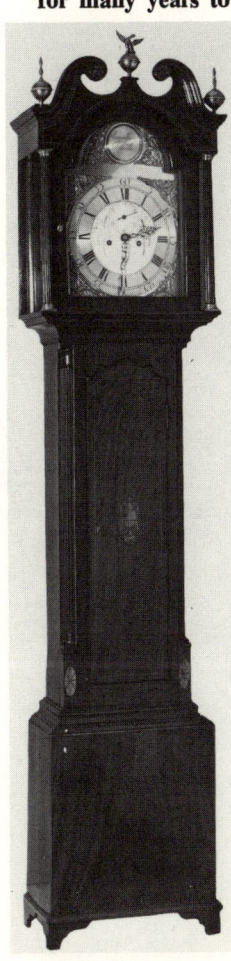

253

Early 18th-century green lacquer long case clock by Williams of King Sutton, c. 1730.

Profit Record	Investment Predictions
1971: PS 1,650	1979–84
1978: PS 2,200	

Individual Notes

Over the past 7 years this 18th-century long case clock increased in value 33%, which is a compounded growth rate of 4.2% per year. Good clocks have always been sought after and pieces of this kind in particular.

Pair of Sheraton period mahogany fold-over top semi-circular card tables, c. 1780.

Profit Record	Investment Predictions
1971: PS 1,500	1979–84
1978: PS 2,250	

Individual Notes

Over the past 7 years this pair of Sheraton card tables have increased in value 50%, which is a compounded growth rate of 6% per year. Pairs of almost anything have become difficult to find and have forced the price up.

Pair of Regency period mahogany fold-over top tea tables, c. 1815.

Profit Record
1971: PS   800
1978: PS 1,500

Individual Notes

Investment Predictions
1979–84

Over the past 7 years this pair of Regency tea tables increased in value 88%, which is a compounded growth rate of 9.5% per year. Pairs such as this are easier to find than earlier tables and are not as highly valued.

...raton period mahogany D-end dining table with center ...ion, c. 1780.

...fit Record
...1: PS 1,300
...8: PS 2,000

...ividual Notes

Investment Predictions
1979–84

This D-end Sheraton dining table over the past 7 years has increased in value 53%, which is a compounded growth rate of 6.3% per year. Elegant twelve-seater dining tables have never been easy to find and do command a high price, and due to their rarity will continue to do so for many years. They are both a solid and very useful investment.

Two from a set of twelve Sheraton period decorate[d] dining room chairs, comprising ten singles and tw[o] carvers, c. 1800.

Profit Record
1971: PS 1,800
1978: PS 3,000

Individual Notes

**Investment Predictions
1979–84**

This set of 12 Sheraton chairs i[n]creased in value 66%, which is [a] compounded growth rate of 7.6[%] per year. Being so decorative a[nd] yet retaining a good clean li[ne] makes it easy to place these chai[rs] in a modern setting. Therefor[e] the lines of these chairs ensure [a] continued stable increase in val[ue] of the next few years.

Two from a set of eight early Chippendale period chestnut dining room chairs, comprising six singles and two carvers, having finely carved ribbon backs and standing on cabriole legs, c. 1750.

Profit Record
1971: PS 2,250
1978: PS 3,500

Individual Notes

**Investment Predictions
1979–84**

This set of Chippendale chairs has increased in value 55%, which is a compounded growth rate of 6.5% per year. The rarity of these chairs makes them something of a collector's item, but there do seem to be more collectors around these days than some years ago.

Unusual Regency period oak Welsh dresser with paneled doors inlaid with mahogany and three drawers, crossbanded in mahogany, c. 1820.

Profit Record
1971: PS 300
1978: PS 800

Individual Notes

Investment Predictions
1979–84

Over the past 7 years this oak dresser increased in value 166%, which is a compounded growth rate of 15% per year. Always a useful piece but the sort of thing that has only recently become fashionable. Appreciation on this type of furniture will definitely increase in value during the next several years and is considered an excellent investment.

Early 18th-century oak Welsh dresser on cabriole legs with shaped doors and frieze to the cornice, c. 1720.

Profit Record
1971: PS   750
1978: PS 1,300

Individual Notes

Investment Predictions
1979–84

Over the past 7 years this 18th-century dresser increased in value 73%, which is a compounded growth rate of 8% per year. Much finer quality than previous Welsh dresser, which is reflected in price, and should be in very high demand in the future.

Chippendale period mahogany secretaire press with paneled doors and blind fret carving to the top, c. 1770.

Profit Record
1971: PS 1,000
1978: PS 1,500

Individual Notes

**Investment Predictions
1979–84**

This secretaire press over the past 7 years increased in value 50%, which is a compounded growth rate of 6% per year. This classical piece, the architectural pediment and finely grained wood combined with the relatively small size, make this item very desirable, which will continue to increase in value steadily.

Sheraton period mahogany secretaire bookcase, c. 1780.

Profit Record
1971: PS 1,300
1978: PS 2,000

Individual Notes

**Investment Predictions
1979–84**

Over the past 7 years this Sheraton bookcase has increased in value 53%, which is a compounded growth rate of 6.5% per year. Yet, quality has never been out of fashion, and although appreciation is sometimes not as rapid, it is always secure.

258

Sheraton period mahogany bureau bookcase with open fret swan neck pediment, c. 1780.

Profit Record
1971: PS 1,600
1978: PS 2,350

Individual Notes

Investment Predictions 1979–84

The period Sheraton bureau bookcase increased in value 46% over the past 7 years, which is a compounded growth rate of 6% per year. The subtle inlay and unusual glazing bars make this piece rare. A steady increase in price should continue.

Charles II tankard, c. 1661.

Profit Record
1972: PS 3,000
1977: PS 4,000

Individual Notes

Investment Predictions 1979–84

Over the past 4 years the above tankard increased in value 33%, which is a compounded growth rate of 4.5% per year. Silver in the higher price ranges peaked several years ago and although silver is always an investment that will appreciate, in today's market less expensive articles are realizing higher returns on investments.

Smaller oak side table, c. 1680.

Profit Record
1971: PS 85
1973: PS 200
1978: PS 375

Individual Notes

**Investment Predictions
1979–84**

Over the past 7 years this small late 17th-century side table increased in value 341%, which is a compounded growth rate of 22% per year. The prices in the smaller early English oak pieces will continue to appreciate and for long-range investment, they are a much safer buy than the larger tables and dressers of the period.

Cabinet, black with inlaid pearl, c. 1765.

Profit Record
1971: PS 1,000
1973: PS 1,600
1978: PS 2,800

Individual Notes

**Investment Predictions
1979–84**

Over the past 7 years this beautiful inlaid cabinet increased in value 180%, which is a compounded growth rate of 16%.

Small walnut chest of drawers, c. 1710.

Profit Record
1971: PS 750
1973: PS 1,750
1978: PS 3,000

Individual Notes

**Investment Predictions
1979–84**

Over the past 7 years the small walnut chest increased in value 300%, which is a compounded growth rate of 22% per year.

Walnut wing chair, c. 1720. Partly covered with old crewel work.

Profit Record
1971: PS   250
1973: PS   900
1978: PS 1,500

Individual Notes

Investment Predictions
1979–84

Over the past 7 years, this early 18th-century wing chair increased in value 500%, which is a compounded growth rate of 29% per year. This dramatic appreciation is due to the rebirth of the chair, and perhaps this one especially was enhanced because of the original crewel work, which has returned to vogue.

Early English chest of drawers, walnut, c. 1710.

Profit Record
1971: PS   200
1973: PS   600
1978: PS 1,200

Individual Notes

Investment Predictions
1979–84

Over the past 7 years this chest of drawers increased in value 500%, which is a compounded growth rate of 29% per year. Chests are becoming more popular due to smaller homes, and the demand for useful pieces of antique furniture therefore increases and can be expected to continue.

261

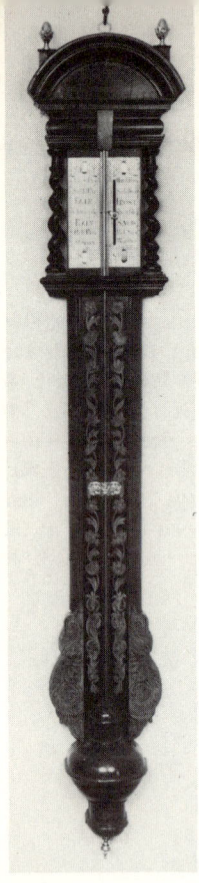

Barometer, c. 1690.

Profit Record			Investment Predictions 1979–84
1971:	PS	300	
1973:	PS	700	
1978:	PS	1,100	

Individual Notes

Over the past 7 years this late 17th-century barometer increased in value 266%, which is a compounded growth rate of 20% per year. During the last decade barometers, as well as clocks, that is actual working instruments, have enjoyed an amazing success. This appreciation should continue undisturbed for the next several years.

Set of 8 walnut side chairs and settee, c. 1720.

Profit Record			Investment Predictions 1979–84
1971:	PS	1,000	
1973:	PS	2,500	
1978:	PS	4,000	

Individual Notes

Over the past 7 years both the chairs and settee increased in value 300%, which is a compounded growth rate of 22% per year. Although the appreciation of these early 18th-century pieces is substantial, perhaps it is not greater because of the changing living style to a more informal mode as well as smaller houses. Although these excellent pieces will continue to increase in value, they will have a smaller market share in the future.

Small mahogany secretary bookcase, English, 1770.

Profit Record			Investment Predictions 1979–84
1971:	PS	250	
1973:	PS	700	
1978:	PS	3,000	

Individual Notes

Over the past 7 years, this late 18th-century secretary bookcase increased in value an outstanding 1,100%, which is a compounded growth rate of 42% per year. Smaller pieces like the above bookcase unit are in large demand, and prices reflect the rarity of good quality smaller units of the period. Prices may level off somewhat, but will continue to increase during the next few years.

Oak refectory table, c. 1610, James I.

Profit Record	Investment Predictions
1971: PS 800	1979–84
1973: PS 1,200	
1978: PS 4,500	

Individual Notes

Over the past 7 years this early 17th-century refectory table increased in value 462%, which is a compounded growth rate of 28% per year. Much of this dramatic appreciation is due to the rarity of authentic James I tables, but also the renewed interest in early English oak played a major part in this increased value.

Oak dresser, c. 1660.

Profit Record	Investment Predictions
1971: PS 200	1979–84
1973: PS 400	
1978: PS 1,250	

Individual Notes

Over the past 7 years this late 17th-century oak dresser increased in value 525%, which is a compounded growth rate of 30% per year. Here again we find the combined influences of rarity and increased demand for early English oak. Prices should stabilize, but increase steadily.

y English coffer, oak, c. 1640.

it Record   **Investment Predictions**
: PS 70   1979–84
: PS 180
: PS 285

idual Notes

Over the past 7 years this 17th-century oak coffer increased in value 307%, which is a compounded growth rate of 22% per year. Early oak, especially English oak, is appreciating rapidly and can be expected to do so for the next several years. This renewed interest can be directly linked to a much more relaxed mode of living.

Early English oak side table with drawer and bottom turned legs and stretchers.

Profit Record
1971: PS 120
1973: PS 225
1978: PS 325

Individual Notes

Investment Predictions
1979–84

Over the past 7 years this side table increased in value 170%, which is a compounded growth rate of 15% per year. This appreciation reflects the collecting trend toward early English oak and will continue for the next several years.

English dresser base, oak with drawers and cupboards, early 18th century.

Profit Record
1971: PS 180
1973: PS 400
1978: PS 550

Individual Notes

Investment Predictions
1979–84

Over the past 7 years this 18th-century dresser increased in value 205%, which is a compounded growth rate of 17% per year. This appreciation will continue due to a renewed interest in early English oak.

Papier-mâché tray, black/gold, c. 1810.

Profit Record
1971: PS 30
1973: PS 45
1978: PS 90

Individual Notes

**Investment Predictions
1979–84**

Over the past 7 years this papier-mâché tray increased in value 200%, which is a compounded growth rate of 20% per year. This appreciation in price is in keeping with the growth of antiques that fall in the category of decorative accessories and will continue during the next several years.

English armchair, walnut heavily carved, c. 1670.

Profit Record
1971: PS 85
1973: PS 200
1978: PS 300

Individual Notes

**Investment Predictions
1979–84**

Over the past 7 years this early English armchair increased in value 252%, which is a compounded growth rate of 20% per year. This pattern is due to continue over the next several years.

Early Italian walnut writing table, c. 1710.

Profit Record
1971: PS 350
1973: PS 550
1978: PS 850

Individual Notes

**Investment Predictions
1979–84**

Over the past 7 years this writing table increased in value 142%, which is a compounded growth rate of 14% per year.

English mahogany free-standing bookcase with rising top, c. 1840.

Profit Record	Investment Predictions
1971: PS 175	1979–84
1973: PS 200	
1978: PS 350	Over the past 7 years this mahogany bookcase unit increased in value 100%, which is a compounded growth rate of 10.5% per year and is predicted to continue at this rate over the next several years.
Individual Notes	

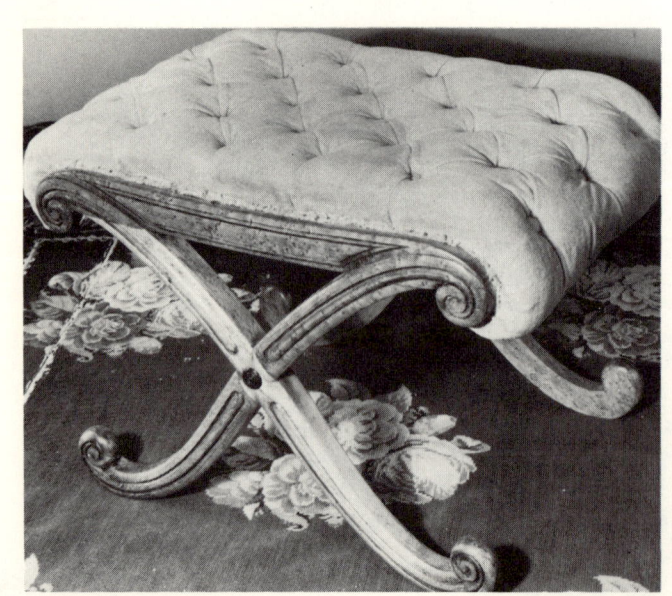

English mahogany open armchair in the Gothic style, c. 1800.

Profit Record	Investment Predictions
1971: PS 100	1979–84
1973: PS 200	
1978: PS 400	Over the past 7 years this early 19th-century armchair increased in value 300%, which is a compounded growth rate of 22% per year. The dramatic increase for a single chair is perhaps due to the fact that the chair as a collectable antique during previous years has been greatly undervalued. The growth rate should continue for another year or two and then stabilize.
Individual Notes	

Simulated maplewood stool, English, c. 1800.

Profit Record	Investment Predictions
1971: PS 65	1979–84
1973: PS 100	
1978: PS 170	Over the past 7 years this stool increased in value 161%, which is a compounded growth rate of 15% per year.
Individual Notes	

Pine display cabinet with reeded sides, c. 1800.

Profit Record	Investment Predictions
1971: PS 195	1979–84
1973: PS 270	
1978: PS 350	

Individual Notes

Over the past 7 years this pine cabinet increased in value 80%, which is a compounded growth rate of 9% per year. Historically, pine has not been highly valued, but as life styles become less formal, rustic antiques, especially pine, are becoming much more popular. Decisive increases should be seen in pine pieces over the next 5 years.

sh mahogany cupboard, c. 1810.

ofit Record	Investment Predictions
71: PS 180	1979–84
73: PS 225	
78: PS 355	

dividual Notes

Over the past 7 years this early 19th-century Irish cupboard increased in value 97%, which is a compounded growth rate of 9% per year. Much of this period of furniture is undervalued, and should show substantial growth rate in the future.

Lady's writing desk.

Profit Record
1971: PS   1,000
1978: PS   1,700

Individual Notes

Investment Predictions
      1979–84

Over the past 7 years this lady's desk increased in value 70%, which is a compounded growth rate of 8% per year. As desks become fashionable, smaller pieces like the above piece should show a greater growth rate.

One of a set of 6 mahogany Biedermeier chairs, c. 1810.

Profit Record
1971: PS   200
1973: PS   350
1978: PS   650

Individual Notes

Investment Predictions
      1979–84

Over the past 7 years, these chairs increased in value 225%, which is a compounded growth rate of 18% per year. This appreciation confirms a renewed interest should continue.

Pair of painted Sicilish festa wine tables with brass tops and carrying handles.

Profit Record
1971: PS 85
1975: PS 120
1978: PS 300

Individual Notes

Investment Predictions
1979–84

These tables show a growth rate of 252% from 1971 to 1978 and a compounded annual growth rate of 20%. This growth rate can be predicted to continue.

Edward Lear, 1812–88. Watercolor. Phila **Egypt Inscribed** "Phila 6th and 7th Feby. 1854." 13 x 20 inches. PS 1,000.

Thomas Sewell Robins, fl. 1829–80. Watercolor Fishing Boats in an Estuary. **Signed with initials. 7¾ x 11¾ inches. PS 350.**

269

Gaspar Verbruggen II, 1664–1730. Flower painting attributed to G. Verbruggen II. Oil on canvas. 19½ x 16½ inches. PS 2,500.

Daniel Seghers, 1590–1661. Flower painting attributed to Daniel Seghers. Oil on panel. 14½ x 10½ inches. PS 2,850.

John Nixon, 1760–1813. Watercolor The Church at Godalming. Signed with initials and dated 1791. 6½ x 9½ inches. PS 280.

Very rare finely carved stick barometer by Charles Molliner, c. 1740. Mahogany with walnut carving. PS 1250.

Nicolaes Maes, 1634–93. Wife of Jan Van Royan, **signed and dated 1663. Oil on panel. 71 x 60 cm. Framed.**

Very rare polychrome Dutch tulip vase, c. 1720. 12 inches high. PS 1200.

Fine 1st period, Worcester sucrier. Blue scale with oriental flowers in cartouches edged with gilt, c. 1770. PS 175.

Rare Spode blue and white plate, "Caramanian" pattern, c. 1810–15. 10 inches diameter. PS 35.

Very rare polychrome 1st period, Worcester dolphin handle cream ewer, c. 1770. PS 225.

271

Pottery figure by Enoch Wood. Girl with flowers, c. 1800. PS 78.

Amethyst and diamond brooch/pendant, Bonekeron (approximately 18 ct. diamonds). PS 3,600.

Strike/repeat carriage clock. Engraved dial mask. Henri Jacot, c. 1870. Overall height including handle 7½ inches (19 cm.). PS 1450.

PORTRAIT MINIATURES

Recently there has been a great revival in the art of the portrait miniaturist. These artists, of the sixteenth, seventeenth, eighteenth, and nineteenth centuries produced small likenesses that, until only recently, were almost totally overlooked. Perhaps the art was originally established to meet the needs that could not be filled by the larger portraits, and today are filled by the modern photographer. Today, portrait miniatures appeal to the collector who is limited by space in the modern home that does not allow large paintings to be either hung or properly displayed, but nevertheless who desires to collect artistic masterpieces at much lower prices.

It is advisable to consult a knowledgeable dealer who specializes in portrait miniatures and who will be invaluable in establishing guidelines for your collection. Since the increased interest in this field of collecting, many fakes have flooded the market, which may cause confusion to the beginning collector. Many libraries have excellent books on the subject, but it is most important to view actual examples of miniatures from different periods, and this can best be done by visiting museums that have portrait miniatures on display. Some of the better collections can be seen at the Victoria and Albert, London; Fitzwilliam, Cambridge; Ashmolean, Oxford; Ham House, Richmond; The Wallace Collection, Brighton; as well as the National Gallery in Washington, D.C.

Prices in this field are usually very stable, but a particularly beautiful piece can appreciate rapidly because of added attention placed on the artist or historical interest stimulated in the subject. For example, one such piece is the £62,000 paid in 1970 for a miniature of the Countess of Somerset by Isaac Oliver. This miniature was formerly in the collection of the Earl of Derby and can now be seen at the Victoria and Albert Museum.

PORTRAIT MINIATURE INVESTMENT HISTORY

Portrait Miniature	Artist	Price 1971	Increases 1978	% Increase	Compounded Growth/yr.
Gouache on Vellum (working life 1560–1616)	Nicholas Hilliard	£5,500	£10,500	90%	10%
Gouache on Vellum (working life 1588–1617)	Isaac Oliver	£1,000	£2,000	100%	11%
Gouache on Vellum (working life 1620–65)	John Hoskils	£1,000	£8,200	700%	35%
Gouache on Vellum (working life 1635–72)	Samuel Cooper	£1,000	£8,500	750%	36%
Watercolor on Ivory (working life 1756–1821)	Richard Cosway	£620	£1,400	125%	12%
Watercolor on Ivory (working life 1775–1829)	George Engleheart	£714	£1,350	89%	9.6%
Watercolor on Ivory (working life 1783–1839)	Andrew Pliner	£550	£980	78%	8.6%

A portrait miniature of a lady, by Thomas Hazlehurst, c. 1800.

Portrait miniature of a boy, artist unknown. Oil on copper, c. 1710.

Portrait miniature of a gentleman, by George Chinnery, 1795.

16 Price Guide to France

VALUE GROWTH CHART

CLOCKS   PRICES QUOTED IN FRENCH FRANCS

ARTICLE	1971	1975	1978	Average Annual Increase	Financial Outlook 1978-84
Gilt spelter mantel clock, c. 1890	400	925	1,500	21%	1
Ebonized wood mantel clock, c. 1880	675	1,600	3,000	24%	1
Carved mantel with deer motif c. 1900	60	270	420	32%	1
Walnut waterfall clock, ornate, c. 1895	230	400	650	16%	3
Cobalt blue porcelain clock set, 3 pcs.	90	200	375	23%	1
Oak mantle, gilt dial, ornate, c. 1895	50	240	400	35%	1
Marble mantel clock, 17", c. 1890	450	975	2,000	24%	1
Gilt spelter mantel, 13", c. 1890	65	145	325	26%	1
Carved oak mantle, silver dial, c. 1900	120	260	425	20%	1
Ornate oak cottage mantle, c. 1890	200	460	750	21%	1
Papier-mâché mantle clock, c. 1880	150	370	675	24%	1
Mahogany grandfather clock, ornate, c. 1860	650	1,250	2,750	23%	1
Carved mahogany grandfather clock, c. 1890	5,900	10,000	18,900	18%	2
Oak, shelf clock, chime, carved, c. 1900	55	145	325	29%	1
Oak, grandfather clock, painted case, c. 1855	900	1,250	2,375	15%	3
Mahogany mantel clock, brass handles, c. 1900	95	200	425	24%	1
Ornate mahogany grandfather clock, c. 1865	950	2,900	4,750	26%	1
Mahogany grandfather clock, inlaid, 1865	990	1,875	3,375	19%	2
Grandfather clock, ornate dial, c. 1860	1,200	1,975	3,125	15%	3
Mahogany wall clock, carved, c. 1865	650	990	1,750	15%	3

VALUE GROWTH CHART

PRICES QUOTED IN FRENCH FRANCS

ARTICLE	1971	1975	1978	Average Annual Increase	Financial Outlook 1978-84
Oak grandfather clock, arch top, c. 1855	890	1,250	2,375	15%	2
Mahogany grandfather clock, ornate, c. 1860	1,100	1,800	2,875	14%	2
Oak grandfather clock, scroll case, c. 1860	950	1,750	2,560	15%	3
Golden oak Gothic wall clock, 1890	900	1,900	3,750	23%	1
WW II operations wall clock	50	195	425	36%	1
Mahogany grandfather clock, carved case, c. 1860	1,000	1,600	2,875	16%	2
Brass case mantle clock, engraved, c. 1890	650	1,450	3,450	27%	2
Term clock, c. 1720	6,000	11,000	18,000	17%	2
Cartel clock, c. 1750	900	2,200	3,400	21%	1
Bull clock, c. 1750	800	1,250	2,700	19%	2
Reproduction bull clock, c. 1820	450	890	1,200	15%	3
18th C. black-japanned bracket clock	5,680	9,000	12,000	20%	1
Small 18th C. ebonized bracket clock	4,000	8,000	11,400	16%	2
Mahogany bracket clock, c. 1760	3,500	6,500	9,500	15%	2
Skelton clock, 31.8 m, c. 1840	2,500	4,500	6,000	13%	3
19th C. enamel & brass carriage clock	780	1,400	2,520	18%	2
19th C. oak bracket on stance	590	1,275	2,760	25%	1
19th C. brass mantel clock (33cm)	400	1,600	2,160	27%	1
19th C. gilt marble lyre clock	1,500	4,200	6,000	22%	1
Enamel brass carriage clock, 1900	780	1,400	2,100	15%	3
19th C. Champleve enamel carriage clock	650	1,600	2,500	21%	1
19th C. ormolu-ebony mantle clock	550	925	1,750	18%	2
Porcelain & gilt mantle clock, 1880	1,500	2,780	5,000	19%	2
Carved oak mantle clock, 1820	640	1,500	3,000	25%	1
19th C. porcelain & gilt mantle clock	500	950	1,400	16%	3
19th C. ormolu & cloisonne enamel clock	2,500	5,900	10,000	22%	1
Gilt & bronze digital mantel clock, 1900	875	2,750	4,250	25%	1
19th C. onyx mantel clock (34cm)	240	565	950	22%	1
19th C. gilt sculptured clock	550	900	1,290	13%	3
19th C. Gilt bronz sculptured clock	340	790	1,080	18%	2
19th C. enamel & onyx mantel clock	780	1,650	3,250	23%	1
19th c. brass cathedral clock	650	1,850	3,000	24%	1
Circular ivory desk clock, 1880	1,100	1,900	3,500	18%	2
19th C. gold, enamel ring watch	1,000	2,500	5,000	26%	1
20th C. gold, enamel slim dress watch	1,700	3,000	4,750	16%	3
18th C. gold, enamel cratelaine	2,500	5,400	9,000	20%	1
19th C. gold, enamel pearl dress watch	3,400	5,900	7,200	11%	4
18th C. gold repoussé cased watch	4,500	7,200	10,000	12%	4
18th C. Morbier clock	200	450	900	24%	1
19th C. Morbier clock	150	375	600	22%	1
18th C. oak case Morbier grandfather clock	240	525	1,250	27%	1
19th C. painted Morbier	300	595	890	17%	3
Gilt spelter mantel clock, c. 1890	400	925	1,500	21%	1
Ebonized wood mantel clock, c. 1880	675	1,600	3,000	24%	1

VALUE GROWTH CHART

PRICES QUOTED IN FRENCH FRANCS

ARTICLE	1971	1975	1978	Average Annual Increase	Financial Outlook 1978-84
Carved mantel clock with deer motif, c. 1900	60	270	420	32%	1
Walnut waterfall clock, ornate, c. 1895	230	400	650	16%	3
Cobalt blue porcelain clock set, 3 pcs	90	200	375	23%	1
Oak mantel clock, gilt dial, ornate, c. 1895	50	240	400	35%	1
Marble mantel clock, 17", c. 1890	450	975	2,000	24%	1
Gilt spelter mantel clock, 13", c. 1890	65	145	325	26%	1
Carved oak mantel clock, silver dial, c. 1900	120	260	425	20%	1
Ornate oak cottage mantel clock, c. 1890	200	460	750	21%	1
Papier-mâché mantel clock, c. 1880	150	370	675	24%	1
Mahogany grandfather clock, ornate, c. 1860	650	1,250	2,750	23%	1
Carved mahogany grandfather clock, c. 1890	5,900	10,000	18,900	18%	2
Ornate mahogany grandfather clock, c. 1865	950	2,900	4,750	26%	1
Oak shelf clock, chime, carved, c. 1900	55	145	325	29%	1
Oak grandfather clock, painted case, c. 1855	900	1,250	2,375	15%	3
Mahogany mantel clock, brass handles, c. 1900	95	200	425	24%	1
Mahogany grandfather clock, inlaid, c. 1865	990	1,875	3,375	19%	2
Grandfather clock, ornate, dial c. 1860	1,200	1,975	3,125	15%	3
Mahogany wall clock, carved, c. 1865	650	990	1,750	15%	3
Oak grandfather clock, arch top, c. 1855	890	1,250	2,375	15%	2
Mahogany grandfather clock, ornate, c. 1860	1,100	1,800	2,875	14%	2
Oak grandfather clock, scroll case, c. 1860	950	1,750	2,560	15%	3
Golden oak Gothic wall clock, c. 1890	900	1,900	3,750	23%	1
WW II operations wall clock	50	195	425	36%	1
Mahogany grandfather clock, carved case c. 1860	1,000	1,600	2,875	16%	2
Brass-case mantel clock, engrav., c. 1890	650	1,450	3,450	27%	2
Term clock, c. 1720	6,000	11,000	18,000	17%	2
Cartel clock, c. 1750	900	2,200	3,400	21%	1
Bull clock, c. 1750	800	1,250	2,700	19%	2
Reproduction bull clock, c. 1820	450	890	1,200	15%	3

VALUE GROWTH CHART

PORCELAIN

PRICES QUOTED IN FRENCH FRANCS

ARTICLE	1971	1975	1978	Average Annual Increase	Financial Outlook 1978-84
Italian Mailocue dish, c. 1510	12,000	15,000	20,000	7.6%	2
18th C. Meissen birds, pair	10,000	14,000	18,000	9. %	2
18th C. Meissen dogs, pair	18,000	20,000	25,000	4.8%	4
Vincinnes cache-pot, c. 1750	18,000	22,000	30,000	8%	2
17th C. Rouen dial, faience	8,500	9,000	12,000	5%	4
Meissen c. 1750 Italian Comedy fig.	7,000	8,500	12,000	8%	2
17th C. Marcelle plate, faience	8,500	9,750	12,000	5%	4
Chantilly sugar box, c. 1730	8,500	9,900	11,000	4%	4
Chinese export armorial disk, 17th C.	7,500	8,200	9,000	4%	4
Vincenno C/S, Blue ground, c. 1750	5,000	6,500	8,000	8%	2
Strasbourg plate, 18th C., painted flowers	6,000	7,000	8,500	6%	3
Royal Bonn pottery vase, floral, 1895	50	145	300	29%	1
Dinner set, 12, beehive mark, c. 1900	400	675	1,250	18%	2
Porcelain wall plaque, scroll design, 1900	25	40	100	22%	1
Signed Kauffmann dinner set, 12, c. 1900	150	325	625	23%	1
Limoges dinner set, 12, floral c. 1900	375	690	1,125	17%	3
Rosenthal small floral vase, c. 1900	20	55	100	26%	1
5 Limoges floral plates, c. 1900	35	95	250	32%	1
Limoges wall plaque, scroll design, 1900	5	25	45	37%	1
5 Limoges blue floral plates, c. 1900	20	45	100	26%	1
Royal Austria fruit bowl, floral, c. 1890	12	39	60	26%	1
Baroque porcelain bowl, Austria, 1900	16	48	75	25%	1
Limoges hor d'oeuvre dish, gold, c. 1884	39	79	180	24%	1
Cake stand, baroque style, "Bonn" 1890	20	54	135	31%	1
Floral decor, salt glaze pitcher, c. 1860	54	145	300	28%	1
Ironstone platter, birds and flowers, 1860	20	49	140	32%	1
Copper luster goblet, c. 1850	35	59	175	26%	1
Copper luster footed sugar bowl, 1855	40	70	180	24%	1
Stoneware pitcher, relief decor, 1860	20	75	160	34%	1
Copper luster sugar bowl, 1860	25	65	145	28%	1
Silver luster pottery goblet, 1860	16	39	80	26%	1
Silver luster creamer, c. 1900	5	20	40	34%	1
Gaudy Welsh pottery tankard, 1860	18	39	75	23%	1
19th C. stoneware pitcher, floral, 1890	39	100	200	26%	1
Parian biscuit barrel, decorated, 1900	45	125	190	23%	1
"Bonn" pottery plant pot, floral, 1890	20	45	75	21%	2
Pratt style porcelain vase, figure decore	2	12	25	43%	1
R. S. Poland hatpin holder and candlestick, 1900	20	56	135	31%	1
R. S. Poland, 3 pcs. trinket set, rose decor, 1900	60	135	200	19%	3
Pottery toast rack, floral decor, 1900	15	30	55	20%	2
Staffordshire pottery dog, c. 1860	18	49	90	26%	1
Stoneware character pitcher, c. 1850	29	59	125	23%	1
3 pcs. porcelain clock set, c. 1900	90	220	425	25%	1
Parian figure of girl, c. 1900	12	36	75	30%	1
Pr. bisque children, c. 1900	75	200	325	23%	1
Pottery swan flower holder, c. 1820	6	22	50	35%	1
3 pcs. pottery cruet set, floral, 1900	19	39	62	18%	3
Pottery match holder, floral, c. 1890	5	12	20	22%	1
German porcelain creamer, floral, 1900	15	36	75	26%	1

VALUE GROWTH CHART

PRICES QUOTED IN FRENCH FRANCS

ARTICLE	1971	1975	1978	Average Annual Increase	Financial Outlook 1978-84
Staffordshire pottery chamber, stick, 1900	6	16	30	26%	1
Porcelain vase, flowers, c. 1890	30	111	160	27%	1
Pr. small floral Porcelain vases, 1900	40	100	175	23%	1
Porcelain clawfooted vase, floral, 1890	3	19	40	45%	1
Pottery cheesedish, floral, c. 1890	39	65	100	14%	3
5 Staffordshire sugar shakers, 1910	90	139	200	12%	4
Toothbrush vase, willow pattern, 1865	25	49	70	16%	2
Flo blue plate, floral decor, 1895	55	95	120	12%	4
Flo blue vases, Yaught decor, 1900	90	135	225	14%	4
Flo blue tea caddy, bridge decor, 1900	20	65	125	30%	1
Blue & white dish, "Abbey" pattern, 1900	4	13	25	30%	1
12 plates, floral decor, gold trim, 1890	55	125	200	20%	2
Flo blue preserve pot, "Abbey", 1900	12	32	60	26%	1
Sèvres signed presentation vase, 1887	2,700	4,200	6,000	12%	4
Sèvres coffee set, 64 pcs., c. 1804	3,700	6,400	9,000	13%	2
Sèvres breakfast tray, c. 1775	650	1,375	2,225	19%	3
Sèvres covered lever with silver, 1790	2,900	4,900	8,500	17%	4
Paris porcelain plaque, 19th C., floral	2,250	4,250	6,000	15%	4
Meissen figure, milkery (11.7cm)	975	1,800	3,350	19%	2
Meissen figure, Kaendler (35.6cm)	1,200	3,000	4,500	21%	1
19th C. Meissen vase, Marcolini	300	675	1,200	22%	1
19th C. Meissen punch pot, rose motif	400	890	1,440	20%	2
19th C. Derby bust of Louis XVI (28.6 cm)	240	540	985	22%	2
St. Cloud figure, woman, white, 1750	650	1,590	2,250	19%	1
St. Cloud pastille burner, c. 1750	2,750	5,950	10,000	20%	2
Meissen figure of sheep (10cm)	850	1,475	2,400	16%	3
Meissen figure of nanny goat (14cm)	700	1,500	2,000	16%	3
Pr. Meissen table oberlishes, floral design	640	1,390	1,750	15%	2
Meissen figure group, "The Lottery"	1,250	3,000	4,750	21%	1
Nymphenburg plate (22.2cm), 1755	850	1,600	2,250	15%	3
Furstenburg cup & saucer, c. 1770	640	1,750	2,125	19%	2
19th C. Dresden portrait plaque of Johnson	250	625	1,000	22%	2
Berlin plaque, "Madonna & Child" 19th C.	950	2,000	3,000	18%	2
Doccia figure candlestick, c. 1770	900	1,450	2,280	14%	3
Venice teabowl, Italian, 1761	500	940	1,250	14%	3
Doccia soup cup & stand, c. 1790	750	1,600	2,250	17%	2
Pr. Balkstedt Russian dancers, 19th C.	550	1,640	3,000	27%	1
Vienna tankard, 19th C.	600	1,750	2,500	23%	1
Vienna tête-à-tête service, 19th C.	2,400	3,870	6,000	14%	2
Vienna "Sargenthal cup & saucer, 1801	1,250	3,200	5,000	22%	1
Vienna dish, "The Judgment," Paris, 19th C.	750	1,500	3,000	22%	1
Rouen pottery pot (16.5 cm)	400	670	1,200	17%	2
Venice pottery drug jar (3.1.8cm)	2,540	4,500	6,250	14%	3
19th C. delft plaque, portrait,	550	1,250	2,000	20%	1

VALUE GROWTH CHART

FURNITURE

PRICES QUOTED IN FRENCH FRANCS

ARTICLE	1971	1975	1978	Average Annual Increase	Financial Outlook 1978-84
Pr. 17th C. Flemish Beechwood chairs	2,400	4,800	7,448	18%	2
Louis XIV 17th C. adjustable wing chair	5,850	9,000	12,500	11%	4
Pr. Louis XV 18th C. armchair	2,400	5,400	7,500	18%	2
18th C. painted settee	17,500	2,850	4,500	18%	2
18th C. Flemish fruitwood settee	950	2,500	5,000	27%	1
Louis XVI 18th C. giltwood canapé	3,000	5,800	7,500	14%	3
Pr. Louis XV carved walnut armchair	3,500	6,000	9,500	15%	3
Pr. Louis XVI 18th C. armchairs	1,150	2,500	3,250	16%	2
18th C. walnut armchairs	3,500	6,000	8,000	13%	4
19th C. papier-mâché chair	75	190	360	25%	1
19th C. papier-mâché side chair	425	790	1,500	20%	1
19th C. mahogany weighing chair	1,800	2,990	4,000	12%	4
19th C. gilt & bronze armchair	995	1,680	3,840	21%	1
Louis XVI 18th C. ormolu dressing table	4,500	7,900	11,500	14%	3
Louis XV writing table	2,700	4,900	8,000	17%	2
Louis XV 18th C. marquetry table	4,000	6,500	10,000	14%	3
Italian 18th C. marquetry table	2,700	5,600	7,000	15%	3
Regency painted 19th C. tripod table	1,275	2,850	5,000	21%	1
19th C. satinwood marquetry table	1,500	3,000	4,750	18%	2
19th C. inlaid papier-mâché table	275	650	1,025	21%	1
19th C. marquetry center table	900	1,575	3,250	20%	1
19th C. center table, sèvres inset	1,200	3,000	4,500	21%	1
19th C. center table, bronze mounts	2,800	4,650	7,500	15%	2
19th C. pietra dura, mounted ebony	3,500	5,500	7,000	10%	4
19th C. ormolu, Kingwood bureau plat	1,500	3,200	5,500	20%	1
19th C. Boulle center table	1,200	2,900	4,800	22%	1
20th C. marble occasional table	250	575	925	21%	1
19th C. marquetry center table	1,750	2,600	4,000	13%	3
20th C. inlaid Damascus game table	590	975	1,600	15%	3
19th C. Louis XV-style, center	2,700	5,500	7,500	16%	2
19th C. lacquer & boulle display cabinet	1,250	2,650	5,000	22%	1
19th C. painted satinwood side cabinet	475	1,200	2,000	23%	1
19th C. carved walnut buffet	620	1,100	1,600	14%	3
19th C. Venetian lacquer bureau bookcase	1,800	3,700	4,500	14%	3
18th C. Dutch walnut bookcase chest	2,500	5,500	8,000	18%	2
Renaissance walnut side cabinet	3,400	7,000	9,000	15%	3
Ivory inset cabinet on stand, 18th C.	2,500	4,850	7,500	17%	3
18th C. neoclassic marquetry commode	4,800	7,900	12,000	14%	3
Louis XV ormolu marquetry commode	4,000	8,500	12,500	18%	2
Pr. Russian marquetry card tables	9,500	16,500	20,500	12%	4
Pr. 18th C. maplewood bureau cabinets	50,000	69,000	80,000	7%	4
18th C. Imperial Russian secretaire	12,000	20,000	35,000	16%	3
Louis XIV boulle commode	71,000	119,000	145,000	11%	4
Louis XVI lacquer bureau plat	200,000	240,000	288,000	5%	4
Louis XV lacquer bureau de dame	89,000	124,000	193,000	12%	3
Louis XVI pictorial commode	22,400	33,780	54,250	13%	3
Louis XV marquetry commode	100,000	135,000	165,000	7%	4
Louis XVI marquetry secretaire	150,000	185,000	205,000	5%	3
6 Empire fauteuils, signed	45,000	70,000	95,000	11%	3
Pr. Louis XV fauteuils	12,000	16,000	22,940	10%	3

VALUE GROWTH CHART

PRICES QUOTED IN FRENCH FRANCS

ARTICLE	1971	1975	1978	Average Annual Increase	Financial Outlook 1978-84
Oak gate-leg table, c. 1900	75	225	400	27%	1
Mahogany desk, brass handles, 1890	220	425	625	16%	2
Mahogany display chest w/glass, 1900	175	400	950	27%	1
Mahogany dining table, c. 1890	75	155	275	20%	2
Carved oak gate-leg table, 1900	85	165	390	24%	1
Mahogany tilt-top table, 1840	125	365	875	32%	1
Mahogany baby's crib, c. 1865	75	200	425	28%	1
Chippendale-style side chair, 1840	55	175	325	29%	1
Walnut serving table, c. 1890	175	325	700	22%	1
Mahogany table, tapered legs, 1890	45	140	200	24%	1
4 Queen Anne-style chairs, c. 1900	145	320	625	23%	1
Small mahogany table, 1880	45	100	175	21%	2
Carved oak dining cabinet, c. 1880	650	1,250	2,000	17%	2
Art nouveau mahogany cabinet	950	1,600	2,250	13%	3
Art nouveau small cabinet, 1890	65	135	250	21%	1
Carved honey oak server, 1880	840	1,275	2,500	17%	2
Golden oak hall stand, c. 1885	550	795	1,125	11%	3
Mahogany floor cheval mirror, 1860	150	360	750	26%	1
Mahogany partner's desk, 1860	650	1,400	2,500	21%	2
Mahogany dining table, 1900	570	870	1,120	10%	4
Jacobean-style cupboard, 1910	175	310	625	20%	3
Washstand marble top, 1885	400	650	1,000	14%	2
Mahogany bureau bookcase, 1900	900	1,675	2,500	16%	3
Inlaid art nouveau cabinet, 1890	500	975	1,375	15%	3
Art nouveau display cabinet, 1895	500	900	1,400	16%	2
Art nouveau oak server, 1890	450	1,000	1,500	19%	2
Oak settle, carved, c. 1800	225	435	800	20%	1
10 pcs. walnut dining set, c. 1900	750	1,950	3,000	22%	1
Oak Bible box, c. 1790	50	275	600	43%	1
Honey oak bureau bookcase, 1905	750	1,200	1,700	12%	3
6 Pcs. oak dining set, 1890	900	1,675	2,250	14%	3
19th C. oak extension table, 1880	450	675	1,000	12%	3
Oak tilt-top table, c. 1850	90	225	475	27%	1
Walnut consul, marble top, 1860	950	1,500	2,250	13%	3
Oak hall stand, c. 1890	150	325	950	30%	1
Cast-iron hall stand, 1880	250	565	725	16%	2
6 rococo gilt armchairs	45,000	70,000	90,000	10%	3
18th C. japanned bureau cabinet	60,000	80,000	99,000	7%	3
Louis XV marquetry bureau de dame	49,000	73,000	93,600	10%	3
Louis XV marquetry table à écrire	45,000	69,000	84,600	9%	4
Louis XV marquetry table à ouvrage	50,000	70,000	80,000	7%	3
Pr. marquetry commodes	36,000	52,000	68,000	10%	3
Louis XV serpentine commode	12,000	20,000	28,800	13%	2
Louis XVI bonheur du jour	14,000	22,000	30,600	12%	3
Marquetry table à écrire	12,000	20,000	26,100	12%	3
Louis XV fauteuil, signed	10,000	15,000	22,000	12%	3
Louis XVI armoire	195,000	290,000	365,000	9%	3
Louis XVI black lacquer secretaire	65,000	100,000	125,000	10%	3
Large oak spinning wheel, c. 1860	69	160	275	22%	2
19th C. mahogany dress table	45	100	250	28%	1
Pedestal oak table, c. 1840	200	425	850	23%	1

VALUE GROWTH CHART

PRICES QUOTED IN FRENCH FRANCS

ARTICLE	1971	1975	1978	Average Annual Increase	Financial Outlook 1978-84
19th C. mahogany desk, leather top	175	365	625	20%	2
Pr. 19th C. oak bed tables	225	465	875	21%	2
Inlaid mahogany table, c. 1860	90	220	450	26%	1
Mahogany night stand, marble top, 1890	75	200	430	28%	1
Mahogany fern stand, carved, 1880	50	145	470	38%	1
19th C. mahogany game table	40	165	300	33%	1
Mahogany scenic inlaid table, 1875	75	220	400	27%	1
Mahogany inlaid chess table, 1880	50	175	350	32%	1
19th C. mahogany washstand, marble top	100	225	500	26%	1
Black oak deacon's bench, 1880	225	590	1,000	24%	1
Oak, high-back hall seat, carved, 1890	1,500	2,200	3,250	12%	3
Hump-back sea chest, dated 1801	340	590	1,000	17%	2
19th C. mahogany bureau bookcase	750	1,590	2,500	19%	2
Normandy cupboard, oak, dated 1800	900	2,700	5,000	28%	1
Oak collector's cabinet, c. 1900	950	1,700	3,200	19%	3
Oak washstand w/mirror, c. 1900	65	245	400	30%	1
Oak hat stand, carved, c. 1900	50	100	225	24%	2
Bamboo umbrella stand, c. 1900	60	110	200	19%	2
Mahogany table, scroll legs, c. 1880	90	210	375	23%	1
Mahogany revolving bookcase, 1900	100	275	450	24%	1
19th C. gilt wood table, c. 1875	95	250	445	25%	1
19th C. ebonized table-top cabinet	65	140	250	21%	2
Oak sideboard & mirror, carved, 1880	1,250	2,990	5,250	23%	2
Paneled oak cupboard, c. 1825	650	975	1,250	10%	3
Oak bureau bookcase, 1900	200	480	875	23%	1
Wall corner cupboard, c. 1810	400	750	1,375	19%	3
Mahogany fern stand, c. 1860	45	155	225	26%	1
Wall cupboard, glass doors, c. 1890	150	295	475	18%	2
Walnut bureau bookcase, c. 1900	900	1,750	3,000	19%	2
Oak Welsh dresser, c. 1860	650	1,900	3,500	27%	1
Credenza w/marble top, c. 1860	350	975	1,500	23%	1
Oak Jacobean chair, c. 1680	400	790	1,250	18%	2
Mahogany tilt-top dining table, c. 1835	875	1,600	2,250	14%	3
Child's roll-top desk, c. 1900	200	425	750	21%	1
Mahogany kneehole desk, c. 1860	175	325	675	21%	1
Oak corner display cabinet, c. 1850	125	265	550	24%	1
Mahogany drop-leaf table, c. 1850	200	460	600	17%	1
Mahogany night stand, leather top, 1890	65	145	275	23%	1
Mahogany fern stand, c. 1880	75	160	279	21%	2
Beechwood carved bench, c. 1900	90	150	325	20%	1
Mahogany shaving stand, c. 1850	200	425	600	17%	2
Rosewood floor cheval mirror, 1850	175	365	750	23%	1
Mahogany blanket chest, c. 1800	980	1,475	2,250	13%	3
Consul table w/coat-of-arms, c. 1850	120	450	700	29%	1
Feathered mahogany desk, c. 1840	450	795	1,300	16%	2
Desk, bracket feet, c. 1785	950	1,800	3,400	20%	1
Rosewood chiffonier, c. 1850	1,000	2,250	3,250	18%	2
Mahogany architect's desk, 1860	2,000	4,500	6,250	18%	2
Paneled blanket chest, c. 1890	125	375	650	27%	1
19th C. carved oak dining table	760	1,560	3,000	22%	1
Oak cupboard on chest, c. 1830	175	420	700	22%	1
Oak consul wall table, c. 1835	225	475	750	19%	2
Mahogany partner's desk, c. 1860	900	1,650	2,400	15%	2

VALUE GROWTH CHART

GLASS — PRICES QUOTED IN FRENCH FRANCS

ARTICLE	1971	1975	1978	Average Annual Increase	Financial Outlook 1978-84
Cranberry art glass pitcher, 1865	65	170	275	23%	1
Cranberry art glass compote, 1865	95	175	300	18%	2
Cobalt blue overlay atomizer, 1900	50	145	265	27%	1
Blue art glass compote, silver base, 1885	100	220	325	18%	2
Art glass muffin dish enameled, 1890	60	135	175	17%	2
Art glass table bell, leaf decor, 1885	45	95	150	19%	2
Art glass decanter, floral decor, 1890	90	160	250	16%	3
Satin art glass vase, floral decor, 1880	20	49	80	22%	1
Lalique glass perfume bottle, 1900	65	110	180	16%	2
Blue glass salad bowl, 1900	15	39	75	26%	1
Green art glass vase, floral, 1885	19	35	60	18%	2
Satin glass sugar shaker, 1890	25	79	130	27%	1
Blue art glass finger oil lamp, 1890	22	55	85	22%	1
Amber art glass pitcher, 1890	33	75	140	23%	1
Art glass sugar & creamer, 1880	25	65	125	26%	1
Orange ribbed art glass vase, 1900	5	12	25	25%	1
3 yellow art glass plates, signed, 1900	140	370	725	27%	1
Pink Bristol vase, cherub decor, 1890	45	89	130	16%	3
Blue & cranberry splatter vase, 1900	45	110	210	25%	1
Cranberry pitcher, c. 1865	78	139	290	21%	2
Cranberry compote, swirl form, 1880	45	160	300	31%	1
Green art glass pitcher, c. 1860	35	70	110	18%	2
Cranberry glass bell, c. 1865	65	189	345	27%	1
Pr. green vases, dragonfly decor, 1890	79	139	240	17%	2
Green glass dish, floral, c. 1890	19	49	100	27%	1
Cranberry tankard, c. 1895	12	30	70	29%	1
Cranberry art glass tumbler	22	46	82	21%	2
Pink sugar shaker, c. 1900	19	30	65	19%	2
Bristol preserve pot, floral, 1890	15	23	45	17%	2
Muffin dish, gold trim, 1895	28	76	130	25%	1
Green splatter posy holder, c. 1900	12	33	60	26%	1
Amethyst art vase, floral, 1890	32	72	150	25%	1
Opaque white art vase, c. 1895	40	89	130	18%	2
Clear art vase, leaf motif, c. 1900	60	149	210	19%	2
Green molded sugar shaker, 1900	19	43	75	22%	1
Blue splatter glass creamer, 1895	5	14	30	29%	1
Opaque red bowl, nickel frame, 1890	7	20	50	32%	1
Cranberry spittoon, c. 1860	22	49	100	24%	1
Cranberry art glass bowl, c. 1890	19	49	85	24%	1
Clear hinged lidded puff pot, 1900	4	19	30	33%	1
Green carnival footed bowl	39	97	150	21%	2
Blue carnival plate, peacock-on-fence	120	310	550	24%	1
White carnival dish, Fenton's pattern	200	375	725	20%	2
Marigold carnival bowl, hob star	10	26	45	24%	1
Cut-glass decanter w/stopper, 1860	55	120	200	20%	2
Cut pickle set, nickel frame, 1890	22	68	125	28%	1
Cut preserve pot, lid, c. 1900	12	30	60	26%	1
Pressed tray, diamond & hob, c. 1900	4	13	25	30%	1
Pressed ice bucket, star, 1896	19	39	100	27%	1
Clear preserve pot, c. 1900	7	23	60	36%	1

VALUE GROWTH CHART

GLASS

PRICES QUOTED IN FRENCH FRANCS

ARTICLE	1971	1975	1978	Average Annual Increase	Financial Outlook 1978-84
Cut sugar shaker, top, 1900	14	34	80	28%	1
Pr. brilliant cut vases, c. 1900	60	134	210	20%	2
Clear atomizer, floral, c. 1910	12	30	65	27%	1
Cut pitcher, diamond, 1900	12	46	100	35%	1
Cut bowl, thumb print, 1890	10	19	40	22%	2
Cut salad bowl, ribbed, c. 1900	12	34	60	26%	1
Cut rose bowl, diamond, 1890	22	39	82	21%	2
Cut sugar shaker, diamond, 1900	19	30	75	22%	2
Cut prism, rib cutting, 1900	2	4	10	26%	1
10 cut tumblers, thumb print, 1900	39	99	160	22%	1
Opaque pressed toothpick holder 1888	32	90	140	23%	1
Swirled cranberry vase, 1890	35	110	175	26%	2
17th C. engraved goblet	1,200	2,250	3,500	17%	2
18th C. venetian covered goblet	2,000	3,800	6,000	17%	2
18th C. French wineglass	140	325	975	32%	1
18th C. baluster-stem goblet	600	975	1,375	12%	4
18th C. composite-stem wine	450	790	1,250	16%	3
18th C. engraved composite-stem	900	1,450	2,500	16%	3
17th C. Daumenglas & cover	750	1,900	2,600	19%	2
17th C. "Facon de Venise" wineglass	550	1,600	2,250	22%	2
Early Jacobite wineglass	1,500	2,750	4,875	18%	2
Gilt blue decanter & stopper, c. 1765	2,400	5,600	7,000	16%	3
19th C. blue & white cameo vase	95	265	500	27%	1
Double-overlay cameo vase, c. 1880	625	1,100	1,600	14%	2
18th C. engraved decanter	2,900	4,900	7,500	15%	2
18th C. two-spouted lamp	195	390	825	23%	1
18th C. lead-glass lamp	1,400	2,600	5,000	20%	2
18th C. chamber lamp	690	1,600	2,125	17%	2
Cameo scent bottle, c. 1884	1,200	2,950	4,300	20%	1
3-color cameo vase, 1885	2,200	4,750	6,500	17%	2
Ivory cameo vase, c. 1885	975	1,670	3,625	21%	1
Ivory cameo vase, c. 1880	1,000	1,875	3,390	19%	2
Cameo-glass bowl, c. 1880	650	1,150	1,625	14%	3
Silver mounted cameo scent bottle, 1884	1,475	2,600	3,850	15%	3
Cameo vase, c. 1885	900	1,200	2,800	18%	3
Enameled Russian vase, c. 1885	700	950	1,250	9%	4
French enameled "Islamic" vase, 20th C.	600	1,400	2,125	20%	1
Mary Gregory glass dish, 1880	450	725	1,060	13%	3
Pr. Bohemian overlay vases, 1865	900	1,275	1,825	11%	3
Pr. Bohemian flashed vases	750	1,450	2,500	19%	2
Pr. enameled vases, 19th C.	250	540	950	21%	2
19th C. enameled vases, floral	475	725	1,100	13%	3
Rock crystal engraved bowl & cover, 1885	135	320	675	26%	1

VALUE GROWTH CHART

COPPER, PEWTER, BRASS

PRICES QUOTED IN FRENCH FRANCS

ARTICLE	1971	1975	1978	Average Annual Increase	Financial Outlook 1978-84
BRONZE STATUES					
Figure of a young girl, 19th C.	850	1,600	2,500	17%	2
Bust of a child, c. 1900, signed	690	1,475	2,250	18%	2
Figure of a hunter, signed, c. 1880	2,700	5,600	7,000	15%	3
Figure of a boy, signed, c. 1898	450	960	1,600	20%	1
Figure of a farmer, signed, 19th C.	1,200	2,200	3,250	15%	3
Duke of Wellington, signed, 19th C.	1,600	2,900	4,000	14%	3
Figure of a sailor, signed, 1925	600	1,300	1,600	15%	3
Figure of a dancer, signed, 19th C.	390	845	1,125	16%	3
Girl dancing, signed, c. 1900	975	1,600	2,500	14%	2
Figure of a nude, signed, 19th C.	560	790	1,300	13%	3
Classical figure, signed, 19th C.	200	500	750	21%	1
Pr. of storks, 19th C.	250	750	1,060	23%	1
Figure of an athlete, signed, 20th C.	675	1,500	2,100	18%	2
Bust of a Bohemian girl, signed, 1900	900	1,750	3,125	19%	2
Young girl skipping, signed, 20th C.	700	1,200	1,975	16%	3
Allegorical figure, 19th C.	975	1,650	2,650	15%	3
Harvester figure, 20th C.	1,000	1,600	2,500	14%	3
Figure of a woman, c. 1900	650	1,200	1,800	16%	2
Pr. of fawns, 19th C.	4,500	7,500	10,000	12%	3
Venetian figure, woman, signed, 17th C.	1,200	2,200	2,800	13%	3
Figure of a nude putto, 16th C.	1,400	2,400	3,125	12%	3
Lion slant, 17th C.	1,600	2,600	4,100	14%	2
Figure of a cherub, 16th C.	675	1,200	1,900	16%	2
Figure of a lion, c. 1600	2,690	4,250	6,000	12%	3
Figure of an owl, 16th C.	3,750	7,500	10,000	15%	3
Figure of Romona, 16th C.	3,200	6,500	9,000	16%	2
Venus & Cupid, 17th C.	2,500	4,200	7,000	16%	2
Bust of William Pitt, signed, 1807	950	1,975	3,125	19%	3
Head of a boy, 16th C.	2,700	5,600	9,000	19%	2
Brass jampan, c. 1860	39	100	175	24%	1
Copper & brass tea urn, c. 1900	125	370	500	22%	1
Brass fender, coaching scene, 1890	49	100	145	17%	2
Copper framed beveled mirror, 1900	36	94	160	24%	1
Brass & iron footman, c. 1865	86	150	225	15%	3
Copper & brass gaslight, c. 1890	100	165	275	16%	3
Brass & iron floor gong, c. 1900	125	245	330	15%	3
Iron & brass scales, c. 1900	20	54	90	24%	1
Brass slipper box, c. 1895	32	79	115	20%	2
Heavy brass gong, c. 1895	69	115	165	13%	3
Brass jardiniere, floral, c. 1900	49	89	120	14%	3
Copper foot warmer, c. 1890	50	89	140	16%	2
Brass coal scuttle, c. 1900	35	80	110	18%	2
Brass magazine rack, 1895	40	94	130	18%	2
Brass stick stance, 1920	30	69	90	17%	2
Cast-iron Caynter scales, 1865	85	165	220	15%	2
Brass & iron fire trivet, 1865	22	39	60	15%	2
Set brass & wood counter scales 1895	45	110	175	21%	1
Cast-iron lidded pan, c. 1890	5	19	30	29%	1
Iron & wood churn, c. 1900	25	67	115	24%	1

VALUE GROWTH CHART

PRICES QUOTED IN FRENCH FRANCS

ARTICLE	1971	1975	1978	Average Annual Increase	Financial Outlook 1978-84
Britannia food covers (3), 1900	25	115	180	33%	1
Cast-iron pot with lid, 1890	15	45	75	26%	1
Pewter teapot, wood handle, 1890	22	45	80	20%	2
Heavy pewter measure, c. 1890	25	100	160	30%	1
Metal flour sifter, c. 1900	5	14	25	26%	1
Pewter pint tankard, c. 1865	40	90	150	21%	2
Pewter sugar & creamer, 1900	19	39	60	18%	2
Britannia teapot, 1895	40	72	115	16%	2
Pewter tankard, c. 1860	10	29	40	22%	2
Copper kettle, iron handle, 1920	22	67	125	28%	1
Twist brass candlesticks, c. 1865	34	79	180	24%	1

Vincennes cache-pot, beautifully decorated, c. 1750.

Profit Record
1971: 18,000 F.F.
1978: 30,000 F.F.

Individual Notes

**Investment Predictions
1979–84**

This rare Vincennes cache-pot, c. 1750, over the past 7 years increased in value 66%, which is a compounded growth rate of 8% per year. Appreciation will continue at the above rate.

A very rare Gubbio dish, c. 1510.

Profit Record
1971: 12,000 F.F.
1978: 20,000 F.F.

Individual Notes

**Investment Predictions
1979–84**

Over the past 7 years this rare Gubbio dish increased in value 66%, which is a compounded growth rate of 7.6% per year. Due to the rarity, the appreciation will be mainly controlled by specific collectors in this field, but should remain stable.

Two very elegant Meissen porcelain dogs, produced about 1740.

Profit Record
1971: 18,000 F.F.
1978: 25,000 F.F.

Individual Notes

**Investment Predictions
1979–84**

These 18th-century Meissen dogs over the past 7 years increased in value 38%, which is a compounded growth rate of 4.8%. Meissen of this period rarely appreciates at dramatic rates, but is still a sound investment.

A pair of beautifully decorated Meissen birds, 18th century.

Profit Record
1971: 10,000 F.F.
1978: 18,000 F.F.

Individual Notes

**Investment Predictions
1979–84**

Over the past 7 years this unique Meissen birds increased in value 80%, which is a compounded growth rate of 9% per year. A similar appreciation is predicted for the future.

16th-century copper plate.

Profit Record
1971: 1,500 F.F.
1978: 4,500 F.F.

Individual Notes

Investment Predictions 1979–84

This beautiful example of an early copper plate over the past 7 years increased in value 200%, which is a compounded growth rate of 17% per year. Good quality early copper pieces are always in demand and will continue to appreciate.

17th-century pewter plate

Profit Record
1971: 3,500 F.F.
1978: 6,500 F.F.

Individual Notes

Investment Predictions 1979–84

This pewter plate over the past 7 years increased in value 85%, which is a compounded growth rate of 9% per year. The appreciation of pewter is stable and should continue.

Long table, 17th century.   2,300 F.F.

Provincial table, 17th century.   3,400 F.F.

Regional buffet, 18th century.   24,000 F.F.

18th-century chest of drawers.   2,600 F.F.

Typical regional 19th-century doug box.   1,100 F.F.

18th-century desk.   3,900 F.F.

French chest of drawers, 18th century.   3,200 F.F.

Typical regional 18th-century "Panetiere."   3,200 F.F.

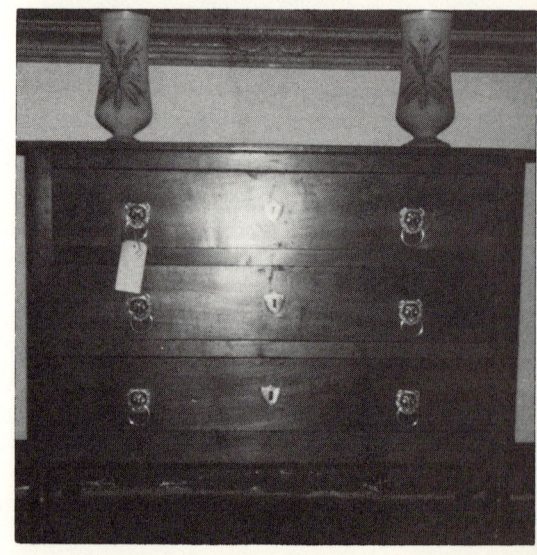

Chest of drawers, 19th century.   1,700 F.F.

Low chest, 17th century. 2,500 F.F.

18th-century clothes press. 6,500 F.F.

18th-century clothes press. 7,800 F.F.

17th-century provincial table. 3,200 F.F.

Two swans of porcelain, natural decoration, by J. J. Kandler, 1747–49. Saxe, 18th century. 105,000 F.F.

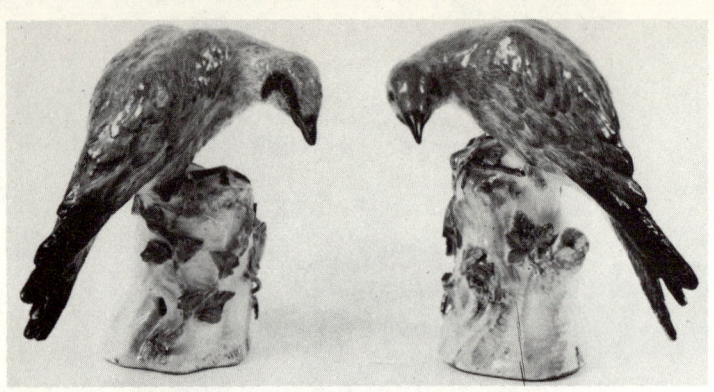

Two grey birds of polychrome porcelain, perched on their tree trunks. Saxe, 18th century. 35,000 F.F.

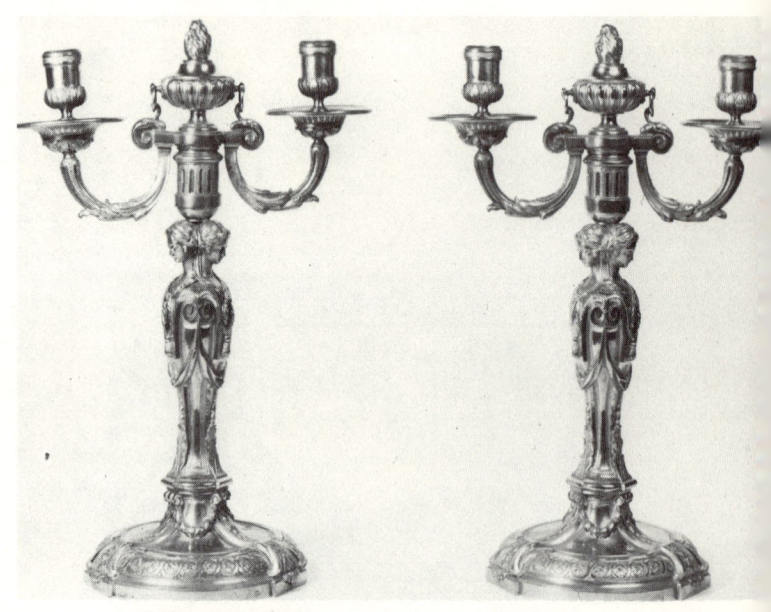

Pair of standing candelabra, each holding two candles, in chiseled and gilded bronze. The shafts are formed from the busts of three young women with garlands of ribbons, tassles, leaves, and roses. The base is circular and the top of the central shaft forms a vase with a frame. (There is a slight crack in one arm.) Louis XVI period. 90,000 F.F.

Pair of sconces for three candles, in sculpted and gilded bronze. The central shaft is ornamented with children symbolizing sculpture and literature, supported by leafy and flowered volutes. Mark: a "C" crowned, 1745–49. Louis XV period. 180,000 F.F.

Pair of small ornate wardrobes. They open by one door and sit on a console with three drawers. 18th century. 1,000,000 F.F.

Chandelier for eight candles, in chiseled and gilded bronze. The central shaft portrays a figure seated on a globe blowing a horn. The pendant is aflame with chequerwork and pearls piled above each other. The arms, candleholders, and basins are decorated with laurel leaves, flowerettes, rose and acanthus leaves. Regency period. Ancient collection of Duc d'Aumont; it is reproduced in the collection "Rodolphe Khan."   300,000 F.F.

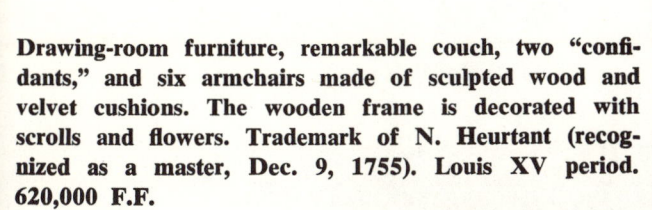

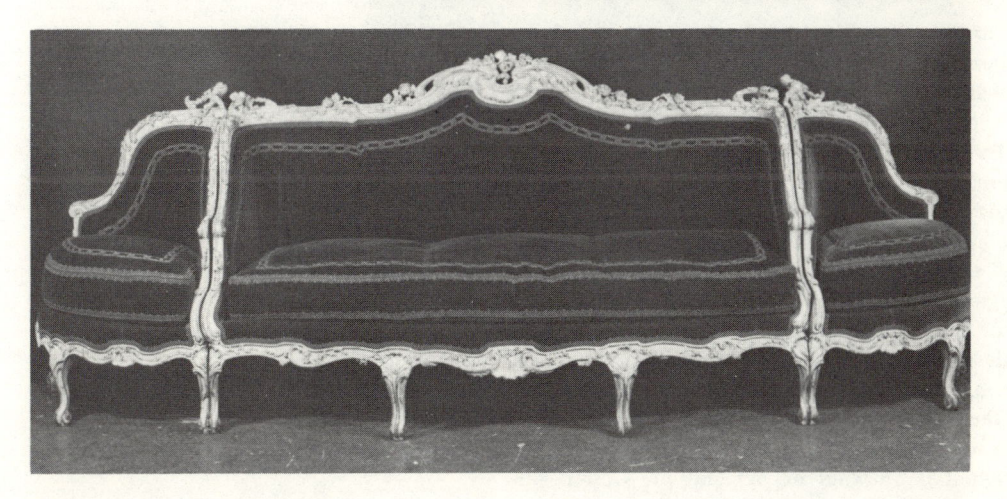

Drawing-room furniture, remarkable couch, two "confidants," and six armchairs made of sculpted wood and velvet cushions. The wooden frame is decorated with scrolls and flowers. Trademark of N. Heurtant (recognized as a master, Dec. 9, 1755). Louis XV period. 620,000 F.F.

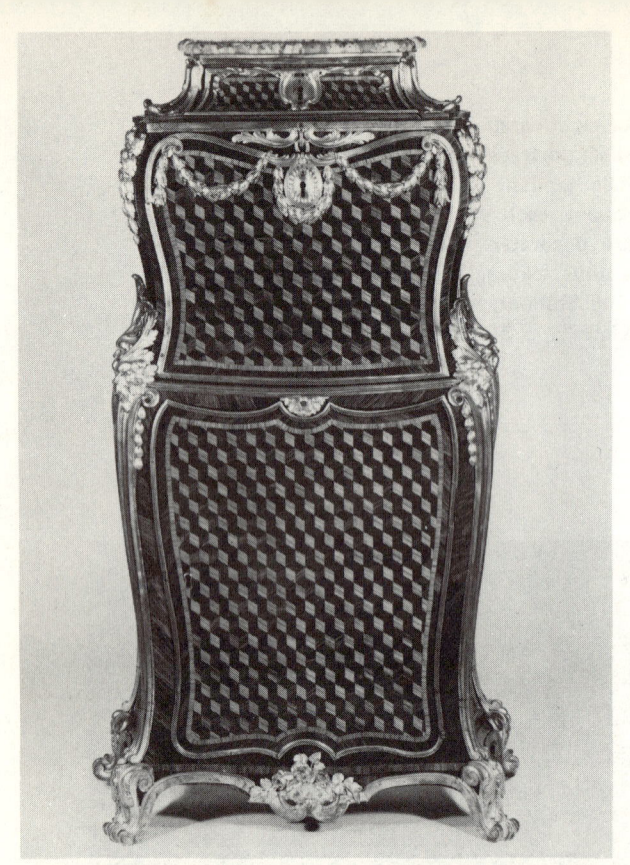

Queen's secretary. A rare, violin-shaped writing desk of wood veneer chequerwork. There is a small drawer in the third superior portion of the desk, and the central portion directly below has a door. Rich chiseled and gilded bronze ornamentation (ribbons, flower garlands, heads of bearded men) grace the form. The undulating line of the base is ornamented with a bouquet of flowers and sits upon four voluted and decorated legs. Mark: J. F. Oeben, a celebrated Parisien cabinetmaker in the time of Louis XV. Louis XV period. 400,000 F.F.

Cabinet. Marble veneering with a mahogany interior superior part presents a central door concealing a (filing, bottle) supported by gilded columns and fla by two secret doors that conceal six drawers. The ext doors are decorated by two motifs. The side doors ex an oval-shaped inlay of a man and a woman loo across at each other. The central door has a meda depicting a shepherdess tying a ribbon around the of a lamb, while a shepherd stands above her playi pipe. Three drawers are beneath this central section lower portion has eight legs with rich, natural ornam tion in gilded and chiseled bronze. The underside is marble. By David Roentgen. Louis XVI period. 400,000 F.F.

Sideboard (furniture partition) made of wood with ebony plaques. Upon the facade and sides are five Japanese lacquer panels with black backgrounds, decorated in light relief with red and gold flower branches, birds and fruits in a framework of red. It opens by three drawers and three doors that conceal sliding shelves. The eight feet are finely grooved and beautifully decorated (friezes of pearls, foliage) in chiseled and gilded bronze. The underside is of embedded grey marble. Mark: Adam Weismeiler (recognized as a master March 26, 1778). Louis XVI period. 800,000 F.F.
(NOTE: This piece of furniture is compared with those lacquer pieces of China executed for the Queens of France, for the Bellevue castle, and now conserved in the Louvre. Two other pieces by Adam Weismeiler are found in the Metropolitan Museum of Art and the Compiegne Castle.)

Rectangular copper relief plaque enameled and gilded. A priest-saint holds a cross and a book, standing under a trilled arch supported by two columns. The figure is engraved and in high relief. His chasuble is enameled a deep blue and decorated with bands of turquoise and red and yellow circles. The background is of lapis lazuli enameling, decorated with vines and multicolor flowers; it is cut by two turquoise bands with multicolor flowers. A large numbus of undulating waves of red, yellow, and turquoise creates a halo behind the saint's head. Limoges. 13th century. 200,000 F.F.

Reliquary formed of riveted copper plates, gilded and enameled. It is modestly decorated with four bust-portraits of angels in red, circular medallion settings of red or green on a green or blue background. Limoges, 18th century. The crest is of the 19th century. 60,000 F.F.

Reliquary of St. Valerie. A rectangular edifice with a sloping roof made of copper plates engraved, enameled, and gilded nailed on a wooden core. All the plaques have a lavender background decorated with large polychrome flowers on vines and gilded figures in higher relief. On the right face, St. Valerie is brought by a guard before the king seated on a throne; on his left an executioner decapitates a kneeling saint. On both sides, the bottom plate depicts five aligned apostles in various postures, holding books. On the other side, women saints meet a seated angel and to the left there seems to be the appearance of Christ's Ghost before Mary. St. Pierre, the 11th apostle, holding a sword, is the sole occupant of one end panel, while the other end panel displays a saint holding a martyr's palm. The reliquary sits on four rectangular legs, and the roof has a serrated crest. (The wooden core rotted and was replaced since the 13th century. Dates to the 13th century. 138,000 F.F.

A central copper plaque of a book binding sculpted, enameled, and engraved. The central figure of Christ on the cross is flanked by St. John and the Virgin Mary. Above his arms in the upper corners are two kneeling angels. The title is engraved in two lines on the cross head: IHS and XPS. The figure of Christ is engraved and in high relief. A halo of lapis lazuli, lavender, white, yellow, and red enameling surrounds his head. The secondary figures are engraved, their heads alone being in high relief. The lapis lazuli background is cut by two bands of turquoise holding rosettes and multicolored disks. Limoges, the first half of the 13th century.   95,000 F.F.

A very large reliquary gilded silver with enameled parts. The notched, rectangular base has four seated children, above which a canopy sustained by eight columns holds a statuette of the Virgin standing with hands clasped in prayer. Above the canopy is a smaller circular pavilion sustained by columns holding a small statue of a kneeling angel holding a rosary. Posed atop the roofing is a small figure of a woman saint in prayer. Spanish, Castellon de la Plana. 17th century.   57,000 F.F.

Large marble torso of an athlete. A drapery folds about the shoulders fixed by a clasp, and encircles the loins. Roman period.   48,000 F.F.

Relief sculpture in limestone. The sculpture depicts four Jewish prisoners accompanied by a soldier in a mountainous landscape. This fragment is from Sennacherib's Palace in Niniva, and emanates from the British Museum's same series representing the siege of the Palestinian town, Lachis. Assyrian Art, 705–681 B.C.   48,000 F.F.

Two pendants depicting views of Venice. Paintings of the Canaletto studio.   410,000 F.F.

295

Watercolor painting. The port of St. Tropez. Signed by Andre Dunoyer De Segonzac. 82,000 F.F.

Watercolor painting La Caleche, by Constantin Guys, 1802–92. 35,000 F.F.

Two pendants depicting a vase of flowers and birds, and a vase of flowers and a dragonfly. Oil paintings on canvas. By Francesco Guardi, Venice, 18th century.
275,000 F.F.

Oil painting on panel, depicting an overheated and tired Arabian horseman and his horse. By Eugene Delacroix, 1841. 580,000 F.F.

Rembrandt self-portrait (24 years of age). Painted in 1629 to 1630, at this time the young master had already developed his own famous style. Wood-carved frame. 1,000,000 F.F.

Oil painting on panel, depicting an overheated and tired Arabian horseman and his horse. By Eugene Delacroix, 1841. 580,000 F.F.

297

Oil on canvas. The Musician's Table. **Signed by Juan Gris,** 1926.   350,000 F.F.

Porcelain dish service of Royal manufacture. Sevres 1834 and 1837. Blue, circular mark of manufacturer with monogram of Louis-Phillipe, "Sevres" and "1834" and "1837." Also, bears marks of artists, gilders, and molders, The decorative subjects are related to the art of cooking, differing for each piece. The borders are friezes of leaves and gold rosettes, and inscriptions are in black gothic letters on a white background.   110,500 F.F.

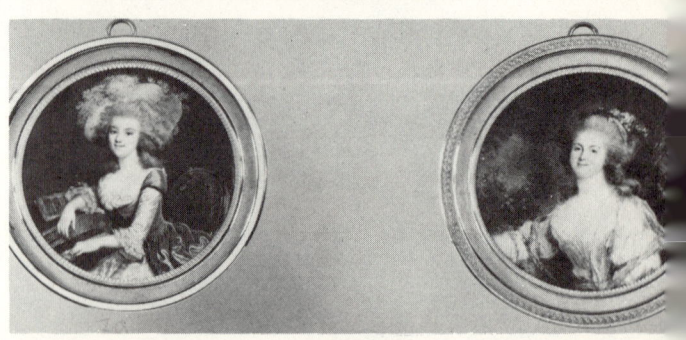

A. The small "Trianon" in the time of Marie Antoinette. Beautiful, round miniature gouache. Signed by Louis Nicolas Van Blarenberghe. Diam. t cm.   75,000 F.F.

B. Alleged portrait of the Princess of Lamballe. Round miniature in a standing frame of gold colors and gilded silver, and chiseled in a frieze of interlocking pearls. By Hall. Diam. 7.2 cm.   25,000 F.F.

C. Alleged portrait of Sophie Arnould, seated before her harpsichord. Round miniature in a standing gold and silver frame, bordered by a filigree of white enamel. Case signed by Laurent, Galerie Montpesier of the Royal Palace. By Hall. Diam. 7 cm.   33,000 F.F.

D. Portrait of Adolphe Hall, the artist's child. Oval miniature in a gold and silver medallion, by Hall. 5 by 4 cm.   90,000 F.F.

Portrait of Jeannine, 1941–42. Oil on canvas. By Nicolas de Stael, 1913–55. 81 x 60   260,000 F.F.

Round, silver soup tureen. Decorated by friezes of palmettes, garlands, laurel leaves. There are two handles attached in three places. The tureen sits on a circular base with four ovoid legs—a silver tray engraved with palmettes and flowers. The arms of the Cadaval family is engraved in this piece. By the Master Goldsmith, Henry Auguste. Paris, 1787.   65,000 F.F.

of silver bottle buckets. The handles are formed by
held in the mouths of lion heads, which bring to-
er the laurel garland enwrapping the bucket. The
nd is interrupted on either side by two medallions
raved with coats of arms. Turin, c. 1780.
00 F.F.

Porcelain jar with grooved, oval base and thick neck. Covered with brown-black glaze, this glaze ends in irregular drips 3 centimeters from the base allowing a lighter yellow-brown glaze to show. The crests of the grooves stand out as cream-colored lines, and the jar has two handles stretching from rim to shoulder. Song of the North. Epoch Song.   110,000 F.F.

Gold, rectangular box with rounded corners. In the center of the cover is a miniature bust-painting of Ferdinand of Bulgaria, placed in a medallion surrounded by 24 rose-shaped diamonds. The corners are also ornamented with fleur-de-lis inset with rose-shaped diamonds. This box is in a case of red velvet, the cover ornamented with a crown. Miniature portrait signed by Zehngraf. Work of Faberge. Master is Henrik Wigstrom. 95,000 F.F.

A large, elegant, gilded silver jar. The ornamentation depicts figures of love playing musical instruments alternating with masqueraders. Above these figures are two engraved medallions dated 1682 and surrounded by inscriptions. The name of Susanna Kalnoki is visible on the circumference. The jar lid is surmounted by a knob resembling a pine tree, and three fish are barely visible underneath the jar. 17th century. 24,000 F.F

Pair of porcelain "cache-pots" from China, Kang Hi period. Decorated with flowers and birds and a gold border enhanced by a coral background. The handles are formed by the heads of the dogs of Fo. The base was gilded and chiseled in the time of Louis XIV.
85,000 F.F.

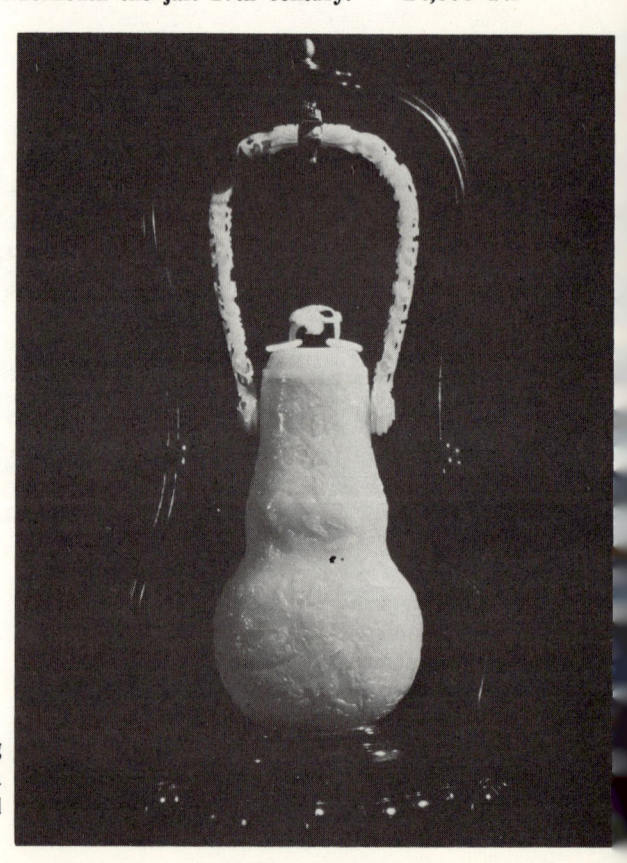

White jade vase with cover. This vase is suspended, having a gourdlike shape of very fine and transparent quality. A light surface relief depicts scenes of divinities grouped amid cloudlike surroundings. 160,000 F.F.

300

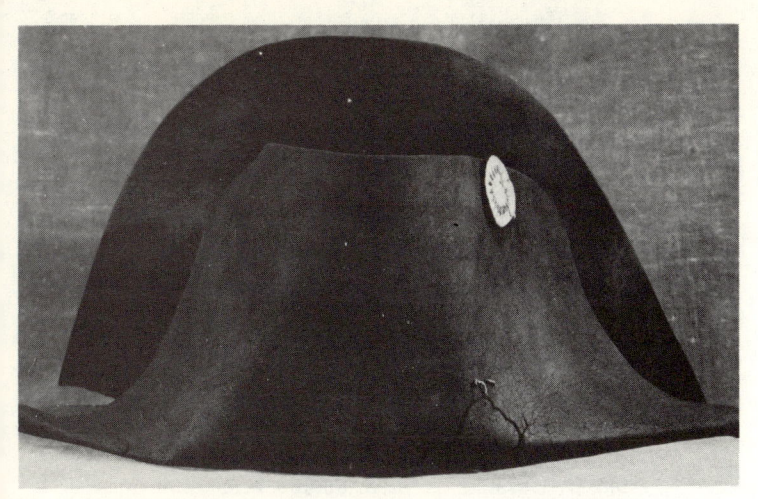

Rare hat of Napoleon. This traditionally shaped hat of thin felt is in a very well-conserved state, ornamented by a small, three-color cocade of white, blue, and red. The front rim is reinforced (like all of the emperor's hats) by a piece of sewn felt, facilitating a better fit. The interior lining of rich, grey silk was remarkably well conserved and is decorated at the base with three rows of concentric stitching. The lining is in excellent condition, but some dirt on the border proves its long usage by Napolean. The piping that surrounded the cocade and button is missing. This hat is accompanied by a manuscript signed "J Dulud" saying:

> This hat belongs to Emperor Napolean. He wore it during the Russian campaign in 1812. This is how it reached my hands. At the time of the disastrous Russian campaign, my spouse was employed in the Emperor's laundry-room; she appealed to the conservator of the wardrobe, Mr. Gervais, and asked for several old hats.
>
> He gave her two of the Emperor's hats which I conserved, having served during this campaign. She gave the other to a person who desired to have one as well. This is the truth. J. DULUD.

170,000 F.F.

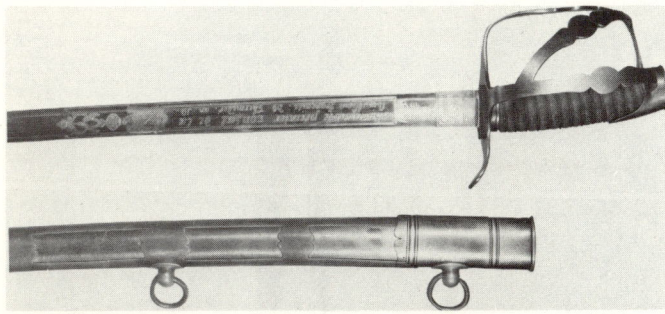

Saber and Scabbard. Very rare and beautiful sword of the "2 Regiment Des Chasseurs A Cheval" (cavalry). The classically formed sword-guard is of bluish iron with a dull-red fuse. On the back side of the blade is marked 43,000 F.F.

A fine and rare example of a 19th-century carved bronze and gilded wall ornaments.   12,000 F.F. the pair.

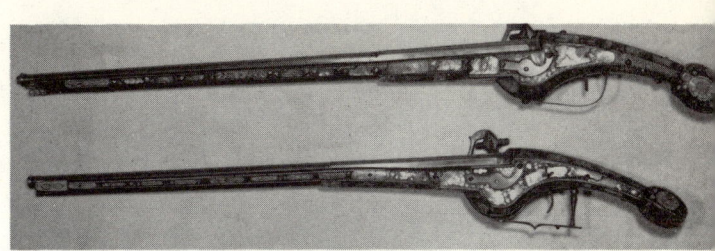

Magnificent and rare French pistol. The very small barrel is channeled down the central portion with a band of rich, gilded decor on a stable background. Like most pistols of this type, the barrel is very prolonged. The pommel holds medallions of pearl engraved with human heads. On one side there is a plate with the initials "G.H." engraved on it, and on a plate on the other side the word "Porteris" is engraved. (There are a few small restorations and deficiencies in the incrustations as well as some light fractures in the framework.) France, Alsace, 1590–95. Caliber is 8 millimeters around.   155,000 F.F.

Splendid and rare French pistol. The very small barrel has magnificent and profuse decoration in its framework—pearl medallions and animals, carvings, and engravings. A plate with the initials "H.F." is visible and the name of the proprietor of the pistol is also engraved in an imbedded plate, "Braun." (There are a few small restorations and deficiencies in the incrustations.) France, Alsace, 1590–95. Caliber is 8 millimeters around.   155,000 F.F.

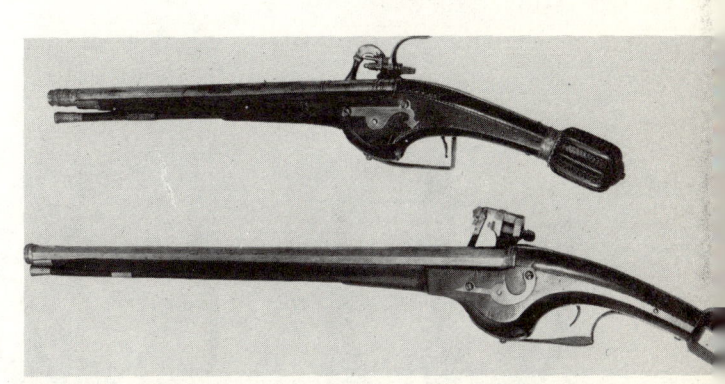

Magnificent and rare pistol of King Louis XIII. France, Lorraine, 1610–15.

Beautiful and rare pistol of King Louis XIII. France, doubtless Paris, 1615–20.

Very fine 19th-century armchair in the Louis XV style. This chair displays beautiful gilt carvings. Price for the pair: 12,000 F.F.

An excellent replica of a commode in the style of Louis XVI. The original can be seen in the collection at the Chateau de Fontainebleau, outside of Paris. The commode commands its importance from the beautiful inlay work ornamented with bronze. Signed F. Linke, Henri Dasson, and G. Durand.   Price 80,000 F.F.

An excellent and very rare example of a commode in the regency style. Beautifully adorned by bronze and expertly inlaid. Produced and signed by Paul Sarmani, Paris. 100,000 F.F.

A very important pair of bronze gilded candelabras, signed Henri Dasson, and dated 1880. Price for the pair: 10,000 F.F.

A very beautiful small table by Martin Carlin, which is modeled after a similar table signed and dated Henri Dasson, 1878.   25,000 F.F.

Kwan-yin sculpture, Chinese in polychrome wood. Sitting with legs bent, her head is slightly inclined to the left with one hand on her knee and one hand raised and bent toward her chin. Ming period.   27,500 F.F.

Triptych panel with gold background. The center panel shows the Virgin Mary and child under a majestic figure of Christ. The right panel shows St. Jacques, St. Jean-Baptiste under the Annunciation Angel; and the left panel shows St. Nicholas of Bari and St. Anthony under the Virgin of the Annunciation. Attributed to Taddeo diBartolo, Siena 1363–1422.   550,000 F.F.

17 Flea Markets of Europe

Although the open markets of Europe date from the Middle Ages, the origin of the term *flea market* can be traced to France in the nineteenth century, where junk dealers gathered at the Porte de Clignancourt to sort through their wares, which were often infested with fleas. This "Marche aux Puces" or market of fleas became a favorite haunt of collectors and dealers alike. Although today these markets often attract tourists, they still remain a vital part of the cities of Europe, where people openly enjoy the age-old practice of bartering while searching for as yet undiscovered treasures.

Bartering is an important and expected part of flea-market shopping. Veteran dealers develop their own bargaining strategies and rigidly stay within predetermined boundaries. Prices vary greatly from country to country and even town to town, and your success in bartering will certainly depend greatly on your pricing knowledge of specific countries and markets. Generally the flea markets located in Southern Europe, such as Spain, Italy, Portugal, and Greece, expect more bartering, and this is built into the pricing of the wares. With any luck at all the price you pay should be no more than half the original asking price. In contrast, markets of Northern Europe expect bartering to a much lesser degree, and although prices will certainly be reduced, they will probably not decline more than ten to thirty percent.

Flea-market shopping has been increasing in popularity during the twentieth century. New markets are started to accommodate this increasing demand, but in this section only the older and more established markets are described.

BELGIUM

Unfortunately, this beautiful country is very often bypassed by travelers to Europe. The cities are quaint, the castles romantic, and the stately homes and museums are filled with famous antiques and artwork. In fact, Belgium offers her visitors a miniature medieval and modern Europe totally within her borders.

Belgium, especially Brussels, has for centuries been known throughout the world as the "cultural crossroads of Europe."

Currency

The monetary unit, the Belgian franc, is divided into 100 centimes. There are coins in 25 and 50 centime dinominations as well as 1, 5, 10, and 50 francs. The banknotes come in 20, 50, 100, 500, 1,000, and 5,000 franc denominations. The Belgian government does not limit the amount of currency you can import or export from the country. The Belgian franc can also be used in Luxembourg, but the Luxembourg franc is not accepted for monetary use in Belgium. 1 Belgian franc = 100 centimes.

INTERNATIONAL CURRENCY CONVERSION CHART

Austria	43 schillings = 100 Belgian francs
Belgium	100 Belgian francs = 100 Belgian francs
Denmark	14 kroners = 100 Belgian francs
France	11 francs = 100 Belgian francs

Germany	6 marks = 100 Belgian francs
Great Britain	1 pound = 100 Belgian francs
Italy	1,500 lira = 100 Belgian francs
Netherlands	7 gulden = 100 Belgian francs
Sweden	12 kroner = 100 Belgian francs
Switzerland	7 francs = 100 Belgian francs
USA	2.75 dollars = 100 Belgian francs

Antique Dealer's Market

Time: Saturday and Sunday
Location: Place du Grand Sablon

This is one of the most exciting markets in Europe and considerably cheaper than the Paris market. The quality of antiques displayed here is wide, and although there are the usual stalls of junk, the emphasis is on good- to fine-quality antiques.

Good-quality brass and copper, as well as provincial clocks and smaller articles, are readily found here and are usually in very fine conditions.

The following is a representative selection of interesting antiques found at this market.

	Belgian Francs
Good selection of brass keys	18–70
Turn-of-the-century grandfathers clocks, pine case	2,500–3,500
Copper tea kettles	600–1,600
Coffee grinders	450–1,200
18th & 19th century bed warmers	700–1,400
Angelica Kauffmann, plate classical figures	900

Brussels Flea Market

Time: 8 A.M. to 1 P.M.; open every day
Location: Place du Jeu de Balle

This is a traditional flea market, although not only featuring antiques, and some very interesting finds can be discovered. Although the market is open every day, Saturday and Sunday are the best days for antique selection, and the earlier the better. The market is widely spread over the entire square, so careful looking through the entire market is essential to find the best buys. It should be noted that prices at this market are slightly less than at the dealer's market. For example, a coffee mill c. 1860, purchased at the dealer's market for 600 Belgian francs, could be found at the Brussels Flea Market for between 20 and 25 percent less.

The following articles are representative of some of the exciting antiques to be found at this market.

	Belgian Francs
Pewter teapots, turn of the century	1,200
Good selection of milk glass	180–700
Brass lanterns	500–1,000
Bread chests	3,500
Provincial wall clocks	1,200–2,500
Brass coffee urn	1,100

GHENT

Time: Friday and Saturday
Location: Place du Vendredi

The beautiful town of Ghent, sometimes known as the "Florence of the North," should not be missed by the art lover.

The market, which is located behind St. Jacobs Church, has an admirable selection of metal wares, copper, brass, pewter, and sometimes good silver pieces.

	Belgian Francs
Pewter coffeepot, c. 1890	1,200
Pewter mold	350
Copper plate	140
Copper brandy warmer, c. 1900	250
Bronze incense burner	450
Selection of silver spoons, English, c. 1890	70–350

FRANCE

Besides the fabulous Paris flea markets, the French provinces are still a most interesting place for the value-minded antique collector, as well as for the dealer looking for buys. These markets, scattered throughout the countryside, are usually well stocked, and the dealers are very friendly and helpful. A knowledge of French is extremely helpful in some of the more rural flea markets, but not absolutely necessary. In fact, France today is one of the best buys in rural flea-market shopping.

Currency

The monetary unit, the French franc, is divided into 100 centimes. There is no restriction placed on the amount of currency in francs that can be brought into the country, but only 100 francs can be taken out.
1 French franc = 100 centimes

INTERNATIONAL CURRENCY CONVERSION CHART

Austria	40 schillings = 10 French francs
Belgium	100 Belgian francs = 10 French francs
Denmark	12 kroners = 10 French francs
France	10 French francs = 10 French francs
Germany	55 marks = 10 French francs
Great Britain	1 pound = 10 French francs
Italy	1,300 lira = 10 French francs
Netherlands	6 guldens = 10 French francs
Sweden	10 kroners = 10 French francs
Switzerland	7 Swiss francs = 10 French francs
USA	2.50 dollars = 10 French francs

Aix-en-Provence (Bouches-du-Rhône)

Time: Tuesday, Thursday, and Saturday mornings, about 8–1
Location: Aix-En-Provence is 766 Kms from Paris. The flea market is located at the Place du Palais de Justice.

Although the market here is rather small, prices are low and quality high. Mostly the antiques are small, decorative accessories.

	Francs
Butter stamp, pineapple design	8
Milk-glass bottles	20–35
Painted bread tray, c. 1820	40

During the month of July, to coincide with the music festival, an International Antiques Fair is held in Aix-En-Provence. Information and exact dates should be addressed to:

Rue Salliers 12
Aix-en-Provence
Bouches du Rhône
France

The Antique Fair is usually held at the Boulevard Carnot, but it is always advisable to check the exact location at either your hotel or the local tourist agency.

This fair is of much higher caliber than the local flea market, and many high-quality antique dealers participate. A visit is very worthwhile, since prices are very reasonable. A good variety of both clocks and watches are always available.

	French Francs
Morez clocks, c. 1810	200–300
Morez grandfather clock, oak case, c. 1820	400–550
Good variety of pocket watches	40–200 & up

Angers (Maine-et-Loire)

Time: Saturday
Location: Angers is 304 Kms from Paris, and the market is at the Place du Pelican.

This market has a very good selection of very reasonably priced antiques with great emphasis on carved furniture, as well as small, decorative articles.

	French Francs
French Provincial hand-carved blanket chest, c. 1800	300–450
Louis XV-style commode, c. 1890	180
Empire card table, lyre base	100
Old brass keys	8–40

Angouleme (Charente)

Time: 2 or 15th of each month
Location: Angouleme is 446 Kms from Paris and the market is held on the Boulevard Berthelot.

Although this flea market is very small, it is an excellent supply source for nineteenth-century brass and copper.

	French Francs
Coach lanterns	20
Brass candlesticks	20 & up
Brass scales with weights	30
19th-century coffee mill	9–30

Argenteuil (Seine-et-Oise)

Time:
Location: Argenteuil is only 14 Kms from Paris and should not be missed by anyone interested in antiques visiting the Paris area. The flea market is held on the Boulevard Heloise.

Prices here are considerably lower than the various Paris markets, but at Argenteuil the good buys must be sorted out from the normal flea-market junk.

	French Francs
Milk-glass lamp	20
Quimper pottery crust set, c. 1900	40
Quimper pottery ink stand	30
Good selection of keys	12 & up
Victorian marble-top night stands	20

Beziers (Hérault)

Time: Friday morning, 9–12
Location: Beziers is 837 Kms from Paris and the market is held at the Place du Champ de Mars.

	French Francs
Brass cigarette box	8
Brass candlesticks, c. 1800–1850	20–40
Coffee grinders, wall type	20
Copper skimmer	8

Bordeaux (Gironde)

Time: Daily
Location: Place Meriadec-Bordeaux is 562 Kms from Paris.

The flea market at Bordeaux makes a worthwhile trip, since prices are extremely low and there is a consistently good selection of antiques.

	French Francs
Rustic grandfather clocks, c. 1890	250–400
Copper bed warmers	40
Brass church candlesticks, 19th century	20–120
Three-legged chairs, cane seats	60–100
Mahogany chests, c. 1800	200–550
Bureau, Louis XVI-style, c. 1890	450

Paris

Paris is famous for its variety of flea markets. Not all are worth the time and effort for the visit, but the better ones are listed below.

Marche—Porte de Clignancourt

Time: Saturday, Sunday, and Monday
Location: Porte de Clagnancourt at the Rue des Rosiers

Although this is the largest and best-known antique market in France, be prepared for very high prices that are not justified. Bargaining may not be so successful because of the large and continuous tourist trade this market receives. The best time for bargains at this market is January through March, when the majority of tourists are gone and local residents and dealers are faithfully paying their income taxes.

Marche—Porte de Vanves

Time: Saturday and Sunday
Location: Paris-southwest, 14th Arrondissement, near the Port de Versailles

This is one of the smaller markets that offers an excellent selection of decorative accessories with the greater emphasis on brass, copper, pewter, candlesticks, small clocks, and crystal. The prices here are much lower than at the Porte de Clignancourt market.

Village Suisse

Time: Monday, and Thursday through Sunday; sometimes open on Thursday evenings
Location: Within easy walking distance of the Eiffel Tower, at the intersection of the avenues De Suffren and De La Motte Picquet

The variety of antiques displayed here is very good and attracts a much wealthier clientele. The Village Suisse is well worth the visit.

Marche La Porte De Montreuil

Time: Saturday and Sunday
Location: Paris, east section, 11th Arrondissement

This is a very interesting market, if you can wade through the piles of worthless junk to the more interesting antique stalls. It is well worth the effort.

The Paris Antique Fair

The "Foire à la Ferraille," which is held at the Boulevard Richard-Lenoir, is held semiannually in the spring and fall, the week preceding Palm Sunday and the first Saturday in October. This fair lasts for about nine days and attracts more than five hundred dealers, and is well worth the visit.

The antique markets of Paris are world famous, and continue to have a changing stock of wares that are well worth taking the trouble to view. Although prices are higher than in provincial markets, the variety of antiques displayed is often justified.

The following is a list of antiques and prices found at the various Paris flea markets and antique fairs.

	French Francs
Brass and copper door and drawer knobs	2–9
19th C. Venetian wineglasses	40
19th C. mantel clocks, marble	100–250
"Oeil de Boeuf," bull's-eye clocks	100

Quimper pottery inkwell	40
Limoges porcelain tea sets	120
Delft tiles, 17th–19th C.	20–200
Bronze figurines	120–400
Pressed wineglass, Austria	20–40
Art nouveau lamps	140–300
Oil lamps, brass	60–100
Perfume bottles	20–80
Chinese export porcelain dish, c. 1810	140
Postcards, c. 1900	1–4
19th C. marble clock with matching candlesticks	180–250
Porcelain dolls, c. 1850	100

Orleans, Loiret

Time: Saturdays
Location: The rear of St. Paul's Church; Orleans is 116 Kms South of Paris

The Orleans flea market is well worth even a detour, especially if you are interested in nineteenth-century provincial furniture and small decorative articles.

	French Francs
19th C. hinged card table	500
Vitrine, Louis XVI style	250–525
Washstands, complete	140–200
Brass keys	4–20
Brass candlabrum, 5 arm	12

Rouen, Seine-Maritime

Time: Sunday morning, and Tuesday, Friday, and Saturday all day
Location: Place St. Marc

Every spring a "Weekend of Antiques" takes place at the Palais de la Halle aux Toiles, and is especially worth a visit. Exact dates can be obtained from any local French tourist agency or Rouen's Syndicat d' Initiative.

Although the weekly Rouen market is small, there is a very good selection of fairly priced antiques displayed.

	French Francs
Blown wineglasses, c. 1800	8–20
Butter mold, wooden, dated 1862	40
Iron, wooden handle, dated 1854	20
Good selection of wall clocks, c. 1890	200–350
Brass letter opener, dated 1802	60
Brass mortar & pestle	30

Strasbourg, Bas-Rhin

Time: Wednesday and Friday morning
Location: Strasbourg is 458 Kms from Paris, and convenient to both Switzerland and Germany

This is a very interesting regional market that displays many worthwhile Alsatian antiques.

	French Francs
Schrank, c. 1850, painted	400
Grandfather clocks	300
Carved chairs	140
Painted pottery	20–100
Pewter charger, c. 1790	100
Beer steins	39–80
Hand-blown 19th C. wineglasses	20 each

Toulouse, Haute-Garonne

Time: Sunday morning
Location: Place St. Sernin; Toulouse is 680 Kms from Paris

Although the large flea market is held on Sunday, a much smaller market takes place each Monday near the Place Arnaud-Bernard.

	French Francs
19th C. brass horse bank	40
7-piece Bavarian fish set	140
400-day anniversary clock	80
Cut-glass wine decanter, c. 1840	60
Pewter tumbler, c. 1820	20
Various French silver tableware	8–20
Handcarved wooden plate, c. 1790	75

Tours, Indre-et-Loire

Time: The biannual antiques market is held the first two weeks each year of both August and May. A weekly market takes place each Wednesday and Saturday.
Location: Tours is 235 Kms from Paris, and the biannual antiques fair is located on the Canal du Berry; while the weekly market takes place at the Place Victoire.

The biannual antiques fair is worth a visit and specializes mostly in furniture, while the weekly market is limited to smaller, decorative items.

	French Francs
French fashion doll	40
Victorian toilet mirror, mother-of pearl inlay	60
Vitrene Louis VI style	400
Provincial grandfather clock	450
Royal Dux vase	20
Spatterware cup and saucer, handleless	30

GERMANY

Germany through the centuries has given to the world some of the most famous people in the cultural arts, and remains one of the most popular countries in the world to visit. Her quaint walled cities, misty seaports, and soaring Alps endear the visitor as well as the native to the charms of Germany.

Currency

The monetary unit, the mark, is perhaps the strongest currency in the world. The German mark (DM) is divided into 100 pfennigs. The West German government has no restrictions on importing or exporting marks, but anyone entering East Germany should inquire at either currency conversion centers or a local travel agency. 1 German mark = 100 pfennigs.

INTERNATIONAL CURRENCY CONVERSION CHART

Austria	70 schillings = 10 DM
Belgium	160 Belgian francs = 10 DM
Denmark	22 kroners = 10 DM
France	18 French francs = 10 DM
Germany	10 marks = 10 DM
Great Britain	1.6 pounds = 10 DM
Italy	2,300 lira = 10 DM
Netherlands	10 guldens = 10 DM
Sweden	18 kroners = 10 DM
Switzerland	12 Swiss francs = 10 DM
USA	4.25 dollars = 10 DM

Hamburg

Time: First Sunday in every month
Location: Altonaer Fish Market, Landingsbrucken

If you happen to be in the Hamburg area, this is an interesting flea market to visit, but a long detour is not advisable.

	Marks
Writing box, hand carved, c. 1820	60
Brass inkwell, white glass inserts	32
Brass tea kettle	16
Royal Bayreuth vase, pastoral scene	29
Variety of beer steins, pewter tops	22–60
Cradle telephones	40–60

Munich

Munich, gateway to the Alps, and home of many of Germany's great breweries, abounds with interesting antique stores as well as the *Auer Dult*.

Time: May, July, and October for one week
Location: The *Auer Dult* is held near the Mariahelfkirche between the Hochstrasse and the Lilienstrasse.

The local German National tourist office should be consulted for exact dates for this market, since they are changed yearly.

	Marks
Brass bells, wooden handles	5
Wall clocks, c. 1890	80–130
Cut-glass candy dish, c. 1900	50
Alpine chest, c. 1800, painted designs	300
Hand-carved side chairs, c. 1890	80–100
Alpine cradle, c. 1850, painted designs	110
RS Prussia dresser tray, pink and red roses	35
Beer steins, pewter tops	22–70

GREAT BRITAIN

England has for many years been known as the supply house of the world to the antique trade. Dealers and shops are numerous both in and around London as well as the countryside, and the friendliness of the British draws people from around the world to this island to look, if not to buy, a small part of her historic past.

Currency

The monetary unit is the pound sterling, and the pound is now divided into 100 new pence. The British government does not place any restrictions on money being imported into England, but not more than 25 pounds can be taken out at one time.
1 pound = 100 new pence

INTERNATIONAL CURRENCY CONVERSION CHART

Austria	40 schillings = 1 pound
Belgium	95 Belgian francs = 1 pound
Denmark	13 kroners = 1 pound

309

France	10 French francs = 1 pound
Germany	6 marks = 1 pound
Great Britain	1 pound = 1 pound
Italy	1,300 lira = 1 pound
Netherlands	6 guldens = 1 pound
Sweden	10 kroners = 1 pound
Switzerland	6 Swiss francs = 1 pound
USA	2.50 dollars = 1 pound

Bermondsey Street Market

Time: Friday 7 A.M.–6 P.M.
Location: Bermondsey Square

This is a terrific flea market for small, decorative accessories, such as silver, ceramics, and small Victorian works of art. Do not be surprised if you arrive at 7:00 and heavy trading has already begun, since this is primarily a dealer's market and business usually begins at sunrise.

	Pounds
Tortoiseshell cigar case	10
Victorian stuffed bird underdome	7
Double-sided tavern sign	60
18th C. mahogany knife box	30
19th C. banjo case barometer	15
Victorian plated soup tureen	40
Victorian three-bottle tantalus	30
Silver sugar tongs, c. 1820	10
Victorian silver-backed mirror and brush set	10

Camden Passage

Time: Saturday and Wednesday 9 A.M.–5 P.M. Most stores in Passage area open every day as well.
Location: Islington Highstreet, N.I.

The quality of wares is high, with a greater emphasis on furniture and works of art.

	Pounds
Edwardian bookcase, walnut	25
19th C. oak fall-front desk, bulbous legs	20
19th C. mahogany music cabinet	10
4 Edwardian chairs, pierced splats, cabriole legs	22
19th C. mahogany plant stand	12
Early Victorian daybed	35
Sheraton mahogany pembroke table	190
Enoch Wood pot, c. 1835	14
18th C. oak cased grandfather clock	70

Cutler Street Silver Market

Time: Sunday 8 A.M.–about noon
Location: Cutler Street

This is predominantly a dealer's market, but the public is welcomed. The market specializes mostly in jewelry, silver coins, and medals.

	Pounds
Victorian silver match case	5
19th C. plated tea caddy	14
Victorian silver teapot	80
Silver sherry label c. 1820	20
Victorian 3-piece silver tea set	72
19th C. Sheffield plated coffeepot	35
19th C. Sheffield plated egg cruet	27
George III shell dish, c. 1775	120

Petticoat Lane

Time: Sunday 9 A.M.–late afternoon
Location: Petticoat Lane and adjoining streets such as Bell Street, Sclater Street, and Cheshire Street

These markets are stocked with mostly inexpensive wares, but fairly good pieces have been discovered here. It is well worth the try.

	Pounds
Victorian mahogany bookcase	30
Victorian mahogany side chair	5
Edwardian jardiniere	12
Victorian ruby glass jug	13
Brass tray, Indian	4
19th C. copper saucepan	5
Early brass irons	6–11
Victorian banjo case barometer	14

Portobello Market

This market is so large that it is divided into many different areas that have various operating times.

Time: Main market, Saturday, 8:30 A.M.–5:30 P.M. Enclosed shops and arcades mostly operate Saturday, 7:30 A.M.–5:30 P.M., while some stores do open on Friday with the same time, so it is best to check.
Location: the Portobello Road from about Galborne Road to Chepstraw

A visit to this market is an education in itself. Several thousand stalls extend along the length of the

Portobello Road, exhibiting wares from a few pounds to many thousand.

	Pounds
Victorian carved oak bureau	60
Set of 4, Chippendale-style beechwood chairs	40
George II mahogany corner cupboard	200
19th C. carved oak sideboard	35
Spode teapot, 19th C.	3
Victorian water jug and basin	6
19th C. rouge marble clock and matching candlesticks	20
Late 19th C. gilt sunburst wall clock	19
Victorian regulator wall clock	45
Edwardian glass sugar custer	3

HOLLAND

The natives of Holland have a proverb, "God made the universe, but the Dutch made the Netherlands." But the Dutch have given more to the world than just some reclaimed land; they have inspired the Great Masters and the delft potters, who have given the world great beauty. The thousands of tourists who flood the country each year try to capture a small amount of the beauty that is Holland.

Currency

The monetary unit is the gulden, and there are 100 cents in the guilden. There are no government restrictions placed on either the importation or export of money from the country. 1 gulden = 100 cents.

INTERNATIONAL CURRENCY CONVERSION CHART

Austria	60 schillings = 10 guldens
Belgium	160 Belgian francs = 10 guldens
Denmark	20 kroners = 10 guldens
France	18 French francs = 10 guldens
Germany	10 marks = 10 guldens
Great Britain	1.8 pounds = 10 guldens
Italy	2,300 lira = 10 guldens
Netherlands	10 guldens = 10 guldens
Sweden	16 kroners = 10 guldens
Switzerland	10 Swiss francs = 10 guldens
USA	4 dollars = 10 guldens

Amsterdam Flea Market

Time: every day except Saturday, 10 A.M.–dusk.
Location: Waterlooplein

Many of the copper and brass articles found at this flea market are reproductions, but not only are they of excellent quality, they are fantastic buys.

	Gulden
Brass candelabrum (reproduction)	25
Brass candelabrum, Louis XVI style	160
Copper brandy warmer, c. 1900	42
Pewter charger, c. 1850	100
Pewter plates (reproduction)	7–14
Corner chair, 3 legs, cane seat, c. 1870	50
Victorian mantel clock	100
Good selection of pewter spoons	3–12

ITALY

For the last two thousand years, Italy has been a pacesetter in literature, government, art, and architecture. It is a vibrant country, despite numerous strikes, pollution, and run-away inflation, and is loved by everyone who visits. The street markets of Italy are alive, the bargaining spirited, and the antiques varied, which make a visit well worth the trip.

Currency

The monetary unit in Italy is the lira. No government restrictions are placed on the amount of lira that can be imported into the country, but only 50,000 lira may be exported. Exact exchange rates should be verified before purchase, because sometimes a more favorable rate can be secured outside the country, for example in either Switzerland or New York.

INTERNATIONAL CURRENCY CONVERSION CHART

Austria	28 schillings = 1,000 lira
Belgium	70 Belgian francs = 1,000 lira
Denmark	10 kroners = 1,000 lira
France	9 French francs = 1,000 lira
Germany	4.50 marks = 1,000 lira
Great Britain	.80 pounds = 1,000 lira
Italy	1,000 lira = 1,000 lira
Netherlands	5 guldens = 1,000 lira
Sweden	8 kroners = 1,000 lira
Switzerland	5 Swiss francs = 1,000 lira
USA	1.75 dollars = 1,000 lira

Bologna

Time: Friday
Location: Via Irnerio

The market is small, but very interesting and a good source for glass, copper, and brass.

	Lira
19th C. decorated glass vase	2,700
Geometric cruet bottle, c. 1810	7,000
Early brass flatirons	1,200–4,000
Victorian iron plant stand	3,500
Late 19th C. hot-water dish, pewter	8,000
19th C. pewter teapot	7,000

Florence

Time: daily except Sunday, 9 A.M.–6 P.M.
Location: Piazza dei Ciompi

Florence, city of art and romance, has a small but very interesting antique market. Almost anything can be found, but the majority of wares are smaller items, for example porcelain, pottery, copper, brass, pewter, and some furniture.

	Lira
Late 19th C. walnut bureau	17,000
19th C. lacemaker's chair	10,000
Pair of alabaster levers	11,000
Victorian chamber pot	1,400
Pair of 19th C. brass candlesticks	7,000
Victorian marble vase	4,500
19th C. pewter coffee pot, c. 1850	9,000
Glass decanter, c. 1890	3,000

Milan

Time: Saturday, 9 A.M.–3 P.M.
Location: Via Calatifimi and Via s. Croce

The Milan market is very interesting, with a wide range of antiques being offered.

	Lira
Pair of embossed bronze candlesticks, dragon motif	9,000
19th C. tulip-shaped pewter tankard	12,000
Good selection of antique brass keys	1,200–4,000
19th C. snuff box with mother-of-pearl	3,500
Late Victorian mahogany toilet mirror	9,000
19th C. flatirons with wooden handles	1,600–4,000
18th and 19th C. beer mugs	4,000–11,000
19th C. copper molds	3,000
Faience bowls and plates, 19th C.	3,000–8,000
Alter candlesticks, 18th and 19th C.	11,000

Rome

Time: Sunday (trading begins here officially at midnight on Saturday evening.)
Location: Porta Portese

Rome, the eternal city, definitely has a flea market to be remembered. Most local residents and dealers visit this market early, even before sunrise. Go early—it is very possible you will find a terrific treasure.

	Lira
Icon, c. 1890, Our Lady Kayanaskaya	60,000
Leatherbound 18th and 19th C. books	1,600–3,000
18th and 19th C. prints	6,000 and up
Silk embroidery picture, 1800	11,000
19th C. scent bottles	5,000 and up
Late 19th C. glass tazza	2,500
19th C. marble mantel clocks	12,000
18th and 19th C. wineglasses	2,500–27,000
19th C. silver-plated urn	14,000
18th C. spinning wheel	16,000

If you are unable to visit the Porta Portese antique market, try the smaller Piazza della Fontanella Borghese market, which is open every day, Monday through Saturday, from about 2 or 3 P.M. until dusk.

SWITZERLAND

Switzerland, world famous for cheese, chocolate, money, watches, and mountains, also has some little-known street markets that are tucked away on picturesque cobble-stoned streets.

Currency

The Swiss franc is definitely the strongest and most sought-after currency in the world. The official monetary unit, the Swiss franc is divided into 100 centimes. The Swiss government places no restriction on the amount of money that enters the country or is taken out; all is welcomed. 1 Swiss franc = 100 centimes.

INTERNATIONAL CURRENCY CONVERSION CHART

Austria	65 schillings = 10 francs
Belgium	150 Belgian francs = 10 francs
Denmark	20 kroners = 10 francs
France	16 French francs = 10 francs
Germany	9 marks = 10 francs
Great Britain	1.6 pounds = 10 francs
Italy	2,200 lira = 10 francs
Netherlands	9 guldens = 10 francs
Sweden	16 kroners = 10 francs
Switzerland	10 Swiss francs = 10 francs
USA	3.50 dollars = 10 francs

Although many of the cities and towns around Switzerland have both planned and unofficial flea markets, the best one takes place in Geneva.

Geneva

Time: Saturday, 8 A.M.–1:30 P.M.
Location: Place Issac Mercier

Although pieces are high here, because nothing is inexpensive in Switzerland, the variety of wares displayed and the condition of everything certainly compensates for the higher prices.

	Swiss Francs
19th C. provincial grandfather clocks	200–425
Alpine painted bread chests	180
Copper tea kettle, c. 1820	20
19th C. coffee grinder	45
Good selection Swiss pocket watches, 19th C.	90 and up
18th and 19th C. beer steins, pewter tops	35–100
19th C. swords	60–100
19th C. alpine pottery cows	16–45
Victorian oak wall barometer	35
Large wooden salad bowls, c. 1850	55

18 Price Guide to Germany

VALUE GROWTH CHART

GLASS STEINS   PRICES QUOTED IN DM

ARTICLE	1971	1975	1978	Average Annual Increase	Financial Outlook 1978-84
Blown, hand-painted enamel scene	62	85	125	10%	3
Footed with brass overlay	100	375	550	27%	3
16″ pedestal, cut decoration	125	150	260	11%	2
Mary Gregory painted enamel	80	162	250	17%	2
½ l. green, richly enameled	37	111	162	23%	3
½ l. cased glass, finely cut with handle	35	80	147	23%	3
½ l. green, enameled student shield	80	145	222	16%	2
½ l. Bohemian etched wildlife scene	30	97	143	25%	4
½ l. Pressed w/lalique relief	50	100	135	15%	2
½ l. cobalt blue, finely etched	55	140	198	20%	3
½ l. pedestal foot sulphide of owl	38	100	140	20%	3
½ l. pressed painted porcelain inset	25	62	105	26%	4
½ l. molded glass w/jeweled top	25	62	92	20%	3
Mary Gregory type amber, dated 1886	52	112	140	15%	2
½ l. pressed w/red and blue enameling	50	110	145	16%	3
½ l. pressed w/hand enameling	30	62	92	17%	3
½ l. pressed with pedestal foot	25	59	72	16%	2
½ l. cut w/foot and applied handle	37	59	89	13%	2
Amber Mary Gregory type-fluted base	47	72	95	10%	2
Liter cranberry w/pewter foot	45	87	145	18%	3
½ l. light blue w/enamel design	42	76	97	13%	2
Liter clear glass, pewter top	25	50	87	19%	3
Small cobalt, etched w/castel	29	55	69	13%	2
¼ l. pressed w/engraved pewter lid	30	52	100	19%	3
½ l. Biedermeier, wide footed	67	112	162	13%	2
½ l. pressed w/jeweled top	25	60	87	19%	3
Blown green, serving stein, 14″	37	62	92	14%	3
½ l. enameled with silver lid	29	95	132	24%	4

VALUE GROWTH CHART
PRICES QUOTED IN DM

ARTICLE	1971	1975	1978	Average Annual Increase	Financial Outlook 1978-84
½ l. amber, footed w/enameling	26	55	89	19%	4
Blown, blue, Mary Gregory type	55	87	112	11%	2
½ l. cut frosted blue w/jewel insert	32	90	130	22%	3
½ l. Bohemian etched German town	50	86	120	13%	3
Blown with ornate helmet type lid	42	69	85	10%	2
Liter glass, pewter lid finely etched	25	55	82	18%	3
16" blue blown serving	35	72	100	16%	3
½ l. cut with richly carved wood type	42	70	137	18%	3
½ l. pedestal, enameled green	22	50	82	20%	4
Liter blown enameled light green	34	55	93	15%	3
½ l. pressed w/pewter lid	13	49	72	28%	4
½ l. pressed w/pewter lid	12	46	74	30%	4
½ l. slender pressed w/lid	22	49	87	22%	3
16" amber blown	50	90	122	13%	2
22" blown, enameled design	47	72	100	11%	2
16" blown w/floral enameling	52	92	125	13%	2
16" blown amber serving	30	72	120	22%	3
½ l. cut pedestal w/pewter lid	56	86	125	12%	3
Liter cut w/pedestal and enamel scene	69	112	137	20%	2
16" light blue enamel painted	62	122	172	16%	3

PORCELAIN STEINS

ARTICLE	1971	1975	1978	Average Annual Increase	Financial Outlook 1978-84
L. w/painted scene & lithopane	47	87	120	14%	2
½ l. decal scene & lithopane	30	62	92	17%	3
½ l. etched with medallions	45	72	119	15%	2
18" serving stein, ornate lid	97	125	200	11%	2
16" ruby enamel serving	69	100	139	10%	2
1 l. pedestal w/painted scene	96	145	190	10%	2
½ l. green enameled hunt scene	30	110	140	25%	4
½ l. intaglio cut, footed	29	56	90	17%	3

VALUE GROWTH CHART

DOLLS AND TOYS
PRICES QUOTED IN DM

ARTICLE	1971	1975	1978	Average Annual Increase	Financial Outlook 1978-84
Pendulum wall clock, 1890	20	55	75	20%	1
Embroidered flowers w/vase	40	60	85	11%	2
8 ps. Woman's toilette set	30	45	65	11%	2
4 ps. pewter coffee set	90	125	165	9%	3

DOLLS

ARTICLE	1971	1975	1978	Average Annual Increase	Financial Outlook 1978-84
French, porcelain head, 1880	200	375	525	15%	2
French, original dress & hat 1825	150	275	375	14%	2

VALUE GROWTH CHART

PRICES QUOTED IN DM

ARTICLE	1971	1975	1978	Average Annual Increase	Financial Outlook 1978-84
German, w/7 dress trousseau	100	325	450	24%	1
Russian, papier-mâché head, 1900	225	400	500	12%	2
Deuel, cloth w/china head	125	200	250	10%	2
Russian mother & child, 1825	100	145	375	21%	1
Polish hand-carved wooden, 1800	75	250	450	29%	1
Clown, rubber head & hands, 1900	50	75	125	14%	3
German, porcelain head, 1890	50	125	200	22%	1
Biedermeier doll c. 1840	500	900	1,500	17%	2
French, large w/porcelain head/hat	300	490	700	13%	2
French fashion, c. 1900	90	170	300	19%	1
Porcelain dollhouse, 1810	75	150	275	20%	1
German dollhouse figures, 1910	75	250	375	26%	1
Small porcelain doll, 1920	50	150	200	22%	1
2 plastic dolls, soft, 1920	25	45	95	21%	1
Plastic Kewpie, original dress	10	40	65	31%	1
Swiss cloth, man & woman, 1900	35	70	100	16%	3
German, costume dress, 1860	90	140	300	19%	2
Wooden, 19th C. Poland	50	125	250	26%	2
French, small w/parasol, 1900	75	150	325	23%	1
Baby, porcelain, 1890	60	85	110	9%	2
2 Porcelain tea dolls, 1890	65	100	135	11%	2
Walking doll, French, 1880	200	375	550	15%	2
Rubber baby, German 1920	25	45	90	20%	3
6 wooden autos, c. 1930	75	150	200	15%	1
12 hand-painted wooden soldiers, 1900	50	79	125	14%	1
Small farmer's dollhouse, 1900	75	100	120	7%	2
Noah's ark, 13 metal fig., 1920	80	100	125	6%	3
Wooden circus, 22 pieces, 1900	45	65	75	8%	2
Hand-carved horses, 4, c. 1870	150	210	300	10%	3
7-piece holy figure set, c. 1900	50	125	200	22%	2
Puppet show w/15 wooden puppets, 1920	75	175	225	17%	1
Dollhouse, Alpine motif, 1900	50	125	150	17%	2
Early wooden puzzle, 1810	20	60	75	20%	2

DOLLHOUSE FURNITURE, c. 1860

Hand-painted chair (4)	22	50	85	21%	1
Secretary desk	50	65	150	17%	2
China cabinet w/glass	25	75	110	23%	1
Spinning wheel	40	60	100	14%	2
Mirrow w/hand carved frame	30	60	90	17%	2
Round table w/2 chairs	25	40	65	15%	2
Sofa	20	50	60	17%	2
Piano w/bench	20	40	65	18%	1
Complete living room, 12 ps.	200	300	425	11%	1
Complete dining room, 10 ps.	100	225	375	21%	1
12 pictures w/frame	100	125	175	8%	3
Bedroom, 10 ps., 1910	25	75	100	22%	1
South German wardrobe	75	100	150	10%	2

VALUE GROWTH CHART

DOLL HOUSE FURNITURE — PRICES QUOTED IN DM

ARTICLE	1971	1975	1978	Average Annual Increase	Financial Outlook 1978-84
DOLLHOUSE FURNITURE, c. 1860					
Wash commode w/bowl & pitcher	125	175	200	7%	3
Hand-painted baby high chair	40	65	80	10%	2
Painted oil lamps, 1910 (2)	40	70	100	14%	1
22 pc. china service, white/gold	55	85	110	10%	2
25 ps. porcelain dinner set	60	75	125	11%	2
7 ps. kitchen canister set, China	40	75	145	20%	1
24 ps. silverware service	70	100	125	9%	1

VALUE GROWTH CHART

GLASS — PRICES QUOTED IN DM

ARTICLE	1971	1975	1978	Average Annual Increase	Financial Outlook 1978-84
BOTTLES					
12 brown & green, maker's mark, 1895	12	27	50	23%	1
8 dark green bitters, c. 1890	8	20	30	21%	1
6 brown, small, c. 1900	4	8	13	18%	2
Green, screw stopper, c. 1890	2	5	8	22%	1
Paneled green, mineral, c. 1890	1	3	5	26%	1
Stippled brown, labeled, c. 1890	2	4	6	17%	2
Plain green, labeled, c. 1890	.5	1	2.5	26%	1
5 pale green, mineral, labeled, 1890	5	9	13	15%	3
12 green, medicine, small, 1860	6	12	18	17%	2
2 square green, labeled, c. 1880	3	5	8	15%	3
4 green mineral, maker's names, c. 1890	4	7	10	14%	3
12 crude green ink bottles, 1865	5	16	25	26%	1
6 mineral, green, labeled, 1850	9	22	30	19%	2
Clear, porcelain & metal top, c. 1890	1	3	5	26%	1
Clear, name in relief, c. 1890	2	5	7.5	21%	1
Square green, c. 1880	2	4	6.5	18%	2
6 green, mineral water, 1890	5	8	15	17%	2
Brown, inverted base, relief, 1900	1	5	7	32%	1
7 square green medicine, 1865	3	7	15	26%	1
16 round green remedy, 1885	16	26	40	14%	3
Green, screw top, labeled, 1890	1	3	5	26%	1
Dark green, screw stopper, c. 1885	3	5	8	15%	2
Green, glass stopper, c. 1890	2	4	6	17%	2
10 clear medicine, small, 1890	3	10	18	29%	1

VALUE GROWTH CHART
PRICES QUOTED IN DM

ARTICLE	1971	1975	1978	Average Annual Increase	Financial Outlook 1978-84
Green wine, labeled, 1880	4	7	12	17%	2
3 brown & green, relief name, 1895	20	36	55	15%	3
6 dark green bitters, names, 1890	7	13	25	20%	1
12 mineral water, c. 1895	12	20	30	14%	3
Amethyst, relief, c. 1890	1	3	6	29%	1
4 green mineral, labeled, c. 1865	2	6	10	26%	1

VALUE GROWTH CHART
CLOCKS — PRICES QUOTED IN DM

ARTICLE	1971	1975	1978	Average Annual Increase	Financial Outlook 1978-84
Graphometer, Paris, 1764	800	1,400	5,400	31%	1
Sundial, Augsburg, 18th C.	900	1,550	4,800	27%	1
Sundial, Paris, 18th C.	700	1,200	3,100	23%	1
Perpetual calendar, 17th C.	400	750	2,100	26%	1
Perpetual calendar, late 17th C.	600	1,350	3,900	30%	1
Astrolab, Persian, 19th C.	1,000	1,200	2,600	15%	2
Nocturnal-dial, 16th C.	1,400	3,200	9,200	30%	1
Universal ring dial, 1675	2,000	2,500	3,900	10%	3
Wooden microscope, 18th C.	1,800	2,000	3,800	11%	3
English compass, 18th C.	400	625	750	9%	3
German sundial, 17th C.	1,000	1,900	2,900	16%	2
Dutch hourglass, c. 1700	900	1,250	1,650	9%	3
French protractor, 1690	250	575	700	6%	2
Nautical kit w/compass, 18th C.	800	1,500	2,300	16%	2
French globe & compass, 1800	2,500	4,000	6,500	14%	2
Telescope, England, 1750	2,000	3,000	4,400	12%	3
Telescope, German, 1835	1,200	2,000	2,600	11%	2
Astronomical telescope, 1850	800	1,250	1,700	11%	2
Culpepper-type microscope, 1790	4,800	6,000	7,000	6%	3
Binocular microscope, 1860	400	575	750	9%	3
Hydrometer, France, 1780	200	375	450	12%	2
Ormolu-ebony mantel, 19th C.	325	545	700	12%	3
Skeleton clock (31.8 cm), c. 1840	900	1,675	2,400	15%	3
Gilt bronze sculptural clock, C.	175	320	480	16%	2
19th C. brass cathedral clock	560	975	1,440	14%	3
19th C. gilt-metal sculptural	145	300	400	16%	2
Enameled & brass carriage, 19th C.	400	725	1,200	17%	2
Vienna porcelain & bronze, 1880	900	1,795	2,880	18%	2
Brass mantle (33 cm), 19th C.	390	675	1,055	15%	3
Onyx mantle, signed 19th C.	140	300	500	20%	1
Gilt spelter mantle, c. 1890	245	500	750	17%	2
Ebonized wood mantle, c. 1880	490	895	1,475	17%	2
Carved Black Forest mantle, c. 1900	50	120	187	21%	1

VALUE GROWTH CHART
PRICES QUOTED IN DM

ARTICLE	1971	1975	1978	Average Annual Increase	Financial Outlook 1978-84
Walnut waterfall, c. 1895	95	195	313	18%	2
3 ps. porcelain, blue, set, c. 1890	60	110	197	19%	2
Ornate oak case mantle, 1890	55	120	205	21%	1
Marble mantle, c. 1890	245	595	975	22%	1
Carved oak mantle, c. 1900	55	135	212	21%	1
Ornate oak cottage mantle, 1890	120	247	362	17%	2
Papier-mâché mantle, c. 1880	65	190	345	27%	1
Plain mahogany grandfather, 1860	490	785	1,250	14%	3
Carved mahogany grandfather, 1810	2,200	4,750	6,250	16%	2
Oak Case shelf, c. 1900	40	79	140	20%	1
Mahogany mantle, c. 1900	59	112	215	20%	1
Oak case grandfather, c. 1865	450	785	1,195	15%	2
Mahogany cased wall, c. 1865	275	560	900	18%	2
Oak Gothic-style wall, 1890	500	1,150	1,875	21%	1
Oak grandfather, carved, 1860	450	697	1,312	17%	1
Mahogany grandfather, 1865	555	795	1,447	15%	2
Feathered mahogany grandfather, 1860	640	860	1,562	13%	3
Carved oak grandfather, 1855	400	720	1,125	16%	2
Cottage, mahogany, c. 1800	63	115	185	17%	2
Crucifix, metal, c. 1625	900	2,250	3,375	21%	1
18th C. cuckoo	500	790	1,500	17%	2
19th C. cuckoo	50	260	400	35%	1
400-Day, c. 1880	75	120	275	20%	2
Vienna regulator, c. 187	90	156	292	18%	2
Picture, c. 1820	65	132	220	19%	2
Oak wall, eagle on top, 1890	79	160	275	20%	1
Oak wall, eagle on top, 1920	64	110	200	18%	2
Mahogany regulator, c. 1825	200	320	400	10%	3

VALUE GROWTH CHART
FURNITURE — PRICES QUOTED IN DM

ARTICLE	1971	1975	1978	Average Annual Increase	Financial Outlook 1978-84
Oak spinning wheel, c. 1860	49	78	125	14%	3
19th C. mahogany table, chess board, 1880	39	84	112	16%	2
Round oak pedestal table, c. 1840	130	295	425	18%	2
19th C. mahogany desk, leather top	65	250	325	26%	1
Carved oak table, scroll design, 1900	79	139	245	17%	2
Victorian inlaid floral table, 1860	39	200	300	34%	1
Pair mahogany right stand, c. 1895	55	127	212	21%	1
Carved mahogany fern stand, c. 1880	78	135	225	16%	2
19th C. mahogany game table	29	79	140	25%	1
Wall fold-down desk, c. 1890	22	45	69	18%	2
Mahogany pedestal game table, 1895	57	98	165	16%	3
19th C. mahogany washstand, 6 pcs., 1860	225	495	750	19%	2
Carved deacon's bench, c. 1865	195	345	625	18%	2
19th C. carved oak high-back hall seat	440	789	1,500	19%	2

VALUE GROWTH CHART
PRICES QUOTED IN DM

ARTICLE	1971	1975	1978	Average Annual Increase	Financial Outlook 1978-84
Red mahogany tea tray, 1900	39	67	155	22%	1
Hump-back sea chest, dated 1820	165	279	500	17%	2
Mahogany bureau bookcase, 1890	395	678	1,312	19%	2
Paneled cupboard, c. 1810	790	1,675	2,500	18%	2
Oak collector's cabinet, 1900	450	765	1,125	14%	3
Ship's oak washbowl stand, 1900	48	78	197	22%	1
Mahogany extension table, c. 1890	245	450	913	21%	1
Mahogany washbowl stand, 1820	49	78	187	21%	1
Ebonized wood table-top cabinet, 1880	62	94	125	11%	3
19th C. gilt wood table, oval, 1890	72	139	220	17%	2
Oak hat stand, carved, c. 1900	39	67	102	15%	2
Revolving bookcase, carved, 1895	68	145	237	20%	1
Mahogany glass door bookcase, c. 1900	225	436	625	16%	3
Mahogany shaving stand, 1880	136	265	412	17%	3
Jacobean style collector's cabinet, 1810	795	1,600	2,600	18%	2
Paneled oak cupboard, c. 1820	165	375	625	21%	1
Oak bureau bookcase, 1900	120	250	436	20%	1
Oak cupboard w/brass handles, 1830	250	435	750	17%	2
Golden oak bureau bookcase, 1900	135	250	412	17%	2
Mahogany fern stand, scrolled, 1890	36	68	107	16%	3
Hanging oak corner cupboard, 1900	69	149	237	19%	2
Pine plate rack, wall, 1860	49	67	125	14%	3
Walnut bureau bookcase, c. 1895	495	799	1,235	14%	3
Oak dresser w/top, c. 1860	675	1,250	1,825	15%	2
Oak credenza marble top, 1865	236	425	812	19%	2
Jacobean chair, c. 1680	295	425	662	12%	3
Mahogany tilt-top dining table, 1825	495	785	1,250	14%	3
Miniature roll-top desk, child's, 1890	139	267	455	18%	2
Kneehole mahogany desk, c. 1860	125	299	420	19%	2
Oak corner display cabinet, c. 1900	490	789	1,225	14%	3
Mahogany drop-leaf table, 1850	99	159	375	21%	1
Carved beechwood bench, c. 1895	55	145	275	26%	1
Mahogany night stand, leather top, 1890	39	76	140	20%	1
Mahogany fern stand, scrolled, 1900	18	29	59	18%	2
Mahogany shaving stand, c. 1885	89	159	345	21%	1
Carved oak blanket chest, c. 1800	556	925	1,375	14%	3
Rosewood cheval mirror, c. 1850	95	167	395	23%	1
Feathered mahogany desk, c. 1840	225	395	685	17%	2
Mahogany bracket feet desk, c. 1785	500	1,275	1,887	21%	1
Rosewood 4-drawer chest, c. 1825	425	900	1,500	20%	2
Oak carved consul table, 1845	120	279	425	20%	2
Mahogany blanket chest, c. 1800	390	725	1,122	16%	2
Mahogany architect's desk, 1860	1,100	2,750	3,250	17%	2
Oak-paneled blanket chest, 1890	139	259	562	22%	1
19th C. oak carved dining table, 1880	579	1,150	1,500	15%	3
Oak consul table, carved, c. 1865	98	169	390	22%	1
Mahogany partner's desk, 1860	556	893	1,422	14%	2
Chippendale-style cabinet, c. 1865	425	789	1,250	17%	2
19th C. glass door display cabinet	139	275	585	23%	1
19th C. mahogany leather-top desk	130	225	380	17%	2
Mahogany desk, brass handles, 1865	125	290	425	19%	2

VALUE GROWTH CHART
PRICES QUOTED IN DM

ARTICLE	1971	1975	1978	Average Annual Increase	Financial Outlook 1978-84
19th C. mahogany dining table, carved	145	320	525	20%	2
Mahogany table, 6 of decor, 1890	39	97	197	26%	1
Mahogany dry sink, c. 1840	55	167	290	27%	1
Rosewood grand piano, 1850	390	760	1,400	20%	2
Art nouveau, oak server, 1890	190	475	750	22%	2
Carved oak settle, c. 1780	250	495	700	16%	2
10 ps. walnut living set, c. 1900	900	1,640	2,225	14%	3
10 ps. oak dining set, c. 1890	675	1,600	2,000	17%	2
Mahogany display cabinet, 1890	225	560	875	21%	1
Oak Bible box, c. 1765	150	490	690	24%	1
6 ps. oak dining set, 1890	500	900	1,250	14%	3
Honey oak bureau bookcase, 1900	350	725	1,000	16%	2
9 ps. Queen Anne-style dining set	550	925	1,750	18%	2
19th C. oak extension table, 1880	125	320	575	24%	1
Oak tilt-top table, c. 1860	420	850	1,125	15%	2
Oak hall stand, c. 1890	125	275	520	23%	1
Cast-iron hall stand, 1880	135	245	462	19%	1
Carved mahogany hall stand, 1860	75	147	312	23%	1
Art nouveau display cabinet, 1895	200	372	472	13%	3
Carved oak chest, dated 1725	225	520	890	22%	1
Mahogany cupboard, c. 1890	210	376	520	14%	2
Rosewood pole screen, c. 1860	75	149	362	25%	1
Mahogany vanity, marble top, 1865	135	260	562	23%	1
Carved mahogany fireplace mantle, 1860	95	160	387	22%	2
Bow-front oak chest, 1900	130	225	400	17%	2
Mahogany consul, marble top, 1840	155	220	475	17%	2
High-back Windsor chair, c. 1850	95	210	338	20%	1
Oak chest of drawers, c. 1890	140	250	419	17%	2
18th C. mahogany sofa	1,500	2,750	3,369	12%	3
18th C. mahogany armchair w/petit point	900	1,750	2,250	14%	3
18th C. needlework side chair	850	1,550	2,124	14%	3
8 elmwood side chairs, 18th C.	2,500	3,250	4,000	7%	4
Pr. Louis XV beechwood armchairs	1,200	2,650	3,750	18%	2
18th C. painted satin settee, gilt	1,300	2,700	3,000	13%	3
18th C. fruitwood settee (157 cm)	975	1,600	2,500	14%	3
18th C. Louis XVI giltwood, canape	1,900	3,675	4,250	12%	3
Pr. Louis XV walnut armchairs	2,300	3,750	5,000	12%	3
Pr. 18th C., Louis XVI side chairs	900	1,375	1,750	10%	3
17th C. oak double gateleg table	1,250	2,250	3,500	16%	2
18th C. oak side table	1,175	2,200	3,000	14%	3
17th C. walnut game table	2,500	4,500	6,000	13%	3
17th C. walnut gateleg table	1,275	1,680	2,750	12%	3
6 ebonized neo-Gothic side chairs, 1830	275	420	625	12%	3
Papier-mâché side chair, 19th C.	300	500	750	14%	2
6 beechwood dining chairs, 1900	195	270	375	10%	4
6 oak side chairs, c. 1900	175	310	420	13%	3
Pr. 18th C. armchairs	1,700	3,200	4,000	13%	3
8 oak dining chairs, c. 1900	690	925	1,200	8%	4
5 walnut dining chairs, c. 1910	250	365	500	10%	4
17th C. mahogany rent table	2,400	3,200	4,000	8%	4
18th C. mahogany gateleg table	1,250	2,750	4,500	20%	1

VALUE GROWTH CHART
PRICES QUOTED IN DM

ARTICLE	1971	1975	1978	Average Annual Increase	Financial Outlook 1978-84
18th C. mahogany occasional table	675	1,250	2,000	17%	2
18th C. mahogany writing table	900	1,475	2,250	14%	2
18th C. Louis XV marquetry table	2,200	3,900	5,000	12%	3
Louis XV marquetry writing table	1,250	2,240	3,500	16%	2
18th C. mahogany game table	1,450	2,000	3,000	11%	4
18th C. 3 pillar dining table	2,250	3,750	5,500	14%	2
18th C. Louis XVI dressing table	2,650	4,000	5,750	12%	4
18th C. mahogany work table	750	1,450	2,000	15%	2
17th C. small oak dresser	900	1,650	2,500	16%	2
18th C. mahogany secretaire book case	2,600	3,950	5,000	10%	3
18th C. bookcase, chest of drawers	1,850	2,900	3,750	11%	3
19th C. mahogany breakfront book case	975	1,850	2,500	14%	3
19th C. mahogany side cabinets	250	590	800	18%	2
19th C. mahogany secretaire book case	1,250	1,875	2,062	7%	4
19th C. mahogany bureau bookcase	900	1,680	2,375	15%	2
17th C. walnut paneled chest	1,900	3,200	4,125	12%	3
Inlaid burr walnut chest, 1850	1,400	2,450	3,000	11%	3
Gothic paneled chest	1,550	2,950	3,375	12%	3
17th C. oak and walnut chest	1,950	2,600	3,125	7%	4
Renaissance side cabinet	1,750	2,650	4,500	14%	2
18th C. Dutch bookcase chest	2,900	4,000	5,600	10%	3
Louis XV ormolu commode	2,900	3,900	6,250	12%	3
18th C. neoclassical commode	2,300	4,300	5,150	12%	3
18th C. parquetry commode	2,600	3,900	5,750	12%	3
19th C. walnut inlaid center table	625	1,450	2,000	18%	2
20th C. marble occasional table	140	265	437	18%	2
19th C. ormalu writing table	1,500	2,300	3,000	10%	3
19th C. boulle center table	1,750	2,650	3,152	9%	3
19th C. Louis XV signed center table	2,350	3,975	4,750	11%	3
Mahogany writing desk, c. 1875	550	900	1,125	11%	3
19th C. mahogany card table	290	560	875	17%	2
19th C. gilt center table	1,750	3,000	4,000	13%	3
19th C. mahogany center table	550	890	1,400	14%	3
19th C. rosewood work table	175	325	550	18%	2
Mother-of-Pearl papier-mâché table	275	500	625	12%	3
19th C. marquetry center table	550	1,250	1,625	17%	2
17th C. fruitwood chest of drawers	925	1,650	2,400	15%	3
17th C. carved chest on chest	1,575	2,990	3,250	11%	3
17th C. oak hutch	3,000	3,900	5,000	14%	2

VALUE GROWTH CHART
PORCELAIN — PRICES QUOTED IN DM

ARTICLE	1971	1975	1978	Average Annual Increase	Financial Outlook 1978-84
Thuringer faience ewer, c. 1740	3,900	5,200	7,500	10%	3
Early Meissen coffeepot, mark R, 1725	2,900	4,850	6,250	12%	3

VALUE GROWTH CHART
PRICES QUOTED IN DM

ARTICLE	1971	1975	1978	Average Annual Increase	Financial Outlook 1978-84
Meissen double-gourd vase, c. 1740	18,750	29,000	45,000	13%	3
Meissen landscape teapot, c. 1725	6,000	9,500	15,000	14%	2
Pr. ormolu sèvres vases, c. 1850	5,900	12,000	17,500	17%	2
24 Coalport bird plates, 20th C.	2,750	5,200	8,000	16%	2
Sèvres yellow ground cream soup, 1780	625	990	1,500	13%	3
Silver & Sèvres ewer & cover, 1768	1,800	3,250	5,000	16%	2
Sèvres presentation vase, 1880	1,375	2,450	3,250	13%	3
Sèvres flowered tray, 1775	375	795	1,250	19%	2
Meissen figure of sheep (10 cm)	600	925	1,250	11%	3
Meissen goat by J.J. Kaendler (10 cm)	325	850	1,187	20%	1
Meissen punch pot, flowered, 19th C.	350	600	750	12%	3
18th C. Meissen floral mug	1,250	2,600	3,500	16%	2
19th C. Meissen marcolin vase	325	495	875	15%	2
Pr. Meissen table obelisks (15.6 cm)	245	565	975	22%	1
Meissen figure (11.7 cm) of soldier	560	1,150	1,750	18%	2
Meissen figure (13.7 cm) by Kandler	950	1,750	2,750	16%	2
Furestenburg coffee cup & saucer, 1770	580	985	1,250	12%	3
Nymphenburg plate, c. 1755	425	780	1,162	15%	3
19th C. Dresden portrait plaque	125	325	562	24%	1
19th C. Berlin madonna plaque	350	675	1,312	21%	1
Vienna tankard w/gilt, 19th C.	475	795	1,412	17%	2
Signed Vienna teacup, dated 1800	750	1,456	2,375	18%	2
Vienna tankard, painted, 19th C.	375	780	1,500	22%	1
Pr. Volkstedt figures, 19th C.	500	956	1,562	18%	2
Vienna chocolate set, 4 ps., 19th C.	975	1,685	3,000	17%	2
19th C. Vienna allegorical plate	750	1,125	1,587	11%	4
Delft picture plaque, 19th C.	425	790	1,062	14%	3
Venice pottery footed plate	275	525	937	19%	2
Tuscan pottery jug (13.4 cm)	675	1,275	1,890	16%	2
Pr. delft pottery cows, c. 1785	2,600	3,650	4,500	8%	4
Siegburg stoneware tankard and top	1,475	2,500	3,375	13%	3
Mettlach stein, signed and dated 1885	145	325	500	19%	2
18th C. unicorn faience jug	925	1,375	2,445	15%	3
Westerwald stoneware jug w/lid	1,475	2,250	3,250	12%	3
Westerwald stoneware jug w/lid (22 cm)	250	465	865	19%	2
18th C. majolica plaque (24 cm)	550	925	1,500	15%	3
Faience yellow ground teapot (15 cm)	250	425	662	15%	3
Schrezheim pottery cabbage tureen	950	1,565	2,475	15%	3
Niderviller cruet stand, 1765	95	198	335	20%	2
19th C. Meissen blue onion plate	27	36	50	9%	3
19th C. Meissen blue onion coffeepot	225	375	500	12%	3
19th C. Meissen floral candy dish	95	190	325	19%	2
19th C. Meissen floral egg	65	175	225	19%	2
19th C. Meissen blue onion cup & saucer	29	52	69	13%	3
18th C. pottery slipware jug	1,250	2,400	3,000	13%	3
17th C. slipware plate	950	2,600	3,400	20%	1
12 Wedgwood pottery plates, 1850	560	940	1,412	14%	2
Chelsea cauliflower tureen, 1760	600	1,275	1,875	18%	2
Chelsea can & handle, c. 1750	475	985	1,250	15%	3
Chelsea tea bowl, c. 1760	625	925	1,560	14%	2
Longton Hall cabbage tureen, 1755	925	1,750	2,185	13%	3
19th C. majolica jardiniere	145	275	472	18%	2

VALUE GROWTH CHART
PRICES QUOTED IN DM

ARTICLE	1971	1975	1978	Average Annual Increase	Financial Outlook 1978-84
Earthenware egg basket, c. 1880	125	269	330	15%	2
Faience cat (32 cm), c. 1865	860	1,150	1,422	7%	4
Stoneware panel, "The Siege," c. 1820	160	325	565	20%	1
Pr. stoneware floral vases, 1860	265	579	950	20%	1
Pr. art nouveau faience vases	565	1,680	2,000	20%	1
Pr. Royal Winde coolers, Chinese export, 18th C.	9,500	1,675	20,500	12%	3
2 Chinese export dutch milk jugs, 1750	325	556	995	17%	2
12 ps. Worcester dessert set	1,875	3,265	5,500	17%	2
Royal Bayreuth vase, painted, D. Coro, 1900	29	47	63	12%	2
Royal Bayreuth silver rim vase, 1900	18	29	48	15%	3
Royal Bayreuth creamer, 1900	16	33	50	18%	2
Royal Bayreuth vase, floral, 1900	19	30	42	12%	3
Royal Bayreuth 3-handled vase, 1900	26	39	55	11%	3
Royal Bayreuth coffeepot, Dutch blue, 1900	29	37	65	12%	2
Royal Bayreuth jewel box, 1900	36	57	83	13%	3
Royal Bayreuth pitcher, 1900	22	47	63	16%	2
R.S. Poland coffee set, 3 ps. 1890	156	300	423	15%	2
Royal Bayreuth creamer, birch form, 1900	39	69	112	16%	2
Royal Bayreuth tankard, c. 1900	12	26	38	18%	2
Royal Bayreuth 3-footed vase, 1900	16	28	40	14%	3
Royal Bayreuth tray, floral, 1900	22	36	48	12%	3
Royal Bayreuth bell, 1900	18	29	42	13%	2
Pr. Royal Bayreuth portrait dishes	36	67	122	19%	1
19th C. majolica pitcher, c. 1910	42	120	197	25%	1
19th C. majolica pitcher, floral, 1890	12	24	32	15%	2
Royal Bonn vase, floral, c. 1895	50	96	155	18%	2
24 ps. Bavarian floral dinner set, 1900	240	369	562	13%	3
Bavarian scenic wall plaque, 1890	19	33	50	15%	3
Signed Kaufmann dinner set, c. 1900	95	196	330	19%	2
Vase, Rosenthal, floral, 1900	16	37	52	18%	2
5 floral Rosenthal plates, 1895	59	122	162	15%	3
Baroque bowl, "C. & F.G. Royal Austria"	10	22	35	20%	1
Bonn cake stand, bird decor, 1890	33	58	72	12%	4
Pottery pitcher, floral, c. 1860	26	52	73	16%	3
Saltglaze pitcher, relief, c. 1860	52	120	157	17%	2
Ironstone platter, floral, 1860	33	54	70	11%	3
Pr. Staffordshire pitcher, birds, 1865	39	99	162	22%	1
Copper luster goblet, c. 1850	22	55	90	22%	1
Stoneware pitcher, white relief, c. 1860	29	49	86	17%	2
6 flo blue plates, "Meissen," c. 1900	19	32	58	17%	2
Staffordshire pottery pitcher & bowl, 1900	39	93	150	21%	1
Blue pottery pitcher & bowl set, c. 1890	26	64	112	23%	1
Royal Doulton pitcher & bowl set, 1900	49	123	162	19%	2
Pottery pitcher & bowl set, floral, 1900	43	73	125	16%	2
Pottery pitcher & bowl set, floral, 1895	52	82	112	12%	3
Pink pitcher & bowl set, roses, 1890	23	47	63	15%	3
Green floral pitcher & bowl set, 1890	12	29	48	22%	1
Pressed glass pitcher & bowl set, 1900	39	74	100	14%	2
Royal Doulton stoneware vase, 1900	96	136	225	13%	3

VALUE GROWTH CHART
PRICES QUOTED IN DM

ARTICLE	1971	1975	1978	Average Annual Increase	Financial Outlook 1978-84
Majolica Jardinier, leaf decor, 1890	37	92	150	22%	1
Cobalt blue lidded stoneware stein, 1895	62	109	144	13%	3
Pr. bowls, German flowers, 1860	29	46	72	14%	3
Pr. Bonn wall plaques, figures, 1900	49	125	172	20%	1
Staffordshire rose bowl, c. 1890	9	27	38	23%	2
Belleek teapot, c. 1890	49	94	157	18%	2
Rosenthal large C & S, floral, 1900	12	23	38	18%	2
Royal Bonn vase, floral, gold trim, 1890	60	110	155	15%	3
Cobalt blue ironstone pitcher, 1850	29	59	90	18%	2
Vienna footed sugar bowl, c. 1855	20	55	82	22%	1
Floral relief stoneware pitcher, 1860	32	59	80	14%	3
Brown silver luster creamer, c. 1900	9	17	23	14%	3
Pratt-style vase, figural decor, 1900	4	9	15	21%	1
Flow Blue pottery, c. 1900	20	39	50	14%	2
Flow Blue soap dish, c. 1890	12	22	33	16%	2
Blue & white dish, "Abbey," c. 1900	3	7	15	26%	1
Flow Blue vase, 1890	29	49	70	13%	3
Flow Blue bowl, 1900	12	26	38	18%	2
Flow Blue baroque wall plaque, c. 1900	9	21	26	16%	2
Flow Blue platter, c. 1900	19	32	40	11%	3
Flow Blue soup tureen, c. 1900	25	61	80	18%	2
Red earthenware pitcher, relief, 1865	12	29	48	22%	2
Copper luster footed sugar bowl, 1855	29	45	95	18%	2
Limoges hors de'oeuvres dish, 1884	33	59	97	17%	2
Pottery pitcher, ivy decor, c. 1860	30	55	73	14%	3
Copper luster pitcher, c. 1859	26	54	90	19%	2
Silver luster goblet, c. 1860	18	30	48	15%	3
Staffordshire tankard, floral, 1860	12	28	38	18%	2
Staffordshire pitcher, floral, 1860	24	39	58	13%	3
Staffordshire ewer, floral, c. 1890	29	42	65	12%	3
19th C. stoneware pitcher, relief	39	67	105	15%	3
Copper luster tumbler, c. 1860	24	39	64	15%	3
Pr. floral pottery vases, c. 1895	33	79	105	18%	2
19th C. grey-blue stoneware pitcher	40	85	107	15%	2
Bonn plant pot, floral, c. 1890	12	20	32	15%	2
19th C. pottery vase, birds	7	16	20	16%	2
Floral pottery tankard, gold trim, 1900	15	32	48	18%	1
Cobalt blue mustard pot, c. 1895	9	19	30	19%	1
Gaudy Welsh tankard, c. 1860	12	27	40	19%	1
Pottery jam pot, floral, c. 1900	10	26	38	21%	1
Floral pottery salad set, c. 1865	28	54	75	15%	2
R.S. Poland hatpin holder & candlestick, 1900	22	59	70	18%	2
R.S. Poland, 3 ps. rose decor trinket set, 1900	39	73	107	16%	3
Pottery plaque, floral, c. 1890	9	22	30	19%	2
Staffordshire toast rack, c. 1900	5	12	17	19%	2
Pr. copper luster horses, c. 1900	26	44	65	14%	3
Pottery dog, glass eye, c. 1865	39	54	70	9%	3
Pr. Bisque female figures, c.1890	89	139	223	14%	2
Pottery character pitcher, c. 1920	2	7	12	29%	1
Creamer, form of birch, c. 1895	9	16	23	14%	2
Rosenthal vase, floral, c. 1890	29	56	80	16%	2
Dish, yellow roses, c. 1900	19	32	55	16%	2

VALUE GROWTH CHART

GLASS   **PRICES QUOTED IN DM**

ARTICLE	1971	1975	1978	Average Annual Increase	Financial Outlook 1978-84
19th C. baccarat primrose weight	790	1,259	1,800	12%	3
19th C. Clichy faceted mushroom weight	825	1,375	1,875	12%	3
19th C. Clichy color-ground weight	990	1,750	2,750	16%	2
19th C. baccarat yellow clematis weight	1,250	2,790	3,750	17%	2
19th C. Clichy 3-color swirl weight	2,250	3,400	4,625	11%	3
Sulphide portrait weight of Bonaparte	240	500	650	15%	2
19th C. enameled humpen (18.4 cm)	55	100	189	19%	2
18th C. Hofkellerei humpen w/cover	95	175	362	21%	1
16th C. enameled Kurfursten humpen	125	220	389	18%	2
16th C. enameled humpen	950	1,675	2,249	13%	2
19th C. enameled humpen and cover	110	275	472	23%	1
Bohemian overlay centerpiece, 1860	250	489	912	20%	1
Silver-lined vase (17 cm), c. 1840	100	220	390	21%	1
Overlay glass scent bottle	95	149	280	17%	2
Venetian scent bottle	45	99	145	18%	2
Bohemian overlay vase (two handles), 1850	200	495	725	20%	1
Mary Gregory enameled dish, 1880	225	500	625	16%	2
Pr. opaque-white vases, floral, 1860	100	325	500	26%	1
Pr. enameled vases, birds, 1860	95	250	472	26%	1
Pr. Bohemian overlay vases, 1850	225	498	975	23%	1
Pr. Bohemian ruby-flash vases, 1845	740	1,250	1,840	14%	3
Pr. Bohemian overlay ruby vases, 1860	250	620	922	20%	2
Pr. Bohemian flash vases (33 cm), 1845	490	925	1,250	14%	3
Rock crystal engraved bowl with cover, 1885	65	220	340	27%	1
Engraved jug & stopper, c. 1875	125	275	445	20%	2
Camea glass scent bottle, 19th C.	950	1,645	2,312	14%	3
Gilt blue decanter & stopper, 1760	875	2,750	4,000	24%	1
17th C. Daumenglas & cover (26 cm)	400	790	1,250	18%	2
Thuringiano armorial goblet (20 cm)	425	940	1,470	19%	2
Dutch Lauenstein goblet, engraved	1,250	2,256	3,500	16%	3
17th C. "Faconde Venise" glass	350	745	1,062	17%	2
Pr. green vase, floral, c. 1890	19	32	75	22%	2
Cranberry pitcher, c. 1865	49	77	125	14%	3
Cobalt blue overlay atomizer, 1890	29	59	100	19%	2
Clear sugar & creamer, floral, 1885	19	34	63	19%	2
12 molded candleholders, c. 1890	29	56	98	19%	2
Cranberry pitcher, c. 1875	49	79	140	16%	3
Cranberry compote, c. 1890	56	99	148	15%	3
Pr. satin-finish vases, painted, 1890	12	27	40	19%	2
Green dish, floral decor, 1890	16	30	45	16%	3
Cranberry tumbler, floral, c. 1880	12	29	48	22%	1
Pink molded sugar shaker, 1900	9	17	30	19%	2
Cranberry cut vase, c. 1900	17	31	40	13%	3
Blue pressed compote, c. 1900	22	43	63	16%	3
Green muffin dish, c. 1890	25	52	72	16%	3
Opaque green posy holder, c. 1885	10	22	30	17%	2
Opaque red glass bowl, c. 1900	7	16	23	18%	2
Opaque white glass vase, c. 1890	17	30	58	19%	2
Green swirled bowl, c. 1900	5	9	13	15%	3
6 cranberry tumblers, c. 1875	26	56	90	19%	2
Cranberry vine decanter, c. 1870	18	49	76	23%	1

VALUE GROWTH CHART
PRICES QUOTED IN DM

ARTICLE	1971	1975	1978	Average Annual Increase	Financial Outlook 1978-84
Cobalt blue posy holder, c. 1890	22	48	60	15%	2
Pr. green, hand-painted vases, c. 1890	36	74	100	16%	2
Amethyst vase, enamel decor, 1890	29	56	75	15%	2
Green crimped footed bowl, c. 1890	19	42	63	19%	2
Green muffin dish, enamel c. 1885	18	49	72	22%	1
Blue pressed compote, c. 1900	22	50	65	17%	2
Pink Molded sugar shaker, 1900	9	17	28	18%	2
Green dish, floral decor, 1890	12	32	50	23%	2
Opaque amethyst vase, floral decor, 1885	10	29	55	28%	1
Green pitcher, cut star, 1895	9	27	40	24%	1
Blue & cranberry vase, c. 1900	35	56	100	16%	2

CUT GLASS

ARTICLE	1971	1975	1978	Average Annual Increase	Financial Outlook 1978-84
Pr. vases, diamond & rib cuttings, 1890	36	79	150	23%	1
Vase, diamond, leaf & panel cutting, 1900	56	89	137	14%	2
Toothpick holder, panel cutting, 1900	2	5	8	22%	1
Pr. candlesticks, fan & rib cutting, 1900	16	22	30	9%	4
Painted celery jar, floral decor, 1900	9	18	28	18%	2
Vase, diamond & fan cut, c. 1900	3	9	15	26%	2
Double decanter set, panel cut, c. 1890	54	89	140	15%	3
Vase, diamond decor, c. 1890	9	16	27	17%	3
Celery vase, thumbprint & fan, 1890	12	29	50	23%	1
Fussy cut vase, thumbprint, c. 1890	39	78	150	21%	1
Pr. signed vases, diamond cut, 1900	40	80	112	16%	3
Biscuit barrel, fan & star, 1900	9	20	35	21%	1
Brilliant cut vases, fussy cut, 1895	20	54	75	21%	1
Vase, diamond & hob star cut, c. 1900	25	49	80	18%	2
Vase, diamond & fan cut, c. 1900	15	32	50	19%	2
Vase, drape & fan cut, c. 1865	40	78	150	21%	2
Footed bowl, diamond & fan, c. 1900	12	29	55	24%	1
Puff pat, fan & thumb cut, 1890	12	30	40	19%	2
Salad bowl, diamond & fan, 1910	9	14	30	19%	2
Perfume bottle, panel & rib, 1890	4	9	15	21%	1
Perfume bottle, silver top, 1900	5	12	16	18%	2
Fussy cut decanter, c. 1865	10	30	55	28%	1
Bowl, diamond cut, c. 1895	9	17	38	23%	1
Toast rack, c. 1900	7	15	23	18%	2
Pr. napkin rings, c. 1900	9	19	28	18%	2
Toothpick holder, c. 1890	7	19	25	20%	2
Pin dish, overall cut, c. 1910	1	5	8	34%	1
8 tumblers, panel & diamond cut, 1890	32	64	90	16%	3
Shaker, star & fan cut, c. 1900	7	16	28	22%	1

Graphometer, "Canivet," Paris, 1764.

Profit Record
1971:   800 DM
1978: 5,400 DM

Individual Notes

Investment Predictions
1979–84

The above instrument over the past 7 years has increased in value 575%, which is a compounded growth rate of 31% per year. Specialized instruments like this one have greatly appreciated in value over the past few years despite a limited market appeal and should continue to do so for many years. Perhaps the yearly increase may slightly decrease, but they are still considered good investments.

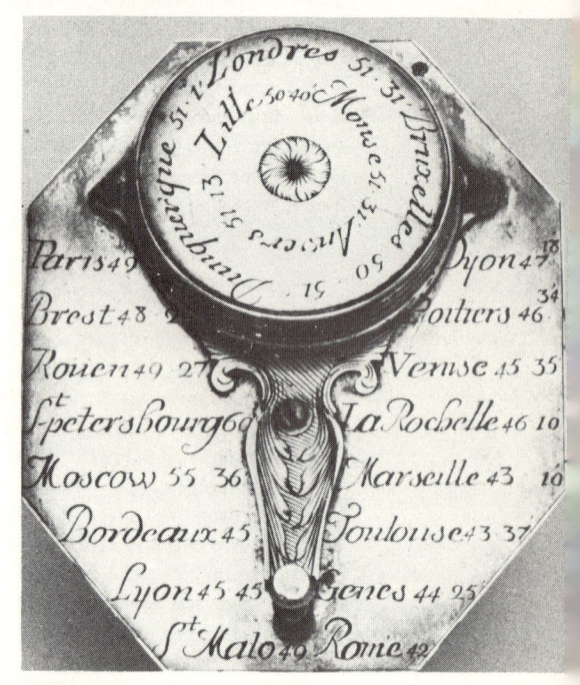

Sundial, Paris, early 18th century.

Profit Record
1971:   700 DM
1978: 3,100 DM

Individual Notes

Investment Predictions
1979–84

This beautifully engraved sundial over the past 7 years increased in value 342%, which is a compounded growth rate of 23% per year. As with other early instruments, the greatest rate of appreciation was seen between 1973 and 1976. Further price increases should level to a more normal rate.

Sundial, Augsburg, early 18th century.

Profit Record
1971:   900 DM
1978: 4,800 DM

Individual Notes

Investment Predictions
1979–84

The sundial over the past 7 years increased in value 433%, which is a compounded growth rate of 27% per year. The greatest appreciation for rare timepieces and instruments was seen between 1973 and 1976, when prices increased almost 300%. Future increases will more than likely be at a slightly reduced rate.

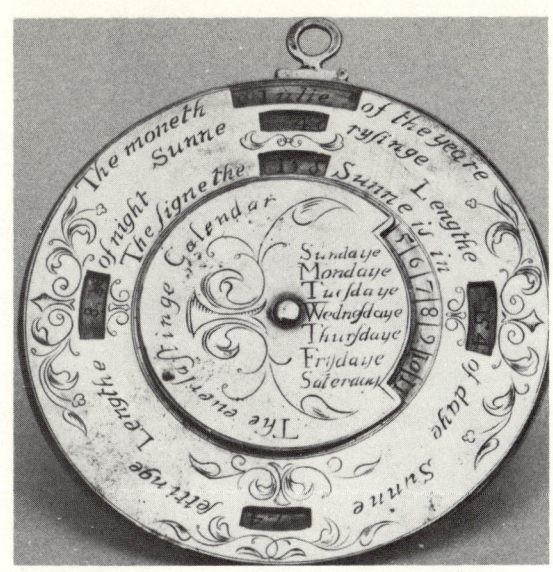

English perpetual calendar, late 17th century.

Profit Record	Investment Predictions
1971: 400 DM	1979–84
1978: 2,100 DM	

Individual Notes

This perpetual calendar over the past 7 years increased in value 425%, which is a compounded growth rate of 27% per year. This calendar was undervalued at 400 DM in 1970, but realized perhaps its greatest appreciation between 1971 and 1976, when it increased 180% in value. Continued price increases should be at a lower rate, but remain stable.

Persian astrolab, early 19th century.

Profit Record	Investment Predictions
1971: 1,000 DM	1979–84
1978: 2,600 DM	

Individual Notes

This early astrolab over the past 7 years has increased in value 160%, which is a compounded growth rate of 15% per year. This is a stable rate of appreciation that can be expected to continue.

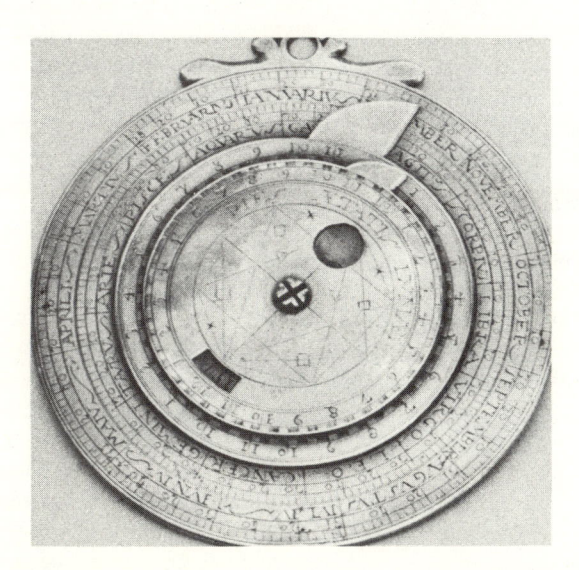

German perpetual calendar, 17th century.

Profit Record	Investment Predictions
1971: 600 DM	1979–84
1978: 3,900 DM	

Individual Notes

This early perpetual calnedar over the past 7 years increased in value 550%, which is a compounded growth rate of 31% per year. As with the other early time instruments that were undervalued during the late 1960s and early 1970s, the greatest appreciation was realized from 1973 to 1976, with a price increase of almost 200%. Future price increases, although stable, will be at a slightly reduced rate.

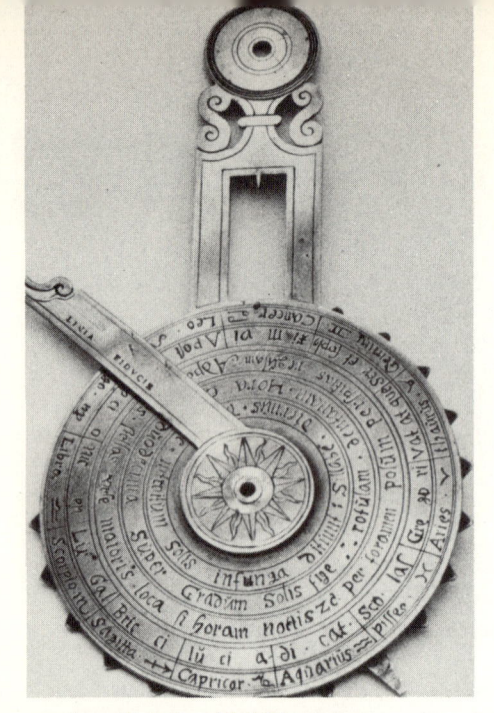

German nocturnal dial, mid 16th-century.

Profit Record
1971: 1,400 DM
1978: 9,200 DM

Individual Notes

Investment Predictions
1979–84

This rare nocturnal dial increased in value over the past 7 years 555%, which is a compounded growth rate of 30% per year. As with other early instruments, the greatest appreciation was seen between 1973 and 1976, and future price increases can be expected to stabilize at a lower rate. Instruments of this type are not sought by collectors for investment but rather to expand specialized collections.

Wooden Mikerescope, Nuremberg, Germany, middle 18th century.

Profit Record
1971: 1,800 DM
1978: 3,800 DM

Individual Notes

Investment Predictions
1979–84

This early Mikerescope over the past 7 years increased in value 111%, which is a compounded growth rate of 11% per year. The appreciation should continue at this rate for some time, but an individual Mikerescope could bring considerably more from a collector at auction.

German universal ringdial, dated 1675.

Profit Record
1971: 2,000 DM
1978: 3,900 DM

Individual Notes

Investment Predictions
1979–84

This unique ringdial over the past 7 years has increased in value 95%, which is a compounded growth rate of 10% per year. The appreciation on this piece should continue in this pattern for some time.

Sailing ship Junot. French ship of the line modeled after the 19th-century prisoner-of-war ship. Frigate with 28 cannons, authentically rigged and in working condition. Beautiful example with minute details encased in a glass cover. 12,000 DM.

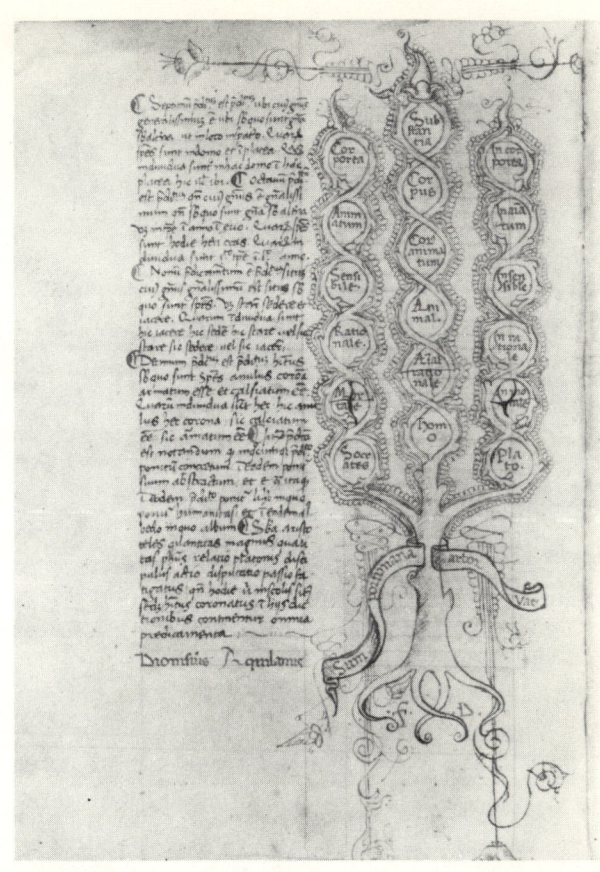

Early geneological study, written in Latin on paper. Venice, 1475. 6,500 DM.

The Four Seasons **etching by Jean Daret (1613 Brussels–1668 Aix-en-Provence). 3,000 DM.**

San Francisco, **Panorama of San Francisco in 1860. Colored lithograph by Henry Payot. 1,500 DM.**

Rome, Saint Peter's Basilica **by L. Rupp, 1830.** View of St. Peter's Square with animated figures in the Biedermeier style.   **750 DM.**

A. Risso–E. Poiteau. Natural history study of oranges, 109 copper engraving in color by Poiteau. Paris, 1818. 6,000 DM.

The Kestner book from P. E. Küppers. The book contains 6 wood prints and 60 lithographs. Hannover, H. Böhme, 1919.   1,200 DM.

James Abott McNeill Whistler (1834 Lowell, Massachusetts, 1903, Chelsea). The Red Robe. **Lithograph 1894. 450 DM.**

Salvador Dali (1904 Figneras—Zebtam Port Ligas).
740 DM.

Doll made in Germany with biscuit porcelain head, movable arms, blue glass eyes in white lace dress.   880 DM.

Large doll, biscuit porcelain head, dark glass eyes, red hair wig and leather body.   1,350 DM.

Large doll, biscuit porcelain head, made in Germany by Armand Marseille, c. 1890. Very beautiful doll in white dress trimmed in lace.   900 DM.

Small doll made c. 1930 by Simon u. Halug.   500 DM.

Baby doll, marked Hluback, Germany about 1900. Blue glass eyes, closed mouth, body made from papier-mâché. Dressed in white piqué dress with red dots.   1,500 DM.

Small children's wagon made from wood with 4 wooden wheels made about 1900 and marked Naether.   460 DM.

Lady doll, replica of a famous actress from 1938.
850 DM.

Small German doll with biscuit porcelain head, black eyes, and original dress.   550 DM.

Children's gramaphone in original carton. Made in Nerona, Germany.   1,000 DM.

Model metal car made by the firm Johann Distler, Nuremberg, c. 1920.   1,450 DM.

Children's sewing machine, c. 1920.   180 DM.

Toy cash register in working condition.   60 DM.

1. Wax's doll about 1880, signed F. Aldis on back. Original dress with gold buttons.   1,650 DM.

2. Grand dame doll about 1850. Blond, firmly styled hair with black ribbon. Very large dark eyes. Hands and legs made from wood.   1,950 DM.

3. Small doll, c. 1850. Cloth body with hands and legs made from papier-mâché. Original dress.   1,100 DM.

4. Wax's doll signed on back, Morrell, c. 1870. 2,200 DM.

Three small porcelain character dolls made about 1900. Very interesting Christmas dolls. One doll is dressed as St. Nicolaus with authentic hat and staff. The second doll is dressed as an angel holding a bell. The last doll is dressed as the devil.   1,600 DM.

1. Two hand-embroidered samplers. The top one includes the alphabet and name, Marie Niederschonce, 1858. The second shows the alphabet decorated with birds, flowers, and houses.   170 DM.

2. Dolls' wash commode with charming 6-piece bowl and pitcher set, porcelain decorated with blue painting. In addition 5 doll hand towels embroidered in red, white, and blue.   500 DM.

3. Bathing doll, "Frozen Charlotte," Germany, c. 1860. 450 DM.

4. Bathing doll, "Frozen Charlotte," unglazed biscuit porcelain, blue painted eyes.   400 DM.

5. Bathing doll, "Frozen Charlotte," Germany, c. 1870. Entire doll made from white glazed porcelain.   580 DM.

6. Bathing doll, "Frozen Charlotte," second half of the 19th century. White glazed porcelain and small porcelain bathtub included.   240 DM.

7. Bathing doll, "Frozen Charlotte," second half 19th century. White glazed porcelain, also porcelain bathtub included with bath thermometer inscribed "Reaumur." 410 DM.

8. Bathing doll "Frozen Charlotte," Germany, c. 1860. Entire doll made from porcelain with a pink glaze. Dressed in white nightdress.   700 DM.

Three doll's suitcases, c. 1880. One made of leather, the other two covered in velvet.   300 DM.

Doll's wardrobe.   250 DM.

Two dolls' corsets, c. 1890.   55, 100 DM.

Set of two large dolls' beer steins made of green glass trimmed in pewter and four small glass humpen, c. 1890. 450 DM.

Biscuit porcelain doll with dark blue open eyes, blond wig, leather wig, and porcelain hands.   1,800 DM.

French "mannequin," c. 1860.   650 DM.

Child's portrait, signed "Toni Sello 98," wall plate from KPM, Berlin.   400 DM.

Doll's coffee service, nine pieces, flower decor.   350 DM.

Doll's wooden table and chairs, c. 1900.   130 DM.

Small doll with lace hat, paperweight blue glass eyes. Marked "Tête Jumeau Nr.6," beautiful example in excellent condition.   2,000 DM.

French doll with trousseau.   1,350 DM.

Stereoscope, c. 1900, by J. Vojta, Prague, with 57 individual photos from cardboard and 110 glass pictures. 2,200 DM.

Open market stand, c. 1890, with 83 small, wooden pieces. 1,650 DM.

Spice shop, c. 1900.   2,200 DM.

Bavarian-style dolls' room, c. 1900.   5,800 DM.

Early 20th-century Meissen Blue Onion pattern, coffee pot.

Profit Record
1971:   90 DM
1978: 300 DM

Individual Notes

Investment Predictions
1979–84

The above Meissen coffee pot over the past 7 years increased in value 19% per year. Meissen porcelain, due to its rarity, has always shown significant price increases, which should continue. The Blue Onion pattern remains popular, and buyer demand will cause good returns on investments in the future

336

19th-century, 2-liter German stein.

Profit Record
1971:   60 DM
1978: 250 DM

Individual Notes

Investment Predictions
       1979–84

The above German stein over the past 7 years increased in value 23% per year. Due to the increased interest in steins prices have climbed steadily during the past few years and promise to continue in the future.

19 Price Guide to Holland

VALUE GROWTH CHART

CLOCKS PRICES QUOTED IN GULDENS

ARTICLE	1971	1975	1978	Average Annual Increase	Financial Outlook 1978-84
Long-case, painted dial	500	1,000	2,200	24%	2
Long-case, brass dial	400	2,300	3,750	37%	1
Lantern, Verge	1,000	5,000	7,500	33%	1
Frisian wall, stool	2,250	5,000	5,750	14%	3
Frisian wall, Staart	1,500	3,950	3,750	14%	3
Banjo barometer, mercury	200	600	875	23%	2
Stick barometer, mercury	400	950	1,350	19%	2
Zaandam	5,000	35,000	25,000	26%	2
Long-case	6,000	35,000	25,000	23%	2
Frisian *Stoelkloks*	1,800	7,500	8,000	24%	2
Late Frisian *Stoelkloks*	1,250	4,500	5,000	22%	2
18th & 19th C. Long-case	1,500	4,000	5,000	19%	1
Long-case (150 years)	750	2,000	2,500	19%	1
English Scenthern	3,000	5,000	10,000	19%	2
French lantern	2,200	4,500	6,500	17%	3
Boule, LXIV	6,000	9,000	15,000	14%	3
Cartouche	1,400	2,000	3,500	14%	2
Comtoise with cog	600	1,200	2,200	20%	1
Normal comtoise	400	600	900	12%	2
Ormolu & cloisonné, set, 1860	990	1,650	3,105	18%	2
French Ormolu, set, by Robin	550	795	1,120	11%	3
19th C. gilded & porcelain, clock set	345	540	990	16%	2
French ormolu & cloisonné, set, 1860	927	1,575	2,227	13%	3
Sèvres 3 ps. set	795	1,450	2,225	16%	2
19th C. marble set	29	52	112	21%	1
19th C. figure set, marble	125	325	405	18%	2
19th C. cathedral set	625	1,290	1,812	16%	2
19th C. ormolu clock & candlesticks	750	1,250	1,800	13%	3

VALUE GROWTH CHART
PRICES QUOTED IN GULDENS

ARTICLE	1971	1975	1978	Average Annual Increase	Financial Outlook 1978-84
Louis XV ormolu set	990	1,850	2,587	15%	3
19th C. white marble set	450	849	1,395	18%	2
19th C. bronze & ormolu set	790	1,685	2,475	18%	2
Louis XV mantel	950	1,680	2,610	15%	3
Bronze & ormolu, c. 1820	600	1,020	1,552	14%	3
Boulle ebonized bracket	245	525	788	18%	2
19th C. ormolu mantel	955	1,649	2,162	12%	3
Regency rosewood bracket	159	345	562	20%	1
19th C. walnut veneered mantel	22	41	63	16%	2
19th C. mahogany mantel	5	12	23	24%	1
Regency mahogany 8-day	110	220	315	16%	2
Edwardian 8-day, oak case	7	19	38	27%	1
19th C. brass bell cased	139	290	427	17%	2
19th C. French ormolu, mantel	225	485	697	18%	2
19th C. figure bronze, mantel	675	950	1,327	17%	2
French porcelain & ormolu	890	1,750	2,160	14%	3
18th C. mahogany balloon	675	990	1,282	10%	3
19th C. boulle & ormolu mantel	525	820	1,125	12%	3
19th C. Dresden mantel	1,350	3,250	4,275	18%	2
Brass architectural mantel	95	265	427	24%	1
19th C. oak mantel	49	110	180	20%	1
19th C. mahogany mantel	29	56	90	18%	2
Regency ormolu figure	550	1,275	1,682	17%	2
19th C. ormolu striking mantel	250	450	675	15%	2
19th C. Sèvres & ormolu clock	620	1,020	1,327	11%	3
19th C. bronze elephant	550	925	1,530	16%	2
19th C. 8-day mantel, oak	49	92	163	19%	2
19th C. mahogany mantel	27	64	90	19%	2
Louis XV globe mantel	2,900	6,400	8,100	16%	2
19th C. barometer, oak case	150	245	337	12%	3
Swiss ormolu & porcelain	490	795	1,325	15%	3
19th C. rococo mantel	250	625	900	20%	1
19th C. rotating globe	450	795	1,125	14%	3

GRANDFATHER CLOCKS

ARTICLE					
18th C. inlaid oak case, 8-day	325	700	945	16%	3
Oak, 8-day long-case	420	725	1,192	16%	2
18th C. carved oak case, 8-day	525	850	1,080	11%	3
18th C. carved oak case, 8-day	325	678	945	16%	2
Round top, mahogany case, 1815	740	1,350	1,867	14%	3
19th C. Westminster chimes	900	1,675	2,475	15%	3
18th C. walnut, 8-day	875	1,725	2,295	15%	3
Walnut, grandmother, 8-day	800	1,250	1,732	12%	3

VALUE GROWTH CHART

PRICES QUOTED IN GULDENS

	1971	1975	1978	Average Annual Increase	Financial Outlook 1978-84
18th C. mahogany, 8-day	625	940	1,282	11%	3
19th C. oak case, 30-hour	125	278	450	20%	1
18th C. oak case, brass face	96	249	427	24%	1
18th C. carved oak case, painted dial	92	178	340	20%	1
18th C. oak case, brass dial	87	225	350	22%	1
19th C. Westminster chime, brass/dial	55	110	160	16%	2
19th C. oak case Westminster chimes	79	140	205	14%	3
19th C. oak case, 8-day, painted dial	95	167	270	16%	2
19th C. painted face, fine detail case	99	220	315	18%	2
Regency mahogany, enamel dial	220	495	697	18%	2
19th C. oak case, brass dial	195	425	765	21%	2
18th C. oak, smaller	245	525	877	20%	1
18th C. inlaid oak, brass dial	220	450	832	21%	1
18th C. oak case, brass arched dial	339	640	855	14%	2
18th C. London, mahogany, 8-day	940	1,675	2,475	15%	3

WALL CLOCKS

	1971	1975	1978	Average Annual Increase	Financial Outlook 1978-84
19th C. gilt sunburst	32	75	110	19%	2
18th C. small dutch wall	275	425	860	18%	2
19th C. papier-Mâché, pearl decor	96	175	248	14%	3
19th C. picture	76	120	180	13%	3
19th C. boulle wall	278	525	900	18%	2
19th C. regulator wall	97	167	337	19%	2
Victorian regulator, mahogany case	95	175	320	19%	2

VALUE GROWTH CHART

PORCELAIN — PRICES QUOTED IN GULDENS

ARTICLE	1971	1975	1978	Average Annual Increase	Financial Outlook 1978-84
3 Nankin, blue & white tureens	450	925	1,237	16%	3
Nankin serving dish w/cover	96	197	382	22%	1
Pr. K'ang Hsi pear-shaped vases	320	645	1,080	19%	2
Pr. 18th C. Canton vases	850	1,456	2,137	14%	2
Pr. 19th C. cylindrical vases	17	36	68	22%	1
Pr. 18th C. Mandarin vases	3,455	5,456	7,562	12%	3
19th C. bottle vase w/domed cover	29	50	80	16%	2
Pr. Imari vases	22	49	112	26%	1
Japanese floral stick stand, 1860	96	149	217	12%	3
19th C. dragon design cracklware vases	18	29	45	14%	3
Ch'ien Lung period, famille rose dish	445	1,250	1,710	21%	1
Porcelain transition period stone cup	95	245	495	26%	1
Pr. Satsuma vases, on stand	550	1,245	1,980	20%	2

VALUE GROWTH CHART

PORCELAIN PRICES QUOTED IN GULDENS

ARTICLE	1971	1975	1978	Average Annual Increase	Financial Outlook 1978-84
STAFFORDSHIRE FIGURES					
Model of Gothic castle	27	44	85	18%	2
19th C. bowl and vase	18	30	55	17%	2
Figure of Duke of Clarence	25	56	90	20%	1
Figure of Marnaurd, 1854	39	100	162	23%	1
19th C. brown clay jug	10	26	45	24%	1
19th C. dancing figure	19	42	68	20%	1
19th C. figure of Prince Albert	27	54	95	19%	2
19th C. figure of Queen Victoria	39	99	170	23%	1
Staffordshire castle, 1845	60	100	157	15%	3
19th C. figure, Duke of Edinburgh	32	79	107	19%	2
19th C. figure, Duke of Clarence	22	59	90	22%	2
Staffordshire family group	18	29	55	17%	2
19th C. courting couple	12	30	59	25%	1
19th C. figure, Robin Hood	25	67	112	24%	1
19th C. figure of sailor	96	149	215	12%	3
Figure group of Highlanders	9	21	45	26%	1
19th C. Dalmatian	20	56	85	23%	1
Faiance delft plate	250	750	1,000	22%	2
Faiance delft pot	250	850	1,000	22%	2
18th C. delft tile, rising duck	6	14	17	16%	3
18th C. delft ship tile	3	9	16	27%	1
Pr. 17th C. delft floral tiles	39	64	108	16%	3
17th C. delft cavalier tile	16	27	40	14%	3
17th C. Lambeth delft tulip charger	450	785	1,485	18%	2
Armoral delft drug jar	45	95	180	22%	1
Pr. 19th C. delft windmill vases	18	36	68	21%	1
Pr. 19th C. delft table ornaments	20	45	70	20%	1
19th C. Satsuma ginger jar	9	23	35	21%	1
19th C. Satsuma pail, floral	32	64	107	19%	2
Pr. Oriental stick stands, decorated	132	364	675	26%	1
19th C. bronze & cloisonné vase	19	43	78	22%	1
Chinese rouleau vase	245	560	945	21%	1
K'ang Hsi onion-shaped bottle	225	629	925	22%	1
17th C. Chinese vase	850	1,745	2,475	16%	3
K'ang Hsi blue & white vase	68	145	270	22%	1
Chinese crackleware vase, dragon decor	65	120	225	19%	2
19th C. Satsuma 2-handled vase	37	75	122	18%	2
Pr. 19th C. cloisonné vases	92	137	215	13%	3
Mu Wang horse plate, K'ang Hsi period	750	1,745	2,520	19%	2
19th C. cloisonné incense burner	450	895	1,215	15%	3
Pr. 19th C. Chinese cloisonné elephant	525	895	1,350	14%	3
Pr. Oriental vases w/covers	235	425	675	16%	2
Pr. 18th C. Canton vases	675	1,625	2,137	18%	2
Pr. K'ang Hsi saucer dishes	69	175	270	21%	1
19th C. Oriental floral stick stand	32	93	157	26%	1
19th C. Satsuma crackleware vase	15	27	45	17%	2
Delft plaque, portrait, 19th C.	295	675	1,025	19%	2
Pr. delft pottery calves, 1785	1,275	2,975	4,375	19%	2

VALUE GROWTH CHART
PRICES QUOTED IN GULDENS

ARTICLE	1971	1975	1978	Average Annual Increase	Financial Outlook 1978-84
16th C. pottery stove, green	1,900	3,250	4,750	14%	3
18th C. oval delft scenic plaque	565	795	1,400	14%	3
16th C. Kraak porcelain bowl	875	1,385	1,972	12%	3
15th C. Svargaloka painted box	112	296	487	23%	1
Lacquer dish, Ming dynasty (25 cm)	675	1,450	1,750	14%	3
15th C. blue & white dish (11 cm), Ming	345	500	625	9%	4
Polychrome dish (15.9 cm) Ming	2,750	3,975	5,000	9%	4
Pr. café-au-lait gourd bottles, 1665	725	1,250	1,500	11%	3
16th C. Ming blue & white dish (30 cm)	625	900	1,250	10%	3
Pr. blue & white Ming dishes (1625)	390	675	362	12%	3
Cloisonné enamel bowl, 16th C.	565	925	1,500	15%	2
Ming blue & white tray (23.8 cm)	390	650	875	12%	3
Pr. blue & white Ming (1621) dishes	365	625	820	12%	3
19th C. famille-verte jardiniere	400	725	987	14%	2
Ch'ien Lung perfume ball (1736)	990	1,650	2,750	16%	2
Pr. blue & white porcelain vases, 19th C.	795	1,495	2,500	18%	2
19th C. Peking overlay glass vases	170	360	500	17%	3
19th C. Ch'ien Lung famille-rose vase	1,000	1,750	2,750	15%	3
Pr. 19th C. famille-rose vases (46.3 cm)	1,450	2,400	3,000	11%	3
19th C. Canton porcelain vase (44 cm)	375	725	1,000	15%	2
19th C. famille-rose (45 cm) vase	425	840	1,312	17%	2
Canton vase (33.4 cm), c. 1880	565	1,140	1,750	18%	2
19th C. blue & white Pilgrim flask	1,275	2,450	3,000	13%	3
Famille-rose dish, 1875 (68.6 cm)	1,400	2,500	3,197	12%	3
19th C. Canton plate (41 cm)	136	275	448	18%	2
18th C. Imari vase (40 cm)	2,300	4,000	5,750	14%	3
19th C. ruby enamel vase (24 cm)	450	845	1,500	19%	2
18th C. Imari vase & cover (50 cm)	1,275	2,600	3,500	16%	2
19th C. Kutani vase (42.5 cm)	490	725	1,312	15%	3
Pr. Satsuma vases, scenic, c. 1900	82	123	163	10%	3
Porcelain pot, bird decor, 1860	29	48	63	12%	3
Crackled porcelain plaque, c. 1865	49	99	138	16%	2
Blue & white Canton bowl, c. 1860	17	29	55	18%	2
Pr. rouge & yellow Satsuma vases, 1860	78	122	185	13%	3
Satsuma jardiniere, floral, 1860	11	23	35	18%	2
Blue & white Canton vase, floral, 1865	33	78	125	21%	1
Satsuma creamer, figural, 1860	19	30	55	16%	2
Bowl, rouge floral decor, 1865	17	29	43	14%	3
Earthenware teapot, c. 1895	9	20	30	19%	2
Imari vase, cobalt blue, floral, 1860	8	18	25	18%	2
Ginger jar, floral decor, c. 1900	11	30	44	22%	1
Small bowl, multicolored, c. 1895	14	32	50	20%	1
Black earthenware vase, c. 1895	39	96	125	18%	2
Satsuma pottery vase, floral, 1865	45	99	120	15%	3
Bowl, rouge floral decor, c. 1860	10	26	38	21%	1
Set of 6 Canton wall plaques, 1860	49	125	185	21%	1
8 floral & scenic plates, c. 1900	39	92	150	21%	1
Ribbed Oriental teapot, c. 1865	30	67	100	19%	2
Floral pitcher, raised decor, 1860	19	46	63	19%	2
Silver luster, Oriental tea set, 1910	9	19	38	23%	1
Black earthenware vase, c. 1895	33	70	98	17%	2
3 blue & white porcelain bowls, c. 1890	42	69	113	15%	3

VALUE GROWTH CHART
PRICES QUOTED IN GULDENS

ARTICLE	1971	1975	1978	Average Annual Increase	Financial Outlook 1978-84
Oriental cup & saucer, floral, 1860	9	22	36	22%	1
3 ps. Oriental tea set, figural, 1865	96	195	325	19%	2
Porcelain pitcher, cook decor, 1845	33	67	98	17%	3
Multicolored Satsuma bowl, 1860	29	69	112	21%	1
2 cobalt-blue bowls, c. 1900	8	19	32	22%	1
4 Satsuma pottery cups, figural, 1860	39	64	105	15%	3
White porcelain bowls, 20th C.	5	16	22	24%	1
Cobalt-blue bowl, floral, 1890	12	27	43	20%	2

VALUE GROWTH CHART
BRASS, PEWTER, COPPER — PRICES QUOTED IN GULDENS

ARTICLE	1971	1975	1978	Average Annual Increase	Financial Outlook 1978-84
Brass & copper milk cans, 18th & 19th C.	500	1,000	1,600	18%	1
Iron money-chest	1,000	1,800	3,000	17%	2
Armor & helmet	600	1,200	1,700	26%	2
Miniature cannon	500	1,200	2,000	22%	
Pewter coffee urn	800	1,400	2,000	14%	1
Hand-covered mirror, brass	1,000	1,400	1,750	8%	1
Iron cauldron, c. 1800	39	72	112	16%	3
Mahogany coal cabinet, 1900	9	15	25	16%	2
19th C. mahogany coal box w/brass	27	46	63	13%	3
18th C. copper coal helmet	42	98	158	21%	1
19th C. brass coal helmet	27	64	98	20%	1
19th C. copper coal skuttle	18	42	73	22%	1
18th C. oval copper skuttle	49	102	180	20%	1
19th C. copper & brass skuttle	19	45	68	19%	2
19th C. circular brass coal bucket	9	17	33	20%	1
Oak coal box, brass handles, 1900	5	9	13	15%	3
Crested brass coal box, 1860	59	92	125	11%	3
Ormolu coal skuttle, 1840	120	245	330	15%	2
18th C. iron basket grate	59	120	158	15%	2
Steel fire-iron set, c. 1845	86	149	215	14%	3
18th C. copper wine flacon	76	158	248	19%	2
Copper kettle, fishtail spout, 1790	29	56	83	16%	3
19th C. brass club fender	99	159	270	15%	3
Copper & brass leg doorman	39	79	125	18%	2
Copper measure, c. 1800	10	31	55	27%	1
18th C. copper kettle, brass handle	24	45	68	16%	2
Copper & brass flagon, 1700	125	198	247	10%	3
Copper & brass tea urn, 1800	68	125	170	14%	2
19th C. copper samovar	68	125	182	15%	3
19th C. plated-on copper samovar	19	58	97	26%	1
19th C. copper ship's lamp	22	48	80	20%	1
19th C. brass table lamp	29	56	112	21%	1
19th C. brass carriage lamp	30	69	107	20%	1
19th C. tin "bulls-eye" lamp	19	28	46	13%	3

VALUE GROWTH CHART
PRICES QUOTED IN GULDENS

ARTICLE	1971	1975	1978	Average Annual Increase	Financial Outlook 1978-84
19th C. brass carriage lamp	23	40	67	17%	2
19th C. brass carbide lamp	19	32	53	16%	2
19th C. brass student's lamp	9	21	35	21%	1
18th C. brass & horn lantern	45	120	180	22%	1
19th C. brass oil lamp, glass shade	21	52	72	19%	2
19th C. brass column table lamp	55	130	197	20%	2
19th C. hot-water dish	21	50	97	24%	1
19th C. tulip-shaped tankard	24	52	90	21%	1
18th C. bulbous measure	225	500	750	19%	2
Pr. of ornate circular tureens	395	725	1,062	15%	3
Pr. 18th C. candlesticks	250	520	775	17%	2
18th C. chalice	68	156	202	17%	2
19th C. half-pint measure	22	40	63	16%	3
18th C. charger	39	97	135	19%	2
19th C. liter tankard	20	54	98	25%	1
18th C. wine pitcher	459	789	1,170	14%	3
19th C. half-liter tankard	14	33	52	21%	1
19th C. wine pitcher	99	154	292	17%	2
17th C. wine flagon	350	625	900	14%	3
18th C. lidded tankard	325	569	832	14%	3
17th C. lidded tankard	200	395	540	15%	2
Set 12, 18th C. octagonal plates	1,500	2,000	3,150	11%	3
19th C. square teapot	19	30	40	11%	3
18th C. liter tankard, engraved	29	72	105	20%	1
Set 12, 18th C. plates	459	1,100	1,750	21%	1
18th C. charger	245	450	762	18%	2
19th C. coffeepot, c. 1850	12	29	45	21%	1
18th C. domed lidded measure	110	279	405	20%	1
Heavy brass jam pan, c. 1860	29	49	88	17%	2
Polished copper foot warmer, 1890	22	46	67	17%	2
Cast-iron counter scales, 1865	33	67	100	17%	2
Polished brass standing gong, 1900	49	100	150	17%	2
Brass-iron fire trivet, 1865	9	21	30	19%	2
Cast-iron fire skillet, 1860	2	6	10	26%	1
Wood & metal washboard, c. 1895	1	5	8	35%	1
9 Britannia metal covers, 1900	27	50	87	18%	2
Pewter food cover, 1890	12	19	25	11%	3
Large pewter plate, 1890	10	22	38	21%	1
Hammered pewter teapot, 1900	9	21	37	22%	1
Continental pewter measure, 1890	27	48	75	16%	3
Pewter teapot, c. 1890	11	21	30	15%	3
Britannia metal teapot, 1900	9	17	27	17%	2
Pewter soup tureen, floral, 1890	45	109	162	20%	2
Pewter inkwell, c. 1865	7	21	40	28%	1
Britannia metal tray, c. 1900	2	6	10	26%	1
Pewter tankard, c. 1860	4	9	15	21%	1
Copper kettle, iron handle, 1900	25	42	60	13%	3
Pr. brass candlesticks, 1860	25	55	100	22%	1
Brass jardiniere, c. 1900	15	29	40	15%	2
Heavy brass table bell, 1900	9	17	22	14%	2
Copper pan, long handle, 1860	19	40	75	22%	1
Brass footed fruit Bowl, 1900	12	20	37	17%	2

VALUE GROWTH CHART

BRASS, PEWTER, COPPER   **PRICES QUOTED IN GULDENS**

ARTICLE	1971	1975	1978	Average Annual Increase	Financial Outlook 1978-84
Brass fire jack, 1890	26	49	70	15%	3
Brass small bed-warming pan, 1900	29	64	112	21%	1
Brass school bell, 1860	29	42	68	13%	2
Brass-embossed tobacco jar, 1900	15	25	37	14%	3
Copper pitcher, c. 1900	16	30	40	14%	3
Ornate brass trivet, c. 1865	17	22	45	15%	2
Copper food warmer, c. 1900	23	44	62	15%	2
Polished copper bed warmer, 1890	9	19	30	19%	2
Ornate brass scroll dish, 1885	7	19	25	20%	1
Brass toddy kettle, c. 1865	100	179	240	13%	2
Brass & iron pierced trivet, 1890	9	19	35	21%	1
Ornate brass gong, c. 1900	56	120	187	19%	2
Polished brass fireplace set, 1885	200	400	500	14%	3
Heavy brass coat hook, c. 1890	9	16	20	12%	3
Cast-iron doorstop, 1865	12	29	45	21%	1
Polished iron saucepan, 1865	5	11	18	20%	1
Polished iron umbrella stand, 1890	56	110	150	15%	2
Wrought-iron footman, 1865	49	73	125	14%	3
Polished iron footman, 1860	24	56	75	18%	2
Brass footman, ornate, 1865	96	154	212	12%	3
Polished iron fire fender, 1900	10	29	40	22%	1
Bronze desk set, c. 1895	120	240	325	15%	2
Polished brass footman, 1860	56	86	113	11%	3
Brass stick stand, c. 1900	20	39	55	16%	2
Brass coal scuttle, c. 1900	19	32	56	17%	2
Copper beveled framed mirror, 1900	27	49	75	16%	2
Pierced brass fender, 1890	10	19	25	14%	3
Copper & brass tea urn, 1890	49	98	150	17%	2
Embossed brass magazine rack, 1900	12	40	57	25%	1
Hammered pewter teapot, 1895	9	29	38	23%	1
Heavy pewter measure, 1890	32	67	82	14%	3
Brass trivet, fish form, 1900	9	17	23	14%	3
Brass chestnut roaster, c. 1890	25	54	90	20%	1
Brass kettle, large, 1895	29	62	100	19%	2
Pr. brass candlesticks, 1865	9	17	27	17%	2
19th C. copper warming pan	33	58	82	14%	3
Six 19th C. horse brasses	24	52	72	17%	2
19th C. engraved brass footman	54	98	157	16%	2
19th C. copper preserve pan	27	68	97	20%	1
19th C. copper saucepan	9	17	27	17%	2
19th C. copper & brass punch urn	125	245	337	15%	3
Brass ship's bell, c. 1812	97	159	247	14%	3
19th C. copper jelly mold	22	48	62	16%	2
Pr. 18th C. brass candlesticks	132	225	292	12%	3
Pr. 18th C. brass candlesticks	145	200	268	9%	4
Pr. 19th C. brass candlesticks	46	92	125	15%	3
Pr. 17th C. bell metal candlesticks	125	240	305	13%	3
Pr. 19th C. ornate metal candlesticks	18	39	68	21%	1
Pr. 18th C. brass candlesticks	98	149	225	13%	3

VALUE GROWTH CHART
PRICES QUOTED IN GULDENS

ARTICLE	1971	1975	1978	Average Annual Increase	Financial Outlook 1978-84
Pr. brass candlesticks, 1800	40	75	125	18%	2
Pr. embossed bronze candlesticks	18	54	97	27%	1
19th C. altar brass candlesticks	27	58	90	19%	2
19th C. brass candelabrum	39	94	145	21%	2
Pr. 19th C. ornate brass candlesticks	38	110	190	26%	1
Pr. 19th C. ornate candelabra	58	125	180	18%	2
Pr. 18th C. brass candlesticks	100	245	337	19%	2
Pr. 18th C. marble & bronze candlesticks	350	725	1,000	16%	2
19th C. brass scales	33	92	157	25%	1
Pr. 19th C. brass scales and weights	56	110	180	18%	2
18th C. brass apothecary scales	49	97	156	18%	2
19th C. cast-iron kitchen scales	25	57	80	18%	2
19th C. steel grover's scales	25	79	125	26%	1
19th C. brass banker's scales	19	48	75	22%	1
19th C. cast-iron coffee pot	16	32	52	18%	2
18th C. iron & brass flatiron	20	49	67	19%	2
18th C. iron & brass flatiron	19	32	55	16%	3

VALUE GROWTH CHART
FURNITURE — PRICES QUOTED IN GULDENS

ARTICLE	1971	1975	1978	Average Annual Increase	Financial Outlook 1978-84
19th C. card table	500	700	800	7%	2
Hand carved oak chest	300	700	1,000	19%	1
18th C. fruitwood settee	975	1,685	2,500	14%	3
8, 18th C. cane seat, side chairs	1,200	2,950	4,000	19%	2
18th C. gilded settee	975	1,500	2,312	13%	3
17th C. oak coffer, carved	139	276	585	23%	1
17th C. paneled oak coffer, carved	245	545	832	19%	2
17th C. Dutch carved chest	980	1,478	2,070	11%	3
Early domed-top coffer, carved	78	198	305	21%	1
18th C. oak chest, 2 drawers	95	195	382	22%	1
18th C. molded front oak corner cabinet	225	450	667	17%	2
18th C. oak chest with 3 drawers	185	450	765	22%	1
19th C. oak coffer on bun feet	19	42	68	20%	1
19th C. oak blanket chest, carved	97	156	292	17%	2
17th C. paneled oak coffer	125	325	585	25%	1
18th C. oak chest on stand	145	300	562	21%	1
Early 19th C. oak marriage chest	56	94	170	17%	2
Early 19th C. carved blanket chest	96	170	278	16%	3
19th C. metal & wood, silver chest	22	50	72	18%	2
18th C. lacquer coffer, cabriole legs	675	1,276	1,710	14%	3
19th C. carved Oriental chest	90	127	225	14%	3

VALUE GROWTH CHART

FURNITURE — PRICES QUOTED IN GULDENS

ARTICLE	1971	1975	1978	Average Annual Increase	Financial Outlook 1978-84
ARMOIRES					
18th C. French provincial, cabriole legs	265	575	900	19%	2
18th C. mahogany clothes press	325	620	1,080	19%	2
18th C. oak French provincial	400	700	1,125	16%	3
17th C. Flemish oak, carved	1,125	2,000	3,195	16%	3
19th C. mahogany linen press	55	149	225	22%	1
19th C. French walnut	300	690	1,170	21%	1
18th C. mahogany hanging wardrobe	220	410	652	17%	3
18th C. inlaid oak cabinet	975	1,845	2,925	17%	3
19th C. oak domed-top linen press	56	120	202	20%	1
19th C. mahogany linen press	56	109	180	18%	2
Walnut cabinet, 3 drawers, 1725	450	725	1,350	17%	2
19th C. stripped pine wardrobe	32	70	112	19%	2
19th C. mahogany linen press	69	155	247	20%	2
Mahogany wardrobe, inlaid, 1810	200	456	787	22%	1
19th C. Empire, mahogany press	156	345	742	25%	1
Carved walnut, ornate, c. 1785	3,250	5,400	9,000	16%	2
18th C. mahogany linen press	190	400	832	23%	1
Mahogany press, paneled, 1760	100	295	495	26%	1
18th C. Dutch marquetry wardrobe	1,200	2,250	4,500	21%	1
Late 19th C. pine wardrobe	10	24	45	24%	1
18th C. serpentine front	250	540	900	20%	1
18th C. mahogany press, splay feet	90	159	315	19%	2
18th C. figured mahogany	224	500	837	21%	1
18th C. French walnut armoire	500	1,200	1,800	20%	1
18th C. mahogany satinwood press	220	490	832	21%	1
19th C. mahogany wardrobe, 2 drawers	150	325	495	18%	2
19th C. breakfront inlaid wardrobe	295	500	787	15%	3
WRITING TABLES					
18th C. mahogany drawing table	900	1,475	2,250	14%	3
Satinwood table, tapered legs, c. 1900	290	645	1,057	20%	1
Satinwood Sheraton style, c. 1900	350	750	1,282	20%	1
19th C. walnut marquetry, cabriole legs	900	1,900	2,925	18%	2
18th C. mahogany architects table	425	695	1,350	18%	2
19th C. figured walnut, French style	1,000	1,750	2,900	16%	3
Oak writing table, 2 drawers, 1650	320	700	1,012	18%	2
Mahogany desk, turned legs, c. 1900	20	43	67	19%	2
Rosewood library table, 1835	100	240	427	23%	1
Rosewood writing table, tapered legs, 1900	25	70	135	27%	1
Tambour-top satinwood table, 1890	1,200	2,700	4,162	19%	2
18th C. mahogany "bonheur de jour"	250	455	925	20%	1
Rosewood "bonheur de jour" 1800	2,950	5,685	7,087	13%	3
Mahogany, drawer & splay feet, 1820	842	1,250	1,552	9%	3
Ladies desk, floral inlay, c. 1890	742	985	1,305	8%	3
Roll-top secretaire, painted, c. 1850	1,500	2,450	3,127	11%	3
Rosewood table, string inlay, 1900	25	70	135	27%	1
19th C. boulle desk on cabriole legs	950	1,600	2,250	13%	2

VALUE GROWTH CHART

PRICES QUOTED IN GULDENS

ARTICLE	1971	1975	1978	Average Annual Increase	Financial Outlook 1978-84
19th C. writing table, mahogany	65	175	270	22%	1
19th C. beechwood, leather lined table	240	575	877	20%	1
Regency rosewood cylinder-front desk	345	900	1,575	24%	1
19th C. writing table, Sheraton style	250	700	1,125	24%	1
18th C. marquetry cylinder top	2,500	4,000	6,750	15%	3
19th C. Kingwood, ornate & Sévres plaques	950	1,785	3,150	19%	2
Mahogany "bonheur de jour," inlaid, 1800	450	900	1,575	20%	1
19th C. mahogany desk, turned legs	50	120	202	22%	1
19th C. French marquetry game table	375	700	1,170	18%	2
Satinwood desk, Sévres panels, 1850	1,250	2,750	3,577	16%	3
Mahogany Carlton House desk, c. 1900	925	2,450	3,375	20%	1

DESKS

ARTICLE	1971	1975	1978	Avg.	Outlook
19th C. mahogany pedestal	90	200	337	21%	1
19th C. mahogany cylinder, 8-drawer	95	145	292	17%	2
19th C. oak kneehole, 6-drawer	40	70	112	33%	1
Mahogany kneehole, brass handles, 1775	450	1,200	1,642	20%	1
Inlaid mahogany kidney desk, 1890	325	745	1,125	19%	2
19th C. oak pedestal desk, 9-drawer	40	125	225	28%	1
18th C. walnut kneehole, bun feet	925	1,700	2,700	17%	2
Mahogany kneehole, brass handles, 1775	645	1,200	1,642	14%	3
19th C. inlaid mahogany pedestal	55	250	405	33%	1
Inlaid walnut kneehole, c. 1720	900	1,550	3,015	19%	2
18th C. Chippendale style, kneehole	750	1,700	2,880	21%	1
18th C. walnut kneehole, bun feet	525	1,200	1,812	19%	2
Walnut kneehole, center cupboard, 1725	1,250	2,500	3,960	18%	2

BUREAUX

ARTICLE	1971	1975	1978	Avg.	Outlook
19th C. Dutch cylinder desk, mahogany	596	925	1,462	14%	3
18th C. Dutch marquetry, serpentine front	2,500	4,900	6,750	15%	3
19th C. Dutch marquetry bombé bureau	2,200	4,000	5,400	14%	3
18th C. Dutch walnut marquetry bombé bureau	3,500	6,250	9,900	16%	2
18th C. Dutch swell-front marquetry	1,250	2,750	4,320	19%	2
18th C. marquetry bureau, paw feet	2,200	3,200	4,300	10%	3
18th C. marquetry limited, shell motif	2,500	4,600	6,525	15%	2
18th C. Dutch marquetry, shaped apron	2,700	4,000	6,300	13%	3
18th C. walnut inlaid, serpentine front	2,400	4,200	6,750	16%	2
19th C. Dutch walnut inlaid bombe	1,275	2,750	3,845	17%	2
19th C. inlaid, serpentine front	1,450	2,275	3,150	12%	3
18th C. Dutch inlaid, splayed feet	2,000	3,600	4,950	14%	3
18th C. Dutch floral inlaid	1,600	2,650	4,320	15%	2
18th C. marquetry, swell-front apron	925	1,650	2,295	14%	3
18th C. Durn marquetry, bombe front	2,700	5,650	8,100	17%	2
18th C. mahogany bureau, 3 drawers	240	500	810	19%	2
18th C. walnut serpentine front	890	1,900	2,610	17%	3
19th C. oak fall front, bulbous legs	25	49	62	14%	3

VALUE GROWTH CHART

FURNITURE — PRICES QUOTED IN GULDENS

ARTICLE	1971	1975	1978	Average Annual Increase	Financial Outlook 1978-84
BUREAUX					
19th C. oak bureau, brass handles	100	250	405	22%	2
19th C. mahogany, cabriole legs	39	70	135	19%	2
18th C. Kingwood cylinder, w/ormolu	1,500	2,950	4,500	17%	2
18th C. oak, bracket feet	450	900	1,327	17%	2
18th C. yewwood, stepped	425	1,200	1,890	24%	1
Oak fall-front, bulbous legs, 1890	26	76	122	25%	1
Oak fall-front cupboard, 1890	12	30	45	21%	1
18th C. mahogany, stepped and concave interior	400	925	1,327	19%	2
18th C. mahogany, brass handles	565	1,260	1,912	19%	2
19th C. mahogany, ogee feet	250	500	765	17%	2
18th C. inlaid mahogany, ogee feet	395	725	1,102	16%	3
18th C. oak fall-front, bracket feet	245	525	922	21%	1
BUREAU BOOKCASE					
18th C. w/cabinet & carving	500	749	1,125	12%	3
19th C. mahogany with cabriole legs	96	164	382	22%	1
Rosewood painted w/mirror, 1820	954	1,675	2,610	15%	3
19th C. veneered walnut, with marquetry	5,000	12,000	16,065	18%	2
18th C. burr walnut bureau	4,900	7,250	11,475	13%	3
Oak on bobbin legs, c. 1900	49	99	157	18%	2
Mahogany cylinder front, c. 1860	56	149	200	20%	1
Mahogany, glass doors, fall front, 1850	95	165	295	18%	2
Mahogany, brass handles, ogee feet, 1800	725	1,290	1,912	15%	3
18th C. Dutch walnut & marquetry	4,200	9,500	12,150	16%	2
18th C. Dutch marquetry bombé front	5,000	11,450	15,120	17%	2
18th C. lacquered & painted Chinese style	4,250	9,540	12,600	17%	2
19th C. mahogany cabinet plain	100	220	300	17%	2
Mahogany book cabinet, 2 shelves	9	26	45	26%	1
CORNER CUPBOARDS					
18th C. oak, paneled doors	125	275	517	22%	1
19th C. mahogany, Sheraton style	250	495	742	17%	2
18th C. mahogany, Sheraton style	425	890	1,237	16%	2
18th C. oak, fielded panel doors	225	500	720	18%	2
Ornate display cabinet, cabriole legs, 1900	20	54	97	25%	1
18th C. hanging mahogany, small	110	255	405	20%	1
Broken arch pediment, mahogany, 1820	96	179	382	22%	1
Inlaid mahogany, tapered legs, 1820	120	225	380	18%	2
Pine, shaped shelves, 1800	256	495	742	16%	2
18th C. pine, dentil cornice	225	495	675	17%	2
18th C. mahogany, diamond glazing bars	420	755	1,237	17%	2
19th C. hanging pine, glass doors	39	79	135	19%	1
18th C. Sheraton style, inlaid doors	249	600	877	20%	1
18th C. lacquered, glazed doors	325	525	742	13%	3
18th C. glazed door, hanging	96	200	382	22%	1

VALUE GROWTH CHART
PRICES QUOTED IN GULDENS

ARTICLE	1971	1975	1978	Average Annual Increase	Financial Outlook 1978-84
18th C. oak, bow front, hanging	245	500	637	15%	3
18th C. japanned, detailed decor	164	395	630	21%	1
19th C. pine corner cupboard	125	260	472	21%	1
18th C. mahogany, bow front, dentil molding	159	275	440	16%	2
18th C. japanned, floral decor	225	450	630	16%	2
18th C. pine, hanging, shell design	159	425	877	28%	1
18th C. bow-fronted, pear-drop molding	220	500	697	18%	2

CUPBOARDS

ARTICLE	1971	1975	1978	Average Annual Increase	Financial Outlook 1978-84
18th C. country oak	159	325	635	22%	1
18th C. Flemish Oak	365	720	1,125	17%	2
16th C. carved walnut	2,250	5,275	7,425	19%	2
17th C. carved oak	420	995	1,890	24%	1
18th C. Dutch oak, carved	375	700	1,100	17%	2
16th C. Dutch oak, carved	2,575	6,330	9,000	20%	1
19th C. carved oak, medicine	12	36	53	24%	1
19th C. mahogany, paneled doors	9	29	45	26%	1
17th C. oak, fielded doors	390	700	1,129	16%	3
16th C. oak, carved panels	5,900	9,450	14,400	14%	3
18th C. oak, fall front, bun feet	230	500	787	19%	2
16th C. painted doors & sides	650	1,245	1,687	15%	3
18th C. Dutch walnut, turned feet	1,249	3,250	5,850	25%	1
19th C. carved oak	25	92	159	30%	1
Ornate mahogany hanging, 1900	12	36	68	28%	1
17th C. oak, paneled doors	450	920	1,462	18%	2

DRESSERS

ARTICLE	1971	1975	1978	Average Annual Increase	Financial Outlook 1978-84
18th C. large oak, 9 drawers	750	1,600	2,250	17%	2
17th C. oak, 2 drawers	450	725	1,350	17%	2
18th C. oak, spoon & dish rack	225	525	945	23%	1
18th C. long oak, brass handles	675	1,275	2,002	17%	2
19th C. oak, wood handles	525	1,250	1,642	18%	2
17th C. oak, turned legs, 3 drawers	995	2,200	3,825	21%	1
17th C. oak, long, 8 small drawers	625	936	1,575	14%	3
19th C. carved oak, painted panels	92	179	295	18%	2
18th C. oak, turned legs, brass handles	395	749	1,350	19%	2
18th C. elm, turned legs, pot board	245	620	1,057	23%	1
18th C. mahogany & oak, 6 drawers	545	1,220	1,980	20%	1
19th C. carved oak	90	172	270	17%	2
18th C. with fruitwood inlays	379	720	1,237	18%	2
Yewwood, cabriole legs, c. 1800	1,276	3,000	4,500	20%	1
17th C. oak, large, bracket feet	675	1,250	1,732	14%	3
19th C. Dutch domed-top, carved	76	150	202	15%	3
18th C. oak, fret-cut legs	625	920	1,282	11%	3
19th C. oak, 2 drawers	59	192	292	26%	1
19th C. oak, square legs	245	520	877	20%	1
18th C. oak, small, pot board	490	795	1,350	16%	2

VALUE GROWTH CHART
PRICES QUOTED IN GULDENS

ARTICLE	1971	1975	1978	Average Annual Increase	Financial Outlook 1978-84
19th C. pine, 2 drawers	125	265	450	20%	1
18th C. small, oak	525	1,000	1,575	17%	2
18th C. oak, tall, pot board	495	900	1,500	17%	2
18th C. oak, paneled doors	390	795	1,327	19%	2
18th C. Dutch, small, oak	565	950	1,462	15%	3
18th C. oak, cabriole legs, wavy frieze	600	1,240	1,620	15%	3
Oak table, fret-cut legs, c. 1820	490	749	1,282	14%	3
Early 18th C. oak, very wide	625	1,150	1,687	15%	3
18th C. honey oak, 7 drawers	495	920	1,550	18%	2
18th C. fruitwood, hanging	145	396	652	24%	1
Small 18th C. oak	449	925	1,305	16%	2
18th C., oak, turned legs	520	745	1,575	17%	2

Baron Cornelis Roeukoeh, signed, dated 1846. Canvas 69 x 92.   135.000 Gilders.

Vincent Van Gogh.   81,000 Gilders.

351

Wouterus Versckush, signed. Canvas 73 x 97.   100,000 Gilders.

Hendrik Johannes Weissenbruch, 1829–1903, signed. Canvas 50.5 x 92.   81,000 Gilders.

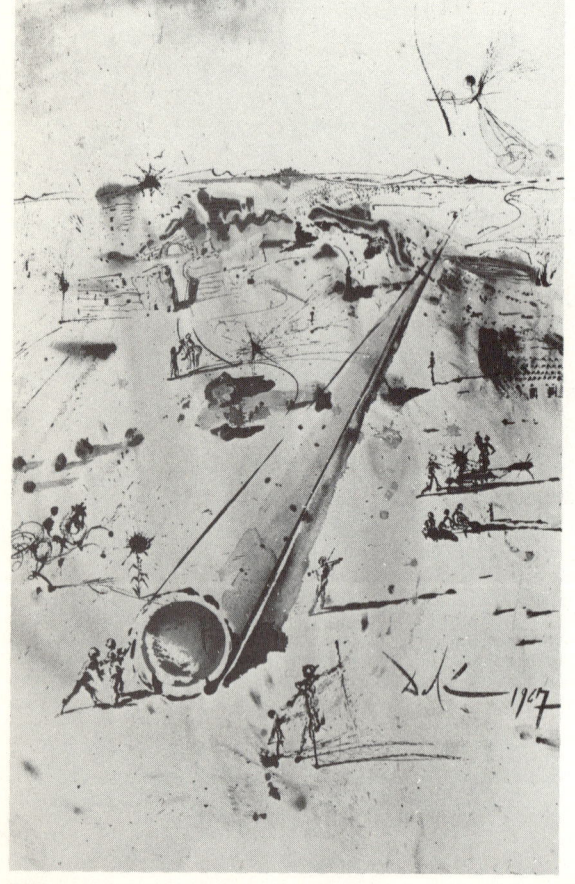

Lithographs of gouaches, all signed and numbered. Above picture is one of 250 numbered copies on handmade paper.   9,200 Gilders.

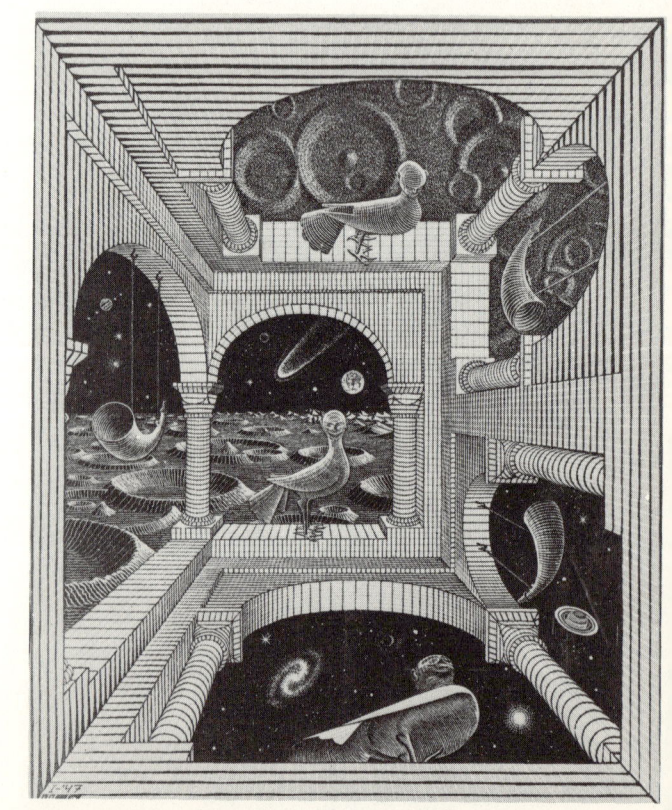

352

M. C. Escher, The Other World, 1947. Wood engraving 31, 7x26 cm. on thin Japanese paper, signed.

L. Zijl, signed bronze statue, 1919.   3,300 Gilders.

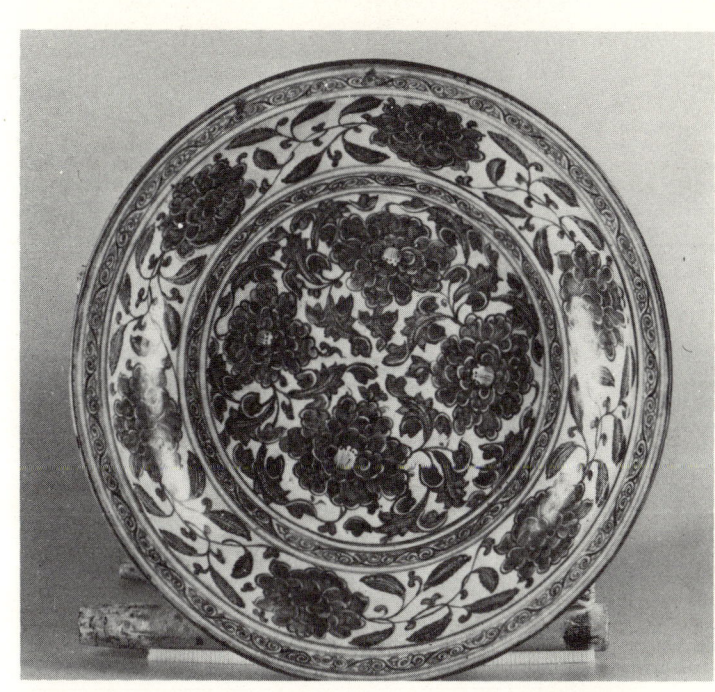

16th-century plate decorated with a chrysanthemum motif designed in a circle.   4,900 Gilders.

Netherlands, Loasdrecht, 18th-century polychrome decor of landscapes with riders.   15,000 Gilders.

J. Mendes da Costa, Beatituda Baruch de Spinoza, bronze statue, 1909.   3,400 Gilders.

A beautiful 17th-century Dutch wardrobe with finely carved decorations and coat of arms.   15,500 Gilders.

A pair of noteworthy armchairs covered in gras and petit-point. G. M. Louis Quinze,   8,200 Gilders.

Set of 6 green glass Roemers, 18th century. 3,400 Gilders.

An exquisite ebony art cabinet inlaid with ivory. 17th century.   6,200 Gilders.

Dutch brass and copper milk cans, with covers.

Profit Record
1970:   500 Gilders
1977: 1,600 Gilders

Individual Notes

Investment Predictions
1977–80

Over the past 7 years these copper and brass milk cans have increased in value 220%, which is a compounded growth rate of 18%. Continued interest promises steady appreciation in the future.

Beautifully hand-carved mirror.

Profit Record
1970: 1,000 Gilders
1977: 1,750 Gilders

Individual Notes

Investment Predictions
1977–80

Over the past 7 years this mirror has increased in value 75%, which is a compounded growth rate of 9% per year. Accessories of this type should continue to appreciate at the above rate at least, if not slightly accelerated, due to the increased interest in home decoration.

Early brass 15th–17-century candlesticks. During the past 8 years candlesticks of this type have increased in value 100%. Appreciation should continue and would be considered an excellent investment. Courtesy Jan Becker, Amsterdam.

Faience Delft plate.   Blue and white Delft pot.

Profit Record
1971:   250 Gilders
1978: 1,000 Gilders

Profit Record
1971:   250 Gilders
1978: 1,000 Gilders

Investment Predictions 1979–84
Both these blue and white Delft pieces increased in value 300% over the past 7 years, which is a compounded growth rate of 22% per year. Good quality Delft is an excellent investment, but the larger pieces seem to appreciate at a much higher rate and will continue.

Pewter Dutch coffee can.

Profit Record
1971:   800 Gilders
1978: 2,000 Gilders

Individual Notes

Investment Predictions 1979–84

This elegant Pewter coffee urn has increased in value over the past 7 years 150%, which is a compounded growth rate of 14% per year. Antiques of this type, if in usable condition, will definitely appreciate in value as more emphasis is placed on the home and entertaining.

Brass cannon.

Profit Record
1971:   500 Gilders
1978: 2,000 Gilders

Individual Notes

Investment Predictions 1979–84

This miniature cannon has increased in value over the past 7 years 300%, which is a compounded growth rate of 22% per year. Antiques of this type are very specialized, and prices are influenced greatly by collector demand, but should appreciate at the above rate.

Curas and helmet.

Profit Record
1971:   600 Gilders
1978: 1,700 Gilders

Individual Notes

Investment Predictions 1978–84

This armor set has increased in value over the past 7 years 183%, which is a compounded growth rate of 16% per year. Antiques of this type usually increase at a slower rate, but can often show drastic appreciation that is controlled solely by buyer demand and interest.

Iron money chest.

Profit Record
1971: 1,000 Gilders
1978: 3,000 Gilders

Individual Notes

Investment Predictions 1979–84

This money chest over the past 7 years increased in value 200%, which is a compounded growth rate of 18% per year. Due to the rarity of these chests, appreciation should be stable if not accelerated if enough interest is stimulated in the market.

Dutch bracket clock.

Profit Record
1971: 1,200 Gilders
1978: 8,000 Gilders

Individual Notes

Investment Predictions 1979–84

This clock over the past 7 years has increased in value 566%, which is a compounded growth rate of 31% per year. Clocks for many years were undervalued, and will continue to appreciate but at a slightly slower rate.

19th-century card table or game table.

Profit Record
1971: 500 Gilders
1978: 800 Gilders

Individual Notes

Investment Predictions 1979–84

Game tables of this type have increased in value over the past 7 years 60%, which is a compounded growth rate of 7% per year. Furniture of this type is an excellent value that should show significant appreciation in the future.

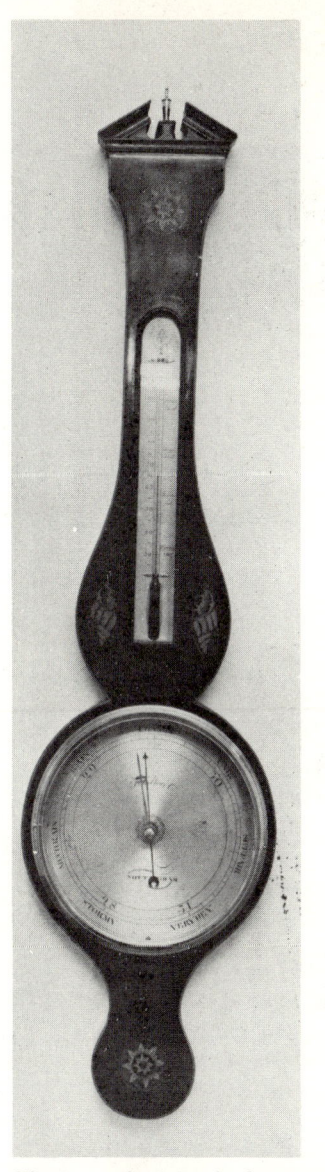

Finely crafted banjo barometers, with mercury.

Profit Record
1971: 200 Gilders
1978: 900 Gilders

Individual Notes

Investment Predictions 1979–84

Barometers of this type over the past 7 years have increased in value 350%, which is a compounded growth rate of 24% per year. Increased interest in barometers has caused great appreciation during the past few years, and should continue for several years to come.

Early lantern clock, Verge.

Profit Record   Investment Predictions
1971: 1,000 Gilders   1979–84
1978: 7,500 Gilders

Individual Notes

This clock over the past 7 years increased in value 650%, which is a compounded growth rate of 33% per year. The rarity of these clocks justifies the constant rate of appreciation.

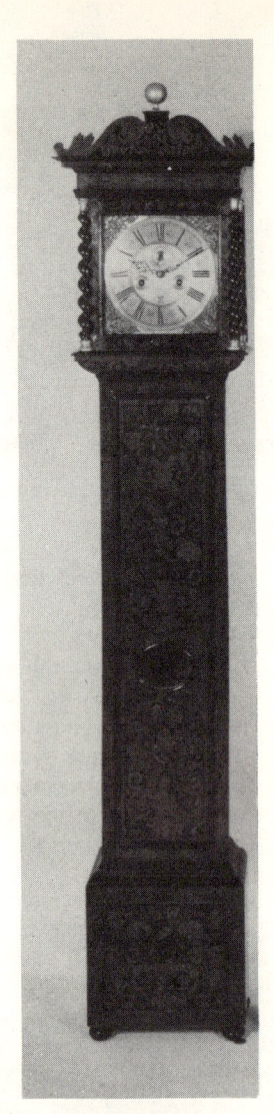

Beautiful inlaid long case clock.

Profit Record   Investment Predictions
1971: 750 Gilders   1979–84
1978: 2,300 Gilders

Individual Notes

Long case clocks of this type over the past 7 years have increased in value 206%, which is a compounded growth rate of 17% per year. The demand for fine clocks will remain high and continue to appreciate.

Bronze mantle clock, French.

Profit Record   Investment Predictions
1971: 200 Gilders   1978–84
1978: 900 Gilders

Individual Notes

Small mantle clocks with a French influence increased in value 350%, which is a compounded growth rate of 24% per year. The appreciation of clocks, especially smaller ones, is extremely stable and should continue.

20 Price Guide to the United States

VALUE GROWTH CHART

FURNITURE — PRICES QUOTED IN U.S. DOLLARS

ARTICLE	1971	1975	1978	Average Annual Increase	Financial Outlook 1978-84
DROP-LEAF TABLES					
19th C. pine	55	95	140	14%	3
18th C. maple	160	320	675	23%	1
Cherry, c. 1845	125	275	400	18%	2
Chippendale, mahogany	250	480	825	19%	2
Chippendale, maple	250	400	590	13%	3
19th C. cherry, 6 turned legs	175	320	565	18%	2
Late 19th C. cherry, rope legs	135	275	450	19%	2
Queen Anne, maple, original	560	985	1,750	18%	2
19th C. cherry	70	150	225	18%	2
Queen Anne, walnut	680	1,250	2,200	18%	2
TEA TABLES					
Mahogany, c. 1780	60	169	250	23%	1
Mahogany, dishtop, 18th C.	450	760	1,500	19%	1
Mahogany, birdcage, 18th C.	225	560	950	23%	1
Mahogany, birdcage, carved	670	1,250	1,875	16%	2
Queen Anne, mahogany	220	400	600	15%	2
Mahogany, carved, 18th C.	325	760	1,200	20%	1
English mahogany, c. 1780	75	150	255	19%	1
Queen Anne, maple, scalloped edge	135	320	500	21%	1
WASHSTANDS					
Mahogany, Duncan Phyfe, c. 1800	55	165	350	30%	1

VALUE GROWTH CHART
PRICES IN U.S. DOLLARS

ARTICLE	1971	1975	1978	Average Annual Increase	Financial Outlook 1978-84
New England, maple, inlaid, c. 1850	45	90	175	21%	1
Late 19th C. oak	30	55	85	16%	3
Late 19th C. Sheraton, painted	60	90	130	12%	3

VALUE GROWTH CHART

PORCELAIN
PRICES QUOTED IN U.S. DOLLARS

ARTICLE	1971	1975	1978	Average Annual Increase	Financial Outlook 1978-84
COLLECTOR'S PLATES					
BING AND GRONDAHL					
Christmas 1912	50	52	55	1%	4
Christmas 1916	55	75	90	7%	3
Christmas 1924	52	55	60	2%	4
Christmas 1930	50	60	65	4%	4
Christmas 1960	55	58	60	1%	4
Christmas 1963	35	55	75	12%	4
Christmas 1964	24	30	35	6%	4
Christmas 1965	25	50	40	1%	4
Christmas 1966	15	25	35	13%	3
Christmas 1967	10	20	30	17%	3
Christmas 1968	10	20	25	14%	3
Christmas 1969	12	15	20	8%	4
Christmas 1970	10	10	15	6%	4
Christmas 1971	10	10	15	6%	4
Christmas 1972		12	20	19%	3
Christmas 1973		15	25	19%	3
Christmas 1974		15	20	10%	3
Christmas 1975		17	20	6%	4
HAVILAND					
Christmas 1971 (First Issue)	65	100	130	10%	3
Christmas 1971 (Second Run)	25	50	65	4%	4
Christmas 1972		20	25	8%	4
Christmas 1973		25	28	4%	4
Christmas 1974		25	30	6%	4
ROSENTHAL					
Christmas 1963	20	60	80	22%	2

VALUE GROWTH CHART
PRICES IN U.S. DOLLARS

ARTICLE	1971	1975	1978	Average Annual Increase	Financial Outlook 1978-84
Christmas 1967	25	50	65	15%	2
Christmas 1968	22	50	60	15%	2
Christmas 1969	25	45	60	13%	3
Christmas 1970	35	50	60	8%	3
Christmas 1971	30	45	55	9%	3
Christmas 1972		35	55	16%	2
Christmas 1973		50	60	6%	3

ROYAL COPENHAGEN

Christmas 1920	40	42	45	2%	4
Christmas 1925	45	50	55	3%	4
Christmas 1948	60	70	75	3%	4
Christmas 1949	65	85	100	6%	4
Christmas 1950	50	65	75	6%	4
Christmas 1951	40	55	60	6%	4
Christmas 1952	65	78	80	3%	4
Christmas 1953	55	62	65	2%	4
Christmas 1954	60	68	75	3%	4
Christmas 1960	45	60	85	10%	3
Christmas 1961	40	65	80	10%	3
Christmas 1962	85	90	100	2%	4
Christmas 1963	32	45	50	7%	4
Christmas 1964	25	35	45	9%	3
Christmas 1965	25	38	45	9%	3
Christmas 1966	27	38	40	6%	4
Christmas 1967	15	30	45	17%	2
Christmas 1968	15	20	25	8%	3
Christmas 1969	15	25	30	10%	3
Christmas 1970	19	20	25	4%	4
Christmas 1971	15	15	20	4%	4
Christmas 1972		10	20	26%	1
Christmas 1973		17	20	6%	4
Christmas 1974		20	22	3%	4
Christmas 1975		20	25	8%	3

BAVARIAN CHINA

PLATES

9½" game plate, quail	18	32	50	16%	2
10" fruit and floral, gold trim	5	9	13	15%	2
7½" portrait of maiden	6	10	14	13%	2
7½" pink and green lilies	3	8	15	26%	1
8½" pink rose, gold trim	8	16	20	14%	2
Dessert, white, gold band	2	4	5	14%	2
9" signed floral	12	23	35	17%	2
8¼" floral and fruit	14	20	30	12%	3
9½" cake, white roses	10	16	35	20%	1

VALUE GROWTH CHART
PRICES IN U.S. DOLLARS

ARTICLE	1971	1975	1978	Average Annual Increase	Financial Outlook 1978-84
9½" cake, open handles, floral	5	9	13	15%	2
7 5/8" signed floral	4	8	12	17%	1
10" pink and yellow roses	9	15	22	14%	2
8¼" portrait, Josephine	6	12	15	14%	2
9½" portrait, Napoleon	19	32	50	15%	2
7½" portrait of a woman	5	12	17	19%	1
8" strawberries, gold trim	6	14	20	19%	1
7½" turkeys	8	12	15	9%	1
9" roses, gold trim	6	15	22	20%	1
9" birds, scalloped edge	4	9	15	21%	1
9" yellow roses, gold trim	9	12	20	12%	3
6½" portrait, Washington	12	17	20	8%	3
6½" portrait, Martha Washington	12	17	20	8%	3
Tea set, hand-painted, rose decor	14	25	39	16%	2
Hat pin holder, marked	6	12	15	14%	2
Toothpick holder, rose decor	4	9	12	17%	2
Sugar bowl, pink roses	3	8	12	22%	1
Covered sugar, lilac decor	5	12	17	19%	1
12 ps. set, child's, signed	19	30	45	13%	2
Salt and pepper, pink roses, gold trim	7	12	18	14%	2

BELLEEK CHINA

ARTICLE	1971	1975	1978	Average Annual Increase	Financial Outlook 1978-84
Basket, handpainted, 5"	45	67	79	8%	3
Basket, woven, heart-shaped	48	70	82	8%	3
5½" marked, Neptune, green trim bowl	46	59	90	10%	2
3½" marked, shellware bowl	19	27	39	11%	2
3½" marked bowl, applied flowers	20	31	37	9%	3
Coffeepot, limpet pattern, marked	15	33	45	17%	1
Coffeepot, tridacna, marked	16	29	40	14%	2
Creamer, marked, embossed flowers	18	22	28	7%	3
Swan creamer, 6", white, marked	34	56	90	15%	2
Creamer, Bacchus heads, grape, 4½"	22	33	43	10%	3
Cup and saucer, pink and gold trim, marked	20	32	40	10%	3
Cup and saucer, Willet, floral, St. Paul	15	37	48	18%	1
Cup and saucer, shell pattern	18	26	33	9%	3
Cup and saucer, Ming pattern	12	15	19	7%	3
Candy dish, open work, roses	32	44	50	7%	3
Maple-leaf-shaped dish, marked, 4¼"	12	19	22	9%	3
Sycamore-leaf-shaped disk, 5"	6	8	10	8%	3
Candy dish, shamrock, marked 5"	19	27	37	10%	2
Shamrock, mug	21	36	42	10%	2
Willet mug, children, c. 1901	44	54	87	10%	2
Willet mug, white	12	15	17	5%	4
Golfer pattern mug	52	72	89	8%	4
Shamrock pitcher, 3"	23	36	45	10%	2

VALUE GROWTH CHART
PRICES IN U.S. DOLLARS

ARTICLE	1971	1975	1978	Average Annual Increase	Financial Outlook 1978-84
Willet, iris pitcher, floral	42	55	62	6%	3
Covered shamrock, sugar bowl	26	39	44	8%	3
White shellware, tea set, 3 ps.	69	120	145	11%	3
Shamrock tea set, 7 ps.	125	180	200	7%	3
Shamrock teapot, basket weave	59	67	75	3%	4
Willet, iris vase, bulbous	139	165	200	5%	4
Vase, white shellware	37	52	60	7%	4

BENNINGTON POTTERY

Bowl, tulip pattern, 8½"	19	30	42	12%	2
Bowl, mottled brown glaze, 8"	17	26	41	13%	2
Bowl, 7½" diam.	15	29	37	14%	2
Bowl, 10" diam.	17	33	41	13%	2
Bowl, 11" diam.	20	34	40	10%	2
Bowl, 13½ diam.	32	56	78	14%	2
Cake mold, 9"	23	37	43	9%	3
Butter churn	44	55	89	11%	3
Blue floral jug, 16"	37	64	100	15%	2
Pitcher, hunt pattern	21	37	55	15%	2
Pitcher, tulip and heart design	37	59	85	13%	2
Pitcher, hunter, dogs, and birds	62	110	150	13%	2
Plates, 8½ diam.	14	22	32	13%	2
Plates, 8¾ diam.	16	27	36	12%	2
Plates, 9¾ diam.	20	33	42	11%	3
Plates, 10½ diam.	22	33	46	11%	3
Plates, 10¾ diam.	30	42	50	8%	3
Syrup jug, spinning wheel pattern	41	59	82	10%	3
Soap dish, 4½"	17	30	37	12%	2
Spittoon, shell	37	59	83	12%	2
Toby mug	38	54	79	11%	2
Vase, water lily pattern, 7"	42	60	70	8%	3
Vase, tulip, c. 1850	36	59	65	9%	3
Vase, corn, 7½"	18	37	40	12%	2

BISQUE FIGURINES

Pr. of tennis players, 15"	33	52	69	11%	3
Girl in Victorian dress, 7½"	15	23	32	11%	3
Nude girl, seated, 3"	8	12	17	11%	3
Cherub on swan sleigh	16	29	39	14%	2
Woman with fan, 10"	14	24	32	13%	2
Madonna and child, 10"	17	28	35	11%	3
Girl and boy with flower basket	12	21	29	13%	2
"The Medic," 4"	19	35	52	15%	2
Nude on lion, white	11	16	20	9%	3

VALUE GROWTH CHART
PRICES IN U.S. DOLLARS

ARTICLE	1971	1975	1978	Average Annual Increase	Financial Outlook 1978-84
Young girl with songbook	8	11	14	8%	3
Nude, seated, white	9	14	18	10%	3
Pr. Punch and Judy, 2½"	19	32	45	13%	2
Pr. Boy and Girl, 7", German	9	15	20	12%	2
Girl and basket, 3"	13	24	30	13%	2
Dutch girl with flower basket	5	7	10	10%	3
Rebecca at the well	21	35	42	10%	3
Little Boy Blue, 9"	7	9	15	12%	2
Little girl holding skirt, 6½"	22	39	48	12%	2
Boy and dog, 6"	9	12	17	10%	3
Little girl with sandwich, 2½"	13	21	27	11%	3
Young girl dancing	24	42	60	14%	2
Little Red Riding Hood, 9"	6	11	14	13%	2
Indian, Germany, 1½"	7	9	12	8%	3
"The Doctor," 4"	19	33	49	14%	2
Little girl pointing finger	5	8	14	16%	1
Pr. little boy and girl, 7"	10	16	22	12%	3
Flower seller, 9"	25	48	60	13%	3
Lovers on settee	14	21	29	11%	3
Group of cherubs	38	54	85	12%	3
Peasant girl gathering flowers	19	26	39	11%	3
Girl and boy on potty, 4½"	8	13	17	11%	3
Nude, Japan, 4"	4	9	12	17%	1
Goose girl	3	6	9	17%	1
Boy and girl reading book	29	58	95	18%	1

BUFFALO POTTERY

ARTICLE	1971	1975	1978	Average Annual Increase	Financial Outlook 1978-84
Covered vegetable bowl	10	12	16	7%	3
Fruit bowl, 4", "Ye Village Tavern"	125	195	280	12%	2
Nut bowl, 8", c. 1909, "Ye Lion Inn"	130	170	200	6%	3
Bowl, "The Start"	40	62	80	10%	3
Bowl, "Ye Village Street," 9"	65	90	120	9%	3
Cup and saucer, "Ye Olde Days," 1909	70	120	150	11%	3
Cup and Saucer, "Fallowfield Hunt," 1909	65	100	159	14%	2
"Ye Lion Inn," mug, 4½"	49	90	125	14%	2
"Ye Lion Inn," mug, 3½"	55	75	100	9%	3
"Beacon Bry," hunt, mug, 1908	60	80	129	12%	2
"Fallowfield Hunt," mug, 3½"	65	125	150	13%	2
Milk pitcher, "Cinderella and Coach," 1909	75	110	125	8%	3
Plate, "At Ye Lion Inn," 6½"	55	75	90	7%	3
Plate, "Fallowfield Hunt," 6½"	50	70	90	9%	3
Plate, "Ye Town Crier," 8½"	55	75	95	8%	3
Plate, "Ye Village Street," 6"	45	60	75	8%	3
Plate, "Dr. Syntax Soliloquizing"	70	110	130	9%	3
Plate, "Dr. Syntax Loses His Wig"	80	140	200	14%	1
Plate, "Village Gossips" 10"	50	79	100	10%	2
Plate, "Fanevil Hall," 10"	14	25	30	12%	2

VALUE GROWTH CHART
PRICES IN U.S. DOLLARS

ARTICLE	1971	1975	1978	Average Annual Increase	Financial Outlook 1978-84
Plate, "Mount Vernon," 10"	10	20	25	14%	1
Plate, "Niagara Falls," 10"	12	21	24	10%	3
Sugar bowl and creamer	32	54	65	11%	3
Teapot argyle	14	28	39	16%	7
Butter tub, apple blossom	9	12	15	8%	3
Sugar bowl, covered, signed	45	72	100	12%	2
Sugar bowl, "Scenes of Village Life"	60	125	165	16%	1
Tobacco humidor	49	100	150	17%	1
Tray, "Ye Lion Inn," 7¾"	60	100	135	12%	2
Tray, "Dancing ye Minuet"	130	170	220	8%	3

CANTON CHINA

ARTICLE	1971	1975	1978	Average Annual Increase	Financial Outlook 1978-84
Basket, latticework	80	120	170	11%	2
Basket and stand, blue and white, 10"	175	300	400	13%	2
Bowl, 9½"	100	145	220	12%	2
Bowl, blue and white, cut corners, 10½"	250	320	400	7%	3
Bowl, 9½", square-cut corners	90	150	225	14%	1
Bowl, blue and white, 10 x 2"	120	225	300	14%	1
Bowl, blue and white, scalloped, 10 x 2"	170	200	250	6%	3
Bowl, covered, vegetable	155	220	260	8%	3
Butter dish, blue, 3 ps.	60	120	150	14%	1
Chocolate pot, blue and white	55	100	120	12%	2
Chocolate pot, blue and white, 5½"	60	95	125	11%	3
Cup and saucer, blue, nameless	20	39	50	14%	1
Demitasse, rose	22	41	50	12%	2
Demitasse, foliage	25	32	45	9%	3
Ginger jar, blue and white, 6"	30	52	90	17%	1
Ginger jar, blue and white, 9"	45	100	145	18%	1
Ginger jar, flat lid, blue	40	59	75	9%	3
Plates, blue and white, 7½"	19	29	35	9%	3
Plate, blue and white, 8½"	29	59	75	15%	1
Plate, blue and white, 9½"	39	54	80	11%	2
Plate, scalloped edge, golden blue, 10"	65	120	150	13%	2
Plate, "100 Butterflies" pattern	58	110	140	13%	2
Covered sugar bowl, blue and white	49	72	120	14%	2
Tea caddy, blue and white, 5"	40	95	150	21%	1
Tea caddy, blue and white, 6"	60	125	160	15%	1
Teapot, dome lid	125	260	400	18%	1
Teapot, blue and white, dome lid	150	250	375	14%	1
Teapot, blue and white, dome lid, 9"	85	120	175	11%	3
Tray, blue, 10 x 11	60	90	120	10%	3
Tray, blue, 10 x 7	75	130	175	13%	2

DELFT

ARTICLE	1971	1975	1978	Average Annual Increase	Financial Outlook 1978-84
Ashtray, windmill scene	9	12	20	12%	2
Square bottle, windmill scene	8	21	30	21%	1
Charger, blue and white, 18th C.	37	56	85	13%	2
Boudoir clock, windmill	49	95	130	15%	1

VALUE GROWTH CHART
PRICES IN U.S. DOLLARS

ARTICLE	1971	1975	1978	Average Annual Increase	Financial Outlook 1978-84
10 pcs. condiment set	39	52	89	13%	2
Creamer, sailboat, 3½"	12	19	22	9%	3
Creamer, cow, windmill	4	10	12	17%	1
Cup and saucer, blue and white, flared top	12	21	29	13%	2
Demitasse, ships	11	19	28	14%	2
Decanter, blue and white, 12"	22	39	69	18%	1
Figurine, man, blue, 10"	13	27	35	15%	1
Inkwell, blue and white	12	19	25	11%	2
Mug, windmill, Holland	9	12	16	9%	3
Plate, boat motif, 8"	12	27	34	16%	1
Plate, blue and white, people, 8½"	6	9	13	12%	3
Plate, windmill motif, 8"	14	26	36	14%	2
Plate, blue, floral motif, c. 1790	22	42	70	18%	1
Plate, Dutch scenes, 12"	17	32	50	17%	1
Spoon rack, blue, scenic	6	16	20	19%	1
Shoe, floral and windmill	9	21	32	20%	1
Shoe, blue windmill, 4½"	12	24	30	14%	2
Shoe, blue windmill, 6½"	13	26	32	14%	2
Tea caddy, blue, scenic	12	32	45	21%	1
Tile, seascape, 5"	5	9	12	13%	2
Tile, floral	6	13	18	17%	1
Tile, costumed men	6	12	16	15%	2
Tile, tulip motif	6	10	15	14%	2
Tile, Children	8	12	19	13%	2
Tile, sailing ships	9	12	18	10%	2
Toothpick holder	8	16	22	16%	1
FLOW BLUE					
Bowl, Amoy	29	42	56	10%	2
Bowl, fairy tales, 10"	18	27	36	10%	2
Rice bowl, Touraine	17	24	32	9%	3
Soup bowl, Ridgway	14	17	20	5%	3
Oriental bowl, 9"	15	21	28	9%	3
Fruit bowl, 12"	28	46	65	13%	2
Regout's flower bowl	14	24	33	13%	2
Oval vegetable bowl, Touraine	19	26	36	10%	2
Washstand bowl, Touraine	26	37	60	13%	2
Covered butter pat	19	28	40	11%	2
Butter pat, Normandy	12	21	29	13%	2
Butter pat, oval, Marie	18	24	32	9%	3
Chocolate Pat, Warwick	27	50	63	13%	2
Creamer, Peking	18	32	50	16%	1
Creamer, Touraine	46	64	90	10%	3
Plate, Touraine, 9"	8	16	29	20%	1
Plate, Watteau, Royal Doulton, 8"	12	17	22	9%	3
Plate, rose, Ridgway, 7"	9	11	14	7%	3

VALUE GROWTH CHART
PRICES IN U.S. DOLLARS

ARTICLE	1971	1975	1978	Average Annual Increase	Financial Outlook 1978-84
Plate, Edgar A. Poe, 10"	22	53	72	18%	1
Platter, Amoy, Davenport 13"	32	70	120	21%	1
Platter, Hong Kong, 14 x 8"	35	63	100	16%	2
Platter, Scinde	29	59	110	21%	1
Sauce dish, Marie	4	7	9	12%	3
Sauce dish, Touraine	9	21	28	18%	1
Tureen, Chinese, Wedgwood	32	54	89	16%	1
Tureen, Madras	27	45	65	13%	2
Tureen, Scinde, large	80	172	290	20%	1
Tureen, covered, Touraine	33	56	90	15%	2
Washstand set, Watteau, Doulton	110	175	220	10%	2
Washstand set, Sobraon	90	120	175	10%	2

LIMOGES

Article	1971	1975	1978	Avg Annual Increase	Financial Outlook 1978-84
Floral banket, T and V	12	19	23	10%	2
Covered bowl, blue and gold, 9½"	24	52	70	17%	1
Portrait bowl, 7"	32	63	100	18%	1
Punch bowl, grape design	70	125	190	15%	2
Punch bowl, pink w/scalloped edge	94	175	250	15%	2
Floral cake set, G.D.A. 7 ps.	26	54	70	15%	2
Floral and blue, candlesticks	19	36	58	17%	1
Art deco, chocolate pat	14	24	35	14%	2
Pink rose, chocolate pat	22	39	62	16%	1
Chocolate pat, white and gold	14	26	38	15%	1
Cup and saucer, Bouillon, J.PL.	3	5	8	15%	1
Cup and saucer, cobalt and gold	12	19	23	10%	2
Demitasse, pink and gold	7	12	19	15%	1
Demitasse, green, gold bands	8	13	16	10%	3
Plate 6, Cupid, gold trim	24	44	72	17%	1
Plate, bird, gold rococo edge	26	52	90	19%	1
Fish plate, swimming, gold edge	11	19	25	12%	2
Luncheon plate, pink floral	1	2	4	22%	1
Plate, spring floral, 7"	2	3	5	14%	1
Plate, roses, gold trim, 8½"	3	5	9	17%	1
Tea set, green, 3 ps. 1906	20	39	60	17%	1
Platter, red rose motif	22	37	49	12%	2
Platter, "The Hunt," 10½" x 18½"	27	52	78	16%	1
Platter, pink floral	16	25	32	10%	2
Dresser tray, roses and gold	11	17	22	10%	2
Dresser tray, vines and floral	9	11	14	7%	3
Soup tureen, white and blue	19	38	47	14%	1
Vase, red roses, 10½"	24	42	64	15%	1
Vase, woman's portrait, 7"	16	24	30	9%	3
Vase, floral, 8"	28	58	72	14%	1

VALUE GROWTH CHART

CLOCKS—AMERICAN PRICES QUOTED IN U.S. DOLLARS

ARTICLE	1971	1975	1978	Average Annual Increase	Financial Outlook 1978-84
Ansonia, iron, mantel	33	56	80	13%	2
Ansonia, desk, 30-hour	17	25	30	8%	3
Ansonia, alarm, 30-hour	10	15	18	9%	3
Ansonia, calendar	48	96	150	18%	1
Ansonia, porcelain case	55	95	125	12%	2
Ansonia, kitchen	29	59	85	11%	1
Ansonia, regulator	139	200	295	11%	2
Ansonia, teardrop	95	175	245	14%	1
Ansonia, school regulator	100	220	275	15%	1
Ansonia, Royal Bonn case	125	220	265	11%	2
Jerome Chauncey, 30-hour	25	59	85	19%	1
Chauncey, shelf, 8-day	150	250	325	12%	2
Chauncey, shelf, walnut, 8-day	125	200	290	13%	2
Connecticut, long-case, 19th C.	240	470	600	14%	2
E. N. Welch, 30-hour	15	25	39	15%	1
E. N. Welch, school, calendar	175	245	375	12%	2
Gilbert Clock Co., porcelain	200	325	475	13%	2
Gilbert, banjo, 8-day	15	39	50	19%	1
Gilbert, oak case, 8-day	35	79	100	16%	1
Gilbert, mantel, lion's head	19	36	55	16%	1
Gilbert, walnut case	45	66	125	16%	1
Ingraham, cottage, walnut case	20	52	69	19%	1
Ingraham, oak case, 8-day	39	72	135	19%	1
Ingraham, rosewood case, 30-hour	45	92	130	16%	1
Ingraham, schoolhouse, oak	60	120	179	17%	1
Ingraham, regulator, 8-day	59	84	125	11%	2
Ithaca, shelf	220	425	620	16%	1
Ithaca, parlour, 14-day	375	850	1,400	21%	1
Ithaca, double dial	150	390	500	19%	1
Ithaca, cottage	220	550	800	20%	1
New Haven, alarm	6	9	12	10%	2
New Haven, shelf, mission	27	62	90	19%	1
New Haven, regulator, oak	129	290	400	18%	1
New Haven, mantel, 8-day	23	47	59	14%	2
New Haven, mahogany, 30-hour	34	64	100	17%	1
New Haven, 7-day, oak	42	74	120	16%	1
New Haven, square case, mantel	21	52	69	18%	1
Sessions, schoolhouse	95	139	200	11%	3
Sessions, mission wall	22	55	79	20%	1
Seth Thomas, kitchen	35	63	95	15%	2
Seth Thomas, schoolhouse	129	200	290	12%	2
Seth Thomas, alarm, 8-day	27	54	70	15%	2
Seth Thomas, rose medallion	1,200	2,000	2,750	13%	2
Seth Thomas, bronze case, glass sides	159	200	325	11%	3
Seth Thomas, banjo, 8-day	67	110	165	14%	2
Seth Thomas, beehive type	29	49	89	17%	1
Seth Thomas, New Orleans	40	73	115	16%	1
Seth Thomas, gallery, 30-day	98	135	200	11%	3
Seth Thomas, gingerbread, oak	52	96	120	13%	2
Seth Thomas, eclipse, wall, 8-day	120	260	300	14%	2
Seth Thomas, silent chime	25	52	85	19%	1

VALUE GROWTH CHART
PRICES IN U.S. DOLLARS

ARTICLE	1971	1975	1978	Average Annual Increase	Financial Outlook 1978-84
Terry & Andrews, beehive	89	167	200	12%	2
Waterbury, double dial	225	490	740	19%	1
Waterbury, porcelain, white	19	42	59	18%	1
Waterbury, gingerbread, walnut	27	79	130	12%	2
Waterbury, kitchen, oak, 8-day	30	58	83	16%	1
Waterbury, walnut case, 8-day	95	139	250	15%	1
Waterbury, desk, 30-hour	12	21	25	11%	2
Western Clock Co., desk type	11	19	23	11%	2
Waterbury, double dial, calendar	125	240	375	17%	1
Waterbury, wall, 30-day	90	130	170	10%	2
Wainwright, 8-day, bracket	240	490	850	20%	1

VALUE GROWTH CHART
CLOCKS—EUROPEAN — PRICES QUOTED IN U.S. DOLLARS

ARTICLE	1971	1975	1978	Average Annual Increase	Financial Outlook 1978-84
FRENCH					
19th C. mantel, marble	32	54	90	16%	1
Carriage, lever escapement	74	98	150	11%	2
19th C. Brocot, Paris, brass case	42	69	110	15%	1
18th C. table, repeater	149	270	575	21%	1
Bulle, electric, mahogany case	29	59	90	18%	1
8-day, ebony inlay case, glass dome	120	220	300	14%	2
18th C. pottery case	86	120	175	11%	1
Carriage, brass case, porcelain face	92	110	170	9%	3
Regulator, 8-day	110	180	235	11%	2
Mantel, ormolu and brass case	155	250	350	12%	2
Wooden case, brass ormolu case	129	240	370	16%	1
Porcelain case, with cherubs	135	197	245	9%	3
14" brass case w/glass sides	100	159	200	10%	3
Morbier, 8-day oak case	90	269	400	24%	1
Morbier, 8-day, without case	120	189	200	8%	3
Carriage, 5", brass case	89	250	400	24%	1
Faience case, c. 1910	30	90	120	22%	1
Carriage alarm, beveled glass	25	95	150	29%	1
Westminster chime, oak case	54	135	200	21%	1
GERMAN					
Grand lonnerier, 8-day, 19th C.	95	220	345	20%	1
Electric shelf, 400-day w/dome	19	29	45	13%	2
Temple, case brass engraved	42	95	140	19%	1
Cuckoo, cuckoo and quail	19	56	80	23%	1
Cuckoo, oak case, single bird	39	78	125	18%	1
19th C. cuckoo, ornate case	125	250	375	17%	1

VALUE GROWTH CHART
PRICES IN U. S. DOLLARS

ARTICLE	1971	1975	1978	Average Annual Increase	Financial Outlook 1978-84
Grandfather, inlaid walnut case	250	450	750	17%	1
Grandfather, oak case, 8-day	120	360	550	24%	1
Ornate, wall, 8-day	140	270	400	16%	2

VALUE GROWTH CHART

REPRESENTATIVE, SELECTED GLASS PATTERNS

GLASS — PRICES QUOTED IN U. S. DOLLARS

ARTICLE	1971	1975	1978	Average Annual Increase	Financial Outlook 1978-84
PATTERN, ASHBURTON					
Bitters bottle	18	26	38	11%	3
Celery vase, scalloped top	36	52	75	11%	3
Champagne glass	20	39	50	14%	2
Cordial	15	27	42	16%	2
Creamers	58	68	125	12%	3
Decanter, pint	20	32	50	14%	2
Decanter, quart	22	36	58	15%	2
Goblets, flaring sides	15	32	45	17%	1
Goblets, straight sides	18	30	42	13%	2
Jugs, pint	32	45	65	11%	3
Jugs, quart	45	56	80	9%	3
Lemonade glass	12	26	40	19%	1
Sugar bowl	32	52	85	15%	2
Wine glass	16	25	38	13%	2
PATTERN, ARGUS					
Ale glass	15	20	27	9%	3
Bitters bottle	12	18	25	11%	2
Celery	30	44	50	8%	3
Champagne	12	30	49	22%	1
Decanter, pint	25	41	50	10%	2
Decanter, quart	28	44	58	11%	2
Egg cup	10	15	18	9%	3
Goblets	12	18	25	11%	2
Sugar bowl	24	32	52	12%	2
Tumblers, footed	16	20	23	5%	3
Wine	14	32	41	16%	2
PATTERN, BABY FACE					
Butter dish	30	48	62	11%	3

VALUE GROWTH CHART
PRICES QUOTED IN U.S. DOLLARS

ARTICLE	1971	1975	1978	Average Annual Increase	Financial Outlook 1978-84
Compotes, covered, small	39	52	71	9%	2
Compotes, open, large	25	36	49	10%	2
Cordials	18	29	36	10%	2
Creamer	28	42	62	12%	2
Goblet	40	56	69	8%	3
Water pitcher	56	73	95	8%	3
Sugar bowl	30	50	68	12%	2

PATTERN, BARBERRY

ARTICLE	1971	1975	1978	Avg Ann Incr	Outlook
Butter dish	16	24	30	9%	2
Celery vase	12	18	25	11%	2
Cordials	8	12	15	9%	2
Creamer	10	16	22	12%	2
Oval dish, 8 x 5½	10	15	21	11%	2
Egg cup	9	12	15	8%	3
Goblet	8	11	14	8%	3
Footed salt	9	11	13	5%	3
Sauce, flat	5	7	9	9%	2
Sauce, footed, round	6	9	12	10%	2
Sugar bowl	18	25	32	9%	2

PATTERN, BEADED TULIP

ARTICLE	1971	1975	1978	Avg Ann Incr	Outlook
Butter dish	10	19	29	16%	1
Cake plate	15	20	26	8%	2
Cordial	7	14	16	13%	1
Creamer	12	15	19	7%	2
Dish, oval	6	9	11	9%	2
Goblet	9	12	16	9%	2
Water pitcher	14	22	29	11%	1
Tray, round	14	20	24	8%	2
Sugar bowl	17	24	30	8%	3

PATTERN, BLEEDING HEART

ARTICLE	1971	1975	1978	Avg Ann Incr	Outlook
Bowls, waste	16	18	20	3%	4
Butter dish	19	32	41	12%	1
Cake plate, stand	18	27	32	9%	2
Compote, high foot	22	37	50	12%	1
Compote, low foot	18	28	43	13%	1
Compote, oval	30	42	53	8%	3
Creamer	24	30	36	6%	3
Goblet, barrel shape	13	19	24	9%	2
Goblet, Bowl straight sides	8	17	21	15%	1
Goblet, thin design	6	19	24	22%	1
Plates, very rare	42	49	54	4%	3
Platter, oval	30	35	37	3%	3
Spoon holder	6	14	19	18%	1

VALUE GROWTH CHART
PRICES QUOTED IN U.S. DOLLARS

ARTICLE	1971	1975	1978	Average Annual Increase	Financial Outlook 1978-84
Sugar bowl	22	33	40	9%	2
Tumbler, water	17	20	23	4%	3
Wineglass	18	21	25	5%	3
PATTERN, CABBAGE ROSE					
Butter dish	17	26	43	14%	1
Cake plate, stand	18	25	32	9%	2
Celery vase	20	33	46	13%	1
Cordials	12	15	19	7%	3
Egg cups	10	17	21	11%	2
Goblet	11	19	23	11%	2
Water pitcher	25	38	50	10%	2
Footed salt	10	14	16	7%	3
Round sauce, 4"	6	9	11	9%	2
Sugar bowl	17	36	43	14%	1
Water tumbler	18	21	24	4%	1
Spoon holder	8	13	17	11%	1
PATTERN, CABLE					
Butter dish	33	42	51	6%	3
Celery vase	33	40	43	4%	3
Champagne	34	45	50	6%	3
Compotes, low foot	27	34	43	7%	3
Cordials	28	31	34	3%	3
Creamer	42	56	62	6%	3
Decanter, pint	38	44	50	4%	3
Decanter, quart	64	73	80	3%	3
Goblets	20	31	39	10%	2
Water pitcher	97	134	150	6%	3
Plate, 6"	34	41	45	4%	3
Footed salt	17	26	32	9%	2
Sauce dishes	7	9	11	7%	3
Spoon holder	9	13	19	11%	2
Sugar bowl	35	48	56	7%	3
Footed tumbler	42	45	49	2%	3
Whiskey tumbler	33	42	48	5%	3
PATTERN, CHAIN					
Butter dish	9	15	22	14%	1
Cordial	5	7	10	10%	2
Creamer	7	12	16	13%	2
Goblet	6	13	17	16%	1
Pickle dish	5	9	12	13%	2
Plate, 7"	6	9	12	10%	2
Plate, 11"	8	12	16	10%	2
Sauce dish, flat	2	3	5	14%	1

VALUE GROWTH CHART
PRICES QUOTED IN U.S. DOLLARS

ARTICLE	1971	1975	1978	Average Annual Increase	Financial Outlook 1978-84
Sauce dish, footed	3	6	8	15%	1
Spoon holder	5	7	13	15%	1
Sugar bowl	9	16	25	16%	1
Wine	6	9	12	10%	2
PATTERN, CLASSIC					
Butter dish	37	52	70	10%	2
Celery vase	22	41	53	13%	1
Compote	28	36	50	9%	2
Creamer	27	35	49	9%	2
Goblet	31	48	55	9%	2
Water pitcher	68	76	84	3%	3
Sauce dish, 4½"	9	14	18	10%	2
Spoon holder	16	25	31	10%	2
Sugar bowl	30	56	70	13%	1
PATTERN, THUMBPRINT					
Ale glass	18	26	35	10%	2
Butter dish	27	55	78	16%	1
Cake stand	35	59	80	13%	1
Castor bottle	8	14	17	11%	2
Celery vase	50	78	112	12%	1
Champagne	22	36	52	13%	1
Compotes, covered, 7"	32	75	100	18%	1
Cordials	15	21	25	8%	3
Creamer	27	42	60	12%	1
Decanter, quart	37	59	100	15%	1
Egg cup	18	26	32	9%	3
Goblets, barrel shape	13	24	33	14%	1
Goblet, knob stem	15	17	20	4%	3
Honey dish	5	8	10	10%	2
Water pitcher	65	125	180	16%	1
Salt, footed	6	12	17	16%	1
Sauce, 4, 4½"	4	9	12	17%	1
Spoon holder	8	24	30	21%	1
Water tumbler	15	21	27	9%	3
Wineglass	17	24	32	9%	3

VALUE GROWTH CHART

STEINS   PRICES QUOTED IN U.S. DOLLARS

ARTICLE	1971	1975	1978	Average Annual Increase	Financial Outlook 1978-84
GLASS STEINS					
Blown, hand-painted enamel scene	85	120	145	8%	3
Footed with brass overlay	250	360	420	8%	3
16" pedestal, cut decoration	200	250	320	7%	3
Mary Gregory painted enamel	100	140	210	11%	3
½ L. green, richly enameled	60	100	150	14%	2
½ L. entaglio cut, with gilt	69	100	125	9%	3
½ L. cased glass, finely cut, w/handle	65	79	100	6%	3
½ l. green, enameled student shield	78	110	170	12%	2
½ l. Bohemian etched wildlife scene	50	79	120	13%	2
½ l. pressed w/lalique relief	78	100	135	8%	3
½ l. cobalt blue, finely etched	89	115	178	10%	2
½ l. pedestal foot, sulphide of owl	70	98	125	9%	2
½ l. pressed painted porcelain inset	30	55	90	17%	2
½ l. molded glass w/jeweled top	27	50	79	16%	2
Mary Gregory type, amber, dated 1886	73	89	110	6%	3
½ l. pressed w/red and blue enameling	60	76	125	11%	2
½ l. pressed w/hand enameling	22	49	62	16%	2
½ l. pressed with pedestal foot	25	45	59	13%	2
½ l. cut w/foot and applied handle	34	46	69	11%	2
Amber, Mary Gregory type, fluted base	82	100	125	6%	3
Liter cranberry w/pewter foot	53	79	127	13%	2
½ l. light blue w/enamel design	35	49	79	12%	2
Liter clear glass, pewter top	22	45	69	18%	2
Small cobalt, etched with castel	42	59	89	11%	3
¼ l. pressed w/engraved pewter lid	37	50	65	8%	3
½ l. Biedermeier, wide footed	90	125	185	11%	3
½ l. pressed w/jeweled top	27	57	85	18%	2
Blown green, serving stein, 14"	42	59	95	12%	2
½ l. enameled with silver lid	45	65	100	12%	2
½ l. amber, footed w/enameling	40	62	85	11%	2
Blown, blue, Mary Gregory Type	89	110	140	7%	3
½ l. cut frosted blue w/jewel insert	79	95	125	7%	3
½ Bohemian etched German town	69	80	95	5%	3
Blown with ornate helmet-type Lid	50	69	90	9%	3
Liter glass, pewter lid, finely etched	27	55	85	18%	2
16" blue blown serving stein	55	89	125	12%	2
½ l. cut with richly carved wood top	49	67	110	12%	2
½ l. pedestal, enameled green	32	52	79	14%	2
Liter blown, enameled light green	45	72	90	10%	3
½ l. pressed w/pewter lid	15	25	45	17%	2
½ l. pressed w/pewter lid	13	27	50	21%	2
½ l. slender pressed w/lid	20	37	65	18%	2
16" armless blown	50	65	100	10%	3
22" blown, enameled design	55	79	95	8%	3
16" blown w/floral enameling	79	92	145	9%	3
16" blown amber serving	50	89	120	13%	2
½ L. 12" cut pedestal w/pewter lid	90	125	165	9%	3
Liter cut w/pedestal and enamel scene	110	189	245	12%	2
16" light blue enamel painted	120	140	165	5%	3

VALUE GROWTH CHART

PRICES QUOTED IN U.S. DOLLARS

ARTICLE	1971	1975	1978	Average Annual Increase	Financial Outlook 1978-84
PORCELAIN STEINS					
Liter with painted scene and lithopane	60	89	100	7%	3
½ l. decal scene and lithopane	35	60	75	11%	2
½ l. cut with etched medallions	75	100	120	7%	3
18" cut serving stein ornate lid	160	195	250	6%	3
16" ruby blown enamel serving	125	175	220	8%	3
Liter cut pedestal w/painted scene	115	190	250	12%	2
½ l. blown green enameled	60	79	90	6%	3
½ l. intaglio cut, footed	34	59	101	17%	2

VALUE GROWTH CHART

FURNITURE — PRICES QUOTED IN U.S. DOLLARS

ARTICLE	1971	1975	1978	Average Annual Increase	Financial Outlook 1978-84
ARMCHAIRS					
Hoop-back Windsor, c. 1780	175	349	645	20%	1
Comb-back Windsor, c. 1780	165	295	575	19%	1
Bamboo turned Windsor, c. 1814	70	160	225	18%	1
Rhode Island Windsor, green paint	175	320	700	22%	1
Cherry banister back, rush seat	320	685	900	16%	2
Oak and yew Windsor	35	62	100	16%	2
Country, carved, splint seat	22	45	63	16%	2
Country maple, ladder back, c. 1750	95	165	375	22%	1
Mahogany, pierced splint, c. 1760	125	240	490	21%	1
Country birch, rush seat, c. 1750	90	175	275	17%	2
George II style, scrolled	150	300	430	16%	2
Pr. mahogany, carved, c. 1860	300	640	1,275	23%	1
17th C. German, walnut	65	195	300	24%	1
Child's, Hitchcock style	55	98	165	17%	2
Balloon back, velvet seat, c. 1850	79	169	225	16%	2
Brace back, 9 spindles	95	189	330	19%	2
Bow back, 7 spindles	22	50	80	20%	1
4 rabbit ears	125	260	450	20%	1
ROCKERS					
Boston, painted black	40	95	150	21%	1
Boston, roll back	35	100	145	22%	1
Painted comb back	49	95	160	18%	2
Splint seat ladderback	10	30	50	26%	1
Bamboo Windsor, 7 spindles	39	68	159	22%	1

VALUE GROWTH CHART

PRICES QUOTED IN U.S. DOLLARS

ARTICLE	1971	1975	1978	Average Annual Increase	Financial Outlook 1978-84
Victorian, upholstered	55	120	200	20%	1
Maple and pine mammy	43	90	156	20%	1
Splint seat ladderback	15	32	50	19%	2
Rolled seat, curved back	39	95	149	21%	1
Child's Victorian	18	42	60	19%	2
Spinning wheel	95	139	235	14%	3
Sausage, turned, ladder back	90	149	375	23%	1
Child's, c. 1900	9	22	35	21%	1
Child's wicker	32	64	90	16%	2
Shaker	95	210	420	24%	1
Caned Seat, Boston	54	90	130	13%	3

SIDE CHAIRS

ARTICLE	1971	1975	1978	Avg	Outlook
Cherry pair, c. 1780	60	210	425	32%	1
Maple, banister back, c. 1745	175	350	920	27%	1
Maple, c. 1750	50	130	275	28%	1
4 Empire, saber leg	90	170	300	19%	2
Mahogany, carved, c. 1760	295	625	1,375	25%	1
Pr. mahogany, ladderback, c. 1800	150	365	725	25%	1
Maple, rush seat, c. 1750	65	195	345	27%	1
Mahogany, inlaid, 1800	125	265	400	10%	2
Maple, banister back, 1750	65	140	200	17%	1
Maple, painted ladderback, 1760	35	59	95	15%	2
Decorated, rush seat, c. 1800	95	160	300	18%	2
6 mahogany, carved, c. 1750	275	490	1,000	20%	1
Mahogany, vase splat, c. 1760	290	695	1,200	22%	1
Spindle back	10	20	39	21%	1
Victorian, Sleepy Hollow, velvet	50	110	169	19%	2
4 mahogany, carved square back, c. 1800	125	290	650	26%	1
Child's Windsor-type high chair	19	49	95	26%	1
Chippendale country, 18th C.	95	190	350	20%	1
Chippendale mahogany, rush seat	100	250	425	23%	1
8 curly maple	150	349	800	27%	1
Victorian, velvet upholstered	19	36	80	23%	1
Louis XV, beechwood	158	295	650	22%	1
Hitchcock, pillowback	45	154	200	24%	1
Empire mahogany	19	40	75	22%	1
Edwardian, rosewood, c. 1910	19	32	65	19%	2

CHESTS

ARTICLE	1971	1975	1978	Avg	Outlook
Marble-top walnut	75	160	240	18%	2
Pine, painted hex signs	65	130	200	17%	2
Cherry hepplewhite, bowfront	175	320	550	18%	2
Inlaid 4 ft. walnut, c. 1800	200	350	500	14%	3
Country walnut, 4 drawers, c. 1760	500	950	1,800	20%	1
New England, mahogany, carved, c. 1800	150	270	450	17%	2
Pine, dovetailed top, 4 drawers	95	210	350	20%	1

VALUE GROWTH CHART

PRICES QUOTED IN U.S. DOLLARS

ARTICLE	1971	1975	1978	Average Annual Increase	Financial Outlook 1978-84
Curly maple, Chippendale, 4 drawers	170	290	390	13%	3
Pennsylvania Dutch, painted, 1800	525	850	1,575	17%	2
Pennsylvania Dutch, painted, Dower, 1820	200	520	850	23%	1
English mahogany, bowfront, c. 1825	600	1,100	1,600	15%	2
Oak, 5 drawers, c. 1900	15	35	55	20%	2
Dutch bridal, painted, c. 1820	125	250	400	18%	2
Blanket, dovetailed	35	65	100	16%	2
Blanket, curly maple, Sheraton, c. 1900	250	490	925	21%	1
Blanket, pine, dovetailed	25	55	90	20%	1
Blanket, Pennsylvania Dutch	35	50	110	18%	2
Blanket, curly maple, c. 1800	200	550	975	25%	1
Blanket, maple, 2 drawers	65	160	400	30%	1
Blanket, 2 drawers, red paint, c. 1760	125	225	450	20%	1
R. I. pine, 2 drawers, c. 1750	175	325	600	19%	2
Pine apothecary, 15 drawers	225	400	700	18%	2
Mahogany, bow front, 19th C.	140	300	625	24%	1
Maple turnip feet, c. 1725	250	650	1,000	22%	1
Pine, 4 drawers w/mirror	65	150	240	21%	1
Pine, 4 drawers, paneled ends	12	39	55	24%	1
Maple, tiger stripe	170	400	825	25%	1
Captain's sea chest, maps	35	100	200	20%	1
Pine sea chest, dovetailed	35	70	155	24%	1
Victorian, walnut, carved	50	140	275	28%	1

CUPBOARDS

Painted poplar, hanging	70	180	340	25%	1
Pennsylvania jelly	125	260	500	22%	1
Pine, 36" wall	60	125	275	24%	1
Cherry, corner, 89" high	250	600	1,375	27%	1
Cherry, 8' high, Blown Glass	325	740	1,500	24%	1
Cherry, Chippendale, bowfront	800	1,425	2,200	16%	2
Pine, corner, bow front	125	325	800	30%	1
Pine, 6 glass panes, orig. paint	75	225	400	27%	1
Pine, corner, 6½', c. 1795	250	600	1,300	26%	1
Pine, Corner, 2 ps., c. 1800	300	575	1,275	23%	1
Jelly, original blue paint	55	150	300	27%	1
Walnut, dovetailed, c. 1840	75	190	275	20%	1
Pine, spice, c. 1820	60	159	300	26%	1

HIGHBOYS

New England, c. 1720, pine	225	650	1,000	24%	1
Philadelphia, c. 1880, mahogany	1,350	2,850	5,000	21%	1
Walnut, Queen Anne	1,250	2,500	3,300	15%	2
Maple, Queen Anne, bonnet top	970	1,850	2,600	15%	2
New England, walnut, 7'	2,500	5,600	8,750	19%	2

VALUE GROWTH CHART

PRICES QUOTED IN U.S. DOLLARS

ARTICLE	1971	1975	1978	Average Annual Increase	Financial Outlook 1978-84
New England, curly maple, c. 1740	2,000	6,450	9,500	25%	1
Pennsylvania, walnut, 9 drawers	850	1,450	2,700	18%	2
New England, cherry, 9 drawers	1,200	2,600	4,000	19%	2
LOWBOYS					
Mahogany, Philadelphia, c. 1850	850	1,500	2,200	14%	2
George II, mahogany, c. 1740	975	1,850	3,600	20%	1
New England, c. 1750	650	1,000	1,700	15%	2
English mahogany, c. 1790	700	1,600	3,000	23%	1
DESKS					
Maple schoolmaster's, c. 1800	70	180	240	19%	2
Oak rolltop	150	340	745	26%	1
Mahogany kneehole, c. 1850	225	560	850	21%	1
Walnut clerk's, c. 1840	55	160	200	20%	1
Walnut lap, c. 1860	12	20	35	16%	2
Painted lady's, c. 1850	125	200	325	15%	2
New England maple, early 18th C.	1,250	2,500	4,500	20%	1
Plantation, mid-19th C.	75	145	375	26%	1
Boston, mahogany, c. 1820	450	1,200	1,600	20%	1
Slant top, pine, c. 1860	50	90	135	15%	3
Oak, c. 1900	25	55	85	19%	2
Cherry rolltop, c. 1860	150	450	800	27%	1
Butler's, c. 1820	200	375	920	24%	1
Mahogany traveling, c. 1860	55	90	145	15%	3
Oak, rolltop, c. 1890	125	350	500	22%	1
Oak station master's, c. 1900	100	300	550	27%	1
Slant-front, Chippendale, cherry	550	1,250	2,000	20%	1
Lady's slant front, pine	225	500	900	22%	1
Inlaid lap desk	22	56	82	21%	1
Rosewood, traveling, lap	25	45	85	19%	2
Slant-front, mahogany, 4 drawers	200	550	1,000	26%	1
Mahogany, block front	325	675	1,100	19%	2
Pine, one drawer, c. 1895	90	175	350	21%	1
Slant-front, walnut, 4 drawers	150	370	850	28%	1
Schoolmaster's kneehole, c. 1900	75	125	245	18%	2
Slant-front, cherry, bracket base	250	400	975	21%	1
New England, Chippendale, curly maple	450	1,200	1,790	22%	1
Hepplewhite, inlay, org.	1,275	2,650	5,000	21%	1
Victorian, lady's writing	75	190	225	17%	2
Pine, 2-drawer	40	85	125	18%	2
DOUGH TROUGHS					
Walnut, dovetailed, splayed legs	50	140	220	24%	1

VALUE GROWTH CHART

PRICES QUOTED IN U.S. DOLLARS

ARTICLE	1971	1975	1978	Average Annual Increase	Financial Outlook 1978-84
Chestnut, lid, pine legs	45	100	185	22%	1
Early New England, pine	45	90	150	19%	2
Early Pennsylvania, Shaker	65	125	300	24%	1
Early New England, pine, tapered legs	25	80	140	28%	1
19th C. poplar w/cover	35	60	100	16%	2
18th C. walnut, carved	68	145	200	17%	2
DRY SINKS					
Walnut, early 19th C.	75	150	220	17%	2
Chestnut, w/drawer	65	140	320	25%	1
Early oak	80	160	375	25%	1
Pennsylvania Dutch, pine	95	180	325	19%	2
Poplar, 2 drawers	50	125	175	20%	1
Pine, 1 drawer	45	100	190	23%	1
Poplar, splash board	75	135	270	20%	1
Walnut, 3 drawers	60	150	230	21%	1
Poplar, 2 doors, low back	45	90	175	21%	1
Pine, 1 drawer, 2 doors	65	139	335	26%	1
Pine, deepwell, 2 doors	70	158	350	26%	1
SECRETARIES					
Walnut, carved, c. 1860	95	165	325	19%	2
Oak, mahogany, inlaid	65	140	180	16%	2
Late 18th C. mahogany, inlaid	950	1,655	3,000	18%	2
Maple, New England, 18th C.	700	1,500	2,450	20%	1
19th C. Sheraton	275	550	900	18%	2
Mahogany, Federal, 2 pieces	450	825	1,150	14%	3
Mahogany, Sheraton, inlaid	475	900	1,200	14%	3
Mahogany, Regency	550	875	1,350	13%	3
Mahogany, Empire, carved	95	260	575	29%	1
Mahogany, Hepplewhite	450	800	1,475	18%	2
Mahogany, Sheraton, original brass	640	1,300	1,600	14%	3
Mahogany, Sheraton, arched	450	790	1,300	16%	2
Mahogany, Sheraton, c. 1820	525	850	1,200	12%	3
SIDEBOARDS					
Walnut, marble top, c. 1860	375	620	975	15%	2
Hepplewhite, inlaid	940	1,475	2,790	17%	2
Bowfront, inlaid, late 18th C.	875	1,500	3,200	20%	1
Serpentine front, Mahogany, 18th C.	1,250	2,200	3,600	16%	2
New England, Maple, 18th C.	650	900	1,500	13%	2
Mahogany, carved, c. 1800	325	550	900	16%	2
Mahogany, Empire	275	425	850	17%	2
Regency style	350	600	950	15%	2

VALUE GROWTH CHART
PRICES QUOTED IN U.S. DOLLARS

ARTICLE	1971	1975	1978	Average Annual Increase	Financial Outlook 1978-84
Hepplewhite, mahogany, 18th C.	1,200	2,200	3,200	15%	2
Sheraton, mahogany	750	1,450	2,000	15%	2
Georgian, early 18th C.	640	1,280	2,700	23%	1
Chippendale, walnut	2,000	3,850	5,800	16%	2

TABLES

CARD TABLES

Article	1971	1975	1978	Avg. Ann. Increase	Outlook
Sheraton, mahogany, c. 1800	450	780	1,500	19%	2
Sheraton, mahogany, carved	550	900	1,400	14%	3
Sheraton, mahogany, top closed	250	560	800	18%	2
Sheraton, mahogany, maple inlay	150	340	600	22%	1
Cherry inlaid, fold top	130	240	375	16%	2
Duncan Phyfe style, mahogany	145	250	500	19%	2
Duncan Phyfe, reeded legs	155	320	625	22%	1
Duncan Phyfe, mahogany, 19th C.	165	300	550	19%	2
Regency, satinwood, 19th C.	225	500	800	20%	1
Queen Anne, mahogany, game top	245	450	925	21%	1
Hepplewhite, mahogany, inlaid	300	580	875	16%	2
Cherry, inlaid, c. 1825	120	325	425	20%	1
Mahogany, inlaid, c. 1795	220	350	500	12%	3
Mahogany, lyre base, 19th C.	145	320	575	22%	1
Philadelphia, walnut, c. 18th C.	180	260	475	15%	3
New England, birdseye maple, inlay	125	300	500	22%	1
Birdseye maple, swell front	240	400	625	15%	2
Chippendale, walnut, ball-and-claw Feet	250	540	875	20%	1
Chippendale, Marlboro-type	290	500	700	13%	3
Empire, mahogany	75	160	250	19%	2
18th C. mahogany, carved	580	900	1,200	11%	3
18th C. mahogany, carved serpentine	975	2,200	3,700	21%	1
19th C. mahogany, floral inlay	95	275	500	27%	1

21 A Pictorial Study of Prices in Belgium, Switzerland, and Denmark

VALUE GROWTH CHART

FURNITURE

PRICES QUOTED IN BELGIAN FRANCS

ARTICLE	1971	1975	1978	Average Annual Increase	Financial Outlook 1978-84
CHESTS					
Small mahogany, bracket feet, c. 1760	2,500	4,950	9,720	21%	1
19th C. inlaid, 6 long drawers	11,450	18,600	32,400	16%	2
19th C. rosewood, tall chest, 12 drawers	2,250	5,250	7,776	19%	1
19th C. mahogany, bow front	750	1,456	2,268	17%	2
18th C. marquetry bachelor's, folding top	12,750	22,450	42,120	19%	1
18th C. mahogany, Chippendale style	3,200	6,540	11,664	20%	1
19th C. walnut, 4 drawers	975	1,545	2,268	13%	3
19th C. mahogany, plinth base	480	925	1,548	18%	2
19th C. mahogany, bow front	540	1,094	1,944	20%	1
18th C. mahogany, enclosed doors	2,500	4,950	6,336	14%	3
17th C. molded front, 4 drawers	4,360	7,250	11,988	16%	2
18th C. Sheraton style, serpentine front	5,750	12,680	18,144	18%	2
19th C. mahogany, bow front	980	1,850	2,700	16%	2
19th C. walnut, 3 long, 2 short drawers	250	540	756	17%	2
18th C. oak, molded, small	3,250	6,840	11,340	20%	1
19th C. mahogany, shell inlay	625	1,250	1,944	18%	1
19th C. Dutch marquetry chest	12,450	22,400	32,400	15%	3
18th C. mahogany, bracket feet	2,250	5,450	9,720	23%	1
19th C. mahogany, straight front	700	1,250	1,944	16%	2
18th C. walnut, bachelor's chest	25,400	56,450	84,240	19%	2
19th C. mahogany, bow front	750	1,475	2,268	17%	2

VALUE GROWTH CHART
PRICES QUOTED IN BELGIAN FRANCS

ARTICLE	1971	1975	1978	Average Annual Increase	Financial Outlook 1978-84
19th C. rosewood, 12 drawers	2,200	5,450	7,776	20%	1
19th C. mahogany, bow front	1,200	2,250	3,096	14%	3
18th C. mahogany, bow front	1,154	2,595	5,184	24%	1
19th C. Empire style, marble top	3,750	6,250	11,988	18%	2
19th C. mahogany, bow front, vase feet	320	625	1,008	18%	2
19th C. mahogany, chest and linen press	975	1,675	2,448	14%	3
18th C. mahogany, straight front	1,100	1,975	2,916	15%	3
19th C. mahogany, fine inlay	790	1,500	1,940	14%	1
18th C. walnut, oysterwood inlay	5,750	15,600	23,652	18%	2
18th C. molded front, walnut	3,250	6,750	11,340	19%	2
19th C. mahogany, straight front	750	1,670	2,592	19%	2
17th C. oak and walnut, carved	6,250	14,700	25,920	23%	1
19th C. mahogany, bow front	975	1,700	2,700	16%	3
Walnut chest, pierced brass handles, 1900	125	300	504	22%	1
18th C. Chippendale style, mahogany	4,525	12,250	19,116	23%	1
19th C. Dutch cabinet, inlaid, spade feet	7,250	17,950	27,216	21%	1
Walnut, pierced brass handles, c. 1865	95	290	525	28%	1
18th C. mahogany, oak drawers	2,250	5,680	11,988	27%	1
19th C. rosewood, 7 drawers	1,875	4,200	6,156	19%	2
18th C. oyster veneered, bun feet	6,750	13,000	21,060	18%	2
18th C. mahogany, bombe front	4,800	18,250	32,076	31%	1
19th C. mahogany, vase-shaped feet	350	725	1,000	16%	3
18th C. honey walnut	5,250	12,000	17,820	19%	2
18th C. low mahogany, bracket feet	2,480	5,680	9,720	22%	1
19th C. walnut, finely inlaid top	1,350	2,250	3,564	16%	2
17th C. oak Bible box, twist legs	900	1,620	2,916	18%	2
19th C. mahogany, bow front	725	1,875	2,900	22%	1
19th C. mahogany, pressed brass handles	820	1,250	1,944	13%	3
19th C. oak, Jacobean style	560	1,100	1,620	16%	3
18th C. walnut, bracket feet	10,250	18,290	31,428	17%	2
Inlaid mahogany low chest, 1900	255	620	900	19%	2
18th C. honey walnut, inlaid top	10,000	17,250	31,400	18%	2
19th C. mahogany, 3 drawers	220	540	972	24%	1
19th C. oak filing chest, 12 drawers	420	725	1,296	17%	2

CHEST-ON-CHEST

ARTICLE	1971	1975	1978	Average Annual Increase	Financial Outlook 1978-84
18th C. bow front, mahogany	9,275	18,200	27,864	17%	2
18th C. walnut, brass handles	28,480	60,250	97,200	19%	2
17th C. walnut, oyster veneered	12,750	29,250	51,840	22%	1
18th C. mahogany, arched top	3,250	7,150	14,256	24%	1
18th C. fruitwood, light and dark woods	4,750	12,350	22,032	25%	1
18th C. oak, paneled front	10,250	16,850	31,428	17%	2
18th C. walnut, bracket feet	25,000	58,250	97,200	21%	1
18th C. lacquer, secretaire drawer	15,000	39,800	68,040	24%	1
18th C. mahogany, 7 drawers	3,200	6,000	12,636	22%	1
19th C. oak, bracket feet, brass handles	2,250	6,250	10,692	25%	1
Mahogany chest-on-chest, c. 1800	8,450	16,400	27,540	18%	2
Chippendale period, pediment top	4,500	12,000	21,060	25%	1
18th C. mahogany, brass top handles	2,890	7,000	12,960	24%	1
17th C. oyster veneered olivewood	25,000	49,250	71,280	16%	2

VALUE GROWTH CHART
PRICES QUOTED IN BELGIAN FRANCS

ARTICLE	1971	1975	1978	Average Annual Increase	Financial Outlook 1978-84
CHINA CABINETS					
19th C. Vernis Martin style w/ormolu	2,250	5,200	7,776	19%	2
Art nouveau style, inlaid, mahogany	3,600	7,000	14,256	22%	1
19th C. mahogany, mirrored display	975	1,650	2,592	15%	3
19th C. rosewood and ormolu	6,200	15,500	34,992	28%	1
18th C. marquetry vitrine	19,500	42,500	84,240	23%	1
19th C. large display cabinet	1,920	3,000	4,860	14%	3
19th C. marquetry, on bun feet	12,750	36,800	64,800	26%	1
19th C. ormolu display cabinet	10,500	21,900	45,036	23%	1
19th C. French, with painted sides	22,550	45,000	87,480	21%	1
19th C. inlaid tulipwood vitrine	12,750	23,500	46,008	20%	1
19th C. mahogany, string inlay	975	1,750	3,564	20%	1
19th C. mahogany, bow front	1,100	2,250	3,240	17%	2
19th C. inlaid mahogany	1,450	2,750	4,212	16%	2
19th C. inlaid mahogany display	950	2,220	3,888	22%	1
17th C. dutch painted display cabinet	28,000	59,000	90,720	18%	2
19th C. marquetry vitrine	14,250	25,000	46,656	18%	2
18th C. serpentine front, French	24,000	56,000	97,200	22%	1
19th C. inlaid, tapering legs	4,700	7,200	11,988	14%	3
19th C. French oval display cabinet	6,250	16,000	33,696	27%	1
18th C. inlaid display, turned legs	37,000	67,000	129,600	20%	1
19th C. inlaid China breakfront	1,378	2,950	5,544	22%	1
18th C. floral inlay, bombe base	27,000	58,250	97,200	20%	1
CARD TABLES					
19th C. rosewood, gilt decorations	2,870	6,250	10,692	21%	1
19th C. brass inlaid rosewood	3,250	7,000	15,552	25%	1
18th C. decorated edges and legs	3,480	7,580	15,120	23%	1
19th C. rosewood splayed feet	2,800	5,650	9,396	19%	2
19th C. mahogany, tapering legs	2,420	6,200	9,720	22%	1
18th C. halfround, mahogany	4,925	9,500	18,468	21%	1
19th C. rosewood, platform base	1,575	3,000	6,480	22%	1
Rosewood, brass inlaid, c. 1800	4,250	9,200	17,820	23%	1
18th C. Sheraton style, halfround	5,250	9,800	20,736	22%	1
Chippendale period, mahogany	5,000	13,250	25,096	26%	1
19th C. figured mahogany, folding top	1,240	2,840	2,212	19%	2
19th C. Burr walnut, serpentine front	6,250	13,250	27,216	23%	1
19th C. mahogany inlay, tapered legs	550	1,250	2,448	24%	1
19th C. halfround, Burr walnut	1,250	3,000	5,832	25%	1
19th C. mahogany, center column	1,100	2,100	3,564	18%	2
Pr. 18th C. inlaid mahogany	3,875	7,975	16,056	23%	1
19th C. mahogany, folding top	575	1,100	2,268	22%	1
19th C. inlaid Burr walnut	1,150	2,250	4,860	23%	1
Pr. 18th C. mahogany, splay feet	4,250	18,250	36,288	36%	1
18th C. Hepplewhite style	2,950	6,550	11,988	22%	1
19th C. rosewood, folding top	2,240	5,600	8,424	21%	1
19th C. mahogany, protruding corners	4,800	11,000	20,088	23%	1

VALUE GROWTH CHART
PRICES QUOTED IN BELGIAN FRANCS

ARTICLE	1971	1975	1978	Average Annual Increase	Financial Outlook 1978-84
19th C. ebonized, inlaid top	740	1,390	2,448	19%	2
18th C. faded mahogany, string inlay	2,580	6,780	13,608	27%	1
19th C. walnut, French style	4,895	11,700	19,440	22%	1
18th C. rosewood, folding top	2,950	6,750	15,228	26%	1
19th C. mahogany, turned center column	1,110	2,175	4,212	21%	1
19th C. oak, with center drawer	940	2,450	5,400	28%	1
19th C. boulle folding top	4,250	9,650	19,440	24%	1
18th C. mahogany, satinwood banding	3,750	7,800	14,904	22%	1
19th C. mahogany envelope	945	7,680	3,888	22%	1
19th C. rosewood, platform, claw feet	1,280	3,180	5,832	24%	1
19th C. Burr walnut, folding top	975	2,250	5,000	26%	1
Pr. Sheraton, satinwood, tapered legs	5,450	11,200	19,440	20%	1
18th C. rosewood, folding top	2,000	3,800	6,156	17%	2
19th C. mahogany, envelope	1,100	2,250	3,564	18%	2
18th C. serpentine front, mahogany	4,850	12,500	17,172	20%	1

DINING TABLES

ARTICLE	1971	1975	1978	Average Annual Increase	Financial Outlook 1978-84
19th C. mahogany, shaped platform	1,250	2,950	4,212	19%	2
19th C. circular, tripod base	1,150	2,750	4,860	23%	1
19th C. Burr walnut, center column	2,250	3,950	8,748	21%	1
19th C. mahogany, on turned columns	2,500	5,650	9,720	21%	1
19th C. circular oak	1,250	2,560	4,860	21%	1
18th C. circular inlaid	15,750	39,000	64,800	22%	1
19th C. oval inlaid walnut	2,250	4,400	7,776	19%	2
19th C. circular mahogany	2,500	5,600	9,072	20%	1
19th C. small mahogany, center	950	2,450	4,212	24%	1
19th C. round Burr walnut	1,850	3,600	6,804	20%	1
19th C. inlaid mahogany	6,450	16,000	29,160	24%	1
19th C. walnut pedestal, inlaid	2,750	5,870	7,128	15%	2
19th C. oval rosewood, pedestal	3,200	7,000	11,340	20%	1
19th C. oval rosewood, loo table	2,800	6,750	11,520	22%	1
18th C. center table, inlaid	3,200	6,500	12,960	22%	1
19th C. snap top, mahogany	2,500	4,000	8,748	19%	2
19th C. rosewood, inlaid and brass	7,280	17,250	29,160	22%	1
19th C. shaped top loo table	6,500	16,400	32,400	26%	1
19th C. octagonal inlaid	4,750	18,000	32,000	31%	1
18th C. crossbanded mahogany	5,200	9,250	21,060	22%	1
19th C. oval walnut on pillar	750	1,500	2,592	19%	2
18th C. crossbanded breakfront	5,450	13,750	25,200	24%	1

Finely inlaid chest of drawers, made in Holland, c. 1800. 65,000 BF.

Dutch vetrine made in 2 parts, 18th century. 230,000 BF.

Vente Du Lundi.   130,000 BF.

William & Mary finely inlaid cabinet, c. 1740. 140,000 BF.

Dutch vitrine finely inlaid, Queen Anne style. 195,000 BF

Still life with fruit, signed A. Coosemans. 180,000 BF.

Dutch silver cabinet finely inlaid, 18th century.
235,000 BF.

ter & Assuerus, Aubusson, end the 17th century.
0,000 BF.

Clock, style of Louis XV, 19th century. 70,000 BF.

387

Elegant Dutch vitrine, 2 parts with commode bottom, 18th century.   110,000 BF.

Sterling silver (6.513 gr) tureen, Jean Baptiste Claude Doliot period restoration.   520,000 BF.

Crucifix clock by Mathias Kasseborer of Ulm, Germany c. 1600. The statue and figures are of gilt metal. The ba[l] surmounting the cross rotates once every 12 hours. 360,000 BF.

Elegant English ebony cabinet with ivory inlay, 18th century.   105,000 BF.

English rare mahogany bookcase, c. 1800.   285,000 BF.

Part of fountain, lead, France or Italy, 18th century. 115,000 BF.

Big gilt mirror, first quality, England, 18th century. 250,000 BF.

Pair of corner gilt consoles, marble tops, Italy, 18th century.   245,000 BF.

Set of four gilt armchairs, England, end 18th century. 300,000 BF.

Sitting Buddha, Chieng saen, Thailand, 14th–15th century. 228,000 BF.

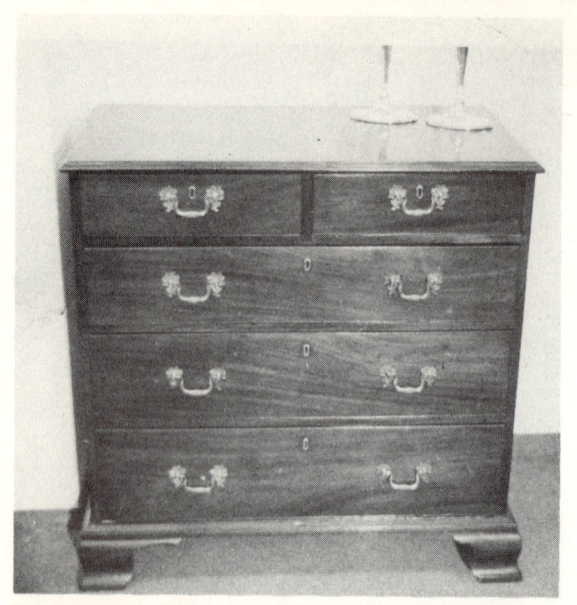

Chippendale chest, c. 1770, with brush slide, original handles.

Profit Record
1971: 4,500 SF
1978: 5,800 SF

Individual Notes

Investment Predictions
1979–84

Over the past 7 years this Chippendale chest increased in value 28%, which is a compounded growth rate of 4% per year. On the average, English furniture does not command high prices in Switzerland. Appreciation in this respect is much slower, but steady.

Phillipp Ramsay Reinagle, Portrait of a Gentleman, signed and dated 1839, oil/canvas, 76 x 64 cm. 6,500 SF.

Sheraton dressing table, c. 1790, serpentine front.

Profit Record
1971: 5,500 SF
1978: 6,500 SF

Individual Notes

Investment Predictions
1979–84

This Sheraton dressing table over the past 7 years increased in value 18%, which is a compounded growth rate of 2.5% per year. English furniture in Switzerland appreciates at a much slower rate than similar pieces in other countries.

Abraham Cooper, 1787–1868, Portrait of a Racehorse, signed with monogram and dated 1824, inscribed "Don John aged 19," 43 x 60 cm. 9,000 SF.

John Wootton, c. 1668–1765. Landscape with ruins and figures. Signed and dated 1758, oil/canvas, 127 x 94 cm. 12,000 SF.

Gold black enamel watch, hours and ¼ repeat, 19th century.

Profit Record
1970: 1,500 SF
1977: 4,500 SF

Individual Notes

Investment Predictions
1978–80

Over the past 7 years this watch increased in value 200%, which is a compounded growth rate of 18% per year. Watches of this type are always in demand and will continue to appreciate at a stable rate.

Minute repeat watch, 18 ct. gold, excellent quality, 19th century.

Profit Record
1970: 2,500 SF
1977: 10,000 SF

Individual Notes

Investment Predictions
1978–80

This beautiful gold watch over the past 7 years has increased in value 300%, which is a compounded growth rate of 22% per year. Collecting watches has become a widely accepted field, and prices should appreciate at a stable rate.

Silver enamel singing bird box with automaton bird.

Profit Record
1971: 1,500 SF
1978: 8,000 SF

Individual Notes

Investment Predictions
1978–80

This exquisite enameled box over the past 7 years increased in value 433%, which is a compounded growth rate of 27% per year. Specialty items like the box above are rare collectors items and their prices are therefore more sensitive to buyer demands, but rarely do prices on boxes of this type go below the yearly growth rate estimated above.

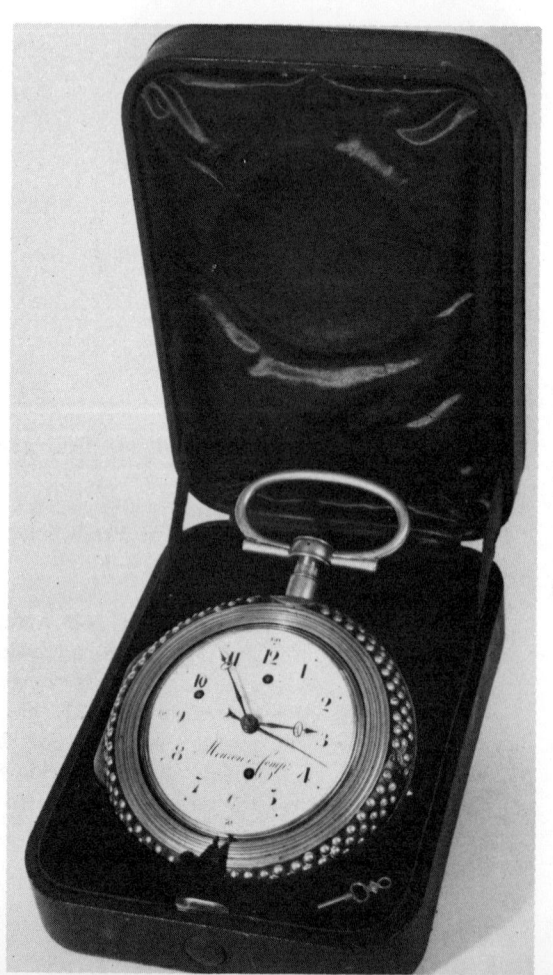

Carriage clock, repeat and alarm made from gilt metal.

Profit Record
1971: 500 SF
1978: 2,000 SF

Investment Predictions
1979–84

This carriage clock over the past 7 years increased in value 300%, which is a compounded growth rate of 22% per year. Before 1969 very little interest was given to carriage clocks, but since 1972 the market has discovered these clocks and they have begun to appreciate. This should continue at a very stable rate for many years

Coach clock with full striking alarm in silver and laque travel box.

Profit Record
1971: 5,000 SF
1978: 17,000 SF

Individual Notes

Investment Predictions
1979–84

This unique coach clock over the past 7 years increased in value 240%, which is a compounded growth rate of 19% per year. The appreciation of both clocks and watches is very stable with yearly increased interest showed by collectors.

392

Early 19th-century Bauern shrank or farmer's closet.

Profit Record	Investment Predictions
1971: 2,200 SF	1979–84
1978: 5,600 SF	

Individual Notes

This unique Swiss farmer's closet, which was undoubtedly used as a kitchen buffet, over the past 7 years increased in value 155%, which is a compounded growth rate of 14% per year. Useful pieces of furniture like this one are increasingly in demand as the kitchen becomes a decorated room of the house, and prices could increase as more interest is stimulated in this area.

Early 19th-century Swiss Bauern shrank or farmer's chest.

Profit Record	Investment Predictions
1971: 2,000 SF	1979–84
1978: 5,000 SF	

Individual Notes

This beautifully painted Swiss farmer's chest over the past 7 years increased in value 150%, which is a compounded growth rate of 14% per year. Pieces of this vintage are eagerly sought, and buyer demand will keep the appreciation stable.

Gold and blue enamel French watch with blue, diamond-studded translucent enamel, 18th century. 60,000 Kroner.

French gold and mother o' pearl snuff box. Maker: Claude de Villers. Paris, 1747.   250,000.

French gold snuffbox. Miniature of battle scenes by Blarenbergh.   175,000 Kroner.

French gold vase watch with music box, 18th century. 75,000 Kroner.

Karl Faberge. Workmaster: Michael Perchin. Gold and mauve translucent enamel clock.   60,000 Kroner.

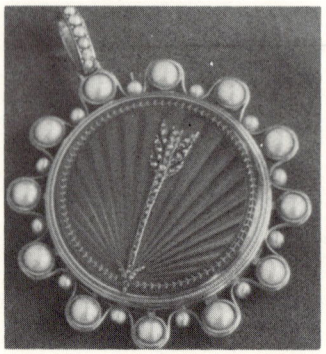

Gold enamel "blind man's" watch set with oriental pearls for numbers. Diamond-studded hand. LeRoy, Paris 18th century.   80,000 Kroner.

Karl Faberge. Workmaster: Henrik Wigstrom Nefrite and Goldmount. 30,000 Kroner.

Gold-mounted Meissen porcelain snuffbox. Herold, c. 1725. 100,000 Kroner.

Silver beaker. Denmark, c. 1600.   Kroner 35,000.

Danish cupboard, c. 1670.

Profit Record
1970: 2,000 Kroner
1977: 6,000 Kroner

Individual Notes

Investment Predictions
1977–80

Over the past 7 years this oak cupboard has increased in value 200%, which is a compounded growth rate of 17% per year. Furniture of good quality such as this chest will continue to appreciate at a stable rate.

395

Bibliography

This is a working bibliography to enable more in-depth study on various subjects. The true student and antique lover is always in search of new clues to further his education.

CLOCKS, BAROMETERS, AND WATCHES

Bell, E. F. *Old English Barometers*. Winchester: The Wykenham Press, 1952.

Cescinsky and Webster. *English Domestic Clocks*. London: Routledge, London, 1913.

Drepperd, Carl. *American Clocks and Clockmakers*. New York: Branford, 1955.

Palmer, Brooks. *The Book of American Clocks*. New York: Macmillan, 1950.

Robertson, J. Drummond. *The Evolution of Clockwork*. London: Cassell, 1931.

FURNITURE

Andrews, Edward Deming. *The People Called Shakers: A search for the Perfect Society*. New York: O.U.P., 1953.

Bjerkol, Ethel Hall. *Cabinetmakers of America*. New York: Doubleday, 1957.

Dacier, Emile. *Le Style Louis XVI*. Paris: Larousse, 1939.

Drepperd, Carl. *Handbook of Antique Chairs*. New York: Doubleday, 1948.

Edwards, Ralph. *Georgian Furniture*. London: Victoria and Albert Museum, 1957.

Edwards, Ralph and P. Mc.Quoid. *Dictionary of English Furniture*. London: Country Life, 1954.

Edwards, Ralph. *Sheraton Furniture Design*. London: Tiranti, 1948.

Fastnedge, Ralph. *English Furniture Styles from 1500 to 1830*. London: Penguin, 1954.

Nutting, Wallace. *Furniture Treasury*. New York: Macmillan, 1948–9.

GLASS

Belknap, E. M. *Milk Glass*. New York: Crown, 1954.

Bergstrom, Evangeline. *Old Glass Paperweights*. New York, 1939.

Bles, Joseph. *Rare English Glasses of the Seventeenth and Eighteenth Centuries*. London: Bles, 1926.

Daniel, Dorothy. *Cut and Engraved Glass 1771–1905*. New York: Barrows, 1950.

Hughes, Bernard G. *Old English, Irish and Scottish Table Glass*. London: Batsford, 1956.

Hunter, Fredrick W. *Stiegel Glass*. New York: Dover, 1950.

Lee, Ruth Webb. *Early American Pressed Glass*. Northboro, Mass.: Lee, 1946.

METALWORK

Brown, R. A. *The History and Origin of Horse Brasses*. R. A. Brown, 1952.

Cotterell, H. H. *National Types of Old Pewter.* Cotterell, 1932.

Kaufmann, Henry J. *Early American Copper, Tin and Brass.* New York: Medill McBridge, 1950.

Sonn, Albert H. *Early American Wrought Iron.* New York: Scribners, 1928.

Twopeny, W. *English Metalwork.* London: Constable, 1904.

NEEDLEWORK

Balton, Ethel Standwood. American Samplers. *Massachusetts Society of the Colonial Dames of America,* 1921.

Webster, Marie D. *Quilts—Their Story and How To Make Them.* New York: Doubleday, 1915.

POTTERY AND PORCELAIN

Barber, E. A. *The Pottery and Porcelain of the United States.* New York: Putnam, 1909.

Bembrose, G. *Nineteenth Century English Pottery and Porcelain.* London, 1952.

Camehl, A. W. *The Blue China Book.* New York: Tudor, 1946.

Dixon, J. L. *English Blue and White Porcelain of the Eighteenth Century.* London, 1952.

Earle, E. M. *China Collecting in America.* New York: Empire State Book Co., 1924.

Honey, W. B. *European Ceramic.* London: 1947.

Honey, W. B. *English Pottery and Porcelain.* London, 1947.

McKearin, Helen. *Early American Pottery and Porcelain.* New York: Parke-Bernet Galleries, 1939.

SILVER

Avery, C. L. *Early American Silver.* New York: Metropolitan Museum of Art, 1920.

Bigelow, F. L. *Historic Silver of the Colonies.* London: Macmillan, 1914.

Jones, E. A. *Old Silver of Europe and America.* London, 1922.

Walts, W. W. *Old English Silver.* London, 1924.

Index

Adam, Robert, 107, 175
Ansbach, 54
American glass, 195-96
Amstel, 62
Arras, 36
Art Nouveau glass, 193
Austin, Nathaniel, 119, 122
Austin, Richard, 119, 122

Baccarat paperweights, 208, 209
Bacchus, 211
Badger, Thomas, 119, 122
Banjo Wallclock, 135
Barnes, Stephen, 119, 121
Bareuther, 87
Barns, Blakeslee, 120, 124
Baroque, 170
Bassett, Francis, 1, 120, 123, 127
Bassett, Frederick, 120
Bateman, Hester, 108
Belcher, Joseph, 120, 125
Belcher, Joseph, Jr., 120
Belleck, 24-25
Bergen, 17
Berlin, 128-30
Billings, William, 120
Bing & Grondahl, 87
Boardman, Luther, 119, 121
Boardman, Sherman, 119
Boardman, Timothy & Co., 120
Boardman, Thomas D., 119
Boardman, Thomas Danforth, 119, 121, 126
Boardman & Company, 120
Boardman & Hart, 120

Boelen, Jacob, 104
Bohemian, 207
Bohemian glass, 190
Bottles, 215-20
Bourg-la-Reine, 37
Bow, 25
Boyd, Parks, 120, 124
Brass, 128-30
Brigden, Timothy, 120, 124
Bristol, 25, 79
Bristol glass, 194-95
Britannia metal, 118

Caen, 37
Calder, William, 120, 125
Capen, Ephraum, 120
Capo di Monte, 70-72
Casuys, Samuel, 103
Caughley, 26
Cauldon, 26-27
Chantilly, 37-38
Charles II, 105-6
Chippendale, Thomas, 174, 175, 180, 184
Clichy paperweights, 204
Clocks, 131-50
Clocks, longcase, 141-43
Cloisonné, 101
Coalpoart, 28
Collins, Arnold, 103
Coney, John, 103-4
Copper, 128-30
Courtille, La, 44
Cozzi, 73
Curtis, Daniel, 120, 124

399

Curtis, I., 119
Curtis, Stephen, 120
Cut glass, 196

Danforth, Edwards, 119
Danforth, John, 119, 121
Danforth, Joseph, Jr., 120
Danforth, Joseph, Sr., 119
Danforth, Josiah, 119
Danforth, Samuel, 119, 121, 127
Danforth, Thomas, I, 119
Danforth, Thomas, II, 119
Danforth, Thomas, III, 119, 121
Danforth, William, 119, 121
Davenport, 28
Delft, 64-68, 86-87
Derby, 29, 78
Derby, Thomas S., 119
Directoire, 173-74
Dummer, Jeremiah, 103-4
Dunhan, Rufus, 119
Dwarf Tallcase clock, 132-33, 135

Edgell, Simon, 120, 125
Ellsworth, William, 120, 124
Enamels, 101-2
Endicott, Edmund, 120
English glass, 193-94
English Registry Marks, 23
Engravings, 74-75

Fabrique de Duc D'Argoulême, 47
Fabrique de la Rue Popincourt, 47-48
Fabrique de la Reine, 46-47
Fabrique de al Rue de Reuilly, 45
Fabrique de Monsieur a Clignancourt, 45-46
Fabrique du Duc d'Orleans, 48
Faubroug St. Dennis, 44-45
Fenn, Gavis, 120
Fenn, Jason, 120
Fenton, 87
Flea Markets, 304-13
Folk art, 151-62
Fraktur, 163-64
Frankenthal, 56
French Provincial, 172-73
Friesland Timepieces, 140
Fulda, 57
Fuller & Smith, 119
Furniture, 168-87
Fürstenberg, 57, 87

Gallé, Emile, 192-93
George I, 106-8
Georgian, 174
German glass, 190
Gilding, 75
Gleason, Roswell, 119, 123, 126
Glass, 188-220
Gothic, 169

Green, Samuel, 119, 123
Griswald, Ashbil, 119, 121

Hallmarks, Silver, 109-15
Hamlen, Samuel, 120
Hamlen, Samuel E., 120
Hand-painting, 75
Hague, The, 63
Harbenson, Benjamin, 120, 125
Harbenson, Joseph, 120
Hardening-on-Fire, 75
Haviland, 38-39, 87
Hepplewhite, George, 176, 183
Herend, 68-69
Hopper, Henry, 120
Höchst, 57-58
Hull, John, 103-4
Hummel, 87
Hurd, Jacob, 104

Imperial, 87
Islamic glass, 189

Johnson, Jehiel, 119, 121
Jones, Gersham, 120, 125

Kilbourn, Samuel, 119, 122, 126
Kloster-Veilsdorf, 58
Krueger, Louis, 120

Lamerie, de Paul, 108
Lane Delph, 30
Lauraguis, 39
Lee, Richard, Sr., 120
Lee, Richard, Jr., 120
Le Nove, 72-73
Lenox, 17
Lewis, Isaac C., 119, 122
Lightner, George, 119, 122
Lille, 39-40
Limoges, 40-41
Liverpool, 30
Longton Hall, 30
Louis XIV, 170-71
Louis XVI, 173
Lowestoft, 31
Ludwigsburg, 58-59
Lyman, William, W., 119

McQuilkin, William, 120
Malineur, George, 120
Madeley, 31-32
Mason Ironstone, 30
Mattlock, 79-80
Medici, 72
Meissen, 59-61
Melville, David, 120, 125
Melville, Samuel, 120, 125
Melville, Thomas, 120, 125
Mennecy-Villeroy, 42

Millefiore paperweights, 207
Miller, Josiah, 120
Minton, 31
Mix, Thomas, 119
Morey, David B., 119
Murray-Curvex printing, 75

Nantgarw, 32
New England Glass Company, 212-13
New Hall, 32-33
Niderviller, 42
Nieuwe, Amstel, 62-63
Norris, George, 120
Nymphenburg, 61
Nyon, 74

Ogee Shelf clock, 132, 137
Olier, R. H., 119
Ostrander, Charles, 120
Oude Amstel, 62-63
Oude Loasdrecht, 62-63

Packaging collectibles, 165-67
Palethorp, John H., 120
Palethorp, Robert, Jr., 120
Paperweights, 206-14
Paquier, Claude du, 18-19
Pewter, 117-27
Pierce, Samuel, 119, 123
Porter, Allen, 119
Porter, Freeman, 119, 126
Printing, 75

Queen's ware, 77

Régence, 171-72
Renaissance, 169-70
Renton & Company, 120
Revere, Paul, 104
Richardson, Joseph, 104
Richardson, Nathaniel, 104
Rockingham, 33
Rococo, 172
Roman glass, 189
Royal Copenhagen, 19-22, 85, 87
Royal Doulton, 33
Rorstrand, 87
Rosenthal, 87
Rouen, 48
Russell, Daniel, 103-4

Saint-amand-les Eaux, 49
Saint Cloud, 48-49, 85
St. Louis paperweights, 209
Sanderson, Robert, 103-4
Sceaux, 49
Schoats, Barthalomew, 103
Schofield, John, 108
Seivres, 49-52, 85-86

Shelf Clock, 133-34, 136-37
Shenango, 87
Sheraton, Thomas, 176
Skinner, John 120, 123
Smith, Eben, 120
Soumain, Simeon, 104
Spiegel, Jacobus Van der, 103
Spode, 34, 83, 87
Stafford, Spencer, 120
Strasbourg, 52
Stiegel glass, 196
Storr, Paul, 108
Sumner, William F., 120
Swansea, 34

Taunton Britannia Manufacturing Co., 120
Terry, Eli, 132, 138
Thomas, Seth, 132
Tiffany, Louis Comfort, 191-93
Tournay, 53
Transferring, 75
Trask, Israel, 120, 123
Trask, Oliver, 120, 123, 126
Tucker, 18

Valenciennes, 53-54
Val St. Lambert, 212
Van Dyck, Peter, 103-4
Vernon, Samuel, 103
Vezzi, 73-74
Victorian, 176-77
Vienna, 18
Vincennes, 43, 78

Ward & Co., H. B., 35, 80-82
Watches, 147-50
Waterford, 195
Water-slide Transfers, 75
Weekes, James, 120, 124
Whitefriars, 211
Whitmore, Jacob, 119, 122
Wildes, Thomas, 120, 124
Will, Henry, 120, 124
Will, William, 120
William III, 105
Williams, Lorenzo, L., 120, 125
Winslow, 104
Woodbury, J. B., 120
Worcester, 35, 80-82

Yale, Henry, 120
Yale, Samuel, 119
Yale, William, 119
Yale & Co. H., 119, 124
Young, Peter, 120

Zaandam clocks, 140
Zürich, 74, 82

401